TRINITY

THEOLOGY IN GLOBAL PERSPECTIVE SERIES

Peter C. Phan, General Editor
Ignacio Ellacuría Professor of Catholic Social Thought, Georgetown University

At the beginning of a new millennium, the *Theology in Global Perspective* series responds to the challenge to reexamine the foundational and doctrinal themes of Christianity in light of the new global reality. While traditional Catholic theology has assumed an essentially European or Western point of view, *Theology in Global Perspective* takes account of insights and experiences of churches in Africa, Asia, Latin America, Oceania, as well as from Europe and North America. Noting the pervasiveness of changes brought about by science and technologies, and growing concerns about the sustainability of Earth, it seeks to embody insights from studies in these areas as well.

Though rooted in the Catholic tradition, volumes in the series are written with an eye to the ecumenical implications of Protestant, Orthodox, and Pentecostal theologies for Catholicism, and vice versa. In addition, authors will explore insights from other religious traditions with the potential to enrich Christian theology and self-understanding.

Books in this series will provide reliable introductions to the major theological topics, tracing their roots in Scripture and their development in later tradition, exploring when possible the implications of new thinking on gender and sociocultural identities. And they will relate these themes to the challenges confronting the peoples of the world in the wake of globalization, particularly the implications of Christian faith for justice, peace, and the integrity of creation.

Other titles published in the series

Orders and Ministry: Leadership in the World Church, Kenan B. Osborne

THEOLOGY IN GLOBAL PERSPECTIVE SERIES

TRINITY

Nexus of the Mysteries of Christian Faith

ANNE HUNT

Maryknoll, New York 10545

Founded in 1970, Orbis Books endeavors to publish works that enlighten the mind, nourish the spirit, and challenge the conscience. The publishing arm of the Maryknoll Fathers and Brothers, Orbis seeks to explore the global dimensions of the Christian faith and mission, to invite dialogue with diverse cultures and religious traditions, and to serve the cause of reconciliation and peace. The books published reflect the opinions of their authors and are not meant to represent the official position of the Maryknoll Society. To obtain more information about Maryknoll and Orbis Books, please visit our website at www.maryknoll.org.

Library of Congress Cataloging in Publication Data

Hunt, Anne, 1952-
Trinity : nexus of the mysteries of Christian faith / Anne Hunt.
p. cm. — (Theology in global perspective)
Includes index.
ISBN-13 : 978-1-57075-629-0 (pbk.)
1. Trinity. 2. Trinity—History of doctrines. I. Title. II. Series.
BT111.3.H86 2005
231'.044—dc22

2005010657

To Kevin,
beloved father and teacher par excellence,
steadfast in his love

Contents

Foreword

by Peter C. Phan

It is a happy coincidence, perhaps even providential, that the volume inaugurating the *Theology in Global Perspective* series concerns the central mystery of the Christian faith and is written by a theologian who is a woman and who hails from Australia. The author's expertise, gender, and nationality bespeak the multifaceted approach of this new series of theological resources. In an increasingly globalized world, theology, especially one that is both catholic (with the lower-case *c*, aiming at inclusiveness) and Catholic (with the capital *C*, rooted in the Roman Catholic tradition), must be ecumenical, intercultural, interreligious, scientifically informed, and praxis-oriented. Of course, not every theme will lend itself to a treatment with an equal consideration of all these five dimensions. Nevertheless, the series intends to promote a theology that embodies all of them as far as possible.

Still, even on the supposition that theology for the twenty-first century must be constructed along these axes, the question remains as to where to begin and how to do so. As for the starting point, systematic theology, as Professor Hunt rightly notes, can, theoretically speaking, begin with any doctrine. Like a circle, Christian faith, which is an organic whole, has no one absolute starting point; any point in the circle can be the beginning of the circumference. Nonetheless, by a fortunate happenstance, the first volume of our series deals with a theme that by any measure occupies the highest place in the hierarchy of truths. It is also highly significant that the doctrine of the Trinity, long banished to the periphery of systematic theology so that Christians were, in Karl Rahner's pithy phrase, by and large "practical monotheists" (that is, Unitarians), has in recent years made a dramatic comeback as the central and pivotal doctrine. Introducing the *Theology in Global Perspective* series with the Trinity, then, affords an excellent opportunity to articulate it in the ecumenical, intercultural, interreligious, scientifically informed, and praxis-oriented way that the series intends.

This new way of doing theology is also embodied in the method with which Professor Hunt develops her theme. She notes that of the three ways to achieve an understanding of the Christian mysteries recommended by Vatican I—(1) by analogy with the truths known naturally, (2) from the interconnections of the mysteries (*nexus mysteriorum*) with one another, and (3) in reference to our ultimate destiny—only the first has been widely used. In contrast, Hunt decides to make use of the second in her own theology of the Trinity, that is, by seeking connections between the trinitarian doctrine and other Christian doctrines. Thus, she is able to articulate "the trinitarian nexus" or the interconnection between the mystery of the Trinity and the other great mysteries of the Christian faith—creation, incarnation, redemption, grace, church, moral life, spirituality, and eschatology, just to name a few. In the elaboration of this *nexus mysteriorum* lie Hunt's creativity and originality.

Readers of Hunt's volume will marvel at the breadth and depth of her scholarship and the liveliness of her imagination. In a clear and engaging style, she introduces them to the teachings of the councils, the fathers of the church of both East and West, and the thought of Catholic, Protestant, and Orthodox theologians. She unfolds the implications of the trinarian doctrine for ecology, worship, spirituality, and the work for justice. She brings the doctrine of the Trinity into dialogue with non-Christian religions.

In spite of logical rigor and precise conceptual tools, Hunt is well aware that talk about the Trinity lives on the conviction, taught by the Fourth Lateran Council, that between Creator and creature there exists more dissimilitude than similitude. To be authentic, God-talk must end up in worshipful silence, since God is the *mysterium tremendum*, which, Hunt helpfully points out, literally means "a mystery to tremble before." But such trembling is also suffused with fascination, joy, and love, since the Trinity is a communion of divine persons so perfectly united in love that they constitute the one God. May we who read this book on the Trinity bend our knees in adoration and praise before this wondrous Mystery.

Preface

This book is designed primarily as a resource for students of theology and specialists in the area, but it will also be of value, I hope, to the interested lay reader. We have tried to keep the style and language accessible to the beginner, assuming only a fairly basic knowledge of theology. In each chapter, we present a brief survey of the historical development of the classical doctrine in the area under study, in order to put into perspective the modern concerns, approaches, and developments from an explicitly trinitarian perspective. Those theologians whose contributions are then examined have been chosen because they approach the various tracts under consideration in an explicitly trinitarian way. We do not claim to offer an exhaustive treatment of every area chosen, nor of every possible area that could have been chosen. Pneumatology, for example, does not feature in a dedicated chapter. What we hope to have offered is a reasonably comprehensive treatment of significant contributions to the areas under examination, so that readers can gain a sense of the issues currently under consideration in that area. We must also admit that the assignment of authors to particular theological areas is not hard and fast; again we have aimed for a general balance and comprehensiveness. A list of recommended readings at the end of each chapter is designed to assist those readers who are interested to engage in the subject in more depth.

In regard to language, we try to avoid noninclusive gender-specific language when referring both to God and to the human person (except in relation to Father and Son where gender-specific language is already in place in the Scriptures, and when quoting material from another source even if that material includes noninclusive language), even though the alternative can often seem clumsy and unwieldy. Alas, there is no easy solution to the issue of language in the contemporary English-language context!

In approaching this exciting and challenging area of trinitarian theology, my questions and concerns are necessarily grounded in the Roman Catholic theological tradition to which I belong. These reflections are humbly offered to the broader Christian community and to members of other faith traditions and, indeed, to any persons interested in exploring the connections. May the work be no less catholic for being Catholic.

Allow me to express my sincere gratitude to those who have assisted in numerous generous ways: first, to my theology students, who inspired the work; to the library staff, and particularly to Rachel Forrest, of Australian

Catholic University, and to Paul Chandler, OCarm, of the Carmelite Library (Melbourne), for unfailing helpfulness and good will in assisting with the provision of the resources for this project; to Bernadette Taylor for assistance with proofreading the text; to Neil Ormerod, who commented on the text in the course of its preparation; to Harvey Egan, SJ, who offered so much useful and nuanced advice on various points; to Bill Burrows and Orbis Books for their interest and assistance in publishing the work; and to Peter Phan for his ongoing encouragement, advice, and support, as well as large doses of good humor. Thanks most of all to Professor Anthony Kelly, CSsR of Australian Catholic University, who has been friend, teacher, and mentor over the years, for his constant encouragement and wise counsel, and for the theological vistas that his extraordinarily expansive and creative vision of the theological landscape has awakened in the many students who have been privileged to learn from him.

Abbreviations and Sources Used in This Work

Collections of Official Church Documents and Teachings

DS Denzinger, H., and A. Schönmetzer, eds. *Enchiridion Symbolorum: Definitionum et Declarationum de Rebus Fidei et Morum.* 36th edition. Freiburg: Herder, 1976.

ND Neuner, J., and J. Dupuis, eds. *The Christian Faith in the Doctrinal Documents of the Catholic Church.* 6th revised and enlarged edition. New York: Alba House, 1996.

Collections of the Writings of Church Fathers

The Ante-Nicene Fathers. 10 volumes. Grand Rapids: Wm. B. Eerdmans, 1974-76.

The Nicene and Post-Nicene Fathers of the Christian Church. American edition. First series. 14 volumes. Grand Rapids: Wm. B. Eerdmans, 1974-79.

The Nicene and Post-Nicene Fathers of the Christian Church. American edition. Second series. 12 volumes. Grand Rapids: Wm. B. Eerdmans, 1973-76.

PG *Patrologiae cursus completus: Series Graeca.* Edited by J.-P. Migne. 161 volumes. Paris: J.-P. Migne, 1857-66.

PL *Patrologiae cursus completus: Series Latina.* Edited by J.-P. Migne. 221 volumes. Paris: J.-P. Migne, 1844-55.

The Documents of Vatican Council II

Unless otherwise noted, all citations are taken from *The Basic Sixteen Documents of Vatican II: Constitutions, Decrees, Declarations.* Revised edition. Edited by Austin Flannery. New York: Costello Publishing, 1996.

AA *Apostolicam Actuositatem.* Decree on the Apostolate of the Laity (November 18, 1965)

AG *Ad Gentes.* Decree on the Church's Missionary Activity (December 7, 1965)

DH *Dignitatis Humanae.* Declaration on Religious Freedom
DV *Dei Verbum.* Dogmatic Constitution on Divine Revelation
GS *Gaudium et Spes.* Pastoral Constitution on the Church in the Modern World
LG *Lumen Gentium.* Dogmtic Constitution on the Church (November 21, 1964)
NA *Nostra Aetate.* Declaration on the Relationship of the Church to Non-Christian Religions
UR *Unitatis Redintegratio.* Decree on Ecumenism
SC *Sacrosanctum Concilium.* Constitution on the Sacred Liturgy
OT *Optatam Totius.* Decree on Priestly Formation

Other Abbreviations

CCC *Catechism of the Catholic Church.* 2nd edition. English translation by various publishers. The second Latin edition was promulgated on August 15, 1997 by Pope John Paul II in the apostolic letter *Laetamur magnopere.* The first edition was promulgated on October 11, 1992.
CIC *Codex Iuris Canonici* (Code of Canon Law of the Roman Catholic Church), promulgated by Pope John Paul II, January 25, 1983. English translation under the auspices of the Canon Law Society of America, *Code of Canon Law: Latin-English Edition* (Washington, D.C.: Canon Law Society of America, 1983).
RH *Redemptor Hominis,* "The Redeemer of Humankind." Encyclical letter of Pope John Paul II, 1979.
STh Thomas Aquinas. *Summa Theologiae.* All translations taken from Blackfriars edition, 60 volumes. New York/London: Blackfriars, 1964-80.

Introduction

Faith Seeking Connections

THEOLOGY IS THE STUDY of God (*theos*). To use Anselm's classic expression, it is the effort of "faith seeking understanding" (*fides quaerens intellectum* in the famous Latin phrase of St. Anselm of Canterbury, [1033-1109]). In more contemporary terms, we could describe it as the science of faith, which seeks to articulate faith's convictions and meaning. Systematic theology then seeks to work the full range of the mysteries of faith into a provisional assimilable systematic whole within the intellectual framework of a given culture. But how is it that we even dare to speak about God? On the one hand, theology avers what the mystics have always known: that God is incomprehensible, utterly beyond our imagination and intelligence, as if abiding in and beyond a cloud of unknowing, forever mystery, sometimes referred to as *mysterium tremendum* (literally, "a mystery to tremble before"[1]). As St. Thomas Aquinas expressed it, we know *that* God is, but not *what* God is. On the other hand, theology nevertheless dares to speak about God! How is it, and on what basis do we proceed to speak and, indeed, to speak in myriad volumes about the mystery of God? It would surely be easier to explain the sound of birdsong to someone who has always been profoundly deaf, or the colors of the rainbow to someone who has been blind from birth, or the feel of the wind to the babe in the womb.

In its Dogmatic Constitution *Dei Filius,* the First Vatican Council (1869-1870) addressed the relation between faith and reason. It explained that the two are ultimately compatible and that human reason can indeed attain at least some understanding of the Christian mysteries. It also enumerated what are recognized as the three classic techniques for advancing theological understanding of the mysteries of Christian faith:

> If reason, illumined by faith inquires in an earnest, pious and sober manner, it attains by God's grace a certain understanding of the mysteries, which is most fruitful, both from the analogy with the objects of its natural knowl-

1. The term has been identified in our time with the work of a great German historian of religion, Rudolf Otto (1869-1937) and his most famous book, *The Idea of the Holy,* trans. John W. Harvey (Oxford: Oxford University Press, 1923; 2nd ed., 1950).

> edge and from the connection of these mysteries with one another (*nexus mysteriorum*) and with our ultimate end. But it never becomes capable of understanding them in the way it does the truths which constitute its proper object. For divine mysteries by their very nature so excel the created intellect that, even when they have been communicated in revelation and received by faith, they remain covered by the veil of faith itself and shrouded as it were in darkness as in this mortal life we are "away from the Lord; for we walk by faith, not by sight" [*2 Cor 5:6–7*].[2]

The three strategies by which we dare to speak with a measure of confidence and competence about the sacred mysteries are thus: (1) by analogy with the truths known naturally; (2) from the interconnection of the mysteries with one another; and (3) in reference to our final end and ultimate destiny.

Theology abounds with analogies.[3] St. Patrick, so the Irish legend goes, used the shamrock to assist in explaining the mystery of the Trinity. It is unarguably a very crude analogy; nevertheless, we see in it the essential pattern of movement from a truth known naturally (the three-leaved shamrock) to the sacred mystery of the three divine persons united in the one God. St. Augustine, centuries earlier, proposed the much more sophisticated analogy of the acts of memory, understanding, and willing in the human person as a way of advancing our understanding of faith's conviction that the one God is Trinity. Moving from a truth known naturally to an understanding of a sacred mystery, analogy functions like an arc or a vector, approximating the mystery. To use Elizabeth Johnson's expression, it is a "naming towards" the divine.[4] It aims to advance our understanding of the mystery, never to prove it or to exhaust its meaning. It serves to elucidate the mystery, while not presuming to encapsulate it. The strategy of analogy, and indeed of the whole enterprise of theology, begins and ends in faith. Moreover, it is grounded in the analogical nature of our existence, in other words, in an understanding that our very being is grounded in the mystery of being, that created being is a participation in divine being. Since all created being is a participation in divine being, the structure and nature of divine being will be reflected in some way in all creation; and thus creation functions, by way of analogy, to reveal the divine mystery.

The Fourth Lateran Council in 1215 contributed an important statement on the use of the strategy of analogy when it definitively expressed the nec-

2. DS 3016; ND 132.

3. Both Anthony Kelly and Neil Ormerod highlight the distinction between analogy and model. See Neil Ormerod, "The Psychological Analogy of the Trinity: At Odds with Modernity," *Pacifica* 14 (2001): 281-94; Anthony Kelly, *The Trinity of Love: A Theology of the Christian God* (Wilmington, Del.: Michael Glazier, 1989), 117-18.

4. Elizabeth A. Johnson, *She Who Is: The Mystery of God in Feminist Theological Discourse* (New York: Crossroad, 1992), 113-17.

essary but limited nature of our language about God in terms of the ever greater dissimilarity than similarity between Creator and creature. In the council's words: "For between Creator and creature no similitude can be expressed without implying a greater dissimilitude."[5] In a much more strident vein, Ludwig Feuerbach (1804-1872) provided a sobering challenge to analogical thinking about God in his rejection of the religious enterprise as a monumental projection, and his pungent accusation that "God is man writ large."[6] It is an accusation that cuts to the quick. Theology must be ever mindful of the risks and the limits of its analogical thinking! The mystery we seek to express is ultimately grounded in faith and shrouded from us, and ever eludes our attempts to express it, even the most erudite. By definition and by virtue of its very nature, the mystery we seek to express simply cannot and will not be contained in any systematic theology, no matter how critically well grounded, refined, elegant, or rigorous.

The First Vatican Council highlighted three classical strategies by which theology speaks about God and the sacred mysteries. The use of analogy is well known and practiced. Yet how rarely, in comparison with the strategy of analogy, do we find the technique of *nexus mysteriorum* and, indeed, the other technique to which Vatican I refers, that of "reference to our ultimate end," explicitly and strategically engaged in systematic theology. The strategy of analogy predominates, almost to the exclusion of the other two techniques. It predominates, even when its use is denied. It is not uncommon, for example, to find theologians who explicitly reject the use of the psychological analogy in trinitarian theology and yet, apparently unwittingly, invoke what is effectively an alternative psychological analogy, the analogy of interpersonal communion.

It is here, with the technique of *nexus mysteriorum*, the interconnection of the mysteries as identified by Vatican I, that this present study appears and seeks to make a contribution. The novelty of this book resides in its exploration of the methodology of interconnection, which has been comparatively neglected in relation to the methodology of analogy in the history of theology. Our precise aim in this book is thus to explore and present the trinitarian nexus or interconnection of the mystery of the Trinity with the other great mysteries of Christian faith. We shall start with the mystery of a triune God in relation to a divine person made human in history and to the created world. Our concern is to explore the theological insights that emerge when the central mysteries of our Christian faith—Christology, creation, grace and the moral life, ecclesiology, the paschal mystery and soteriology, the world

5. DS 806; ND 320.

6. See Ludwig Feuerbach, *The Essence of Christianity*, trans. George Eliot (1854); modern ed. Amherst, N.Y.: Prometheus Books, 1989).

religions, spirituality and worship, and eschatology—are approached from an explicitly trinitarian perspective and situated in a distinctly trinitarian context. In our exploration, we shall call on and synthesize a number of contemporary approaches and review a range of recent contributions in this precise area. Theology as "faith seeking understanding" here finds expression as "faith seeking connections." We seek through our study to show how our understanding of the Trinity informs and enriches the theological enterprise. Similarly, the technique of interconnection promises a richer understanding of the Trinity itself when its connection with the other mysteries is explored.[7]

Technically, a systematic theology could be constructed from any point: Jesus Christ, grace, eschatology, creation, church, the Kingdom of God, or soteriology, but here we will use an understanding of God as Trinity as the linchpin. Karl Barth, one of the great Protestant theologians of the twentieth century, whose work marks a watershed in German Protestant trinitarian theology, placed the mystery of the Trinity at the head of his revelation-centered Christian theology, recognizing its decisive and controlling role in regard to the whole theological enterprise.[8] His contemporary, Karl Rahner, one of the great theologians in the Roman Catholic tradition, sparked a renewal of interest in trinitarian theology with his controversial *Grundaxiom* that the economic Trinity is the immanent Trinity and vice versa[9] and with his suggestion that "despite their orthodox confession of the Trinity, Christians are, in their practical life, almost mere 'monotheists.' [In other words, unitarians.] We must be willing to admit that, should the doctrine of the Trinity have to be dropped as false, the major part of religious literature could well remain virtually unchanged."[10] Despite the flourishing of trinitarian theology per se in recent years, however, there remains more generally, I suggest, a kind of trinitarian forgetfulness or, for want of a better term, a lack of trinitarian imagination in Western theology. The profoundly trinitarian intuition of Christian faith, so vibrant in the very early church, is lacking. One still finds theology units on, for example, the topics of creation or grace, where no explicit reference is made to the mystery of the Trinity. Our aim is to awaken that trinitarian intuition and to foster an explicitly trinitarian imagination that extends and enriches the entire theological enterprise.

7. Consider, for example, my own *The Trinity and the Paschal Mystery: A Development in Recent Catholic Theology*, New Theology Studies 5 (Collegeville, Minn.: Liturgical Press, 1997), in which the mystery of the Trinity is explored from the perspective of Jesus' paschal mystery.

8. Karl Barth, *Church Dogmatics*, vol. 1, *The Doctrine of the Word of God: Prolegomena to Church Dogmatics*, part 1 (Edinburgh: T&T Clark, 1975), 295-304. For an excellent study of trinitarian theology in German Protestant thought, see Samuel M. Powell, *The Trinity in German Thought* (Cambridge: Cambridge University Press, 2001).

9. Karl Rahner, *The Trinity*, trans. Joseph Donceel (London: Burns & Oates, 1970), 21-24.

10. Ibid., 10-11.

1

The Development of Trinitarian Theology in the Patristic and Medieval Periods

BEFORE WE PROCEED to explore the interconnection of the mystery of the Trinity with other mysteries of Christian faith, we shall first familiarize ourselves with the biblical foundations of trinitarian faith, and with the development of trinitarian doctrine and theology, as expressed in the patristic and medieval periods. There in the tradition we find extraordinarily rich veins of trinitarian spirituality.

FAITH'S EXPERIENCE OF THE THREE: THE ORIGINATING EXPERIENCE

Andrei Rublev's magnificent fifteenth-century icon, sometimes known as "The Hospitality of Abraham," depicts with rare beauty the story, narrated in Genesis 18:1-15, of the three visitors to Abraham, near the oaks of Mamre. In that story, Abraham offers hospitality and refreshment to his guests and they tell Abraham that Sarah will bear a son. At another level of interpretation of the image, the icon depicts the holy Trinity, the divine community of the three coequal divine persons of the Trinity. Indeed, the icon was painted for the iconostasis of the Monastery of the Holy Trinity in Russia. The three angelic figures, with their beautifully elongated and winged bodies, sit in gentle repose and communion around the table. Their faces are turned in tender loving deference to one another. A sense of serenity and harmony exudes from the icon. With its exquisite interplay of color and light, the icon speaks of the unity and the diversity of the divine persons, their distinctiveness and their equality, the otherwardness of their attention, and the very rhythm and splendor of trinitarian life and love. It is hardly surprising that Rublev's icon proved to be his crowning achievement, so highly esteemed that it was later deemed to be the model for all representations of the Trinity.

But such a trinitarian interpretation of the visitation of the three to Abraham would not have been possible or even conceivable in Old Testament times. It was only from the vantage point of the divine self-revelation, as attested in the New Testament, that the story of Abraham's hospitality to his three mysterious guests was able to be perceived through a trinitarian lens. Scholars debate the degree to which the New Testament writers were cognizant of "the trinitarian problem" of the existence of the Three in the one Godhead—for problem it indeed is once the question of the Three in the one nature of God's being, and of how this could be so, emerges in consciousness. But there is widespread agreement that there is no sense of a plurality of persons within the Godhead prior to the revelation of God that is given in Jesus. The Old Testament is nevertheless highly significant in the later development of trinitarian conceptuality, for it provided a framework and terminology with which to speak of plurality in God. We turn now to survey briefly faith's experience of the threeness of God as attested in the Scriptures.[1]

The Old Testament speaks, for example, of God as Father, though Father is not a common title in the Old Testament and, when it does occur, it more often refers to the Father of Israel as a nation. The Old Testament also speaks of the Son of God, at first in reference to the people as a whole and sometimes in reference to a king or a judge or an upright Jew. Whether Son of God was used in reference to the Messiah before the time of Jesus is unclear. Messianic expectations included notions of a messianic kingdom and a personal Messiah, although not a divine Messiah. The Old Testament also speaks of the Word and the Wisdom of God, but without personification. In other words, Word and Wisdom in the Old Testament do not refer to personal divine beings as such. Neither Word nor Wisdom is a person to be addressed. They do not connote any kind of plurality in the Godhead. Nor is there evidence of paternity and filiation within the Godhead in the Old Testament. Similarly Spirit, originally meaning wind or breath, as in the breath of life, and at times linked with Messiah, is not regarded as a person as such. Spirit is rather an attribute or activity of God.

While the Old Testament evinces no sense of plurality in the Godhead, what it does provide is, first, a climate within which plurality was later conceivable and, second, a terminology with which to express that plurality. It is no accident, then, that, in the light of trinitarian revelation in the life, death, and resurrection of Jesus, the New Testament writers employ notions of God

1. For helpful surveys of the biblical basis of Christian faith in the Trinity, see Arthur Wainwright, *The Trinity in the New Testament* (London: SPCK, 1962); Edmund J. Fortman, *The Triune God: A Historical Study of the Doctrine of the Trinity* (London: Hutchinson; Philadelphia: Westminster, 1972), 3-33; Boris Bobrinskoy, *The Mystery of the Trinity: Trinitarian Experience and Vision in the Biblical and Patristic Tradition* (Crestwood, N.Y.: St. Vladimir's Seminary Press, 1999), 13-143. For magnificent recent studies of the resurrection and of the development of devotion to the risen Jesus, see Larry W. Hurtado, *Lord Jesus Christ: Devotion to Jesus in Earliest Christianity* (Grand Rapids: Wm. B. Eerdmans, 2003); and N. T. Wright, *The Resurrection of the Son of God,* Christian Origins and the Question of God 3 (London: SPCK, 2003).

as Father, Son, Word, Messiah, Wisdom, and Spirit to describe and name the experience of the plurality of God in New Testament times. The Old Testament provided terminology and conceptuality for the threefold experience of God in Jesus Christ.

Turning to the New Testament, there are in fact very few texts that make reference to the three *dramatis personae* in the one text. The most notable example is the Matthean baptismal commissioning at the end of Matthew's Gospel: "Go therefore and make disciples of all nations, baptizing them in the name of the Father, and of the Son, and of the Holy Spirit" (Matt. 28:19). There are, of course, a number of scriptural cameos that iconically attest to an experience of the Three: the infancy narrative, the baptismal theophany, the story of Jesus' temptations, the transfiguration, the farewell discourses in John's Gospel, the ascension, Peter's speech at Pentecost, the martyrdom of Stephen, and most importantly, of course, the narrative of Jesus' paschal mystery of death and resurrection.

While the full threefold reference can rarely be found in single passages, there are many texts that refer to two of the Three. Certainly, the Father, Son, and Holy Spirit each emerge in clear distinction from the other two. Jesus' relationship to the Father is clearly unique, unlike any other, as quintessentially expressed in the remarkable intimacy with which in prayer he invokes the Father as Abba.[2] The Father–Son relationship is evidently a highly privileged one in the New Testament, and is especially strongly depicted in John's Gospel. The Holy Spirit emerges with considerable vibrancy and with a distinct personal reality, particularly in the Paraclete passages in John's Gospel and in Paul's letters.[3]

The Synoptic Gospels and the Acts of the Apostles provide clear witness to the belief that God is one. God is sometimes called Father. Jesus is referred to as Son of God in a way that indicates more than messianic sonship. Mark's Gospel, for example, describes Jesus as "the Son of God" (Mark 1:1; 15:39), while, in Matthew's account, Peter declares: "You are the Christ, the Son of the living God" (Matt. 16:16).[4] At times the texts seem to indicate that Jesus is subordinate to the Father; at other times, the title Son of God seems to

2. See Joachim Jeremias's classic study *The Prayers of Jesus*, Studies in Biblical Theology, 2nd series 6 (London: SCM Press, 1967). Wolfhart Pannenberg, in regard to Jesus' use of Abba, refers to L. Snidler's argument that there is evidence of the use of Abba in the Talmud, and to Helmut Merklein's claim that it is the frequency and normalcy of Jesus' use of Abba that is distinctive and original or unique. See Pannenberg, *Systematic Theology*, vol. 1, trans. Geoffrey W. Bromiley (Grand Rapids: Wm. B. Eerdmans, 1991), 260.

3. Some biblical scholars argue that John's Gospel comes closer than any other New Testament writing to a trinitarian position. See, e.g., Fortman, *Triune God*, 30. Arthur Wainwright notes that the threefold pattern is absent from the Letter to the Hebrews (*Trinity*, 255).

4. N. T. Wright points out that "'Son of god' is a notoriously fluid title in early Christianity. It is all too easy to jump to conclusions about what it meant to the original writers and their first readers" (*Resurrection*, 724). For Wright's discussion of the meanings of "Son of God," see *Resurrection*, 723ff.

refer to a divine sonship, in other words, that the Son is strictly divine as the Father is divine. The title Son of Man is often used by Jesus himself. It does not affirm divine sonship, but it is associated with the power to forgive sins and with power over the Sabbath. The title Lord is only rarely applied to Jesus in the Synoptic Gospels. When it is used in relation to Jesus in Acts, it would seem to ascribe more than messianic lordship to the risen Jesus. Stephen prays: "Lord Jesus, receive my spirit. . . . Lord do not hold this sin against them" (Acts 7:59-60). While the Holy Spirit is usually depicted as a divine force or power in the Synoptics and Acts, the distinct personal existence of the Holy Spirit is suggested in the theophany at the baptism, the baptismal command, and the descent of the Holy Spirit at Pentecost. If we define "trinitarian" to refer to the existence of three coequal persons in the Godhead, there is no trinitarian witness as such in the Synoptics and Acts. There are, however, undoubtedly traces of what we could call triadic patterns that attest to a sense of three *dramatis personae* in God. Matthew's Gospel, for example, begins with the infancy narrative and concludes with the baptismal command. Jesus is more than a mere man and enjoys a unique relationship with the one whom he calls Abba, Father. There are thus clear intimations of a trinitarian pattern. In summary, there are definite traces of a triadic pattern in the Synoptics and Acts, but there is no trinitarian doctrine as such, and there is no sense of "a problem" with the Three.

In Paul's letters, God (*ho theos*) is Father and Jesus is Our Lord Jesus Christ. Paul would seem to be reluctant to call Jesus God, preferring the title Lord. Indeed, that Jesus is Christ and Lord is the very kernel of Paul's gospel. Paul often refers to Jesus as Son of God, frequently in the Old Testament sense of the one divinely chosen for a divine mission. In other words, it has a soteriological function rather than an ontological reference—though it is sometimes more than merely functional—and affirms the divinity of the Son in relation to the Father (God), as when, for example, Paul speaks of "when the time had fully come, God sent forth his Son" (Gal 4:4). Paul too is at times subordinationist, but the Son is never a creature in Paul's witness. The full divinity of Jesus is attested in terms of Jesus' origin, power, and sonship, a divine sonship that is proved in the resurrection. Whether and to what degree Paul is aware of the problem of Christ as Son, in terms of his relationship to the Father, are unclear. His concern is to trace the pattern of salvation history. Paul gives the Holy Spirit a fuller treatment than any other New Testament writer. He notably underscores the role of the Holy Spirit in Christian life. Paul closely associates Christ and the Holy Spirit in the work of sanctification, but without identifying them and without articulating the relationship between them. Paul writes of the double mission of Son and

Spirit: "But when the fullness of time had come, God sent his Son . . . so that we might receive adoption as children. And because you are children, God has sent the Spirit of his Son into our hearts, crying 'Abba! Father'" (Gal. 4:4-6). The Spirit is not merely a divine impersonal force but a distinct personal being. Although Paul's writings provide many triadic texts, indicating an essentially economic understanding of the Three in the work of salvation, the relations of the Three to each other and to the unity of being of God is approached only tangentially, if at all.

In John's Gospel, Father is the most favored name for God, and the Father–Son relationship is strongly depicted. Jesus is the Word, and John emphasizes the participation of the preexistent Word in creation. In the prologue, the Word is God. After John 1:18 ("No one has ever seen God. It is God the only Son . . . who has made him known"), John makes no further reference to the Word. It is Jesus as the Son of God that emerges most clearly in John's Gospel. As John writes, "these are written so that you may come to believe that Jesus is the Messiah, the Son of God" (John 20:31). For John, this title, Son of God, has not just ethical or soteriological but metaphysical and ontological implications. John clearly calls Jesus God in John 1:18 and John 20:20. Thomas calls the risen Jesus, "My Lord and my God" (John 20:28). But the Johannine text "the Father is greater than I" (John 14:28) will later be used to justify and bolster the argument that the Son is subordinate to—indeed a creature of—the Father. The person of the Holy Spirit emerges clearly in the Paraclete passages (14:16, 17, 26; 15:26-27; 16:7-15), and John attests to a distinctly personal reality more explicitly than anywhere else in the New Testament. The Holy Spirit is the Paraclete, the Consoler, the Advocate, the Intercessor. More clearly than any other writer, John evinces and emphasizes an understanding of the divinity of the Son and of the Holy Spirit as person, thus laying the foundations for a doctrine of the Trinity. In summary, John comes closer to a trinitarian position than any other New Testament writer, demonstrating a certain degree of awareness of the trinitarian problem.

In the context of feminist concerns regarding the strongly masculine imagery in naming the persons of the Trinity, Geoffrey Wainwright argues that the names Father, Son, and Holy Spirit are given to us in revelation and are not to be lightly set aside:

> In sum, it seems to me that the trinitarian name of God is *given* to us with Jesus' address to "Abba, Father," his self-understanding and career as "the Son," his promise of the Holy Spirit. Christian reflection upon the divine self-revelation and the experience of salvation it brought led to the conclusion of an eternal divine Tri-unity. Classical Christian worship . . . has

> normatively employed the given name of the one God—Father, Son, and Holy Spirit—whenever the Trinity has been solemnly invoked. Thus the historic identity of the Christian faith is at stake if that structure is obscured or the best name we have is abandoned.[5]

But while we can agree that the names Father, Son, and Holy Spirit are given in revelation and are not to be lightly set aside, issues remain regarding an authentic interpretation of those names and, no less importantly, of their use in the Christian tradition and in Christian life. As William Hill explains, in a discussion of the New Testament matrix of the Trinity:

> Father, Son and Spirit are not so much proper names in the New Testament, with immediate connotations of personhood, as they are symbols of God arising spontaneously out of the religious experience that in its tripartite character is indigenously Christian. God is grasped by those who "follow after Jesus" as utterly transcendent (but lovingly and trustingly so in the mode of a caring father), as mediated and available to us in the reality of a human life (i.e., as saving us through the humanity of Jesus), and as immanent in the world (i.e., as a force working invisibly in the depths of human consciousnesses forming the believing community).[6]

The New Testament does not contain a doctrine per se of the Trinity, in the sense of an understanding of three distinct coequal subjects within the one Godhead; indeed, it leaves open the issue of the relation of the Son and Spirit to the Father, as later controversies amply demonstrate. What the New Testament does is to attest strongly to a profound sense in the early Christian community of the threeness of God, with references that are admittedly probably more liturgical than confessional and certainly not creedal. Triadic resonances and an abundance of fragmentary arcs and intimations throughout the New Testament combine to reinforce the threefold pattern that emerges there. While the Scriptures do not give an explicit *doctrine* of the Trinity, however,

---

5. Geoffrey Wainwright, "Trinitarian Worship," in *Speaking the Christian God: The Holy Trinity and the Challenge of Feminism*, ed. Alvin F. Kimel (Grand Rapids: Wm. B. Eerdmans, 1992), 218-19. Aquinas holds that "Father" is a distinctly personal name. *STh* I, q. 33, aa. 2-3. For discussions on this issue, see Gerald O'Collins and David Kendall, who argue for the traditional naming of the three persons of the Trinity as irreplaceable, while also not endorsing its exclusive use (*The Bible for Theology: Ten Principles for the Theological Use of Scripture* [Mahwah, NJ: Paulist Press, 1997]). For an excellent study of the understanding of the fatherhood of God in the early church, see Peter Widdicombe, *The Fatherhood of God from Origen to Athanasius* (Oxford: Clarendon Press, 1994). For a well-balanced and informed study of the issue from a feminist perspective, see Elizabeth A. Johnson, *She Who Is: The Mystery of God in Feminist Theological Discourse* (New York: Crossroad, 1992). See also Anne Hunt, *What Are They Saying about the Trinity?* (Mahwah, N.J.: Paulist Press, 1998), 22-34.

6. William J. Hill, *The Three-Personed God: The Trinity as a Mystery of Salvation* (Washington, D.C.: Catholic University of America Press, 1982), 26.

they do more than simply pave the way for it: they attest to the vibrant lived experience in the early Christian community of the threefold structure of God's self-revelation; they witness to the threefoldness of God as expressed in liturgical and sacramental practice; they provide clear intimations of a trinitarian pattern; they establish a rhetoric for the expression of trinitarian faith; and they provide the basis for later development of trinitarian doctrine.

THE EARLY DISTILLATION OF TRINITARIAN FAITH

An eleventh-century Anglo-Saxon drawing shows the Trinity of Father, Son, and Holy Spirit (depicted as a dove, seated on the head of Mary, who sits next to the Father and Son, with the child Jesus on her lap).[7] In that icon, Satan is depicted as a devil beneath the heavenly throne. Represented on Satan's right and left are the two arch-villains in the history of Christianity: Judas and Arius. The traitor Judas is well known in the Christian tradition. The story of his betrayal is annually recited in the Easter Triduum. But who was Arius, the reader may well ask, and what was the heinous crime that warranted his depiction in art as one comparable in villainy to Judas, who betrayed the Lord for a mere thirty pieces of silver?

Arius (d. ca. 336) was a presbyter from Alexandria in the early fourth century of the Christian era. To summarize the matter very briefly, he denied the full divinity of the Son. That betrayal was his crime, a crime—so the unknown artist depicts it—comparable with Judas's betrayal. Arius, concerned to protect the divine unity, immutability, and impassibility, reasoned that the Word, while preexistent in regard to the world, is a created intermediary, a kind of demi-god, neither fully God nor fully human. He argued that the Logos is not eternal, that it is foreign to the divine nature, that it is not God as the Father is truly and fully and eternally God. He argued that the Logos is a creature, created out of nothing, and had a beginning. "There was when he was not," Arius argued, and this expression effectively served as the Arian slogan. Only a lesser god, of reduced divinity, was capable of suffering, Arius reasoned. How else could God suffer? Hence Arius adopted a subordinationist stance in regard to the question of the divinity of Jesus Christ, the incarnate Son and Word. Arius's religious imagination simply could not accommodate a God who did what Jesus Christ had done.[8]

---

7. *The Father and the Son and the Dove of the Holy Spirit with the Virgin Mary and the Christ Child*, British Library, Cotton MSS Titus D. xxvi and xxvii.

8. For discussions of the Arian controversy, see Lewis Ayers, *Nicaea and Its Legacy: An Approach to Fourth-Century Trinitarian Theology* (Oxford: Oxford University Press, 2004); R. P. C. Hanson, *The Search for the Christian Doctrine of God: The Arian Controversy 318-381* (Edinburgh: T&T Clark, 1988); Rowan Williams, *Arius*, 2nd ed. (London: SCM Press, 2001).

So great was the fracas in Emperor Constantine's only recently united Roman empire that this theological debate threatened to split the empire asunder. There were enough troubles on the boundaries of the empire without troubles within. Constantine proceeded to bring imperial pressure to resolve the dispute and restore religious unity and peace. He called a universal council of the newly imperially sanctioned church at Nicaea in June 325. It was to be the first-ever formal council of bishops representing the whole church to resolve a question of doctrine (and hence began the tradition of *ecumenical councils*). The council was opened by Constantine, and he maintained a keen interest in the proceedings, determined above all to have a clear resolution to the controversy. According to tradition, about three hundred bishops gathered at Nicaea, including Athanasius, most of them from the East. The controversy focused on the generation of the Word or Son from the Father. The real issue was Christian realism: Is the Son truly God or is that designation merely a courtesy title? The issue was brought to a head when pressed to its soteriological consequences: Are we really and truly saved or are we not? The council resolved that the Son is truly God and not by way of a courtesy title. In response to the Arian slogan, the council replied that "there was not when he was not." He was the eternally begotten Son of God. He was not a creature of the Creator. He was not created out of nothing. The resolution was articulated in the Creed or Symbol of Nicaea. In that creed, the council used the unscriptural word, *homoousios,* "from the same being/substance," to state that the Son is truly, fully, equally and eternally God, as the Father is God. The Son is begotten, eternally, from the very being or substance of the Father. The creed of the Council of Nicaea stated:

> We believe in one God, the Father almighty, maker of all things, visible and invisible.
>
> And in one Lord Jesus Christ, the Son of God, the only-begotten generated from the Father, that is, from the being [*ousia*] of the Father, God from God, Light from Light, true God from true God, begotten, not made, one in being [*homoousios*] with the Father, through whom all things were made, those in heaven and those on earth. For us human beings and for our salvation he came down, and became flesh, was made man, suffered, and rose again on the third day. He ascended to the heavens, and shall come again to judge the living and the dead.
>
> And in the Holy Spirit.[9]

9. DS 125; ND 7. Four anathemas are included at the end of the creed: "As for those who say: 'There was a time when He was not' and 'Before being begotten He was not,' and who declare that He was made from nothing [*ex ouk ontōn*], or that the Son of God is from a different substance [*hypostasis*] or being [*ousia*], that is, created [*ktistos*] or subject to change and alteration,—[such persons] the Catholic Church condemns." DS 8; ND 126.

Arius and his supporters were exiled. The Council of Nicaea was not, however, the end of the matter. The bishops returned to their communities, but the trouble was that there was no unanimity of understanding as to what the *homoousios* really meant; its meaning had not been clearly defined. The problem was compounded by the fact that the language of the church in the East was Greek, while that in the West was Latin, with difficulties in translation further exacerbating the problem. In some ways, *homoousios* was redolent of what was known as modalism, the heresy that understands the three divine persons of Father, Son, and Holy Spirit as merely different "modes" or manifestations of God's presence at different times in salvation history. A good number of bishops, having supported the anti-Arian *homoousios* at the council, became concerned that *homoousios* had modalist overtones and did not adequately protect the real distinctions between the divine persons. They were therefore inclined to favor a more explicitly antimodalist term, *homoiousios* (of *like* substance). Meanwhile the question of the divinity of the Holy Spirit had also emerged as an issue of dispute. Is the Holy Spirit truly, fully, and eternally God, as the Father is? The emperor Theodosius called another council, this time at Constantinople in 381. Here too Athanasius played a significant role, and here too the soteriological perspective served to clarify the matter. As Athanasius explains: "But if, by participation in the Spirit, we are made 'sharers in the divine nature,' we should be mad to say that the Spirit has a created nature and not the nature of God. For it is on this account that those in whom he is are made divine. If he makes men divine, it is not to be doubted that his nature is of God."[10] Thanks to the unifying conciliating work of Athanasius, the Council of Constantinople reiterated the *homoousios* and clarified that the Holy Spirit was also truly, really, and fully God, stating that the Holy Spirit "is Lord and Giver of Life. He proceeds from the Father. He is worshipped and glorified." The Nicene-Constantinopolitan Creed proclaimed:[11]

> We believe in one God, the Father almighty, maker of heaven and earth, of all things visible and invisible.
>
> And in one Lord Jesus Christ, the only-begotten Son of God, generated from the Father before all ages, Light from Light, true God from true God, begotten, not made, one in being [*homoousios*] with the Father, through whom all things were made. For us and for our salvation He came

10. Athanasius, *Epistle* 1.24, in *The Letters of Saint Athanasius Concerning the Holy Spirit*, trans. C. R. B. Shapland (New York: Philosophical Library, 1951), 126-27.

11. The reader may well notice a number of differences in word order and sentence structure between the two creeds. For a discussion of the relationship of the Constantinopolitan Creed to the Creed of the Council of Nicaea, see J. N. D. Kelly, *Early Christian Creeds*, 2nd ed. (London: Longmans, 1960), 296-331.

down from the heavens, and became flesh from the Holy Spirit and the Virgin Mary and was made man. For our sake too he was crucified under Pontius Pilate, suffered and was buried. On the third day he rose again according to the Scriptures, he ascended to the heavens and is seated at the right hand of the Father. He shall come again in glory to judge the living and the dead; to his Kingdom there will be no end.

And in the Holy Spirit, the Lord [*to Kyrion*] and Giver of life, who proceeds [*ekporeuomenon*] from the Father,[12] who together with the Father and the Son is worshipped and glorified, who has spoken through the prophets. [And] in one Holy Catholic and apostolic Church. We acknowledge one baptism for the forgiveness of sins. We expect the resurrection of the dead and the life of the world to come. Amen.[13]

At this point then, in 381, the trinitarian faith of the church was distilled and proclaimed in what came to be called the Nicene Creed, which Christians continue to recite today as the symbol par excellence of our faith.[14] Trinitarian doctrine was effectively settled. The task of meaning-making and interpretation remained, however, as indeed it does for every generation. Theology at this stage moves from a dogmatic stage, wherein doctrine is formulated and promulgated, into what we might describe as a more properly theological stage, wherein our faith seeks understanding of the mysteries we proclaim.

THE CAPPADOCIANS IN THE EAST AND AUGUSTINE OF HIPPO IN THE WEST

The challenge in trinitarian theology is how to talk coherently and intelligibly about the reality of God as both three and one. Clearly, precision in terminology and clarity in conceptuality are required. Conceptual clarity demanded terminological clarity. Two terms in fourth-century Greek emerged in Christian theological usage in the East, *ousia* and *hypostasis*, both of which refer to something that subsists. However, the terms were effectively

12. Note that the phrase "and the Son" (Latin: *filioque*) is not included in this creed. Its later unilateral inclusion in the Western church contributed in large measure to the continuing division between the East and West. (See appendix for a brief survey of what is called the Filioque Controversy.) Note, however, that the creed does not say that the Holy Spirit proceeds from the Father *alone*.

13. DS 150; ND 12. The Second Council of Constantinople (553) would later reiterate: "If anyone shall not confess that the nature [*physis, natura*] or essence [*ousia, substantia*] of the Father, of the Son and of the Holy Ghost is one, as also the force and the power; [if anyone does not confess] a consubstantial [*homoousios*] Trinity, one Godhead to be worshipped in three subsistences [*hypostaseis, subsistentiae*] or Persons [*prosopa, personae*]: let him be anathema" (*Nicene and Post-Nicene Fathers,* 2nd series, 14:312).

14. The creed made its way into the Western church in a slightly different form.

synonymous at that time. The Council of Nicaea, for example, uses both, without distinction.[15]

The Cappadocians—Basil of Caesarea (d. 379), his brother Gregory of Nyssa (d. 394), and their little-known sister and ascetic Macrina (d. 379), and their friend Gregory of Nazianzus (d. 390)—came from Cappadocia in the East, part of what is now modern Turkey.[16] They contributed significantly to the development in the East of the terminology and conceptuality with which to speak about the mystery of the Trinity.[17] Gregory of Nazianzus, for example, explains:

> God is three in regard to distinctive properties, or subsistences [*hypostases*], or, if you like, persons [*prosōpa*]: for we shall not quarrel about the names, as long as the terms lead to the same conception. He is one in respect of the category of substance, that is, of godhead. . . . We must avoid any notion of superiority or inferiority between the Persons; nor must we turn the union into a confusion, nor the distinction into a difference of natures. (*Oratio* 39.11)[18]

In his *Oration on the Great Athanasius,* Gregory of Nazianzus teaches: "We use in an orthodox sense the terms one Essence [*ousia*] and three Hypostases [*hypostaseis*], the one to denote the nature of the Godhead, the other the properties of the Three" (*Oratio* 21.35).[19] Basil of Caesarea compares the distinction between *ousia* and *hypostasis* to the distinction between the general and the particular, and explains: "Therefore in respect of the godhead we acknowledge one *ousia* . . . but we also confess the particular *hypostasis* so that we may have an unconfused and clear conception of Father, Son, and Holy Spirit" (*Epistle* 236.6).[20] Although the process was a long and circuitous one, thanks in large measure to the Cappadocians, *hypostasis* (person) gradually

15. See the anathemas at the end of the creed of the Council of Nicaea, where *hypostasis* and *ousia* appear to be used synonymously.

16. For an introduction to the Cappadocians generally, including Macrina, and to Gregory of Nazianzus, in particular, whom the Fathers acclaimed as "Gregory the Theologian," see John McGuckin, *Saint Gregory of Nazianzus: An Intellectual Biography* (Crestwood, N.Y.: St. Vladimir's Seminary Press, 2001).

17. See, e.g., John D. Zizioulas, "The Doctrine of the Holy Spirit: The Significance of the Cappadocian Contribution," in *Trinitarian Theology Today: Essays on Divine Being and Act*, ed. Christoph Schwöbel (Edinburgh: T&T Clark, 1995), 44-60.

18. This translation is from *The Later Christian Fathers: A Selection from the Writings of the Fathers from St Cyril of Jerusalem to St Leo the Great,* ed. Henry Bettenson (London: Oxford University Press, 1970), 118.

19. "On the Great Athanasius," in *Nicene and Post-Nicene Fathers,* 2nd series, 7:279.

20. This translation is from Bettenson, *Later Christian Fathers*, 77. See also *Basil,* Letter 38, "Concerning the difference between ousia and hypostasis" (traditionally attributed to Basil although also found in the works of Gregory of Nyssa and possibly written by him) in *Nicene and Post-Nicene Fathers,* 2nd series, 8:137-41.

emerged as the term with which to refer to the Three in their distinction from each other within the One God, while *ousia* (substance) emerged as the term to refer to the Oneness of God. In 381, the Council of Constantinople, in the letter addressed by the Synod of Constantinople to the Western bishops, spoke of the mystery of the Trinity in terms of three *hypostases* and one *ousia* (though the distinction is not expressed in this way in the creed of the council as such).[21]

The Cappadocians distinguished between the Three in terms of their origin and mutual relations: the Father is font or cause; the Son is begotten of the Father; and the Holy Spirit proceeds from Father.[22] While recognizing that the person of Father is source or font or fountainhead of the Godhead, they insisted that the Son and Holy Spirit are not subordinate. They recognized, in a counter against the charge of tritheism, that the unity of the three persons is expressed in their unity of activity or common work.[23] They explained the mystery of the unity of the three hypostases in the one divine *ousia* in terms of the notion of coinherence in each other.[24] In the eighth century, John Damascene would speak in terms of perichoresis.[25] The Council of Florence (1438-

21. Council of Constantinople, The Synodical Letter, in *Nicene and Post-Nicene Fathers,* 2nd series, 14:188-90. For a careful study of the history of the so-called but arguably overstated "Cappadocian solution" (one *ousia* and three *hypostaseis*) to the fourth-century trinitarian controversy, see Joseph T. Leinhard, "*Ousia* and *Hypostasis*: The Cappadocian Settlement and the Theology of 'One *Hypostasis*,'" in *The Trinity: An Interdisciplinary Symposium on the Trinity,* ed. Stephen T. Davis, Daniel Kendall, and Gerald O'Collins (Oxford: Oxford University Press, 1999), 99-121.

22. Gregory of Nyssa, for example, distinguishes between the processions of Son and Spirit: "And again we conceive of a further difference from the cause: the one [i.e. the Son] is derived immediately from the first cause, another [i.e. the Spirit] through that which is thus immediately derived. So the status of the Only-begotten attaches incontrovertibly to the Son, while the Spirit is unambiguously derived from the Father: the mediation of the Son safeguards his character as Only-begotten, without precluding the Spirit's relationship to the Father by way of nature." "Quod non sunt tres dei," from Bettenson, *Later Christian Fathers*, 154. Basil writes of "the Holy Spirit . . . conjoined as He is to the one Father through the one Son." Basil, *On the Holy Spirit* in *Nicene and Post-Nicene Fathers,* 2nd series, 8:28; see also 8:29.

23. Wolfhart Pannenberg notes, in contrast, that theology in the second and third centuries had based the distinction between the persons on the idea of different spheres of operation. See Pannenberg, *Systematic Theology*, 1:278. As Pannenberg points out, this notion of the common activity of the three divine persons meant, first, that the common activity was not constitutive of the divine persons or their relations and, second, that another basis had to be found for the trinitarian distinctions, which the Cappadocians then located in the relations. Pannenberg also points out that Gregory of Nyssa had to concede that the unity of action did not necessarily mean unity of substance. See Pannenberg, *Systematic Theology*, 1:395 n. 110.

24. See Basil, *Letter* 38.8, in *Nicene and Post-Nicene Fathers,* 2nd series, 8:141.

25. John of Damascus, "Exposition of the Orthodox Faith," 1.8; 3.5; and 4.18, in *Nicene and Post-Nicene Fathers*, 2nd series, 9:11, 49, 90, 91. Hilary of Poitiers also expressed the notion of coinhering relations in God. See *De Trinitate* 3.1; 4.1; 9.69, in *Nicene and Post-Nicene Fathers,* 2nd series, vol. 9. Note that the word perichoresis does not share etymological roots with *perichōreuo* ("dance around") but rather relates to *perichōreō*, meaning "to encompass" or "to permeate," although the notion of dancing around is considered to be a most apt image for the divine unity. Walter Kasper observes that the concept of perichoresis (mutual indwelling or interpenetration) first occurs in Gregory of Nazianzus,

1445) later articulated the doctrine of the perichoresis, or circumincession, the coinherence or mutual indwelling of the divine persons, as an explication of the true identity of substance in the Trinity.[26]

Augustine of Hippo in the West (354-430) brought a new level of conceptuality to trinitarian theology and had a profound influence on the development of Latin trinitarian theology in particular.[27] His book *The Trinity (De Trinitate)*, although not the only trinitarian writing by Augustine, is his most significant work on this subject. It was written between approximately 400 and 420.[28] Appealing to the text from Isaiah that "unless you believe, you will not understand" (Isa. 7:9), Augustine's aim, he explained, was to show how faith, assisted by reason, can proceed toward an understanding of the mystery of the Trinity, in other words, the unity and equality of the Three and their real distinction. Augustine begins with a discussion of the unity of God, but this does not mean that Augustine understands the divine essence to be prior to the divine persons. In *Letter* 120 (ca. 410), where Augustine explicitly addresses the question of the unity of the Godhead and the distinction of the persons, he expressly argues against the notion that the substance of the Trinity is anything other than the Father, Son, and Spirit:

> The Father, the Son and the Holy Spirit are the Trinity, but they are only one God; not that the divinity, which they have in common, is a sort of

in relation to the two natures in Christ (*Epistle* 101.6; see *Nicene and Post-Nicene Fathers,* 2nd series, 7:440) and that it is John Damascene who first applies the term *perichōrēsis* to the Trinity of divine persons (*The God of Jesus Christ,* trans. Matthew J. O'Connell [New York: Crossroad, 1988], 284).

26. DS 1331; ND 326. The Greek word, *perichōrēsis*, is translated into Latin as *circumincessio* (from *incedere*, "to permeate and interpenetrate") and *circuminsessio* (from *sedere* and *sessio*, "to be seated"). The former conveys a more active and dynamic indwelling and coinherence and is usually the preferred Latin form. Actually, the notion of perichoresis is arguably best rendered by the combination of *circumincessio* and *circuminsessio.*

27. For a classic study of Augustine, see Peter Brown, *Augustine of Hippo: A Biography* (Berkeley and Los Angeles: University of California Press, 2000). For helpful discussions of Augustine's trinitarian theology, see Edmund Hill, *The Mystery of the Trinity,* Introducing Catholic Theology 4 (London: Geoffrey Chapman, 1985); Basil Studer, *The Grace of Christ and the Grace of God: Christocentrism or Theocentrism*, trans. Matthew J. O'Connell (Collegeville, Minn.: Liturgical Press, 1997); Lewis Ayers, "The Fundamental Grammar of Augustine's Trinitarian Theology," in *Augustine and His Critics: Essays in Honour of Gerald Bonner*, ed. Robert Dodaro and George Lawless (London: Routledge, 2002), 51-76; Michel René Barnes, "Rereading Augustine's Theology of the Trinity," in *The Trinity: An Interdisciplinary Symposium*, 145-76; Neil Ormerod, "Augustine's *De Trinitate* and Lonergan's Realms of Meaning," *Theological Studies* 64 (2003): 773-94.

28. Other discussions in regard to the Trinity can be found in Augustine's earlier *Letter* 11, in *Nicene and Post-Nicene Fathers,* 1st series, 1:228-30; in "A Treatise on Faith and the Creed" (*De fide et symbolo*), in *Nicene and Post-Nicene Fathers,* 1st series, 3:327-31; in Tractate 39, in *Nicene and Post-Nicene Fathers,* 1st series, 7:222-24. See Barnes, "Rereading Augustine on the Trinity," 145-76, where Barnes also discusses *Sermon* 52, and No. 69 of Augustine's Eighty-Three Different Questions, *Div. Quaest.* (See *Fathers of the Church,* vol. 7.)

> fourth person, but that the Godhead is ineffably and inseparably a Trinity. (*Letter* 120)[29]

Later in this same letter, Augustine reiterates this point:

> You know that in the Catholic faith it is the true and firm belief that the Father and the Son and the Holy Spirit are one God, while remaining a Trinity, because they are inseparably of the one and the same substance, or, if this is a better word, essence. . . . It remains for us, then, to believe that the Trinity is of one substance and that the essence is nothing else than the Trinity itself.[30]

Augustine made a number of highly significant contributions to the development of trinitarian theology in the Latin church.[31] He distinguished between the visible (incarnation and Pentecost) and invisible missions of the Son and the Holy Spirit. With remarkable insight, he recognized that the missions reveal the processions; in other words, the missions are the processions revealed in time. He distinguished between mission and procession, in terms of temporal and eternal, *ad extra* and *ad intra*. He distinguished between substantial and relational categories (categories relating to substance and categories relating to the relations), and this distinction provided a coherent framework within which to accommodate both the distinction among the Three (in terms of relational categories) and the unity of the one God (in terms of substantial categories). He recognized that the unity of the one God requires that all the works of the Trinity *ad extra* are indivisible, as from one principle. He maintained, however, that each of the divine persons possesses the divine nature in a particular manner and, thus, in the operation of the Godhead *ad extra*, it is proper to attribute to each of the Three a role that is appropriate to the particular divine person, by virtue of the trinitarian origin of that person. Through this strategy of appropriation, wisdom is appropriated to the Son, love to the Holy Spirit; and the work of creation to

29. From Saint Augustine, Bishop of Hippo, *Letters*, vol. 2 *(83-130)*, trans. Wilfred Parsons, *Fathers of the Church* 18 (Washington, D.C.: Catholic University of America Press, 1953), 300-317, at 311.

30. Ibid., 314, *ut ipsa essentia non aliud sit quam ipsa trinitas.*

31. The relationship between Augustine's work and that of the Cappadocians remains a matter of interest and debate. It would seem that Augustine, who by his own admission did not read Greek easily, had Latin translations of at least excerpts from the writings of Athanasius, Basil of Ceasarea, and Gregory of Nazianzus. In *De Trinitate* 3.1, Augustine refers to some works in Greek. Augustine also refers to Hilary of Poitiers' work on the Trinity in 6.1. For a helpful overview of contemporary systematic appropriations of Augustine's trinitarian theology and a critique of the assumption of Théodore De Régnon's nineteenth-century Greek/Latin paradigm, see Michel René Barnes, "Augustine in Contemporary Trinitarian Theology," *Theological Studies* 56 (1995): 237-50.

the Father, redemption to the Son, and sanctification to the Spirit.[32] Augustine settled somewhat reluctantly for the term "person" for the three hypostases, recognizing the need to say something in response to the question of what to call the Three. As the Cappadocians had done, he distinguished the Three in terms of relations of origin or mutual relations within the one Godhead (Father unbegotten; Son begotten; the Holy Spirit their common gift, bond of communion, the mutual love of Father and Son). He too understood their unity in a perichoretic way. As he explains, they are "each in each, and all in each, and each in all, and all in all, and all are one" (Augustine, *De Trinitate* 6.12).

As well as clarifying a number of vital terms and concepts in trinitarian theology, Augustine invoked the use of a number of so-called psychological analogies, drawn from reflection on the experience of the self-conscious human subject, as a way to understand the mystery of the Trinity. His use of the psychological analogies, whereby the inner-trinitarian processions of Word and Spirit are tentatively explained chiefly in terms of our conscious experience of the mental acts of knowing and loving, was fundamentally based on the biblical understanding of the human person as created in the image of God (Gen. 1:26). Always acutely aware of their limitations, he intended these psychological analogies simply to be helpful in advancing our understanding of how it is that God could be both One and Three.

In his *De Trinitate,* Augustine presents more than twenty triadic psychological analogies for exploration, of which we shall mention only a few (Augustine, *De Trinitate* 9-11; 14). From the analogy of mind or memory, knowledge, and love (*mens, notitia, amor*), Augustine moves to memory, understanding, and will (*memoria, intellectus, voluntas*), and memory, understanding, and love (*memoria, intellectus, amor*), to memory, knowledge, and love of self (*mens meminit sui, intelligit se, diligit se)*, and thence to the human self engaged in remembering God, understanding God, and willing or loving God (*memoria Dei, intelligentia Dei, amor in Deum*). Augustine at this point concludes: "Now this trinity of the mind is God's image, not because the mind remembers, understands and loves itself; but because it has the power also to remember, understand and love its Maker" (*De Trinitate* 14.15).[33]

32. Augustine, while not actually using the term "appropriation," wrestles with the issue in *De Trinitate,* books 6 and 7. Thomas Aquinas, following Augustine, also engages the strategy of appropriation. See Timothy L. Smith, "The Context and Character of Thomas's Theory of Appropriations," *The Thomist* 63 (1999): 579-612; Anthony J. Kelly, "A Multi-Dimensional Disclosure: Aspects of Aquinas' Theological Intentionality," *The Thomist* 67 (2003): 335-74.

33. In 14.6 Augustine adds a poignant note: "if it is with reference to its capacity to use reason and understanding in order to understand and gaze upon God that it was made to the image of God, it follows that from the moment this great and wonderful nature begins to be, this image is always there, whether it is so worn away as to be almost nothing, or faint and distorted, or clear and beauti-

Here, in the consubstantial, coequal, really distinct dynamic acts of the inner self-remembering, understanding, and loving God, Augustine finds the image of the triune God in the human person. The procession of the Son corresponds to that of understanding (*intelligentia*) from the mind (*mens*) or memory (*memoria*), while the procession of the Holy Spirit corresponds to the procession of love (*amor*). Note, however, that Augustine insists:

> I do say that the Father is memory, the Son understanding, and that the Holy Ghost is will. . . . I do not say that these things are to be equated, even by analogy, with the Holy Trinity, that is to say are to be arranged according to some exact rule of comparison. This I do not say. But what do I say? See, I have discovered in you three things which we see as exhibited separately but whose operation is inseparable. (*Sermon* 52.10.23)[34]

Augustine wrestled with the question of how to distinguish the procession of the Holy Spirit from the procession of the Son by generation or begetting from the Father. He concluded that the procession of the Holy Spirit is only able to be distinguished from the Son if we say that he proceeds from the Father *and* the Son (*filioque*, meaning "and the Son"), in a common spiration, as from one source or principle (*De Trinitate* 5.15). Augustine thus laid the foundation for the inclusion of "and the Son" (*filioque*) to the section in the Nicene Creed concerning the procession of the Holy Spirit, an inclusion that was to prove so vexatious and so costly, contributing in large measure to the schism between the Church in the East and in the West.[35]

THOMAS AQUINAS: GOD IS THE PERFECTION OF BEING, *ACTUS PURUS, IPSUM ESSE*

Strongly influenced by the burgeoning of Aristotelian philosophy in the emerging university centers of Europe in the thirteenth century, Thomas Aquinas (ca. 1225-1274) refashioned the richly experiential and intuitive approach to the mystery of the Trinity that was the Augustinian inheritance.[36]

ful." See also Walter H. Principe, "The Dynamism of Augustine's Terms for Describing the Highest Trinitarian Image in the Human Person," *Studia Patristica* 18 (1982): 1291-99.

34. In *Prayers of St. Augustine*, ed. Barry Ulanov (Minneapolis: Seabury Press, 1983), 127.

35. The Second Council of Lyons (1274) and the Council of Florence (1438-1445) later defined that the Holy Spirit proceeded from the Father and Son as from one principle, that is, by one single spiration. DS 850, 1300-1302, 1330-31; ND 321, 322-24, 325-26.

36. For a most helpful introduction to Aquinas's trinitarian theology, see Herbert McCabe, "Aquinas on the Trinity," in *God Still Matters*, ed. Brian Davies (London: Continuum, 2002), 36-53; and Aidan Nichols, *Discovering Aquinas: An Introduction to His Life, Work and Influence* (London: Darton, Longman & Todd, 2002). For more detailed discussions of Aquinas's trinitarian theology,

In the *Summa Theologiae*, his theology primer for beginners,[37] Aquinas, concerned for systematic intelligibility of the sacred mysteries in a way that was never part of Augustine's intention, first reverses Augustine's more historical order of approach, which begins with the missions of Son and Spirit, and instead begins his explication of the mystery of the Trinity with a consideration of the processions, then moves to the relationships of the divine persons *ad intra*, and *finally* to their missions *ad extra*.[38]

For Aquinas, God is *Esse*, the perfection of "be-ing"or "is-ness." (The Latin *esse*, "to be," is a verb, not a noun.) Indeed God is *Ipsum Esse*, sheer actuality, sheer being, in which we participate to a limited degree. This sheer liveliness of God in God is expressed in terms of insight and joy or delight. The fullness of insight naturally expresses itself in a word that is intelligible to itself, and sheer joy or bliss issues lovingly from the delight in that word. (Here our own human experience of "getting a joke" or the "Eureka experience" of Archimedes' fame when "we get it" serves as an apt analogy. Think of your own experience of the sheer joy that accompanies the intellectual experience of "getting it," the delight that we feel when whatever it is makes sense to us and "we get it"!)

Aquinas then takes up Augustine's experientially based psychological analogy, in terms of the mental acts that issue in word and love, and transposes it into a metaphysical understanding of God as the perfection of spiritual being, Pure Act, *Actus Purus*.[39] In God as Pure Act of Be-ing, *Ipsum Esse*, to be, to know, and to love perfectly coincide. They are distinct yet inseparable. The immanent act of self-understanding issues in the inner word, the

---

see, e.g., W. J. Hankey, *God in Himself: Aquinas' Doctrine of God as Expounded in the Summa Theologiae* (Oxford: Oxford University Press, 1987); Rowan Williams, "What Does Love Know? St Thomas on the Trinity," *New Blackfriars* 82 (2001) 260-72; Anthony Kelly, "Multi-dimensional Disclosure"; and two magnificent recent studies of magisterial import, Jean-Pierre Torrell, *Saint Thomas Aquinas*, 2 vols., trans. Robert Royal (Washington, D.C.: Catholic University of America Press, 2003), esp. vol. 2, *Spiritual Master*, 1-224; and Gilles Emery, *Trinity in Aquinas*, with a foreword by Jean-Pierre Torrell (Ypsilanti, Mich.: Sapientia Press, 2003).

37. So Thomas himself describes his work in the prologue to the *Summa Theologiae*.

38. For a helpful comment on Aquinas's trinitarian thought, see Bernard Lonergan, *Verbum: Word and Idea in Aquinas*, ed. David B. Burrell (London: Darton, Longman & Todd, 1968), 206-15. Anthony Kelly provides a contemporary overview in "Multi-dimensionsal Disclosure."

39. William Stevenson, in "The Problem of Trinitarian Processions in Thomas's Roman Commentary," *The Thomist* 64 (2000): 619-29, argues that Aquinas, after an initial exploration, rejects the analogy of memory, understanding, and will and turns to the analogy based on intelligible emanations to explicate the divine processions; see *STh* I, 27. Stevenson observes that Aquinas's treatment of the *imago Dei* is separated from his consideration of the trinitarian processions by sixty-seven questions, and figures in terms of theological anthropology as distinct from trinitarian theology. In other words, Stevenson argues, Aquinas's treatment of the Trinity in the *Summa* involves a much more radical appropriation of Augustine. Neil Ormerod argues that Augustine's *De Trinitate* chapter 9 is the real foundation for Thomas's treatment of the processions in the *Summa*. See Neil Ormerod, "Augustine and the Trinity—Whose Crisis?" *Pacifica* 16 (2003): 28.

verbum—thus, the first procession whereby the Father conceives the Word or generates the Son. The Word is God understanding God, God's self-understanding (*STh* I, q. 34, a. 2, ad3). It is conceived by God; it has the same nature as God (*homoousios*); it is God. The two are distinguished from each other in their relation to each other. Turning now to consider the second procession, we know from our experience that knowledge is not disinterested or without affectivity. Recall our sense of the joy that comes with understanding. In this sense, the intellect is inclined to what is known and to what is good; it takes delight in its understanding. The emanation of the Word is thus followed by the procession of Love, a bliss, a joy, and a delight in the self-understanding that is expressed in the eternal Word. This, then, is the procession of the Holy Spirit. The Holy Spirit is God loving God; God's self-love. Thus, in the generation of the Word, God knows Godself and, in the procession of the Holy Spirit, God loves Godself. Here then is Aquinas's explication of the two processions in God: the procession of the intellect, God's self-knowledge, which is the generation of the Son or Word, and the procession of joy or delight in that self-knowledge, God's self-love, which is the spiration or procession of the Spirit. As Aquinas explains:

> There are in God two processions, namely the procession of the Word and another. To see why, one must bear in mind that in God procession corresponds only to an action which remains within the agent himself, not to one bent on something external. In the spiritual world the only actions of this kind are those of the intellect and the will. But the Word's procession corresponds to the action of the intellect. Now in us there is another spiritual process following the action of the will, namely the coming forth of love, whereby what is loved is in the lover, just as the thing expressed or actually understood in the conceiving of an idea is in the knower. For this reason besides the procession of the Word another procession is posited in God, namely the procession of Love. (*STh* I, q. 27, a. 3)

Aquinas thus proceeds to an elegant and refined rendering of an understanding of the divine processions in terms of the Aristotelian categories of the intellect and will, the dynamic activities of knowing and loving.[40] In Aquinas's hands, Augustine's more intuitive and subjective interior approach to the psychological analogy, that was grounded in his reflections on the experience of human consciousness, is rendered anew with exacting method-

40. Note that Aquinas, in *STh* I, q. 93, a. 7, ad 3, following Augustine, locates the image in the *activities*—not the faculties—of memory, intellect, and will, explicitly correcting Peter Lombard in this regard.

ological rigor, considerable metaphysical refinement and arguably unmatched explicative power. As wrought by Aquinas, the psychological analogy was to serve as the most privileged and esteemed method of explication of the mystery of the Trinity for centuries, almost to the point of dogma! It was, for example, affirmed in the catechism of the Council of Trent and in a number of papal documents, and served, unchallenged, as common doctrine until relatively recently.

The Augustinian-Thomistic analogy of human understanding and loving for explicating the mystery of the Trinity as three coequal, consubstantial (same substance) divine persons, so coinhering in each other as to be one, is superb! It fits well with the biblical teaching that the human person is created in the image of God and therefore reflects in a preeminent way the mystery of God's being. It resonates strongly with the scriptural references to the revealed processions of God's Word and Love. It acknowledges God as the perfection of consciousness and intentionality. It accords with an understanding of human being as participating, in limited degree, in the divine consciousness. It comes closer than any analogy to the mystery of the divine perichoresis (the mutual indwelling or coinhering of the Three).

RICHARD OF ST. VICTOR: GOD AS TRINITY OF LOVE, *IPSUM AMARE*

Although it was Thomas Aquinas's explication of the mystery of the Trinity in terms of the psychological analogy that was to enjoy virtual hegemony through the succeeding centuries, in this brief survey of the development of trinitarian theology it is also appropriate that we advert to other important contributions. One of those comes from the medieval mystic Richard of St. Victor (d. ca. 1173).

We have noted that Augustine's exploration of the experience of the human person as analogy for an understanding of the mystery of the Trinity yielded more than twenty variations of what came to be called the psychological analogy. One of the analogies that he presented for consideration in his book *De Trinitate* is the analogy of interpersonal love: the trinity of love that comprises the loving subject (the lover), the object loved (the beloved), and the relation or bond of love (*vinculum caritatis*), the love which unites them (*De Trinitate* 8.14; 9.2; 15.10). Augustine, however, quickly set this analogy aside. As an interpersonal as distinct from an intrapersonal analogy, it risked a tendency to tritheism. Compared to the intrapersonal psychological analogy, and its explication of the Trinity in terms of the human acts of subjectivity, the interpersonal analogy of love was far less intellectually satisfying: the three elements (lover, beloved, and their love) are clearly not consubstantial (same substance); nor do they together render very satisfactorily the mystery of the trinitarian perichoresis (the mutual coinherence or indwelling of the Three). Augustine considered the intrapersonal psychological analogy to be far superior. Yet, while the analogy of interpersonal love fails to satisfy at the level of consubstantiality and coequality of the three elements and their mutual coinherence, there is surely something that is really and deeply true that is encapsulated in the analogy of interpersonal love. After all, the Scriptures attest that God is love. So do the mystics. We too know from our own limited and flawed experience that we are our "best selves" when we are "in love." Surely the analogy of interpersonal love is especially apt in rendering the mystery of the mystery of the God who is Love, the God who is Trinity.

It is here that the medieval mystic Richard of St. Victor—whom Dante Alighieri (1265-1321), in the *Divine Comedy*, described as "in contemplation more than man"[41]—emerges in the history of trinitarian theology, with a retrieval of the analogy of interpersonal love, the analogy that was at best tangential in Augustine's exploration of the mystery of the Trinity and which he set aside in favor of the intrasubjective psychological analogy of the acts of memory, understanding, and love. Richard of St. Victor's interest found its focus not in the experience of human consciousness and the operations of knowing and willing but rather in the experience and the nature of interpersonal love.[42] Richard thus undertakes a psychological exploration of interpersonal self-transcending love. His focal image is that of human love as a reflection of divine love. The paradox inherent in Richard's theology is that he uses reason to explore the experience of human love and to demonstrate the mystery of the Trinity. In the process, he brings an exemplaristic metaphysics to his theology: God is the exemplar of human (and all) being; the human being is as image of God; human self-transcending love provides an image of trinitarian love. He also brings a metaphysics of participation to his theological endeavors: the limited perfection expressed in human experience is a sharing in the absolute perfection of the Godhead.

Richard's exploration of the mystery of the Trinity begins with the notion that God is the fullness and perfection of all goodness. Richard then reasons

---

41. Dante, *Divine Comedy*, "Paradise," Canto X, line 121, in *The Divine Comedy of Dante Alighieri*, trans. Charles Eliot Norton (Chicago: Encyclopaedia Britannica, 1952), 121.

42. For a helpful introduction to Richard of St. Victor's trinitarian theology, see Zachary Hayes, *Saint Bonaventure's Disputed Questions on the Mystery of the Trinity: An Introduction and a Translation* (St. Bonaventure, N.Y.: Franciscan University, 1979), 13-24. Although Hayes's primary interest is the influences shaping Bonaventure's theology, he provides a helpful introduction to Richard of St. Victor's contribution and its influence on Bonaventure's theology.

that, of all things that are good, charity is the greatest good, for nothing exceeds charity in goodness. God must therefore possess charity in the highest degree. As Richard explains: "where the fullness of divinity is found, there is the fullness of goodness, and consequently the fullness of charity" (*De Trinitate* 5.7).[43] An analysis of charity, as the supreme form of the good, then serves in Richard of St. Victor's trinitarian theology to demonstrate—indeed almost to prove—that there must be a plurality of persons in the Godhead.

Richard argues that charity necessarily involves another, apart from oneself. Indeed, the greatest charity is self-transcending love for another person, who is one's coequal. Hence, he argues, there must be self-transcending love for another coequal person (*condignus*) within God. Moreover, the lover and beloved wish to share their love. Mutual love, to be perfect, must be shared with a third; therein lies its consummation and perfection. In other words, since love by nature involves relation to each other, the perfection of love demands that the two persons in love share that love with a third person. Two persons in the Godhead would lack the perfection of that charity which can only be achieved by sharing their love with a third. Without the third, the perfection of love would be lacking. Richard explains:

> Sharing of love cannot exist among any less than three persons. Now, as has been said, nothing is more glorious, nothing more magnificent, than to share in common whatever you have that is useful and pleasant. But this cannot be hidden from supreme wisdom, nor can it fail to be pleasing to supreme benevolence. And as the happiness of the supremely powerful One and the power of the supremely happy One cannot be lacking in what pleases Him, so in Divinity it is impossible for two persons not to be united to a third. (*De Trinitate* 3.14)[44]

Supreme charity, Richard reasons, thus demands consummation of their love by being shared with a third coequal one. In other words, the fulfillment of their mutual love requires not just love (*dilectio*) but a shared love (*condilectio*) for a third subject; hence the necessity of a third person (*condilectus*). All three share the one love, each in the mode of love unique to that person (*De Trinitate* 5.16).

The interpersonal analogy of love—a marginal element in Augustine's theology—is thus taken up in a new and original style of trinitarian theology by Richard of St. Victor. In Richard's hands the analogy of interpersonal love

43. See Richard de Saint-Victor, *La Trinité,* trans. Gaston Salet (Paris: Éditions du Cerf, 1959), 316-17.

44. See *Richard of St Victor, Book Three of the Trinity*, trans. Grover A. Zinn (New York: Paulist, 1979), 388.

shifts from the triad of lover, beloved, and their mutual love (*vinculum caritatis*) to a triad of symmetrical and consubstantial interpersonal relations between coequals, where there is no hierarchy and where each person is at once lover and beloved. Given that it speaks deeply to and from human experience, it is hardly surprising that Richard of St. Victor's psychological analogy of interpersonal love has enjoyed considerable appeal in modern attempts to reinvigorate an understanding and appreciation of the mystery of the Trinity. Despite its perennial appeal, it was, however, never to achieve the status and influence of the intrapersonal psychological analogy, as developed by Augustine and refined by Thomas Aquinas and sanctioned in papal documents. It did, however, profoundly influence the trinitarian theology of another great medieval theologian, Bonaventure, a theologian whom Karl Rahner described as one of only a small number of Christian thinkers who evince "an authentic trinitarian mysticism."[45]

BONAVENTURE: GOD IS GOOD AND GOODNESS IS SELF-DIFFUSIVE

Bonaventure (ca. 1221-1274) is known in the tradition as the Seraphic Doctor. Pope Leo XII referred to him as "the prince of mystical theology."[46] Bonaventure was a contemporary of Thomas Aquinas and followed Francis of Assisi, the founder of the Order of Franciscans, as seventh minister general of the Friars Minor.[47] His extended period of leadership of the order earned him the title of "second founder of the Franciscan Order." Bonaventure's inspiration found its profound source in the religious experience of Francis of Assisi. Indeed, as Hans Urs von Balthasar explains: "His world is Franciscan, and so is his theology," and yet, as von Balthasar also explains, "Bonaventure does not only take Francis as his centre: he is his own sun and his mission."[48]

Inspired by Francis of Assisi, who, through his experience of Christ, had emphasized the nature of God as good and loving, and by the New Testament, which attests to goodness as the proper name of God: "No one is good

---

45. Karl Rahner, *The Trinity*, trans. Joseph Donceel (London: Burns & Oates, 1970), 10.

46. *New Catholic Encyclopedia*, 2nd ed. (Detroit: Thomson/Gale in association with the Catholic University of America, 2003), s.v. "Bonaventure."

47. For helpful introductions to Bonaventure's trinitarian theology, see Hayes, *Saint Bonaventure's Disputed Questions*, 13-66; idem, "Bonaventure: Mystery of the Triune God," in *The History of Franciscan Theology*, ed. Kenan B. Osborne (Bonaventure, N.Y.: Franciscan Institute, 1994), 39-125. For an introduction to Bonaventure's mystical writings, see Zachary Hayes, *Bonaventure: Mystical Writings* (New York: Crossroad, 1999).

48. Hans Urs von Balthasar, *The Glory of the Lord: A Theological Aesthetics*, vol. 2, *Studies in Theological Style: Clerical Styles*, ed. John Riches, trans. Brian McNeil (San Francisco: Ignatius Press, 1984), 263.

but God alone" (Luke 18:19; Matt. 19:17), Bonaventure's trinitarian theology begins with the notion of God as good. Bonaventure, like Aquinas, then draws on the Augustinian inheritance, but, unlike Aquinas, he also draws on the Pseudo-Dionysian view that goodness, which is naturally and necessarily self-diffusive (*bonum diffusivum sui*), is the pre-eminent attribute of God.[49] Since God is good, and since goodness is by its very nature self-diffusive and fecund, God is necessarily self-communicative and fecund (luxuriantly fruitful). For Bonaventure, this provides the metaphysical basis for the first emanation or procession in God (the Son/Word). The first person, the Father, is "fountain fullness" (*fontalis plenitudo*), "the fountain of plenitude," "the first principle," from whom all comes. The first procession emanates as a natural emanation (*per modum naturae*, i.e., by way of nature), which necessarily and naturally flows from the dynamic fecundity of the divine nature. (Augustine and Aquinas, by way of contrast, envisage the first procession by way of intellect. For Bonaventure, however, the first procession proceeds from the fecundity of the Father. While both understand the first procession "by way of nature," they understand it in quite different ways. For Augustine and Aquinas it is an intellectual procession; for Bonaventure it is a natural procession, which flows from the divine fecundity.[50]) Bonaventure then turns to Richard of St. Victor's reflections on love to understand the emanation or procession of the Spirit, *per modum amoris,* by way of love (or *per modum voluntatis*, by way of will). Bonaventure thus brings together a notion of goodness and the concept of love in his trinitarian theology.

The notion of primacy emerges strongly in Bonaventure's trinitarian theology: the Father is the first and ultimate source of all being; the fullness of divine fecundity resides in him. The Son or Word or Image is the inner self-expression of God and proceeds from the Father by way of exemplarity. Word is Bonaventure's preferred term for the second person, for it expresses the relations of the second person as exemplar both in relation to the Father *and* in relation to creation.[51] In regard to the emanation of the Holy Spirit,

49. See Ilia Delio, "Bonaventure's Metaphysics of the Good," *Theological Studies* 60 (1999): 228-46; see also eadem, "Does God 'Act' in Creation? A Bonaventurian Response," *Heythrop Journal* 44 (2003): 328-44; eadem, *Simply Bonaventure: An Introduction to His Life, Thought, and Writings* (New York: New City Press, 2001).

50. For very helpful comments on Bonaventure's understanding of the generation of the Son in relation to that of Augustine and Aquinas, see Hayes, *Saint Bonaventure's Disputed Questions*, 45. Hayes explains: "Bonaventure also sees the intellect to be involved. But his guiding light is the concept of primal, fecund goodness. Intellect precisely as intellect is not fecund; it is so only in as far as it springs from the fecund nature of God. Thus, the primary principle of the Son's generation is the divine nature; the natural fecundity of the neo-Platonic tradition dominates this understanding. The Augustinian tradition is integrated within this framework. That which flows from the divine essence naturally does so as a perfect self-expression of the Father; it is the Word of the intellect."

51. See Zachary Hayes, "Christ, Word of God and Exemplar of Humanity," *Cord* 46 (1996): 3-17.

Bonaventure appropriates the argument from love from the Victorine tradition and understands the Holy Spirit as "bond of love."[52]

Bonaventure's trinitarian theology also explicitly includes creation in its purview in a remarkably thought-provoking and inspiring way. Creation is another aspect of the self-expressiveness of the goodness that is God. Bonaventure recognizes that, in regard to creation, the cosmos emanates, in and through the Word, from the trinitarian exemplar and itself reflects the trinitarian order at various levels and degrees.[53] The Trinity, as source of all, necessarily leaves its stamp on all creation, Bonaventure argues. Thus, the world as a whole is a vast symbol of the Trinity. It is like a book that reflects its trinitarian author at each and every turn. Bonaventure suggests that it reflects its trinitarian Creator at three levels: as vestige (expressing the Trinity in a distant and unclear way); as image (reflecting the Trinity in a closer and more distinct way); and as similitude (that most intense reflection, which is found in the rational spirit that is conformed to God through grace, which intensifies and transforms the image found in the human person into ever deeper and more personal conformity to the eternal Exemplar). Bonaventure explains that creation is a vast symbol of the triune God:

> The creation of the world is a kind of book in which the Trinity shines forth, is represented and found as the fabricator of the universe in three modes of expression, namely, in the modes of vestige, image, and similitude, such that the reason for the vestige is found in all creations, the reason for the image in intelligent creatures or rational spirits alone, and the reason for similitude in the Godlike only. Hence, as if by steplike levels, the human intellect is born to ascend by gradations to the supreme principle, which is God. (Bonaventure, *Breviloquium* 2.12)[54]

This notion of the cosmos as the artwork of its trinitarian Creator has profound implications for our understanding of our relationship to and responsibility regarding the cosmos and provides a rich resource for an ecologically attuned theology in later developments of trinitarian theology.[55]

---

52. For a detailed discussion of Bonaventure's understanding of the Holy Spirit as the bond of mutual love of the Father and Son, see Walter Principe, "St. Bonaventure's Theology of the Holy Spirit with Reference to the Expressions 'Pater et Filius diligent se Spiritu Sancto,'" in *S. Bonaventura*, vol. 4, *Theologica* (Rome: Collegio S. Bonaventura Grottaferrata, 1974), 243-69.

53. As Zachary Hayes points out, Bonaventure's understanding of exemplarity operates at two interrelated levels—first, there is a trinitarian exemplarity and, second, a christological exemplarity. See Hayes, "Bonaventure: Mystery of the Triune God," 72.

54. Trans. Erwin E. Nemmers (London: B. Herder Book Co., 1946), 75.

55. See, e.g., Denis Edwards, *Jesus, the Wisdom of God: An Ecological Theology* (Homebush NSW: St Paul's, 1995).

JAN VAN RUUSBROEC: TRINITY AS WHIRLPOOL: LOVE RETURNS WHAT IT RECEIVES

We would not wish to conclude our survey of the development of trinitarian theology without at least brief reference to the mystical tradition. There is, of course, no one tradition of trinitarian mysticism. But among a number of medieval thinkers whom we could mention, including not least William of St. Thierry (ca. 1080),[56] Hildegard of Bingen (1098-1179),[57] and Joachim of Fiore (1135-1202),[58] two figures in particular stand out for the brilliance of their trinitarian insight, Jan van Ruusbroec (or Ruysbroeck) and Julian of Norwich.

The Flemish mystic Blessed Jan van Ruusbroec (ca. 1293-1381) is known in the tradition as the Admirable Doctor. Karl Rahner also describes him, alongside Bonaventure, as exemplifying "an authentic trinitarian mysticism,"[59] while Louis Dupré describes him as "Western Christianity's most articulate interpreter of the trinitarian mystical tradition."[60] Although Jan van Ruusbroec is the author of a number of very influential theological treatises and is esteemed as one of the great mystical theologians of the late medieval period—indeed many would count him the greatest—his writing, in Middle Dutch, is relatively little known in contemporary theology, particularly in the English-speaking world.[61]

---

56. Odo Brooke comments: "The greatest contribution of William of St Thierry is to have evolved a theology of the Trinity which is essentially mystical, and a mystical theology which is essentially Trinitarian" (*Studies in Monastic Theology* [Kalamazoo, Mich.: Cistercian Publications, 1980], 8). Where for Augustine the psychological analogy serves as analogy for the inner-trinitarian processions, for William, the trinitarian image of God in the human person grounds the dynamism by which the human person is impelled to union with God. For a study of the Augustinian basis of William's spirituality, also see David N. Bell, *The Image and Likeness: The Augustinian Spirituality of William of Saint Thierry* (Kalamazoo, Mich.: Cistercian Publications, 1984).

57. For a recent study of Hildegard of Bingen, see Anne H. King-Lenzmeier, *Hildegard of Bingen: An Integrated Vision* (Collegeville, Minn.: Liturgical Press, A Michael Glazier Book, 2001).

58. With a highly innovative theology of history, Joachim of Fiore is regarded as one of the most creative thinkers in Western thought. In Dante's *Paradiso* (Canto XII, lines 139-41), Bonaventure describes twelve figures, famed for their wisdom, who together form the second ring of the heavenly lights, and among them he includes Joachim of Fiore, as "endowed with prophetic vision." Joachim's attack on Peter Lombard's trinitarian theology was condemned at the Fourth Lateran Council in 1215, as was his own trinitarian doctrine. For Joachim, history has a trinitarian structure because God is Trinity; the inner-trinitarian relations are expressed in history, with three successive stages corresponding to the three divine persons. See DS 803-6; ND 317-20.

59. Rahner, *Trinity*, 10.

60. Louis Dupré, *The Common Life: The Origins of Trinitarian Mysticism and Its Development by Jan Ruusbroec* (New York: Crossroad, 1984).

61. For a selection of his work in English, see *Jan van Ruusbroec, The Spiritual Espousals and Other Works*, trans. with introduction by James A. Wiseman, Classics of Western Spirituality (New York: Paulist Press, 1985), and Corpus Christianorum Continuatio Mediaeualis, vols. 103, 104, 107 (Turnhout: Brepols, 1998-2002).

Ruusbroec takes up Bonaventure's notion of the divine fecundity as the source of the generation of the Son, the eternal Word.[62] The Son is generated from the fecundity of the Father and is the exemplar of all created things. The Spirit proceeds or flows forth as the mutual love of the Father and Son. But here Ruusbroec introduces an innovative element to trinitarian thinking: he reasons that it is the very nature of love to return what it has received, thus enabling the other to give again. As Ruusbroec explains: "From this comes a love, that is, the Holy Spirit, and it is a bond from the Father to the Son and from the Son to the Father. By this love, the Persons are embraced and penetrated and have flowed back into that unity out of which the Father without cease is giving birth" (*Realm of Lovers*).[63]

The Spirit thus emerges in Ruusbroec's thinking not simply as the passive love that proceeds from the mutual contemplation of the Father and Son, and as such as the one who is given, but who does not give. As Rik Van Nieuwenhove explains, for Ruusbroec, the Spirit is rather the active principle of return, *regiratio* (flowing back or return), both within the Trinity, where the divine persons return to their divine unity from which they proceed again unceasingly, and in the created cosmos, whereby all creation is drawn back to its trinitarian source. Within the Trinity, the Holy Spirit, according to Ruusbroec, "flows from them both. For He is one will and one love in both of them, and out of them both eternally flowing-out and flowing back into the nature of the Godhead" (*Twelve Beguines*).[64] Ruusbroec thus envisages the inner-trinitarian dynamic as an unceasing circular movement, rather like a fathomless eddy or bottomless whirlpool; indeed, this trinitarian image is especially dear to him.[65] A remarkably dynamic trinitarianism results,

---

62. For discussions of Ruusbroec's trinitarian theology, see Rik Van Nieuwenhove, *Jan van Ruusbroek: Mystical Theologian of the Trinity*, Studies in Spirituality and Theology (Notre Dame, Ind.: University of Notre Dame Press, 2003); idem, "In the Image of God: The Trinitarian Anthropology of St Bonaventure, St Thomas Aquinas, and the Blessed Jan van Ruusbroec," *Irish Theological Quarterly* 66 (2001): 109-23; idem, "The Franciscan Inspiration of Ruusbroec's Mystical Theology: Ruusbroec in Dialogue with Bonaventure and Thomas Aquinas," *Ons Geestelijk Erf* 75 (2001): 102-15; Paul Verdeyen, *Ruusbroec and His Mysticism*, trans. André Lefevere (Collegeville, Minn.: Liturgical Press. A Michael Glazier Book, 1994); Paul Mommaers, *The Land Within: The Process of Possessing and Being Possessed by God According to the Mystic Jan van Ruysbroeck*, trans. David N. Smith (Chicago: Franciscan Herald Press, 1975), esp. 65-76; James Wiseman, "The Birth of the Son in the Soul in the Mystical Theology of Jan van Ruusbroec," *Studia Mystica* 14 (1991): 30-44; Hans Urs von Balthasar, *Theo-Drama: Theological Dramatic Theory*, vol. 5, *The Last Act*, trans. Graham Harrison (San Francisco: Ignatius Press, 1998), 457-62.

63. Jan van Ruusbroec, *The Realm of Lovers*, Corpus Christianorum Continuatio Mediaeualis 104 (Turnhout: Brepols, 2002), 1535-38.

64. Jan van Ruusbroec, *The Twelve Beguines*, Corpus Christianorum Continuatio Mediaeualis 107A (Turnhout: Brepols, 2000), 2a, 563-65.

65. See, e.g., *The Spiritual Espousals*, Corpus Christianorum Continuatio Mediaeualis 103 (Turnhout: Brepols, 1998), c, 215; b, 987 (a flowing ebbing sea); *Realm of Lovers*, 2253; *Twelve Beguines*, 2a,

wherein the divine persons flow back into their shared being through the Spirit in a never-ending dynamic of ebb and flow. The application to trinitarian theology of this notion of *regiratio*, based on an analysis that it is the nature of love to return what it has received, is arguably unique to Ruusbroec's approach and pervades his theology and indeed shapes the trinitarian character of his mysticism of union with God.[66]

JULIAN OF NORWICH: AS TRULY AS GOD IS OUR FATHER, SO TRULY GOD IS OUR MOTHER

Our brief survey of the development of trinitarian theology must also refer to the writings of Dame Julian of Norwich (ca. 1342).[67] An anchorite mystic about whom we know very little (indeed, not even her name with any certainty), Dame Julian provides no explicit or systematic exposition of trinitarian theology as such, but the mystery of trinitarian love thoroughly permeates her writings in a remarkable and profound way.[68] Counted among the theological classics of mystical literature, Dame Julian's *Revelations of Divine Love* is based on the revelation to her of sixteen "showings" about the love of God. The mystery of the Trinity figures in her very first vision and prompts her reflection on the mystery:

> Suddenly the Trinity filled my heart fully of the greatest joy, and I understood that it will be so in heaven without end to all who will come there. For the Trinity is God, God is the Trinity. The Trinity is our maker, the Trinity is our protector, the Trinity is our everlasting lover, and the Trinity is our endless joy and our bliss, by our Lord Jesus Christ and in our Lord Jesus Christ. (*Showings,* Long text, chap. 4)[69]

---

525. The image of the whirlpool was also dear to the beguine mystic Hadewijch (ca. 1210-1260). See Bernard McGinn, *The Flowering of Mysticism: Men and Women in the New Mysticism 1200-1350* (New York: Crossroad, 1998), 211.

66. For discussions of Ruusbroec's notion of *regiratio*, see Van Nieuwenhove, *Jan van Ruusbroek: Mystical Theologian of the Trinity*.

67. The visionary Hildegard of Bingen (1098-1179) also records a remarkable vision of the Trinity, now a well-known image of the Trinity, in which the outer circling light represents the Father, an inner red-gold circle represents the Holy Spirit, while a central human figure in sapphire blue represents the eternal Word. Hildegard's writing on the mystery of the Trinity is, however, not as well developed as that of Dame Julian.

68. For discussions of Julian's work, see Grace M. Jantzen, *Julian of Norwich: Mystic and Theologian* (London: SPCK, 1987), esp. 108-26; Brant Pelphrey, *Christ Our Mother: Julian of Norwich* (Wilmington, Del.: Michael Galzier, 1989); Kerry Hide, *Graced Origins to Graced Fulfillment: The Soteriology of Julian of Norwich* (Collegeville, Minn.: Liturgical Press, 2001).

69. All translations from *Julian of Norwich Showings*, trans. Edmund Colledge and James Walsh, Classics of Western Spirituality (New York: Paulist Press, 1978).

All our life is in these three, she explains: "In the first we have our being, and in the second we have our increasing, and in the third we have our fulfilment" (*Showings*, Long text, chap. 58).

A striking element in Julian's trinitarian thinking that is particularly pertinent to us here is the emergence of the notion of the motherhood in God as Trinity. For, as Julian herself explains, "I saw the working of the whole blessed Trinity. In seeing this I saw and understood these three properties: the property of the fatherhood, the property of the motherhood and the property of lordship in one God" (*Showings*, Long text, chap. 58). Julian thus insists, "As truly as God is our father, so truly is God our mother" (ibid., chap. 59). Admittedly, the maternal image of God is well grounded in Scripture in, for example, the image of the spirit of God hovering over creation (Gen. 1), of God as the woman who will never forget her child (Isa. 49:15), and the Matthean mother hen (Matt. 23:37). There are also traces of the notion in the tradition.[70] St. Anselm, for example, in his "Prayer to Saint Paul," reflects on the image of Christ on the cross, in terms of Christ as mother, travailing in the pain of giving birth to her children.[71] Recall too that the symbol of the pelican, who feeds her young with her own blood, has traditionally represented Christ's motherly love in the Eucharist. But the image of God as mother emerges in a unique way in Julian's writings. She links motherhood to the very nature of God, but she relates it particularly closely to Christ, as the deep wisdom of God and our mother. She explains that "our saviour is our true mother, in whom we are endlessly born and out of whom we shall never come."[72] Julian thus explains: "And so in our making, God almighty is our loving Father, and God all wisdom is our loving Mother, with the love and goodness of the Holy Spirit which is all one God, one Lord."[73]

Having surveyed the development of the main themes of trinitarian theology over the centuries, we are in a position to appreciate the wealth of resources in the tradition that are available to us in our task of rendering trinitarian meaning in our times. We shall now turn to consider the major areas of development in contemporary trinitarian theology.

---

70. See, e.g., Caroline Walker Bynum, *Jesus as Mother: Studies in the Spirituality of the High Middle Ages* (Berkeley: University of California Press, 1982), esp. 110-69; Kerry Hide, "The Deep Wisdom of the Trinity Our Mother: Echoes in Augustine and Julian of Norwich," *Australasian Catholic Record* 4 (1997): 432-44.

71. Anselm, "Prayer to Saint Paul," in *The Prayers and Meditations of St Anselm*, trans. with introduction Benedicta Ward (Harmondsworth: Penguin, 1973), 153-56.

72. Julian of Norwich, *Showings*, Long text, chapter 57.

73. Ibid., chapter 58.

FOR FUTHER READING

Ayers, Lewis. *Nicaea and Its Legacy: An Approach to Fourth-Century Trinitarian Theology*. Oxford: Oxford University Press, 2004.

Barnes, Michel R. *The Power of God: Dunamis in Gregory of Nyssa's Trinitarian Theology*. Washington, D.C.: Catholic University of America Press, 2001.

Bobrinskoy, Boris. *The Mystery of the Trinity: Trinitarian Experience and Vision in the Biblical and Patristic Tradition.* Crestwood, N.Y.: St. Vladimir's Seminary Press, 1999.

Emery, Gilles. *Trinity in Aquinas.* With Foreword by Jean-Pierre Torrell. Ypsilanti, Mich.: Sapientia Press, 2003.

Fortman, Edmund J. *The Triune God: A Historical Study of the Doctrine of the Trinity.* London: Hutchinson; Philadelphia: Westminster, 1972.

Hankey, W. J. *God in Himself: Aquinas' Doctrine of God as Expounded in the Summa Theologiae*. Oxford: Oxford University Press, 1987.

Hill, Edmund. *The Mystery of the Trinity*. Introducing Catholic Theology 4. London: Geoffrey Chapman, 1985.

Hill, William J. *The Three-Personed God: The Trinity as a Mystery of Salvation*. Washington, D.C.: Catholic University of America Press, 1982.

Hurtado, Larry W. *Lord Jesus Christ: Devotion to Jesus in Earliest Christianity*. Grand Rapids: Wm. B. Eerdmans, 2003.

Kelly, J. N. D. *Early Christian Creeds*. Second edition. London: Longmans, 1960.

———. *Early Christian Doctrines*. Revised edition. New York: Harper & Row, 1978.

Lonergan, Bernard J. F. *Verbum: Word and Idea in Aquinas*. Edited by David B. Burrell. London: Darton, Longman & Todd, 1968.

———. *The Way to Nicea: The Dialectical Development of Trinitarian Theology*. London: Darton, Longman & Todd, 1976.

de Margerie, Bertrand. *The Christian Trinity in History*. Translated by Edmund J. Fortman. Studies in Historical Theology 1. Still River, Mass.: St. Bede's Publications, 1982.

Meyendorff, John. *Byzantine Theology: Historical Trends and Doctrinal Themes*. London: Mowbrays, 1974.

O'Collins, Gerald. *The Tripersonal God: Understanding and Interpreting the Trinity.* New York/Mahwah, N.J.: Paulist Press, 1999.

O'Donnell, John J. *The Mystery of the Triune God*. Heythrop Monograph Series 6. London: Sheed & Ward, 1988.

Rahner, Karl. *The Trinity*. Translated by Joseph Donceel. London: Burns & Oates, 1970.

Studer, Basil. *Trinity and Incarnation: The Faith of the Early Church.* Edited by Andrew Louth. Translated by Matthias Westerhoff. Edinburgh: T&T Clark, 1993.

Torrance, T. F. *The Trinitarian Faith*. Edinburgh: T&T Clark, 1988.

Torrell, Jean-Pierre. *Saint Thomas Aquinas.* Vol. 2, *Spiritual Master.* Translated by Robert Royal. Washington, D.C.: Catholic University of America Press, 2003.
Wainwright, Arthur. *The Trinity in the New Testament.* London: SPCK, 1962.
Wright, N. T. *The Resurrection of the Son of God.* Christian Origins and the Question of God 3. London: SPCK, 2003.

2

Contemporary Approaches to Trinitarian Theology

THE INTRASUBJECTIVE PSYCHOLOGICAL ANALOGY as described by Augustine and refined by Thomas Aquinas served for centuries, right through to the twentieth century, as the explication par excellence of the mystery of the Trinity, the two inner-trinitarian processions, and the missions of the Word and Spirit in human history.[1] While not technically dogma as such, it enjoyed a remarkable authority, finding its way into in the catechism of the Council of Trent and into papal statements. Sadly, however, the manual or textbook approach to theology in the post-Reformation period involved the gradual reduction of the whole theological enterprise to proving a doctrinal point. It proceeded by way of select theses, which were proved in a syllogistic form, with Scripture reduced to proof texts, and the larger theological tradition reduced to the "opinions" of authorities. This approach was starkly different from the medieval *quaestio* method, which was more intent on understanding than apodictic proof. A truncation of trinitarian theology occurred, which resulted in a series of proofs for five notions, four properties, three persons, two missions, one nature—in a way that detached the central mystery of faith from history of salvation and its contemplative significance.[2] The manual approach did no justice to Aquinas's achievement and, indeed, effectively undermined it. The explicatory power of Aquinas's trinitarian theology was then further eroded in the twentieth century with the emergence of a thought world that was very different from that of Aquinas and the medievals. The result is that Aquinas's explication of the mystery of the Trinity by way of the psychological analogy, despite its refined logic and highly systematic elegance, no longer renders meaning effectively in our world. For a start, we in the twenty-first century are simply no longer confident or competent in the realm of classical metaphysics in which terms Aquinas constructed and expressed his *Summa*

1. For a discussion regarding its use in Protestant German Circles, see Samuel M. Powell, *The Trinity in German Thought* (Cambridge: Cambridge University Press, 2001).

2. See Yves Congar, *The History of Theology*, trans. Hunter Guthrie (Garden City, N.Y.: Doubleday, 1968), 177-81.

Theologiae. The metaphysics of being, soul, natures, and faculties that he engaged is not comprehensible, let alone persuasive or congenial, to modern empirically organized consciousness, which looks instead for more existentially satisfying religious meaning. Our culture instead demands that the teachings of Christianity be expressed in more experiential and existentially meaningful terms. As Bernard Lonergan recognized:

> The defects of Scholasticism were the defects of its time. . . . A theology is the product not only of faith but of culture. It is cultural change that has made Scholasticism no longer relevant and demands the development of new theological method and style, continuous indeed with the old, yet meeting all the genuine exigences both of Christian religion and of up-to-date philosophy, science, and scholarship.[3]

Moreover, we live in a culture where belief in God is simply not a deeply determining feature in the way that it was in Aquinas's time. Indeed, in our culture, a sense of the *absence* of God is a deeply determining feature and the very question of the existence of God is itself problematic. In other words, what was unproblematic for Aquinas is acutely problematic for us. Hence the emergence of an acute dissatisfaction with the psychological analogy, as classically expressed, and an urgent demand for the development of a new theological method and style and for new renderings of the perennial truths of Christian faith.

KARL RAHNER: THE TRINITY AS MYSTERY OF SALVATION

The German theologian Karl Rahner SJ (1904-1984) was one of the greatest systematic and pastoral theologians of the twentieth century, and his contribution to systematic theology was prolific.[4] Of particular interest to us here is that he, together with the eminent Protestant theologian Karl Barth, thrust trinitarian theology out of the obscurity into which it had fallen in the textbook approach of previous centuries and into renewed prominence. Rahner in particular heralded the shift in modern trinitarian theology away from the psychological analogy as privileged means of explication of the mystery and toward a focus on the mystery of the Trinity as mystery of salvation.

---

3. Bernard Lonergan, "Unity and Plurality: The Coherence of Christian Truth," in *Third Collection: Papers by Bernard J. F. Lonergan, S.J.*, ed. Frederick E. Crowe (New York: Paulist Press, 1985), 246-47.

4. See the survey of Rahner's work in *The Cambridge Companion to Karl Rahner*, ed. Declan Marmion and Mary E. Hines, Cambridge Companions to Religion (Cambridge: Cambridge University Press, 2005).

Rahner observed that, in the textbook trinitarian theology of his times, the doctrine of the Trinity was effectively isolated from the other major tracts of systematic theology and, moreover, that it was also remote from the actual events of salvation history, with the unity of God treated prior to the tri-unity of God, and in essentially metaphysical terms and categories, resulting in a seemingly arcane doctrine with little or no practical significance for Christian life. Rahner wryly commented: "One might almost dare to affirm that if the doctrine of the Trinity were to be erased as false, most religious literature could be preserved almost unchanged through the process."[5] Rahner went on to observe:

> And it cannot be objected that the *Incarnation* is such a theologically and *religiously* central element in Christian life that on that account the Trinity is always and everywhere irremovably present. For when the Incarnation of God is spoken of theological and religious intention is today concentrated on the fact that "God" has become man, that "a" person of the Trinity has assumed flesh—but not on that fact that this person is precisely that of the Word, Logos. One could suspect that as regards the catechism of the head and the heart, in contrast to the catechism in books, the Christian idea of the Incarnation would not have to change at all, if there were no Trinity.[6]

But, Rahner reminds us, the incarnation is an event that is proper to the Son/Logos alone.[7] Jesus is the Word incarnate, the Son, the second divine person. Trinitarian theology therefore has an utterly central place in systematic theology. Rahner thus called for a major revision of the theology of the Trinity and for a restoration to its properly central and privileged place in systematics.[8]

Rahner particularly lamented the separation and the ordering of the tracts treating the doctrine of God and the doctrine of the Trinity in classical trinitarian theology, a sequencing that makes it seem that the doctrine of the Trinity is mere supplement to the former.[9] He was also critical of psychological speculation in classical trinitarian theology, arguing that

---

5. Karl Rahner, "Remarks on the Dogmatic Treatise '*De Trinitate*,'" in *Theological Investigations*, vol. 4 (London: Darton, Longman & Todd, 1966), 79.

6. Ibid.

7. Recall that Aquinas argues that any of the divine Three could have become incarnate. *STh* III, q. 3, a. 5.

8. See Karl Rahner, *The Trinity*, trans. Joseph Donceel (London: Burns & Oates, 1970).

9. For a critique of Rahner's comments regarding the separation of the treatises, *De Deo Uno* and *De Deo Trino* and, more generally, of contemporary misrepresentations and misunderstandings of Thomas's trinitarian theology, see Gilles Emery, *Trinity in Aquinas*, with a foreword by Jean-Pierre Torrell (Ypsilanti, Mich.: Sapientia Press, 2003), esp. 165-208.

> [psychological speculation has] the disadvantage that in the doctrine of the Trinity it does not really give enough weight to a starting point in the history of revelation and dogma which is within the *historical and salvific* experience of the Son and of the Spirit as the reality of the divine self-communication to us, so that we can understand from this historical experience what the doctrine of the divine Trinity really means. The psychological theory of the Trinity neglects the experience of the Trinity in the economy of salvation in favor of a seemingly almost gnostic speculation about what goes on in the inner life of God. In the process it really forgets that the countenance of God which turns towards us in this self-communication is, in the trinitarian nature of this encounter, the very being of God as he is in himself, and must be if indeed the divine self-communication in grace and in glory really is the communication of God in his own self to us.[10]

God is known, Rahner insisted, where God has revealed Godself, and that is as manifest in the life of the Word incarnate, the Word existing as the man, Jesus Christ. God's self-communication is truly a real *self*-communication. Rahner thus insisted that the economic Trinity—in other words, the Trinity of divine persons as we know it in the economy of salvation—reveals the immanent Trinity, the inner-trinitarian mystery of God. Moreover, in his famous *Grundaxiom* ("basic axiom"), Rahner insisted that the economic Trinity is the immanent Trinity and *vice versa*.[11]

In his own theology, Rahner pressed to an analysis of the conditions for the possibility of incarnation and grace. He recognized that creation, the creation of what is other than God, is the condition for the possibility, the necessary presupposition, of God's divine self-communication to what is other than God. Indeed, creation itself is a moment in the divine self-communication. Rahner recognized the intrinsic link between the procession of the Word, as the self-expression of the Father *ad intra*, and the procession of the world from God *ad extra*. In a way that is reminiscent of Bonaventure's theology, Rahner also recognized the intrinsic link between the role of the Word as God's self-expression in creation and in the incarnation. He argued that the incarnation of the Word requires that creation is ordered to the possible incarnation of the Word. Creation of the cosmos is the beginning of trinitar-

---

10. Karl Rahner, *Foundations of Christian Faith: An Introduction to the Idea of Christianity*, trans. William V. Dych (New York: Crossroad, 1987), 135. In this greatly acclaimed book, arguably the closest Rahner comes to a systematic architectonic presentation of his theology, Rahner offers an excellent summary of his trinitarian theology at the end of this short section on the Trinity. See p. 136-37.

11. Rahner, *Trinity*, 21-24. The *vice versa* provoked considerable discussion, particularly in regard to the freedom of the immanent Trinity, and Rahner would later omit reference to it. His essential point was that the immanent Trinity is revealed in the economic Trinity. For a critique of a contemporary suggestion that the economic/immanent distinction be abandoned, see Thomas G. Weinandy, *The Father's Spirit of Sonship: Reconceiving the Trinity* (Edinburgh: T&T Clark, 1995), 129-36.

ian self-revelation and, from its beginning, the cosmos exists in the order of grace. Here too Rahner resonates with Bonaventure's profound sense of the *imago Trinitatis* in and throughout the cosmos.

Rahner also appreciated that, similarly, the human person is ordered to the possibility of the incarnation and to personal union with the indwelling Trinity. In grace, the human person encounters not simply something but Someone, nothing less than God indeed, in God's triune self, whereby the three divine persons indwell in the graced human person. As Rahner explains: God "does not merely indirectly give his creature some share of himself by creating and giving us created and finite realities through his omnipotent *efficient* causality. In a *quasi-formal* causality he really and in the strictest sense of the word bestows *himself*."[12] Rahner would thus persuade us that grace is primarily uncreated grace, the indwelling of the three divine persons in the graced human person.

The world and the human person come into being as the condition for the possibility of God's self-communication. In this way, Rahner's theology identifies and explores the intrinsic link between Trinity, grace, incarnation, and creation (with application, as we shall pursue later in our study, to contemporary ecological concerns for the care of the cosmos).[13] The Trinity emerges in his theology as the primordial mystery of Christian faith, as mystery of salvation no less, and thus as the nexus wherein all other tracts of systematic theology are intrinsically connected. At the core of Rahner's argument is the reality of God's *self*-communication, as truly the communication of God's very self, and thus the identity of the economic Trinity and the immanent Trinity.

LIBERATION APPROACHES TO THE TRINITY: THE TRINITY IS OUR SOCIAL PROGRAM

In the context of the change in cultural consciousness which Lonergan describes and under the impetus of Rahner's radical challenge to trinitarian

12. Ibid., 36.

13. For Rahner's succinct but remarkably profound understanding of the use of analogy in speaking about God, where he grounds analogous language in transcendental experience of the human person as spirit-in-the-world, see *Foundations*, 71-73. "We ourselves, as we can put it, exist analogously in and through our being grounded in this holy mystery which always surpasses us. But it always constitutes us by surpassing us and by pointing us towards the concrete, individual, categorical realities which confront us within the realm of our experience. Conversely, then, these realities are the mediation of and the point of departure for our knowledge of God" (ibid., 73). In other words, given an understanding of the human person as spirit-in-world, whatever we know or love as finite and particular ("categorical") we know and love against the "horizon" of holy mystery. Concomitantly, in knowing or loving anything finite, we simultaneously also implicitly know or love God. Rahner describes analogy as "the tension between a categorical starting point and the incomprehensibility of the holy mystery, namely God" (ibid.).

theology, we can begin to understand the disaffection with the classical Augustinian-Thomistic explication of the mystery of the Trinity in recent times, and the emergence of what we might call social models of the Trinity,[14] with their very strong emphasis on the personal, relational, and social aspects of being, and on the distinctly practical significance of trinitarian faith for Christian life in the world.[15] Eschewing the Augustinian-Thomistic intrapersonal psychological analogy, most contemporary theologians have turned to an interpersonal psychological analogy, a social model, in an attempt to render the mystery of our faith in the Trinity in meaningful and effective ways for our times. As Gary D. Badcock explains: "the social doctrine of the Trinity begins with the idea of the Trinity as a *community* of Father, Son and Holy Spirit, whose relations are conceived to be genuinely personal, and in the nature of love, rather than relational in the more abstract, ontological sense of the 'relations of opposition.'"[16] Among the most notable is the work of Latin American liberation theologian Leonardo Boff.[17] His primary concern is not the systematic intelligibility of the mystery, as it was for Aquinas. Trinitarian faith, he insists, is as much a matter of orthopraxis as of orthodoxy. It implies and indeed demands a commitment to social transformation, to a socially and politically responsible praxis. It has to be good news in the here and now of our lives, and preeminently so in the lives of the poor.

Boff's foremost interest is thus to render the mystery of the Trinity meaningful and liberating for the poor. How in their situation is the revelation of the Trinity genuinely good news, he asks, and good news *in their world right now*? Boff finds the answer to that most vital question in an understanding of the Trinity by means of what we may call the social model, wherein the mystery of the Trinity of the three divine persons is envisaged as a commu-

14. By social models or approaches, we mean those trinitarian theologies which focus on the Trinity as a community of persons and seek to explicate the social and political ramifications of that understanding of the Trinity for human community.

15. Consider, for example: Leonardo Boff, *Trinity and Society*, Liberation and Theology 2, trans. Paul Burns (London: Burns & Oates, 1988); Elizabeth A. Johnson, *She Who Is: The Mystery of God in Feminist Theological Discourse* (New York: Crossroad, 1992); Catherine Mowry LaCugna, *God for Us: The Trinity and Christian Life* (New York: HarperCollins, 1991); Jürgen Moltmann, *The Trinity and the Kingdom: The Doctrine of God*, trans. Margaret Kohl (San Francisco: HarperCollins, 1991); Denis Edwards, *Jesus, the Wisdom of God: An Ecological Theology* (Homebush, NSW: St Paul's, 1995); John Zizioulas, *Being as Communion: Studies in Personhood and the Church* (Crestwood, N.Y.: St. Vladimir's Seminary Press, 1985).

16. Gary D. Badcock, *Light of Truth & Fire of Love: A Theology of the Holy Spirit* (Grand Rapids/Cambridge: Wm. B. Eerdmans, 1997), 246.

17. Boff, *Trinity and Society*; idem, "Trinity," in *Systematic Theology: Perspectives from Liberation Theology* (Readings from *Mysterium Liberationis*), ed. Jon Sobrino and Ignacio Ellacuría (Maryknoll, N.Y.: Orbis Books, 1993, 1996), 389-404; idem, *Holy Trinity, Perfect Community* (Maryknoll, N.Y.: Orbis Books, 2000).

nion of coequal subjects that is characterized by relationality and mutuality. The beautiful fifteenth-century icon of the Trinity by the Russian icon painter Andrei Rublev exquisitely expresses this great mystery of love, this holy society, so to speak, that proponents of the social model so highly favor and esteem. In essence, Rublev's icon depicts a communion of three coequals that is characterized by mutuality and reciprocity, mutual giving and receiving, wherein each of the divine persons exists in and with and for the others, and which excludes any sense of subordination or marginalization. The society that is the Trinity, Boff would persuade us, serves as a prototype of human society, thus motivating social and historical progress, here and now. Here, precisely in the social interpersonal dimension of trinitarian being, Boff finds the good news for the poor that he seeks.

Motivated and impelled by the conviction that "the Trinity is our social program,"[18] Boff argues that our goal then is to build a human society along the lines of the society that is the Trinity, so that human community models the trinitarian community. From this perspective, the Trinity itself, as understood by means of the social model, serves as model for human community, relationships, and social structure. The mystery understood in this way itself functions as an analogy for human community. Boff effectively reverses the direction of the analogy here. His concern is, as we have said, not the systematic explication of trinitarian theology but the social ramifications of the mystery for the human community. Society, he insists, is summoned to transform itself after the model of the trinitarian communion.

This understanding of Trinity, based on a social model of the Trinity, effectively inspires a model of society and indeed of church that is characterized by equality, inclusion, participation, and hospitality, without subordination or marginalization. Such a community—be it in society, or in the church—necessarily insists on more equitable, egalitarian, and participative social and political structures. It would respect and protect diversity, esteeming unity, not uniformity. There would be no subordination of one person relative to another in a society that was modeled on the Trinity as mystery of inclusion and participation, equality and mutual self-giving. There would be neither glaring inequality nor grossly uneven distribution of wealth and resources, such as prevails in our world today. A spirit of hospitality and reconciliation would prevail.

For Boff, and for proponents more generally of the social model of the Trinity, orthopraxis is the crucial issue. Indeed Boff would appear to be at

---

18. Miroslav Volf explains that it was the Russian Nicholas Fedorov who first formulated the expression: "the Trinity is our social program." Miroslav Volf, "'The Trinity Is Our Social Program': The Doctrine of the Trinity and the Shape of Social Engagement," *Modern Theology* 14 (1998): 403.

pains to demonstrate his knowledge of and fidelity to orthodoxy. It is in the area of orthopraxis that his contribution to contemporary theology, and that of his Latin American theological colleagues, has radical and costly consequences and where it has drawn radical and critical responses, particularly in regard to the engagement of Marxist tools of analysis of social structures.[19]

Elizabeth Johnson and Catherine LaCugna both approach trinitarian theology from a feminist liberation perspective.[20] Their concern, like Boff's, is liberation in the here and now of our world, but their particular concern is liberation for women. The problem, from the perspective of feminist theologians, is that the Father–Son metaphor, so clearly privileged in the Scriptures, and the fact of Jesus' maleness have been used, wittingly or unwittingly, to abuse and oppress women. These images have been used to legitimate women's subordination and their exclusion from full participation in the life of the church in general, and from the ordained ministry in particular. The fundamental question that emerges from the perspective of feminist theology is whether the historical fact of Jesus' maleness, which is undeniable, is itself an essential element of his identity as Savior. Or does his identity as Savior reside in other elements of his person?

Although some feminist theologians have left the field, bemoaning the patriarchal structures and institutions of the church and its tradition as beyond remediation, Elizabeth Johnson, whose work we shall briefly examine here, embarks on a sophisticated retrieval of the tradition, appealing to the resources within the tradition, albeit hidden or overshadowed, in order to deconstruct the strategies and arguments by means of which clerical male domination has been legitimated and women's inferior status perpetuated. "The symbol of God functions,"[21] to use her expression: it functions, even if unconsciously, by shaping our understanding of ourselves, our relationships to each other and to God, and the way in which we structure our collective life. Moreover, the symbol functions, irrespective of its theological validity and therein lies the problem. A masculinist conception of God, when not augmented by other conceptions that include female imagery to depict the Godhead, effectively functions, even if unwittingly, as the linchpin of patriarchy,

19. In a notification to Boff in 1982, the Vatican Congregation of the Doctrine of the Faith said that his book *Church, Charism and Power: Liberation Theology and the Institutional Church* (New York: Crossroad, 1985), which is critical of the church's hierarchy and institutions, is "a danger to church doctrine." Boff was silenced. He later left the Franciscans. See "Doctrinal Congregation Criticizes Brazilian Theologian's Book," *Origins* 14/42 (1985): 683-87.

20. Johnson, *She Who Is*; Catherine Mowry LaCugna, "The Trinitarian Mystery of God," in *Systematic Theology: Roman Catholic Perspectives*, vol. 1, ed. Francis Schüssler Fiorenza and J. Galvin (Minneapolis: Fortress Press, 1991), 149-92; eadem, *God for Us*.

21. Johnson, *She Who Is*, 5.

legitimizing male domination. Johnson thus proceeds to cut incisively to the core, to the heart of the strategy of analogy in theology, as long understood in the tradition.[22] Let us recall the strategy of analogy: First, we proceed from truths known naturally to the mysteries. Second, negation is inherent in our analogical language about God, as the Fourth Lateran Council highlighted: our language about God is necessarily limited, and there is a greater dissimilarity than similarity inherent in our descriptions of God.[23] Third, no words can fully encapsulate and express the divine mystery. God remains ineffable, incomprehensible, ever beyond our language and concepts. Thereby, with this deft stroke, Johnson relativizes all of our God talk and relativizes the use of male imagery to represent and name God. God is not male! It is as simple as that. The church community should therefore insist on engaging a much-augmented field of metaphors with which to speak rightly of God.

In her retrieval of the Christian understanding of the Trinity, Johnson returns to Scriptures and reclaims the biblical image of Wisdom-Sophia. Her aim is an exploration of the trinitarian mystery which clearly demonstrates that Jesus' maleness is not an essential aspect of his identity and role as Savior and God incarnate. Indeed, she examines the use of the Father–Son metaphor in the New Testament and observes that the frequency of Jesus' use of the paternal metaphor increases in direct relation to the chronology of the writing the texts, so that the usage in John's Gospel greatly exceeds that in earlier Gospels, thereby indicating the influence of patriarchalism in the writing of the Scriptures, Johnson argues.[24] She then elaborates an understanding of the three divine persons in terms not of Father, Son, and Holy Spirit, which is the traditional ordering and naming of the Three, but of Spirit-Sophia, Jesus-Sophia, and Mother-Sophia. Again, her concern is to avoid masculinist notions of the divine persons. Johnson argues that an androcentric emphasis on Jesus' maleness warrants the charge of heresy. Jesus is male, certainly, but his maleness, she argues, is not theologically determinative of his identity as Christ and Savior. His maleness is simply a particularity of his person; it is not determinative of his identity as Christ. It is not his maleness but his option for the poor and marginalized that ushers in the new creation and the new order of justice; that indeed is the scandal of particularity that really matters, Johnson insists.

Why the title *She Who Is?* Johnson recalls the work of Thomas Aquinas, who draws on narrative in the Hebrew Scriptures, where God is revealed in

22. See Elizabeth A. Johnson, "The Incomprehensibility of God and the Image of God Male and Female," *Theological Studies* 45 (1984): 441-65.

23. DS 806; ND 320.

24. Johnson, *She Who Is*, 80-81.

an epiphany to Moses, and describes Godself as YHWH (Exod. 3:14), a Hebrew expression that is traditionally rendered in English as "I am who I am" or "I am." In Aquinas's hands, this becomes in Latin *Qui est (The One Who Is)*, which in English becomes *He Who Is*, with *He* supposedly serving to express both *He* and *She*, though the *She* is perennially truncated. But *Qui est* is just as legitimately translated as *She Who Is*, Johnson argues:

> SHE WHO IS: linguistically this is possible; theologically it is legitimate; existentially and religiously it is necessary if speech about God is to shake off the shackles of idolatry and be a blessing for women. In the present sexist situation where structures and language, praxis and personal attitudes convey an ontology of inferiority to women, naming toward God in this way is a gleam of light on the road to genuine community.[25]

If the reader finds the name *She Who Is* rather odd and disturbing, that only goes to show just how strongly entrenched masculinist imagery and terminology are in our understanding of God. But God is not male. God is neither male nor female. When we use masculinist imagery we are speaking analogically, not univocally. As the Fourth Lateran Council reiterates: the dissimilarity exceeds the similarity in our analogy. Johnson's crucial point is that woman is just as much *imago Dei* as is man. God is just as truly *She Who Is* as *He Who Is*.

Where Boff is not particularly concerned to correct the notion of God inherent in the orthodox statements of trinitarian faith and is far more concerned with its practical ramifications for Christian life, Johnson deftly and competently constructs a feminist trinitarian theology that offers a solid critique of classical trinitarian theology and offers a complementary imaging of God. Like Boff, Johnson too is deeply concerned for orthopraxis. But in her case, orthopraxis requires a radical reappraisal of the role and standing of women in the church and, concomitantly, in society; and because orthodoxy has served to legitimate the oppression of women, its classical expression requires a reappraisal.

We have briefly surveyed what we might call "the social model" of the Trinity as it appears in the liberation trinitarian theologies of Latin American liberation theologian Leonardo Boff and feminist liberation theologian Elizabeth Johnson. In conclusion, it is fair to say, theologically, that the social model of the Trinity risks a certain tendency to tritheism and that it struggles to render satisfactorily the mystery of the divine unity, which, in the Orthodox tradition, is expressed in terms of the divine perichoresis, that mystery of a love so perfect as to express itself in complete mutual coinher-

25. Ibid., 243.

ence and mutual indwelling. But both Boff and Johnson undoubtedly make a genuinely significant contribution to contemporary trinitarian theology. As for any model of the great mystery of the Trinity, however, the social model too undoubtedly functions best when complemented by other models or analogies.

TRINITY AS MYSTERY OF COMMUNION AND PERSONHOOD

Orthodox theologian John Zizioulas, Metropolitan of Pergamon in the Ecumenical Patriachate of Constantinople, brings a distinctly original perspective to the engagement of the social model of the Trinity, with his remarkably influential book, *Being as Communion: Studies in Personhood and the Church.*[26] Whereas Leonardo Boff and Elizabeth Johnson stress the practical ramifications of our Christian faith in the Trinity in regard to the very structures of the society in which we live, including the church, for Zizioulas the implications for church are the very heart of the matter. In his thought, trinitarian theology and ecclesiology are intimately and inextricably related. An understanding of the Eucharist, as the preeminent point of the nexus between trinitarian theology and ecclesiology, plays a prominent role in Zizioulas's theology. He recalls the ancient understanding in the early church of the Eucharist as an event of communion that is constitutive of the church. There in the celebration of the Eucharist, the church tastes the very life of the Trinity and realizes its being as an image of God's being.[27] The Eucharist, then, is constitutive of the very being of the church. Its celebration by the community manifests and indeed realizes the church as the people of God.[28]

Zizioulas understands that, from the moment a human being becomes a member of the church, he/she takes on God's way of being. That way of being is the way of relationship—with the world, with others, with God. Church, then, is an event of communion, and it is as a communion of persons that the church is an image of God. Since God's being is relational, the being of the church is relational. Since God's being is persons in communion, so the church's being is persons in communion.

---

26. See n. 15 above; idem, "On Being a Person: Towards an Ontology of Personhood," in *Persons, Divine and Human: King's College Essays in Theological Anthropology*, ed. Christoph Schwöbel and Colin Gunton (Edinburgh: T&T Clark, 1991), 33-46; idem, "The Church as Communion," *St Vladimir's Theological Quarterly* 38 (1994): 3-16; idem, "Communion and Otherness," *St Vladimir's Theological Quarterly* 38 (1994): 347-61.

27. Zizioulas, *Being as Communion*, 21.

28. For a discussion of this aspect of Zizioulas's thought, see Paul McPartlan, *The Eucharist Makes the Church: Henri de Lubac and John Zizioulas* (Edinburgh: T&T Clark, 1993).

Zizioulas appeals to the theology of the Cappadocians in the East as the foundation of his theology and particularly to the notion that the Trinity has its source in the person of the Father, as personal originating principle from whom the Son and Spirit proceed.[29] Zizioulas argues:

> If God exists, He exists because the Father exists, that is, He who out of love freely begets the Son and brings forth the Spirit. Thus God as person—as the hypostasis of the Father—makes the one divine substance to be that which it is: the one God. . . . What therefore is important in trinitarian theology is that God "exists" on account of a person, the Father, and not on account of a substance.[30]

From this perspective, an ontology that treats divine substance apart from the divine persons is a contradiction in terms. Zizioulas insists:

> The Holy Trinity is a *primordial* ontological concept and not a notion which is added to the divine substance or rather which follows it, as is the case in the dogmatic manuals of the West and, alas, in those of the East in modern times. The substance of God, "God," has no ontological content, no true being apart from communion. In this way, communion becomes an ontological concept in patristic thought . . . it is communion which makes beings "be": nothing exists without it, not even God.[31]

The insistence on the monarchy of the Father in the begetting of the Son and the breathing out of the Spirit means that being is traced back to person, not to substance, with profound existential ramifications for our understanding of personhood. Personhood thus emerges as a relational category in Zizioulas's trinitarian theology and indeed as the highest ontological principle, with primacy over the category of substance. Indeed, in the concept of personhood, which, Zizioulas argues, the world owes to Greek patristic thought, human

---

29. For a critique of Zizioulas's work particularly in regard to the Cappadocian Fathers, see Lucian Turcescu, "'Person' Versus 'Individual,' and Other Modern Misreadings of Gregory of Nyssa," in *Re-Thinking Gregory of Nyssa*, ed. Sarah Coakley (Malden, Mass.: Blackwell, 2003), 97-109; David Bentley Hart, "The Mirror of the Infinite: Gregory of Nyssa on the *Vestigia Trinitatis*," in *Re-Thinking Gregory of Nyssa*, 111-31.

30. Zizioulas, *Being as Communion*, 41-42. In a footnote (n. 37), Zizioulas summarizes what he describes as the basic ontological position of the theology of the Greek fathers: "No substance or nature exists without person or hypostasis or mode of existence. No person exists without substance or nature, *but* the ontological 'principle' or 'cause' of being—i.e that which makes a thing to exist—is not the substance or nature but the *person* or hypostasis. Therefore, being is traced back not to substance but to person."

31. Ibid., 17.

existence is given "its most dear and precious good."[32] Concomitantly, difference between persons emerges not as the cause of disunity but as the ground of communion. Otherness, Zizioulas recognizes, is constitutive of unity, not consequent upon it. Otherness and communion coincide in the mystery of personhood. He explains:

> The mystery of being a person lies in the fact that here otherness and communion are not in contradiction but coincide. Truth as communion does not lead to the dissolving of the diversity of beings into one vast ocean of being but to the affirmation of otherness in and through love.[33]

In this understanding of being, there is no being without communion, and no communion without persons, and no communion without difference. Communion, personhood, and relationality emerge as ontological categories in Zizioulas's trinitarian theology. Communion, being as being-in-relation, is affirmed as the essential nature of ultimate reality.[34]

HE IS THE IMAGE OF THE INVISIBLE GOD: JESUS CHRIST'S PASCHAL MYSTERY AS ICON OF THE TRINITY

The Augustinian-Thomistic approach to trinitarian theology privileges the psychological analogy in its explication of the mystery of the Trinity and of how it is that there are two processions within the Godhead. The Canadian theologian Bernard Lonergan (1904-1984) has taken up the analogy and transposed it into a more contemporary key, situating it in terms of an analysis of human interiority and the fundamental dynamism of human intentionality, the dynamism of questioning, thinking, judging, restlessly seeking

---

32. Ibid., 65. Zizioulas notes that "although the person and 'personal identity' are widely discussed nowadays as a supreme ideal, nobody seems to recognize that *historically* as well as *existentially* the concept of the person is indissolubly bound up with theology" (ibid., 27).

33. Ibid., 106.

34. From the Protestant tradition, Colin Gunton also argues vigorously for an understanding of the Trinity in terms of personhood, and not of substance. See, e.g., *The Promise of Trinitarian Theology* (Edinburgh: T&T Clark, 1991); idem, *The One, the Three, and the Many: God, Creation, and the Culture of Modernity* (Cambridge: Cambridge University Press, 1993). Gunton is strident—indeed, I believe, unreasonably so—in his criticism of the Western tradition of trinitarian theology, particularly in regard to Augustine. For a critique of the treatment of Augustine's theology in contemporary theology, see Michel René Barnes, "The Use of Augustine in Contemporary Trinitarian Theology," *Theological Studies* 56 (1995): 237-51; idem, "Rereading Augustine's Theology of the Trinity," in *The Trinity: An Interdisciplinary Symposium on the Trinity*, ed. Stephen T. Davis, Daniel Kendall, and Gerald O'Collins (New York: Oxford University Press, 1999), 145-76; for a critique of Gunton's treatment in particular, see Neil Ormerod, "Augustine and the Trinity—Whose Crisis?" *Pacifica* 16 (2003): 17-32.

fulfillment in and commitment to the good, the true, the beautiful, the holy.[35] Nevertheless, the approach by way of the psychological analogy remains somewhat unpalatable to more general contemporary sensibilities, despite its virtues in explicating the mystery of trinitarian being in a highly rigorous and elegant way. Admittedly, the social implications for human conduct are less immediately obvious. Hence, the emergence of the social models of the Trinity, which attend not to the more taxing questions of terminological and conceptual rigor in explaining the mystery but to its tangible practical ramifications for human being in the world. Not orthodoxy but orthopraxis is their concern and indeed their virtue. These social models of the Trinity are now enjoying considerable appeal in Christian thought. Their emergence has also prompted and assisted renewed efforts to appreciate the Orthodox tradition of theology in general, and of trinitarian theology in particular. On reflection, however, one cannot but observe that the person of Jesus Christ, his teaching, and the events of his life, death, and resurrection are rather strangely remote from all of the trinitarian considerations we have considered thus far. Yet, as the Scriptures attest, "He is the image of the invisible God" (Col. 1:15). Christ, not the human person or community as such, is the preeminent and unsurpassable image of God. It is a strange turn of theological history that trinitarian theology has been shaped along lines that are so remote from the revelation of God given to us in the person of Jesus. In reaction to this situation, Hans Urs von Balthasar (1905-1988) and Jürgen Moltmann (1926-) both make remarkable contributions to trinitarian theology.

We turn first to consider Balthasar's work. Even though he is critical of the Augustinian-Thomistic tradition that takes the human mind and its acts of intellect and will as the prime analogy of divine life, he does not disallow the validity or legitimacy of the psychological analogy as an approach to understanding the mystery. But, for him, it simply pales in comparison with the revelation that is given to us in the person of Jesus, preeminently in the paschal mystery of his death, descent into hell, and resurrection. Balthasar

35. Bernard Lonergan, *De Deo Trino I: Pars Dogmatica* and *II: Pars Systematica* (Rome: Pontificia Università Gregoriana, 1964). See also idem, "Consciousness and the Trinity," *Philosophy and Theology* 7 (1992): 3-22; idem, *Verbum: Word and Idea in Aquinas*, ed. David B. Burrell (London: Darton, Longman & Todd, 1968); and Quentin Quesnell, "Three Persons—One God," in *The Desires of the Human Heart: An Introduction to the Theology of Bernard Lonergan*, ed. Vernon Gregson (New York: Paulist Press, 1988), 150-67. Anthony Kelly carries forward Lonergan's effort to transpose the psychological analogy by way of a more phenomenologically based account of religious and Christian experience. In Kelly's transposition, the human experience of self-transcending subjectivity, with its peak state of being-in-love, becomes the analogy for the divine Being-in-Love and thus for an understanding of the triune God. See *The Trinity of Love: A Theology of the Christian God* (Wilmington, Del.: Michael Glazier, 1989).

would have us take a full about-turn and direct our attention not to ourselves as made in the image of God but to Jesus, the Word incarnate, where God has revealed Godself to us. Why look at ourselves when God has revealed Godself to us? To explore the mystery of the Trinity by directing our attention to the psychological analogy, Balthasar argues, is to be looking in the wrong direction. It is as simple a matter and as dim a reflection as that! Moreover, Balthasar would have us adopt a quite different stance in our theologizing. He urges us to "a kneeling theology," in other words, a theology that is mediated by prayer and adoration and imbued with a sense of the sheer glory of God.[36] Faith, as he understands it, is first of all a seeing and a beholding and, indeed, an adoring, long before it is an act of seeking understanding.

Balthasar thus turns his attention to Jesus' paschal mystery, there to mine its trinitarian depths.[37] Moreover, he recognizes that the trinitarian mystery is preeminently revealed at the midpoint of the *Sacrum Triduum*, in Jesus' descent into hell. This is indeed a remarkable claim, given that there is little warrant for it in the Scriptures (1 Pet. 3:19; 4:6). In making this astonishing claim, Balthasar is deeply influenced by his friend and mentor Adrienne von Speyr, who, over a period of years, had a series of mystical experiences, including some regarding Jesus' descent into hell.[38] Inspired by her, he insists that Holy Saturday is "the mysterious middle between cross and resurrection, and consequently properly in the centre of all revelation and theology."[39] There in the descent, he argues, the glory of the Lord is preeminently revealed, the glory that is the love that God is (1 John 4:8). Balthasar explains: "It is 'glory' in the uttermost opposite of 'glory,' because it is at the same time blind obedience, that must obey the Father at the point where the last trace of God

36. Peter Henrici, "A Sketch of Balthasar's Life," *Communio* 16 (1989): 307-50, at 329; see also Edward T. Oakes, *Pattern of Redemption: The Theology of Hans Urs von Balthasar* (New York: Continuum, 1994), 7-8, 96, 183.

37. For a much more detailed examination of Balthasar's work in regard to the paschal mystery and the Trinity, see Anne Hunt, *The Trinity and the Paschal Mystery: A Development in Recent Catholic Theology*, New Theology Studies 5 (Collegeville, Minn.: Liturgical Press, 1997), 49-61. See also Thomas G. Dalzell's excellent study, *The Dramatic Encounter of Divine and Human Freedom in the Theology of Hans Urs von Balthasar*, 2nd ed., Studies in the Intercultural History of Christianity 105 (Bern: Peter Lang, 2000); Guy Mansini, "Balthasar and the Theodramatic Enrichment of the Trinity," *Thomist* 64 (2000): 499-519.

38. Of Adrienne von Speyr and her influence on his work, Balthasar writes: "Her work and mine are neither psychologically nor philologically to be separated: two halves of a single whole which has as its center a unique foundation" (*My Work: In Retrospect* [San Francisco: Communio Books, Ignatius Press, 1993], 89, also 19, 30, 105-7). See also Hans Urs von Balthasar, *First Glance at Adrienne von Speyr*, trans. Antje Lawry and Sergia Englund (San Francisco: Ignatius Press, 1981); and *The Von Balthasar Reader*, ed. Medard Kehl and Werner Löser, trans. Robert J. Daly and Fred Lawrence (Edinburgh: T&T Clark, 1985), 403-4.

39. *Von Balthasar Reader*, 404.

seems lost (in pure sin), together with every other communication (in pure solitariness)."[40]

The paschal mystery is the mystery of love; it is explicable only as love. For Balthasar: "Love alone is credible."[41] In no other way does what is revealed make any sense at all. Balthasar proceeds to think of God's being, and hence the trinitarian processions, not in terms of absolute and perfect being—*Actus Purus*, for Thomas Aquinas—but rather in terms of the self-emptying, self-sacrificing, and intrinsically dynamic nature of love. As Balthasar explains: "The cross alone is God's final exegesis, who here proves himself once for all as love."[42] The cross is the revelation of God's glory, albeit a hidden glory, but the glory of inner-trinitarian love.

Balthasar recognizes that the paschal mystery and the mystery of the Trinity are inextricably interconnected. Indeed, Balthasar's highly dramatic sense of the interpenetration of the mysteries is as compelling as it is unique. There in Christ, particularly in the paschal mystery, with Holy Saturday as its midpoint, we see, according to Balthasar, the form of God's love for the world, and there, correspondingly, the doctrines of the Trinity, Christology, and soteriology have their center.

As for all of the theologians whose work we are considering, we must refer our readers to more detailed studies of Balthasar's exploration of the Trinity from the perspective of the paschal mystery.[43] We shall comment briefly, however, on his understanding of the descent into hell. For Balthasar, Holy Saturday and the descent into hell are not the appearance of the victor in the kingdom of the underworld, as some of the early church fathers had surmised.[44] Rather, Balthasar recognizes that the descent represents Jesus' solidarity with the sinner in his/her death, in his/her radical separation from God, in his/her hellish desolation and utter loneliness as a being-only-for-oneself, and in his/her complete powerlessness to redeem oneself. For Balthasar, the essential mystery of the descent into hell is that God himself (in the person of the incarnate Son) experiences God-forsakenness and God-estrangement. It is this that constitutes the mystery of our salvation and indeed the glory of the Lord. Here, then, in the mystery of the descent into hell, is the point of nexus of Christology, the paschal mystery, the Trinity, and soteriology. For this God-forsakenness, this abandonment of the Son by the Father in the descent, is possible only because, at this their point of greatest

40. Hans Urs von Balthasar, *The Glory of the Lord: A Theological Aesthetics*, vol. 7, *Theology: The New Covenant*, ed. John Riches (San Francisco: Ignatius Press, 1982-), 233.

41. See Hans Urs von Balthasar, *Love Alone: The Way of Revelation: A Theological Perspective* (London: Burns & Oates, 1968).

42. Hans Urs von Balthasar, "God Is His Own Exegete," *Communio* 13 (1986): 284.

43. See, e.g., Hunt, *Trinity and the Paschal Mystery*, 57-89.

44. See J. N. D. Kelly, *Early Christian Creeds*, 3rd ed. (Harlow: Longman Group, 1972), 378-83.

separation, Father and Son are united in undying love by the Holy Spirit. In the resurrection, the revelation of the Trinity is decisive. It reveals that, even in that moment of their extreme and utmost separation, Father and Son are united.

It is in the paschal mystery, through which our salvation was wrought, that God's very being is revealed. The paschal mystery is none other than the drama, played out in the realm of creation, for us and for our salvation of the eternal trinitarian love itself: the Father's bestowal of his love on the Son, the self-giving love—even unto death and descent—of the Son, and the outflowing of the Spirit, the personification of their love.[45] The soteriological "for us" of the paschal mystery is grounded in the self-giving self-yielding love of the divine persons of the Trinity. The paschal mystery reveals that the nature of our triune God is positively constituted by this eternal kenotic self-giving and receiving between the divine persons. In their triune exchange of life and love, we see that to be a person in the Trinity is to be a pure relation, a being-for-one-another. God's glory is revealed in the paschal mystery as eternally and limitlessly gratuitous, self-sacrificing love. The distinctly kenotic character of divine love thus emerges strongly in Balthasar's theology. The triune God is constituted by a kenotic self-giving and receiving between the persons: this, indeed, is the glory of God. "For it is precisely in the Kenosis of Christ (and nowhere else) that the *inner* majesty of God's love appears, of God who 'is love' (1 John 4:8) and therefore a trinity."[46]

Jürgen Moltmann is unquestionably one of the most influential of the German Protestant theologians of the twentieth century. His work has proved seminal in the development of contemporary trinitarian theologies.[47] Moltmann also rejects the traditional approach to trinitarian theology and insists that trinitarian theology should be grounded in the events of the economy of salvation. Like Balthasar, Moltmann reminds theology that God is known where God is self-revealed, and that, for Moltmann, is in Jesus' paschal mystery, particularly Jesus' death on the cross. He explains: "The content of the doctrine of the Trinity is the real cross of Christ himself. The form of the crucified Christ is the Trinity."[48] Moltmann argues that the event of the cross can be understood only in trinitarian terms:

---

45. Balthasar writes: "The whole thrust of this book has been to show that the infinite possibilities of divine freedom all lie *within* the trinitarian distinctions and are thus free possibilities within the eternal life in God that *has always been realized.*" *Theo-Drama: Theological Dramatic Theory*, vol. 5, *The Last Act,* trans. Graham Harrison (San Francisco: Ignatius Press, 1998), 508.

46. Balthasar, *Love Alone*, 71.

47. For a helpful discussion of Moltmann's work in the wider context of the tradition of German Protestant trinitarian thinking, see Simon M. Powell, *The Trinity in German Thought* (Cambridge: Cambridge University Press, 2001).

48. Jürgen Moltmann, *The Crucified God: The Cross of Christ as the Foundation and Criticism of Christian Theology,* trans. R. A. Wilson and John Bowden (London: SCM, 1974), 246.

> If a person once feels the infinite passion of God's love that finds expression here, then he understands the mystery of the triune God. God suffers with us—God suffers from us—God suffers for us; it is this experience of God that reveals the triune God. It has to be understood, and can only be understood, in trinitarian terms.[49]

Moltmann, a prisoner of war in World War II, wrestles with the question of suffering and of theodicy. For Moltmann, the only acceptable answer is that God suffers. Moreover, God's suffering, he argues, can be understood only in trinitarian terms.[50] That "God suffers with us—God suffers from us—God suffers for us" is thus fundamental to his understanding of the Trinity. The cross—with the suffering of the Son for us and the suffering of the Father who gave up the Son—therefore lies, he argues, "at the centre of the Trinity."[51] He argues that the cross has, so to speak, "a retroactive effect" on God.[52] God is thus eternally defined in terms of the suffering of the cross. Like Balthasar, Moltmann understands that only love makes sense of the divine suffering of the cross. God is love; hence, God is characterized by the relationality of love. Moreover, as Moltmann explains: "The question of theodicy is not a speculative question; it is a critical one. It is the all-embracing *eschatological question*."[53] Moltmann's theology is thus both profoundly trinitarian in its inspiration and strongly eschatological in its outlook. Indeed, he is convinced of the radical eschatological orientation of the whole theological enterprise. For him, the resurrection makes Christian faith eschatological—hence his own radically eschatological approach and the notion that the present is characterized and shaped by the future. In other words, the present is understood proleptically, as the prolepsis of the future into the present. This eschatological view of reality, Moltmann insists, demands expression in Christian praxis. It also demands a certain dialectical character in our God talk, as does the mystery of Jesus' death and resurrection, for death and resurrection are seemingly total opposites.

An understanding of the cross as a trinitarian event leads Moltmann to an understanding of the trinitarian history of God wherein God affects and is affected by history and experiences a history with the world.[54] There is, he insists, no question, however, of a process theology at work in his theology,

---

49. Moltmann, *Trinity and the Kingdom*, 4; see also 21-60.
50. Ibid., 4 and 25.
51. Ibid., 83.
52. Ibid., 160-61.
53. Ibid., 49.
54. For a thought-provoking critique of Moltmann's trinitarian theology, see David Coffey, *Deus Trinitas: The Doctrine of the Triune God* (New York/Oxford: Oxford University Press, 1999), 105-30.

whereby God needs history in order to realize Godself.[55] What Moltmann intends is not dissolution of God into history but a real involvement of God in history. The goal of the history of God is the unity of all things in God and with God, when all will be "all in all" (1 Cor. 15:28). The eschaton, in Moltmann's theology, is thus God's future, the consummation of the trinitarian history of God, as well as that of creation.

Moltmann would therefore have us understand that divine being is ruptured on the cross, in a drama that is constitutive of God's being and history. The cross takes place in the history between the Father and Son. It is "the concrete history of God," the event of the love of the Son and the grief of the Father, from which issues the Spirit, who opens up the future and creates life.[56] The event of the cross—the grief of the Father, the surrender of the Son, and the power of the Spirit—is taken up into the very being of the triune God, where it is constitutive of God's triune being and history. Moltmann would persuade us that God is *this* trinitarian event, the event of the cross: the Father who delivers up his Son, the Son who is abandoned, the Holy Spirit who is the bond of union between them. As Moltmann explains: "What happened on the cross was an event between God and God. It was a deep division in God himself, in so far as God abandoned God and contradicted himself, and at the same time a unity in God in so far as God was at one with God and corresponded to himself."[57] Here is the basis for our hope, in the face of all the suffering of history. Christian hope, according to Moltmann, is grounded in the suffering of God, who raises Jesus from the dead.[58]

The question remains, however, whether Moltmann has in this way so merged God with the world as to compromise God's transcendence and independence from the world. Indeed, in an attempt to avert precisely this problem, Moltmann introduces the notion of the doxological Trinity. The doxological Trinity is not only creator of all that is and source of salvation but

---

55. Moltmann, *Trinity and the Kingdom of God*, 107. David Coffey also engages skilfully and critically with process theology; see *Deus Trinitas*, 84-104.

56. Moltmann, *Trinity and the Kingdom of God*, 90.

57. Moltmann, *The Crucified God*, 244.

58. For Balthasar, by contrast, the event of the cross and the paschal mystery is grounded in the eternal primordial trinitarian event itself, whereby the Father begets the Son. God is, in the paschal mystery, what God is eternally. The cross does not constitute the trinitarian being; rather, it is the form or modality, in the realm of creation, of that supra-temporal innertrinitarian event of mutual self-giving and self-yielding love. The event of the paschal mystery, and the radical separation it involves, is eternally allowed for, included and exceeded in the eternal supra-temporal drama of trinitarian life, wherein the Father begets the Son. Balthasar understands that, at the same time, the immutability of God is not something static and that the events in the economy are taken up into and "enrich" the trinitarian relations. See Hans Urs von Balthasar, *Theo-Drama,* 5:506-21; and, for a discussion of this aspect of Balthasar's theology, Guy Mansini, "Balthasar and the Theodramatic Enrichment of the Trinity," *Thomist* 64 (2000): 499-519.

the one who inspires our adoration. Revealed in salvation history as God is in Godself, it is the object of our worship and praise—and not merely for salvation's sake.[59]

We have now surveyed, although very briefly, the major areas of development in contemporary trinitarian theology. We now turn to our exploration of the *nexus mysteriorum*, the nexus of the mysteries, the strategy of interconnection, seeking to locate the major tracts of theology expressly in the setting of trinitarian theology. Our interest is to fathom the theological insights that emerge, as well as what difficulties are averted and what new possibilities unfold, when the mysteries are explored at this nexus.

FOR FURTHER READING

Balthasar, Hans Urs von. *Dare We Hope "That All Men Be Saved"?* With a Short Discourse on Hell. Translated by David Kipp and Lothar Krauth. San Francisco: Ignatius Press, 1987.

———. *The Glory of the Lord: A Theological Aesthetics.* Vol. 7, *Theology: The New Covenant.* Edited by John Riches. Translated by Brian McNeil. San Francisco: Ignatius Press, 1989.

———. *Life out of Death: Meditations on the Easter Mystery.* Translated by Davis Perkins. Philadelphia: Fortress Press, 1985.

———. *Love Alone: The Way of Revelation: A Theological Perspective.* Edited by Alexander Dru. London: Burns & Oates, 1968.

———. *Mysterium Paschale: The Mystery of Easter.* Translated with an Introduction by Aidan Nichols. Edinburgh: T&T Clark, 1990.

———. *The Von Balthasar Reader.* Edited by Medard Kehl and Werner Löser. Translated by Robert J. Daly and Fred Lawrence. Edinburgh: T&T Clark, 1985.

Boff, Leonardo. *Trinity and Society.* Liberation and Theology 2. Translated by Paul Burns. London: Burns & Oates, 1988.

Coffey, David. *Deus Trinitas: The Doctrine of the Triune God.* Oxford/New York: Oxford University Press, 1999.

Hill, William J. *The Three-Personed God: The Trinity as a Mystery of Salvation.* Washington, D.C.: Catholic University of America Press, 1982.

Hunt, Anne. *The Trinity and the Paschal Mystery: A Development in Recent Catholic Theology.* New Theology Studies 5. Collegeville, Minn.: Liturgical Press, 1997.

———. *What Are They Saying About the Trinity?* Mahwah, N.J.: Paulist Press, 1998.

Johnson, Elizabeth A. *She Who Is: The Mystery of God in Feminist Theological Discourse.* New York: Crossroad, 1992.

Kelly, Anthony. *The Trinity of Love: A Theology of the Christian God.* New Theology Series 4. Wilmington, Del.: Michael Glazier, 1989.

59. Moltmann, *Trinity and the Kingdom of God,* 152-53.

LaCugna, Catherine Mowry. *God for Us: The Trinity and Christian Life*. New York: HarperCollins, 1991.
Moltmann, Jürgen. *The Coming of God: Christian Eschatology*. Translated by Margaret Kohl. London: SCM, 1996.
———. *The Crucified God: The Cross of Christ as the Foundation and Criticism of Christian Theology*. Translated by R. A. Wilson and John Bowden. London: SCM, 1974.
———. *History and the Triune God: Contributions to Trinitarian Theology*. Translated by John Bowden. London: SCM, 1991.
———. *The Trinity and the Kingdom of God: The Doctrine of God*. Translated by Margaret Kohl. London: SCM, 1981.
O'Donnell, John J. *The Mystery of the Triune God*. Heythrop Monograph Series 6. London: Sheed & Ward, 1988.
Rahner, Karl. *Foundations of Christian Faith: An Introduction to the Idea of Christianity*. Translated by William V. Dych. New York: Crossroad, 1987.
———. "Remarks on the Dogmatic Treatise '*De Trinitate*.'" In *Theological Investigations*, 4:77-102. Translated by Kevin Smyth. Baltimore: Helicon Press, 1966.
———. *The Trinity*. Translated by Joseph Donceel. London: Burns & Oates, 1970.
Weinandy, Thomas G. *Does God Change? The Word's Becoming in the Incarnation*. Still River, Mass.: St. Bede's Publications, 1985.
———. *The Father's Spirit of Sonship: Reconceiving the Trinity*. Edinburgh: T&T Clark, 1995.

3

Trinity and Christology

But who do you say that I am? (Mark 8:27)

CHRISTOLOGY CONCERNS THE QUESTION of the person of Jesus, an understanding of who he is, and what he means for us today. The writer of John's Gospel tells us that "the world itself could not contain the books that would be written" (John 21:25) to tell the full story of Jesus Christ, the Word made flesh among us. It is hardly surprising then that there is no conceptually or intellectually unified doctrine of Christology in the New Testament and that a number of Christologies are found there.[1] In fact, it took some centuries before questions concerning the nature and person of Jesus Christ rose to the fore in the early church and demanded doctrinal resolution. Nor are we, in our generation, under any delusion or pressure to think that our particular account of the mystery will be exhaustive. The task of Christology is necessarily an unending enterprise. As for theology more generally, Christology must respond in each new age and context to new sensibilities, new modes of consciousness, and new issues and pastoral concerns.

Who is Jesus, the Christ? That is our question. The Gospel reports that Jesus himself asked the question: "Who do you say that I am?" (Mark 8:27) For centuries the church has taught that he is "true God and true man," and "perfect in Godhead and perfect in manhood," but what does this mean for us in our culture and in our times? The connection between Trinity and Christology is the focus of our attention in this chapter. Now, one might well presume that, of all the doctrines in the Christian tradition, this is the one that is quite literally unimaginable outside of a trinitarian context. Yet, as we shall see, the development of the classical christological doctrine, while undoubtedly grounded in Christian faith in the triune God and designed to protect the realism of Christian faith in Jesus' humanity and divinity, followed in the direction established in the development of trinitarian doctrine and took a strongly metaphysical turn that left it strangely remote from its trini-

1. James D. G. Dunn, *Christology in the Making: A New Testament Inquiry into the Doctrine of the Incarnation* (Philadelphia: Westminster, 1980).

tarian origins and bearings and, moreover, from the mystery of Jesus' life, death, and resurrection. The explicit connection of the doctrines of Trinity and Christology is in fact by no means to be presumed; our exploration here seeks to explore the intrinsic connection between the two.

TRINITARIAN DOCTRINE AS PRECURSOR

It was the Arian controversy and the question of the generation of the Son or Word, and the concomitant question of the ontological status of Jesus as the incarnate Son—Was he truly God or was he a lesser being?—that first erupted in the history of the development of Christian doctrine. The conviction that Jesus Christ is the Son of God—truly God and truly human, God become human in order to achieve our salvation—that he was "God incarnate," was implicit in the most primitive kerygma of the church. He is "God revealing himself as a man," as Ignatius of Antioch expressed it (*Ephesians* 7.2; 19.3).[2] When pushed to the test, however, the scriptural witness by itself did not provide an unambiguous answer to the question of Jesus' ontological status and whether he was truly and fully God.

In those disputes culminating at the Council of Nicaea in 325, it was the genius of Athanasius to move beyond the search for proof texts to resolve this vital question and instead to consider the full scope of the biblical testimony in regard to the identity of Jesus and to the salvation wrought by him. Athanasius brought an explicitly soteriological perspective to resolve the question of Jesus' divinity, recognizing that the resolution of the controversy regarding the generation of the Son and his ontological status was to be found in the answer to the one question that really mattered—Is humankind saved or is it not? This was the question to cut to the core. Either the Son of God, who had become united with what was human, was fully divine—and therein was the source of our hope in salvation, resurrection, and eternal life—or he was not divine, and in that case we were not saved and our condition of estrangement from God through sin was not really altered.

The Council of Nicaea resolved the question of Jesus' status with a resounding affirmation of the divinity of Jesus, that he is "God from God, Light from Light, true God from true God," a notion that is further reinforced with the use of the nonbiblical word *homoousios* (same substance). But notice that the utterly critical question of the status and identity of Jesus resulted in the articulation of *trinitarian* as distinct from *christological* doc-

2. In *Early Christian Fathers*, trans. and ed. Cyril C. Richardson (New York: Collier Books, Macmillan, 1970), 90, 93.

trine. Indeed, the conciliar form of trinitarian doctrine was virtually settled at the Council of Nicaea in 325, with the Council of Constantinople in 381 elaborating on the person of the Holy Spirit, all long before the Council of Chalcedon in 451, which addressed specifically christological questions. In other words, trinitarian doctrine took shape long before Christology. When questions concerning the person of Jesus eventually emerged, trinitarian doctrine effectively provided the conceptual framework for christological doctrine.

THE CHRISTOLOGICAL DISPUTE AND THE CHALCEDONIAN RESOLUTION

After the Council of Nicaea, two schools of theological thought, with different styles of scriptural exegesis, arose in regard to Jesus—one in Antioch in Syria, the other in Alexandria in Egypt. The person of Jesus and the nature of the constitution of his person in terms of his humanity and his divinity eventually emerged as an issue of dispute. Antioch, on the one hand, placed greater emphasis on the humanity of Jesus and developed a "Word-man" Christology, wherein it was understood that the Word indwelt in Jesus as in a temple, so to speak, an approach that, while recognizing both human and divine dimensions of Jesus' person, involved a certain tendency to dualism. The Alexandrian school, on the other hand, placed greater stress on Jesus' divinity (and on an understanding of salvation in terms of deification) and developed an understanding of Jesus in terms of his descent from the heavens. With a "Word-flesh" approach to the mystery of Jesus, and a greater emphasis on the oneness of the union of divine and human, this approach involved a certain tendency to devalue Jesus' humanity.

The tension between the two schools erupted in a bitter dispute concerning the issue of Mary, the mother of Jesus, and the titles proper to her. Nestorius, a monk of the Antiochene dogmatic tradition, was the newly enthroned archbishop of Constantinople. According to the historian Evagrius, around Christmas in 428, Nestorius delivered a series of sermons in the cathedral publicly disputing the propriety of calling the Virgin Mary "Mother of God," *Theotokos*.[3] While not denying the divinity of Christ, Nestorius argued that,

3. For a detailed account of the Nestorian controversy, see *The Ecclesiastical History of Evagrius Scholasticus*, trans. with introduction by Michael Whitby, Translated Texts for Historians 33 (Liverpool: Liverpool University Press, 2000). See also John A. McGuckin, *St. Cyril of Alexandria: The Christological Controversy: Its History, Theology, and Texts*, Supplements to Vigiliae Christianae 23 (Leiden: E. J. Brill, 1994).

strictly speaking, Mary is not properly called *Theotokos*, the bearer or mother of God, but rather that she should more properly be called *Christokos*, Mother of Christ, or *Theodochos*, receiver of God. Nestorius argued that Mary was the mother of Jesus but not the mother of God, for, while Jesus as a human being was born of her, the divine Logos was not born of her. From Nestorius's perspective, it was not possible that the divine Logos as such was born of a human mother.[4] Cyril, the powerful bishop of Alexandria, responded vigorously to this assault on Mary as the mother of God and on Jesus' divinity and the reality of the incarnation. He denounced Nestorius to Pope Celestine. The two major christological parties, with their roots in the theological traditions of Alexandria and Antioch, clashed in the battle between these prominent personalities, Cyril and Nestorius. Considerable discord ensued.[5] The dispute that developed was essentially a christological one. Was Jesus truly and fully human and was he also truly and fully God?

Emperor Theodosius II called another general council. The dispute came to a head at Ephesus, in twin rival councils, with both sides meeting separately and each excommunicating the other. The council at which Cyril presided was later deemed, under the pope's authority, to be the legitimate one. No dogmatic definition in a formal sense issued. But, in what was a triumph for Cyril, Nestorius's teaching of "two distinct natures in Christ" and of "two persons" or "two sons" (i.e., the Son of God and the son of man, as if in effect set side by side) was condemned, and the propriety of the title *Theotokos* confirmed. Nestorius was condemned as "the new Judas"[6] and banished.

Cyril, in a softening of his stance, conceded the use of the expression "two natures" and with it the distinction between the human attributes proper to Christ's humanity and the divine attributes proper to his divinity. While maintaining that there were not two independently existing sons in Jesus, he argued for the "hypostatic [i.e., personal] union" in Jesus Christ of the divine Logos and the human being. "One, out of two," he declared.[7] In other words,

4. See "Nestorius' First Sermon Against The *Theotokos*," in *The Christological Controversy*, trans. and ed. Richard A. Norris, Sources of Early Christian Thought (Philadelphia: Fortress Press, 1980), 123-30.

5. Gregory of Nyssa, for example, commented: "If in this city [Constantinople] one asks anyone for change, he will discuss with you whether the Son is begotten or unbegotten. If you ask about the quality of the bread you will receive the answer, 'the Father is greater, the Son is less.' If you suggest a bath is desirable, you will be told 'there was nothing before the Son was created'" (*De filii deitate* [PG 46:557], cited by W. H. C. Frend, *The Rise of the Monophysite Movement: Chapters in the History of the Church in the Fifth and Sixth Centuries* [Cambridge: Cambridge University Press, 1972], xii).

6. See Frend, *Rise of the Monophysite Movement*, 18, which cites *Acta Conciliorum Oecumenicorum*, I. I. 2, p. 54.

7. See "Cyril of Alexandria's Second Letter to Nestorius," in *Christological Controversy*, 131-35.

there are not two persons, the Son of God and the son of man. Cyril thus insisted on the *one* subject or subsistent reality in Jesus, the divine Logos incarnate. Some of Cyril's opponents were not convinced, however, and were concerned that Cyril was teaching a kind of mixture or confusion of Jesus' two natures, in which the divinity of Christ was changed or altered or modified in some way. They staunchly held to their traditional teaching of "two natures." As in the trinitarian controversy, the resolution of the dispute was not assisted by a measure of ambiguity and imprecision in the meaning of the terms *ousia* (substance), *hypostasis,* and *physis* (nature), and by the lack of an adequate conceptual framework within which to express the mystery and to obviate dangers of misinterpretation. Imperial pressures and ecclesiastical and political rivalries exacerbated the situation.

Despite the Council of Ephesus, the dispute between the two parties continued unabated. Under pressure from the emperor, a compromise was reached between the positions of Alexandria and Antioch with a Formula of Union in 433.[8] The discord continued, however, and the christological controversy was reignited in 446 in Constantinople when Eutyches, a vigorous defender of the Alexandrian tradition, denied that Christ has two natures *after* the incarnation and argued instead that Christ has only "one nature after the union" (and hence the later term for this approach, *monophysitism*, meaning one nature). Pope Leo I wrote a letter to Flavian, who was then bishop of Constantinople, where Eutyches was presbyter.[9] Condemning the teaching of Eutyches, Leo employed the terminology that the North African Tertullian had previously used to describe Jesus Christ, the Son of God made human, in terms of two natures (*duae substantiae*), human and divine, in the one person (*una persona*) (*Against Praxeas* 27).[10] Against the monophysitism of Eutyches, who taught "one nature after the union," Leo stressed the distinction between the two natures, in the unity of the one person (*unitas personae*) of Jesus. Leo argued that, since Jesus was born of both God and Mary, he is truly God and truly human and that he possesses, in the unity of his person, both a divine nature and a human nature, together with their associated divine and human traits.

Once again a period of turmoil and discord prevailed in the church, though it was largely in the East. The Council of Chalcedon was convened to bring the controversy to a conclusion. What was needed was not a new creed as such—indeed such was expressly excluded by the council[11]—but a

8. DS 272; ND 607.

9. See "Pope Leo I's Letter to Flavian of Constantinople," which came to be called *Tomus Leonis*, in *Christological Controversy,* 145-55. DS 291-94; ND 609-12.

10. In *Ante-Nicene Fathers,* 3:624.

11. The introduction to the "Definition of Faith" of the Council of Chalcedon states: "We therefore decree . . . that primary authority shall belong to the exposition of the correct and blameless faith

statement to avert misinterpretation or misrepresentation of the faith defined at Nicaea (which all accepted as a binding norm for the expression of faith) and Constantinople (which, along with Ephesus, was received as "ecumenical" at the Council of Chalcedon).[12] Several hundred bishops gathered at Chalcedon under the supervision of imperial commissioners. Again, as in the trinitarian debate, argument focused on the ontological aspects of the question (in other words, the composition of Christ's being and the manner in which his humanity and divinity were united in him) and not on soteriological, anthropological, or historico-salvific aspects or on the paschal mystery of Jesus' death and resurrection. As in the earlier trinitarian disputes, however, it was soteriological considerations that assisted in resolving the question about Jesus' full humanity. As Gregory of Nazianzus succinctly expressed it: *Quod non assumptum—non salvatum est;* what is not assumed is not healed; what is united with God is saved (*Epistle* 101).[13] But, as also occurred in the development of trinitarian doctrine, there was a weakening of the soteriological and historical roots of christological doctrine. The result, as we see below, was a rather abstract and essentialist formulation of christological dogma that is remote from the actual events of salvation history. The ontologizing of Christology thus followed the ontologizing of trinitarian theology.

The final statement of the Council of Chalcedon was a carefully crafted tapestry of various elements from the different Christological traditions and cenetrs of church life, Alexandria and Antioch, Constantinople and Rome. It drew on Cyril's letters to Nestorius, the Formula of Reunion, and Leo's Tome. Following Cyril, it maintains the unity of Christ, who is fully human and fully divine. Following the Formula of Reunion, it asserts that Christ exists "in two natures" without confusion or division. Following Leo's Tome, it asserts that Jesus is one hypostasis, a single subject, in two natures, human and divine. The

---

composed by the three hundred and eighteen holy and blessed fathers who gathered in Nicaea when Constantine, of devout memory, was emperor; and that authority shall belong to the decrees which derived from the one hundred and eighty holy fathers in Constantinople, which they laid down for the destruction of the heresies which had grown up at that time and for the corroboration of our same catholic and apostolic faith" (*Christological Controversy*, 156).

12. The development of the notion of the "ecumenical council," of which Nicaea was for a long time the only recognized example, facilitated the development of a conciliar magisterium as the standard and the means by which to resolve doctrinal matters. Nicaea was deemed the norm or standard against which to assess the orthodoxy of theological doctrine. The method to resolve the christological controversy at both Ephesus and Chalcedon was to assess the competing positions in terms of their conformity with the faith of the "318 Fathers." The Council of Chalcedon regarded its work as an exposition of the church's creed, an elaboration of the church's faith defined at Nicaea, while providing a statement that left no room for misinterpretation or confusion in regard to the heresies of Nestorius and Eutyches.

13. In *The Later Christian Fathers: A Selection from the Writings of the Fathers from St Cyril of Jerusalem to St Leo the Great,* ed. and trans. Henry Bettenson (London: Oxford University Press, 1970), 108.

mia physis (one nature) formula was abandoned, and also Cyril's notion of "from (*ek*) two natures" (i.e., before the union). It explicitly condemns both Nestorius and Eutyches and, concomitantly, the extreme expression of Antiochene theology on the one hand and of Alexandrian theology on the other. In the assertion of the distinction between the two natures, it rejects the radical monophysitism of Eutyches. In the emphasis on the union, it rejects Nestorius's position and any notion of the division of the one Christ into two persons or *prosōpa*. Hypostasis (person) is the term used to designate the subject of the union of the two natures. The pronouncement of the Council of Chalcedon begins by restating the creeds of Nicaea and Constantinople and then proclaims a doctrine of Jesus Christ's double *homoousios*:

> Following, therefore, the holy Fathers, we unanimously teach to confess one and the same Son, our Lord Jesus Christ, the same perfect in divinity and perfect in humanity, the same truly God and truly man composed of rational soul and body, the same one in being (*homoousios*) with the Father as to the divinity and one in being (*homoousios*) with us as to his humanity, like unto us in all things but sin *[cf Heb 4:15]*. The same was begotten from the Father before the ages as to his divinity and in the latter days for us and for our salvation was born as to his humanity from Mary the Virgin Mother of God (*Theotokos*).
>
> We confess that one and the same Lord Jesus Christ, the only-begotten Son, must be acknowledged in two natures, without confusion or change, without division or separation. The distinction between the natures was never abolished by their union but rather the character proper to each of the two natures was preserved as they came together in one person (*prosōpon*) and one hypostasis. He is not split or divided into two persons (*prosōpa*), but he is one and the same Only-begotten, God the Word, the Lord Jesus Christ, as formerly the prophets and later Jesus Christ himself have taught us about him and as has been handed down to us by the Symbol of the Fathers.[14]

The Council used the word *homoousios*, which had proved so contentious after the Council of Nicaea and which the Council of Constantinople had not used in its elaboration on the person of the Holy Spirit. Eutyches had denied that Jesus is *homoousios* with us in his humanity (though he did allow it of Mary in relation to us). The Chalcedonian doctrine acknowledges unity and distinction and, at the same time, clearly excludes separation, confusion,

14. DS 301-2; ND 614-15.

division, or alteration of the divine and human natures. It asserts an emphatic diphysitism, proclaiming that he is one "in two natures"—not *from* two natures but *in* two natures. The natures are preserved with their distinctive properties in and after the union, without confusion or alteration. Nature provides the principle of distinction and duality, while the unity of Christ is located at the level of person or *prosōpon* or hypostasis. He is "one person." The emblem of Chalcedon, the basic formula of Christology, was thus encapsulated: he is one person in two natures.

The stalwart adherents of what would later be termed monophysitism, remained concerned that the Chalcedonian resolution allowed for the emergence of the doctrine of "two sons." From their staunchly anti-Nestorian perspective, Chalcedon seemed like a rehabilitation of Nestorius, a new kind of Nestorianism, because of its two-natures statement. (But note the strong references in the creed and in the Chalcedonian statement that Jesus Christ is the *one* Lord.) The resolution at Chalcedon finally proved costly indeed, leaving a tragic legacy of controversy and division in the church. The lack of adequate conceptual apparatus remained a continuing problem. Other issues, such as monothelitism (one will) and monoergism (one energy) later emerged (to be rejected as unorthodox). The Third Council of Constantinople (680-681) would later clarify the distinction between the two wills and also between the energies and operations of the two natures in Christ.[15] The meaning of the phrase "in two natures" in the one subject of their union, hypostasis, had yet to be clarified but would require greater clarity of meaning of the terms *hypostasis* and of *physis*.

CONTEMPORARY APPROACHES TO CHRISTOLOGY

The Councils of Nicaea, Ephesus, and Chalcedon provided the philosophical and terminological framework for classical christological doctrine for the centuries to come. But how best *in our times* to understand and to speak of the identity of Jesus, given that the technical philosophical categories of nature, substance, and even person no longer communicate in our world what they did in the time of the ecumenical councils when trinitarian and christological doctrine was formulated? Modern consciousness finds them static and essentialist in tone. Much more empirically than philosophically oriented in comparison to our early Christian forebears, it also finds this kind of explication of the mystery of Jesus terribly remote from the historical life, death, and

15. DS 556-58; ND 635-37.

resurrection of Jesus, all the more so given all that is newly available to us through modern critical biblical exegesis. Moreover, we moderns, newly attuned to the world—the whole cosmos—as a complex web of interrelationships and processes, find the classical treatment singularly lacking in cosmic scope and significance. As John Paul II affirmed, explicitly adverting to the cosmological dimensions of the significance of the incarnation: "The Incarnation, then, also has a cosmic significance, a cosmic dimension: the 'first-born of all creation' becoming incarnate in the individual humanity of Christ, unites himself in some way with the entire reality of man, . . . with the whole of creation."[16]

Vatican II noted that the human race has passed from a static concept of reality to a more dynamic, evolutionary one and that the new situation calls for new efforts of analysis and synthesis (GS 5). This shift from a static concept of reality to a more dynamic, evolutionary one heralds the need for a recasting of classical christological dogma from the rather remote, ahistorical, and static framework into terms more accessible and meaningful in the contemporary context. It is not that we are rejecting the essential meaning and the truth of the classical understanding of the mystery of Jesus. Rather, we want and need to move beyond the classical framework in which it is expressed, precisely in order to protect the underlying truth and meaning, which Chalcedon sought to express. As Pope John XXIII explained and Vatican II confirmed, "the deposit and the truths of faith are one thing, the manner of expressing them—provided their sense and meaning are retained—is another" (GS 62). By way of contrast to the classical approach, Vatican II also speaks of the need to grow in understanding of the mystery of the person of Jesus (e.g., LG), and situates the significance of the incarnation in terms of the dignity of human being: "For, by his incarnation, he, the Son of God has in a certain way united himself with each individual. He worked with human hands, he thought with a human mind. He acted with a human will, and with a human heart he loved" (GS 22).

The task of Christology is necessarily an unending enterprise. The Council of Chalcedon marks neither the beginning nor the end of the process of doctrinal development. Just as the early Christians expressed their faith in Jesus Christ in different ways, each generation, employing its own philosophical tools and scriptural insights, and in its own particular historical and cultural context, is called to articulate its faith in Jesus Christ as "the way, and the truth, and the life" (John 14:6) in meaningful, credible, and accessible

---

16. On the Holy Spirit in the Life of the Church in the World, *Dominum et Vivificantem*, a. 50; see http://www.vatican.va/holy_father/john_paul-ii/encyclicals/>.

ways. But with the impetus provided by both Karl Rahner and Karl Barth, and renewed focus on the Trinity as it is revealed to us and for us in the economy, and on Jesus' identity not just as God-man but as the incarnate Son, contemporary Christology is newly challenged to explore the intrinsic connection between Christology and Trinity and to articulate an expressly trinitarian Christology.

CHRISTOLOGY FROM A TRINITARIAN PERSPECTIVE

Christoph Schwöbel hits the mark when he suggests that what he describes as the current crisis in modern Christology in regard to its intelligibility and credibility might be due precisely to the neglect of its trinitarian foundations and connections.[17] For Schwöbel, the fact that the clarification of the trinitarian logic of the Christian understanding of God preceded the articulation of orthodox Christology is highly significant and indicates that Christology necessarily presupposes the trinitarian understanding of God. He observes that, in the course of the christological controversy, christological thought lost its trinitarian foundations, together with the ontology of personhood of the Cappadocians. Schwöbel asks: Might not a solution to the christological crisis lie in a trinitarian understanding of the divine and a trinitarian understanding of what it is to be human? Might exploration from an explicitly trinitarian perspective open up new possibilities for a christological imagination? Schwöbel finds in the fact that trinitarian logic and doctrine emerged before christological doctrine a hint that an elucidation of the mystery of Jesus Christ is necessarily situated in the context of an expressly trinitarian understanding of God. When isolated from the trinitarian structure and logic of Christian faith as revealed in the message, life, death, and resurrection of Jesus Christ, christological doctrine, Schwöbel observes, verges on the nonsensical and its problems become intractable. He argues that the neglect of the trinitarian framework also results in the disjunction between Christology and soteriology.[18]

Schwöbel therefore proposes a trinitarian Christology, a Christology explicitly based on the trinitarian logic of Christian faith and worship, and an explicitly trinitarian hermeneutic. He argues that the Christian community and worship serve as the starting point and immediate context for Christology. After all, he explains, the Christian community celebrates the trinitarian

---

17. Christoph Schwöbel, "Christology and Trinitarian Thought," in *Trinitarian Theology Today: Essays on Divine Being and Act,* ed. Christoph Schwöbel (Edinburgh: T&T Clark, 1995), 113-46.
18. Ibid., 136-37.

being of God as the condition of its own being and its own participation in the divine communion, and it is in that trinitarian framework that the Christian community proclaims and professes that Jesus is Lord. It is there too that the Holy Spirit makes believers co-present with Christ, and Christ co-present with the believers. Schwöbel thus calls for a restoration of a trinitarian framework for Christology. He insists, however, that this is *not* the same as the metaphysical framework of trinitarian theology that traditionally served as the framework for Christology and resulted in the two-natures doctrine of classical Christology.

In line with the shift to a more relational ontology that, as we have seen in our brief introductory overview, is so strong a feature of contemporary trinitarian theologies,[19] Schwöbel explains that to construct Christology in a trinitarian framework calls for "a paradigm shift from natures to persons."[20] From that new perspective, the question of the divinity of Christ is interpreted not in terms of his possession of a divine nature but rather in terms of his relations, as the Son, to the Father and to the Holy Spirit; for it is those relations, Schwöbel argues, that constitute Christ as agent of salvation. From this perspective, he is divine not because he possesses a divine nature but because God the Father relates to him, in the Spirit, as the Son and thereby distinguishes himself as the Father from the Son and is, in this way, in personal communion with him, in the Spirit. Similarly Christ is divine in relating to God the Father, in the Spirit, and thereby distinguishing himself as the Son from the Father and, in this way, is in personal communion with the Father and the Spirit.

The divinity of Christ is then explicated in terms not of the possession of a divine nature but rather in terms of his relationship as Son with the Father and with the Holy Spirit. The Christ event is then recognized as the enactment of his divine Sonship, in relation to the Father and led by the Spirit, in the modality of a truly human life. In his very person, God and alienated creation are reconciled. Similarly, in regard to the humanity of Christ, to be human does not mean possessing a human nature, but to be a human person, to actualize the relational being of humanity in becoming a person in relation to other persons. When we speak of the humanity of Jesus, we mean that the Son of God has not just come into a human person but has truly become a human person. That Jesus is truly human reveals the created destiny of human being to be in relation to God. The soteriological significance of Jesus' humanity lies in the promise of the Gospel that in him humanity is restored

19. See, e.g., Anne Hunt, *What Are They Saying about the Trinity* (Mahwah, N.J.: Paulist Press, 1998).
20. Ibid., 139.

to its created destiny. It is not just that he shares in our humanity, but that we share in his humanity and participate by grace through the Spirit in his relationship with the Father. Schwöbel appeals to John Zizioulas's notion that to be the *imago Dei* is to be persons in communion.[21]

Schwöbel argues that this shift from natures to persons, from substance metaphysics to a metaphysics of relations, affords a refashioned trinitarian hermeneutic for Christology and that "this paradigm shift from natures to persons" would seem to lie "at the heart of a trinitarian hermeneutic for Christology."[22] Schwöbel also observes that, when the locus of the divinity of Christ is recognized not in the possession of a divine nature but in the relationship of the Son to the Father, in and through the Spirit, then questions as to how the divine and human natures coexist in the one person recede from our concerns and the question becomes instead how these relations of Sonship can be exercised and enacted in the reality of a human life. Here the Gospel narratives come to the fore, he argues, presenting different perspectives on and different theological interpretations of Jesus' life, a life constituted by and conducted in the Spirit, in obedience to the Father, for the coming of God's kingdom and the salvation and reconciliation of all creation.

We arrive then, Schwöbel proposes, at a renewed understanding of the hypostatic union, the doctrine of the union of divine Son and the humanity of Christ in the one person of Jesus Christ. The true humanity of Christ is constituted by its assumption by the Son. Conversely, it is only in being the hypostasis of the humanity of Christ that the divine Son is the incarnate Son. The identity of Jesus Christ is then described in terms of the union of the person of the Son, who is constituted as the Son through his relation to the Father in the Spirit, with the humanity of Jesus, which is constituted in its relational structure, precisely through its hypostatic participation in the person of the Son in its relations to the Father and the Spirit. Humanity is, in this way, restored to its created destiny, in Jesus Christ, the second Adam. The hypostatic being of the Son is the eschatological promise for the whole of creation, realized in the person of the incarnate Son. It is the paradigm for the reconciled being of the whole of creation, the ground of its possibility, and the promise of its realization.

In this relational ontology, Jesus Christ's being is thus situated in two sets of relationships: the trinitarian relations of Father, Son, and Holy Spirit, which are constitutive of his identity and divinity as the Son, and the relational being

---

21. John D. Zizioulas, *Being as Communion: Studies in Personhood and the Church*, with a foreword by John Meyendorff (Crestwood, N.Y.: St. Vladimir's Seminary Press, 1985).

22. Schwöbel, "Christology and Trinitarian Thought," 139.

of humanity, which finds its fulfillment in the relationship of God's daughters and sons through the Son and the Spirit to the Father. Here, Schwöbel notes, the classical understanding of the union of the two natures "without confusion, without change, without division, without separation" serves an important critical function in a trinitarian Christology, as a safeguard of the important distinction between the being of the creator and created being.[23]

Similarly, in Schwöbel's reconnection of Christology with soteriology in this expressly trinitarian reconstruction, our salvation is to be in communion with God without change, without fusion, without division, and without separation. Distinction is preserved in the hypostatic relation; it is not a question of fusion or of unrelated coexistence of the two natures. The Kingdom of God, as realized in the very person of Jesus Christ, thus emerges as the life of the whole of creation in communion with its triune creator, a communion "without confusion, without change, without division, without separation." The personal being-in-communion, which God is eternally, is the ultimate eschatological reality for the whole of creation.

Schwöbel proposes that this paradigm shift from natures to persons also has important repercussions for our understanding of the doctrine of the Trinity, as it requires, he argues, abandoning the rigid distinction in classical trinitarian theology between the processions in the immanent Trinity and the missions in the economy. Schwöbel proposes that the distinction be replaced with an understanding of the trinitarian relations that sees the relations as mutual and reciprocal (and not just as originating) and which thus integrates both personal distinction and personal communion of Father, Son, and Spirit.[24]

A trinitarian approach to Christology and to the salvation that is God's plan for the universe, such as that outlined by Schwöbel, certainly refocuses attention on the relational dimension of divine and human being. In doing so, it also offers the possibility of averting a number of problematic issues that have emerged in contemporary Christology, by allowing for a more expansive horizon than the traditional metaphysical approach affords, thus enabling Christology to accommodate and to respond much more creatively and graciously to newly emerging insights and sensibilities. The concerns of feminist theology, liberation theology, and eco-theology, for example, as well as those of ecumenism, a theology of world religions, and indeed the meaning of Christian faith and life in the world, can be more comfortably accommodated in this kind of Christology, with its emphasis on the relational dimension of both divine and human being.

While Schwöbel's proposed reformulation of Christology in an expressly

23. Ibid., 143.
24. Ibid., 140.

trinitarian perspective offers new possibilities for Christology, it also raises questions and concerns, particularly in regard to the fundamental coherence of the argument at a cognitive level. Admittedly, it admirably engages the emerging existential awareness of person as an intrinsically relational being, and so addresses contemporary consciousness, which recognizes and prizes relationality as intrinsic to and constitutive of authentic personhood. But in eschewing the dimension of substance, it effectively leaves the notion of person without metaphysical grounding. Without some notion of substance, the notion of person and of relation is simply not philosophically grounded. In thus seeking to ameliorate an emphasis in the traditional doctrine on "nature" to the detriment of "person", Schwöbel's proposal risks problems of its own, namely, explaining the being of Jesus Christ overly one-sidedly in terms of relation, to the exclusion of other important dimensions of personhood, such as substantiality (the *in-itself* and *not-in-another* dimension of being) and interiority. As William Norris Clarke explains, personhood involves both substantiality (the *in-itself* dimension of being) and relationality (the *toward-others* aspect). Clarke thus argues:

> Hence we are faced, on the one hand, with a richer older metaphysical tradition of the person that left the relational dimension underdeveloped and, on the other hand, the more recent phenomenological tradition that has highly developed the relational aspect of the being of the person but lost its metaphysical grounding. What is urgently needed is a creative integration of these two valuable but incomplete lines of thought into a more complete and well-rounded philosophy of the person.[25]

Constructing a Christology from a trinitarian perspective also alerts us to the importance of attending to it from a pneumatological perspective.[26] The interpersonal relationships between Jesus and the Father and between Jesus and the Spirit are both intrinsic to the mystery of the person and work of

25. William Norris Clarke, *Person and Being*, The Aquinas Lecture, 1993 (Milwaukee: Marquette University Press, 1993), 5. See also idem, "Person, Being and St. Thomas," *Communio* 19 (1992): 601-18; idem, "To Be Is to Be Self-communicative: St. Thomas' View of Personal Being," *Theology Digest* 33 (1986): 441-54; idem, "The 'We Are' of Interpersonal Dialogue as the Starting Point of Metaphysics," *Modern Schoolman* 69 (1992): 357-68; idem, "Thomism and Contemporary Philosophical Pluralism," in *The Future of Thomism*, ed. Deal W. Hudson and Dennis Wm. Moran (Notre Dame, Ind.: American Maritain Association, University of Notre Dame Press, 1992), 91-108. See also Gerald A. McCool, "An Alert and Independent Thomist: William Norris Clarke, S.J.," in *The Universe as Journey: Conversations with W. Norris Clarke*, ed. Gerald A. McCool (New York: Fordham University Press, 1988), 13-47; Gerald A. McCool, "The Tradition of St. Thomas since Vatican II," *Theology Digest* 40 (1993): 324-35.

26. Yves Congar's remarkable three-volume work, *I Believe in the Holy Spirit*, trans. David Smith (London: Geoffrey Chapman, 1983), attests to the central place of pneumatology in Western theology. See Elizabeth T. Groppe, "The Contribution of Yves Congar's Theology of the Holy Spirit," *Theological Studies* 62 (2001): 451-78.

Jesus. The Gospels attest to the reality that the life and ministry, the death, descent, and resurrection of Jesus are inseparable from the Holy Spirit. The hypostatic union of the human and the divine in the person of Jesus Christ is realized through the Holy Spirit and, indeed, is made accessible to us through the Holy Spirit. As Irenaeus recognized, the Word and the Spirit are the two hands of God (Irenaeus, *Against Heresies* 4.20.1).[27] Christology and pneumatology are inextricably related, and a Christology that is not deeply imbued with pneumatology is seriously impoverished.[28]

Here David Coffey's efforts to construct a "Spirit Christology" provoke fresh questions for contemporary trinitarian theology.[29] Coffey, who holds the William J. Kelly Distinguished Chair of Theology at Marquette University, situates his trinitarian theology in the context of the dominant model of the Trinity, to which he variously refers as the "procession" or "distinction" or "mission" model, according to which, in accordance with the descending scheme of Johannine Christology, the Son proceeds from the Father, and the Holy Spirit from the Father and (or through) the Son (*filioque* or *per filium*). This mission-procession scheme finds expression in the Gospel in the incarnation, life, death, resurrection, and ascension of Jesus, the incarnate Son. The order or taxis is Father–Son–Holy Spirit. The taxis in regard to believers, whereby the Spirit, Spirit of Christ, unites believers with Christ by faith, thus giving them a share in his divine Sonship and thus in his fellowship with God, is the reverse: Holy Spirit–Son–Father.

One of the problems Coffey identifies with this "procession" model is that it recognizes, at best, only a secondary and derivative role for the Holy Spirit in the incarnation, thus contributing to the impoverishment of a theology of the Holy Spirit. Coffey argues that the New Testament offers not just one but two models of the Trinity and that "a balanced theology of the Trinity, one that aims to be ecumenically constructive, must encompass *all* the biblical evidence."[30] Coffey proposes an alternative model, one that is more closely

---

27. In *Ante-Nicene Fathers*, 1:487.

28. John Zizioulas comments in regard to Vatican II and its pneumatology in regard to ecclesiology: "One of the fundamental criticisms that Orthodox theologians expressed in connection with the ecclesiology of Vatican II concerned the place which the council gave to Pneumatology in its ecclesiology. In general, it was felt that in comparison with Christology, Pneumatology did not play an important role in the council's teaching on the Church. More particularly, it was observed that the Holy Spirit was brought into ecclesiology *after* the edifice of the Church was constructed with Christological material alone" (*Being as Communion*, 123).

29. David Coffey, "Spirit Christology and the Trinity," in *Advents of the Spirit: An Introduction to the Current Study of Pneumatology*, ed. Bradford E. Hinze and D. Lyle Dabney (Milwaukee: Marquette University Press, 2001), 315-38 (see also Ralph Del Colle's response, pp. 339-46); idem, "Our Return to God through Christ in the Spirit," *Compass* 23 (1989): 33-36; idem, "The Holy Spirit as the Mutual Love of the Father and the Son," *Theological Studies* 51 (1990): 193-229; idem, *Deus Trinitas: The Doctrine of the Triune God* (Oxford/New York: Oxford University Press, 1999).

30. Coffey, *Deus Trinitas*, 45.

aligned with the ascending Christology of the Synoptic Gospels, a model that, in his earlier writings, he called the "bestowal" model, in which the Holy Spirit is bestowed by the Father and the Son on each other. Coffey later refers to this model as the "return" or "union" model, since Jesus, having been sent forth from the Father, is conceived by means of the Father's bestowal of the Holy Spirit. Jesus returns to the Father through his life and death in the power of the Holy Spirit.[31] Here, the taxis is Father–Holy Spirit–Son (or to state it more fully Father–Holy Spirit–Son–Holy Spirit–Father). This "return" or "union" model, Coffey insists, is more comprehensive than the "procession" model, in that "it includes the sending forth in the sweep of the larger movement of return."[32] Coffey argues that this "return" model is identical to Augustine's understanding of the Trinity, wherein the Holy Spirit is the mutual love of the Father and the Son. In this model, the return of believers to God, because the Holy Spirit is mediated to them by the Son, follows the order: Holy Spirit–Son–Father.

Coffey offers a novel approach to a Spirit Christology, and a thorough assessment of his contribution has not yet been done.[33] We turn now to the work of Jacques Dupuis (1923-2004), a Belgian Jesuit priest and professor emeritus of the Pontifical Gregorian University, who offers a highly nuanced approach that is in careful accord with the classic conciliar statements of christological orthodoxy, with radical implications for a theology of world religions.

JACQUES DUPUIS' TRINITARIAN CHRISTOLOGY: JESUS' UNIQUENESS AS "CONSTITUTIVE" AND "RELATIONAL"

Jacques Dupuis SJ strives for what he explicitly describes as a "trinitarian Christology" upon which to build a theology of religions. We shall confine our attention to his Christology in this chapter and examine his theology of religions later. Readers will recall that Schwöbel argues that the neglect of the

---

31. Unlike Coffey, who argues for two trinitarian models, Thomas G. Weinandy, in *The Father's Spirit of Sonship: Reconceiving the Trinity* (Edinburgh: T&T Clark, 1995), argues that, in the immanent Trinity, the Father begets the Son in or by the Holy Spirit, and the Spirit proceeds simultaneously from the Father. Weinandy comments: "Now Coffey verges on the present thesis when he states that the Son proceeds from the Father's love for him. . . . However, because Coffey does not give any active role to the Spirit in the begetting of the Son, he does not fully see that it is in the Father spirating the Spirit that the Son is simultaneously begotten in and by the Spirit; that is, in the love of the Father. The Holy Spirit conforms the Son to be the Son and so allows him to love the Father by the same Spirit (Love) in whom he is begotten" (ibid., 70 n. 31). For Coffey's critique of Weinandy's argument, see "Spirit Christology and the Trinity," 334-35.

32. Coffey, *Deus Trinitas*, 5.

33. Ralph Del Colle offers a study of Coffey's theology in *Christ and Spirit: Spirit Christology in Trinitarian Perspective* (New York: Oxford University Press, 1994) but, given subsequent developments in Coffey's thought, a more critical and comprehensive assessment is yet to be completed.

trinitarian framework also results in the disjunction between Christology and soteriology. It is a soteriological perspective and concern which informs Dupuis' remarkable endeavors to construct a theology of religions, wherein the reality of religious pluralism finds a positive meaning as part of God's salvific plan. Indeed, Dupuis insists that "Christology needs to keep in touch with its soteriological foundation at every step of its elaboration."[34]

Dupuis proceeds to argue for a Christology that is expressly based on the Trinity and an understanding of the interpersonal relationships between Father and Son and between Son and Holy Spirit.[35] He explains:

> Such a Christology will place in full relief the interpersonal relationships between Jesus and the God whom he calls Father, on the one side, and the Spirit whom he will send, on the other. These relationships are intrinsic to the mystery of Jesus' person and of his work. Christology ought to be imbued with these intra-Trinitarian relationships in any situation; but this requirement obtains all the more in the context of a theology of religious pluralism.[36]

Indeed, Dupuis is critical of past failures in Christology to attend to this interpersonal dimension, resulting in the mistaken development of a closed and restrictive Christocentrism. As Dupuis explains:

> Christology has often sinned by impersonalism. To remedy such a shortcoming, the personal trinitarian dimension of the mystery must be present everywhere. A Christology of the God-man is an abstraction; the only Christology that is real is that of the Son-of-God-made-man-in-history. The personal intra-trinitarian relations must, therefore, be shown to inform every aspect of the Christological mystery.[37]

Despite this criticism of the traditional approach, Dupuis' Christology is deeply grounded in the orthodox faith, as expressed by the Council of Chalcedon (431) and reiterated by the Third Council of Constantinople (680-681). Indeed, he frequently appeals to the classical statements of christological orthodoxy, which express the mystery of Christ in terms of the two natures existing "without confusion or change, without division or separation." Dupuis

34. Jacques Dupuis, *Who Do You Say I Am? Introduction to Christology* (Maryknoll, N.Y.: Orbis Books, 1994), 140.

35. See Jacques Dupuis, *Christianity and the Religions: From Confrontation to Dialogue* (Maryknoll NY: Orbis Books, 2002), 90-95.

36. Jacques Dupuis, *Toward a Christian Theology of Religious Pluralism* (Maryknoll, N.Y.: Orbis Books, 1997), 205; see also idem, *Christianity and the Religions*, 91.

37. Dupuis, *Who Do You Say I Am?*, 36.

therefore argues that, within the one person of Jesus Christ, we can distinguish between his two natures, human and divine, and thus between the operations of his uncreated divine nature and his created finite human nature.

In reference to Jesus Christ, Dupuis eschews the language of "absolute" and "definitive" and prefers to speak in terms of "constitutive," "universal," and "decisive." First, our knowledge of God is not absolute or definitive, he argues; it is necessarily limited.[38] Second, the absolute Savior, Dupuis argues, is the Father, who is the ultimate source of the risen Lord and of all reality. Hence, Dupuis insists, the uniqueness and universality of Christ the Savior are "constitutive." As the Son of God incarnate, Jesus is the center of history and the key to the entire procession of salvation, and his resurrection confers universal significance on his human existence. In this sense, he is "constitutive" of universal salvation. Dupuis consistently stresses that Jesus' constitutive uniqueness as universal Savior rests on his personal identity as the Son of God. In refusing to speak of Jesus Christ as absolute and definitive, however, Dupuis is definitely not implying that Jesus Christ is relative and that he is one Savior among several. As Dupuis explains:

> In accordance with the mainline Christian tradition, the constitutive uniqueness and universality of the Jesus-Christ-event must be maintained. Such uniqueness must not, however, be construed as absolute; what is absolute is God's saving will. Neither absolute nor relative, Jesus' uniqueness is "constitutive" and "relational" . . . in the sense that the singularly unique event of Jesus Christ is inscribed in the overall ambit of God's personal dealing with humankind in history, and, therefore, related to all other divine manifestations to people in the one history of salvation.[39]

Based on the Chalcedonian understanding of the hypostatic union within which the two natures are acknowledged to exist "without confusion or change, without division or separation," Dupuis then proceeds to distinguish between the Word of God *in se* and the Word of God incarnate.[40] He reiter-

38. Dupuis refers to John Paul II, *Fides et Ratio*, par. 2., in regard to "the fullness of truth [which] will appear with the final Revelation of God."

39. Jacques Dupuis, "Trinitarian Christology as a Model for a Theology of Religious Pluralism," in *The Myriad Christ: Plurality and the Quest for Unity in Contemporary Christology*, ed. T. Merrigan and J. Haers (Leuven: Leuven University Press, 2000), 96-97.

40. Gerald O'Collins observes that Dupuis' critics accuse him of separating the Word of God and the man Jesus into two separate subjects. O'Collins notes, however, that Dupuis' critics "have never produced chapter and verse to back up this accusation." See "Jacques Dupuis: His Person and Work," in *In Many and Diverse Ways: In Honor of Jacques Dupuis*, ed. Daniel Kendall and Gerald O'Collins (Maryknoll, N.Y.: Orbis Books, 2003), 23.

ates that the Word of God and Jesus are personally identical. He insists, nevertheless, as with Chalcedon, that we can distinguish, but never separate, the two natures and their respective operations.[41] While the humanity of Jesus and the person of the Word of God cannot be separated, the two natures of Jesus Christ remain distinct in their union in the one person; they are not identical.

Dupuis repeatedly emphasizes that, in Jesus Christ, "God effected a self-manifestation in a manner that is decisive and can be neither surpassed nor repeated."[42] But he also insists that the centrality of the incarnational dimension of God's economy of salvation must not be allowed to obscure the universal abiding presence and action of the divine Word and the Spirit. This leads Dupuis to argue that, while God's self-communication culminates in the revelation of God in the person of Jesus Christ, the presence and action of God's Word are not restricted to the historical event of the incarnation. In other words, Dupuis would persuade us that the incarnation, life, death, and resurrection do not exhaust the presence and activity of the Word (and similarly that of the Spirit) in salvation history. Dupuis argues that both Word and Spirit are active in the world and in salvation history both before and after the Christ-event.[43] The action of the Word and the Spirit endures, as Dupuis explains:

> It seems therefore possible to talk of an action of the Word of God, not only before the incarnation of the Word but also after the incarnation and the resurrection of Jesus Christ, distinct from the salvific action through his humanity, provided that this continued action of the Word be not "separated" from the event in which the insuperable "concentration" of the self-revelation of God according to the one divine plan for the universal salvation of humankind takes place.[44]

The human existence of Jesus clearly belongs to a particular time in history, but, despite its historical particularity, the Christ-event has lasting and universal significance. However, the presence and action of the Word and

41. Among a number of references to the early fathers, Dupuis refers to Leo's celebrated Tome, in which Leo distinguishes between the divine activity of the Son and the human activity. For examples, see Dupuis "'The Truth Will Make You Free': The Theology of Religious Pluralism Revisited," *Louvain Studies* 24 (1999): 241.

42. Dupuis, *Who Do You Say I Am?*, 141.

43. Dupuis always refers to the Christ-event in its totality. As he explains: "Let me state immediately that whenever I write of the Christ event, I take it in its totality: from the incarnation to the Paschal mystery, which in turn comprises not only the death on the cross, but the resurrection, ascension, Pentecost (which is also a Christological mystery) and, indeed, the parousia" ("Truth Will Make You Free," 243).

44. Dupuis, *Christianity and the Religions*, 144.

Spirit—as in the Augustinian-Thomist doctrine of the divine missions—is not restricted to the incarnate existence of the Word in the person of Jesus Christ. Dupuis maintains that the Christ-event neither limits nor exhausts the universal action of the Word and Spirit. The Word of God exists eternally and was present and active throughout salvation history before the incarnation. The Word remains God and continues to act as God, after the incarnation and resurrection. In other words, Dupuis argues that the divine activity of the Word, while always related to the humanity assumed at the incarnation, is not limited to that humanity. The divine action of the Word as such remains, and it extends, Dupuis argues, beyond the human action of the risen Christ (and it is here that Dupuis runs the risk of separation of Jesus and the Word). "What is being affirmed," Dupuis explains, "is that, even after the incarnation and the resurrection, a divine action of the Word *as such* remains, which extends beyond the human action of the risen Christ."[45] From the very beginning of creation, Dupuis argues, God has revealed Godself to humankind, through God's Word and God's Spirit. As Irenaeus in the second century expressed it: God the Father saves "with two hands"—the Word and the Spirit (*Against Heresies* 40.20.1). In this way, then, Dupuis presses for an appreciation of the trinitarian rhythm of God's activity throughout salvation history. The two hands of God are united and inseparable, but distinct and complementary in the one unified divine plan for salvation.

We shall later return to Dupuis' theology of the world religions, where Dupuis draws out the significance of the distinction between the two natures, their operations and energies, in regard to the universal salvation achieved by the divine Word before and after the incarnation. Dupuis' understanding of what he describes as the "hypostatic independence,"[46] or the personal dis-

---

45. Dupuis, "Truth Will Make You Free," 238. Dupuis' book *Toward a Christian Theology of Religious Pluralism,* prompted an investigation by the Vatican Congregation for the Doctrine of the Faith. The notification states: "For the unity of the divine plan of salvation centred on Jesus Christ, it must also be held that the salvific action of the Word is accomplished in and through Jesus Christ, the Incarnate Son of the Father, as mediator of salvation for all humanity. It is therefore contrary to the Catholic faith not only to posit a separation between the Word and Jesus, or between the Word's salvific activity and that of Jesus, but also to maintain that there is a salvific activity of the Word as such in his divinity, independent of the humanity of the Incarnate Word" (a. 2). For a helpful discussion of Dupuis' work, in the light of the concerns raised by the Congregation, see Gerald O'Collins, "Christ and the Religions," *Gregorianum* 84 (2003): 347-62; idem, "Jacques Dupuis: His Person and Work," 18-29. Dupuis responds to his critics in "The Truth Will Make You Free," 211-63. He reiterates that at no stage does he resile from the uniqueness and universality of Jesus Christ. He explains: "I have proposed a Trinitarian Christology as a useful model for a theology of religions, one able to combine and hold together the uniqueness and universality of Jesus Christ in the order of salvation and a true positive and salvific value of the other religious traditions for their followers" (p. 226). He repeatedly affirms the unique and transcendent character of Christian revelation. For further discussion, see our later chapter in this book, "Trinity and the World Religions."

46. Dupuis, "Trinitarian Christology," 86.

tinction between God's "two hands," the Word and the Spirit, whose actions in salvation history are distinct but inseparable and complementary, opens up new possibilities for a Christian understanding of the world religions in the context of the divine salvific plan.

CONCLUSION

As we come to a conclusion of our overview of Christology from an explicitly trinitarian perspective, it is salutary to note that Christoph Schwöbel concludes his christological reflections by directing everything back to the paschal mystery. Developing a trinitarian Christology, he reminds us, requires that we understand God, God's being and attributes, not from the point of the contrast between created being and the being of the creator, not from some metaphysically fashioned notions of the Godhead and its perfections, but from that point where God has revealed God's triune self to us in a preeminent way, the paschal mystery. This implies, he argues, "seeing the life, death and resurrection of Jesus Christ not as the *Kenosis* of the attributes of God, but as their *Plerosis* in the person of the Son. Discourse about the being and attributes of God is not the presupposition of a trinitarian account of the person and work of Christ, but one of its results."[47] Constructing a Christology from a trinitarian perspective, Schwöbel insists, means approaching it from those events where the Trinity has revealed itself to us, in the paschal mystery. In that event of triune surrender, of mutual self-giving and self-yielding love, we have the revelation of inner-trinitarian reality and relationality and of the mystery of Christ. It is to the paschal mystery that we shall turn our attention in our next chapter.

FOR FURTHER READING

Coffey, David. *Deus Trinitas: The Doctrine of the Triune God.* Oxford/New York: Oxford University Press, 1999.

Dunn, James D. G. *Christology in the Making: A New Testament Inquiry into the Doctrine of the Incarnation.* Philadelphia: Westminster, 1980.

Dupuis, Jacques. "'Christianity and the Religions.'" *Louvain Studies* 24 (2003): 363-83.

———. *Christianity and the Religions: From Confrontation to Dialogue.* Maryknoll, N.Y.: Orbis Books, 2002.

47. Schwöbel, "Christology and Trinitarian Thought," 145.

———. *Jesus Christ at the Encounter of World Religions.* Maryknoll, N.Y.: Orbis Books, 1991.

———. *Toward a Christian Theology of Religious Pluralism.* Maryknoll, N.Y.: Orbis Books, 1997.

———. "Trinitarian Christology as a Model for a Theology of Religious Pluralism." In *The Myriad Christ: Plurality and the Quest for Unity in Contemporary Christology.* Edited by T. Merrigan and J. Haers, 83-97. Leuven: Leuven University Press, 2000.

———. "'The Truth Will Make You Free': The Theology of Religious Pluralism Revisited." *Louvain Studies* 24 (1999): 211-63.

———. *Who Do You Say I Am? Introduction to Christology.* Maryknoll, N.Y.: Orbis Books, 1994.

Fuller, Reginald H., and Pheme Perkins. *Who Is the Christ? Gospel Christology and Contemporary Faith.* Philadelphia: Fortress Press, 1983.

Hill, Brennan. *Jesus the Christ: Contemporary Perspectives.* Mystic, Conn.: Twenty-Third Publications, 1991.

Hurtado, Larry W. *Lord Jesus Christ: Devotion to Jesus in Earliest Christianity.* Grand Rapids: Wm. B. Eerdmans, 2003.

Johnson, Elizabeth A. *Consider Jesus: Waves of Renewal in Christology.* London: Geoffrey Chapman, 1990.

Loewe, William. *The College Student's Introduction to Christology.* Collegeville, Minn.: Liturgical Press, A Michael Glazier Book, 1996.

Macquarrie, John. *Jesus Christ in Modern Thought.* London: SCM; Philadelphia: Trinity Press International, 1990.

McDermott, Brian O. *Word Become Flesh: Dimensions of Christology.* New Theology Studies 9. Collegeville, Minn.: Liturgical Press, A Michael Glazier Book, 1993.

Meyendorff, John. *Christ in Eastern Christian Thought.* New York: St. Vladimir's Seminary Press, 1975.

O'Collins, Gerald. *Christology: A Biblical, Historical, and Systematic Study of Jesus.* Oxford: Oxford University Press, 1995.

Rahner, Karl. "Current Problems in Christology." In *Theological Investigations,* 1:149-200. New York: Seabury Press, 1974.

Schwöbel, Christoph. "Christology and Trinitarian Thought." In *Trinitarian Theology Today: Essays on Divine Being and Act,* edited by Christoph Schwöbel, 113-46. Edinburgh: T&T Clark, 1995.

Studer, Basil. *Trinity and Incarnation: The Faith of the Early Church.* Edited by Andrew Louth. Translated by Matthias Westerhoff. Edinburgh: T&T Clark, 1993.

Wright, N. T. *The Resurrection of the Son of God.* Minneapolis: Fortress, 2003.

4

Trinity, the Paschal Mystery, and Soteriology

He is the image of the invisible God, the first-born of all creation . . . all things have been created through him and for him. (Col 1:15-16)

THE PASCHAL MYSTERY and its connection with the mystery of the Trinity has proved a most fruitful area of exploration in recent decades, with notable contributions in particular by Jürgen Moltmann and Hans Urs von Balthasar, who approach it in order to probe more deeply the trinitarian mystery of God.[1] It is an exploration that has been prompted by the emergence of protest atheism, fueled by the immense suffering and terrors experienced in the twentieth century. Meanwhile, the flourishing of historical-critical biblical scholarship in recent times has made possible a fresh approach to the New Testament witness to the life, death, and resurrection of Jesus and a peeling away of the philosophical accretions that have accumulated around the articulation of Christian faith over the centuries.

In the light of this relatively recent reconnection of these two mysteries, it is surprising to realize that trinitarian theology and the paschal mystery of Jesus' death and resurrection have for most of the two millennia of the tradition usually been treated quite separately from each other. The death and resurrection of Jesus were usually treated under the theological rubric of redemption. Despite recognition of their intimate connection in liturgy, where the notion of the paschal mystery was well established in the early church, the death and resurrection were not treated in such a way that they were obviously related to each other in the one paschal mystery. As we shall

1. See Jürgen Moltmann, *The Crucified God: The Cross of Christ as the Foundation and Criticism of Christian Theology*, trans. R. A. Wilson and John Bowden (London: SCM, 1974); idem, *The Trinity and the Kingdom of God: The Doctrine of God*, trans. Margaret Kohl (San Francisco: HarperCollins, 1991); Hans Urs von Balthasar, *Mysterium Paschale: The Mystery of Easter*, trans. with an introduction by Aidan Nichols (Edinburgh: T&T Clark, 1990). For a discussion of their work see Anne Hunt, *The Trinity and the Paschal Mystery: A Development in Recent Catholic Theology*, New Theology Studies 5 (Collegeville, Minn.: Liturgical Press, 1997), 57-89, 164-71; eadem, *What Are They Saying about the Trinity?* (Mahwah, N.J.: Paulist Press, 1998), 49-61.

see, this renewed connection in theology—indeed this privileging of the paschal mystery as utterly central to Christian faith and theology—has resulted in a recognition of the enormous significance of the paschal mystery, not just as mystery of our redemption, not merely the means by which we have been saved, but as properly revelatory of the very being of God.

Here we turn to consider the work of two very different theologians, Sebastian Moore and François Durrwell. The paschal mystery has a central place in their theologies and, while they both approach it from a trinitarian perspective, they treat it in very different ways. Moore adopts a profoundly psychological approach, seeking to grasp the revolution in consciousness that the disciples experienced (i.e., their own paschal experience) and that the process of conversion of the human person involves. Durrwell, on the other hand, approaches the interconnection from the perspective of what is called "biblical theology" and recognizes the paschal mystery of Jesus as icon of divine being, the enactment, so to speak, in the realm of creation of the inner-trinitarian mystery of the Father's generation of the Son. We might summarize their approaches in terms of subjectivity: Moore is concerned with human subjectivity, while Durrwell addresses divine subjectivity.

SEBASTIAN MOORE: THE GRASSROOTS EXPERIENCE OF THE TRINITY

One might, without much ado or delay, easily relegate Sebastian Moore's work to the realm of spirituality and concomitantly dismiss it from the more rigorous arena of properly systematic theology. Indeed, many do! His writing is sketchily developed; the terminology is loose and not well defined; the usual raft of scholarly references is notably absent; he daringly breaks into poetry at various points; and the focus of his attention is not so much God per se as the process of conversion and the associated psychological changes in the consciousness of the human subject. At first glance, Moore's work is simple and uncritical and seemingly even naive; but, in fact, it demands a kind of psychological workout (as Stephen Duffy comments[2]) that requires a sophisticated level of self-awareness and a very serious effort to examine one's own interiority. Moore's contribution is in fact neither naive nor uncritical, but rather the fruit of a refined postcritical religious consciousness and a keenly honed methodological awareness of the dynamics of consciousness that aims at a distinctly post critical retrieval.

2. Stephen Duffy, "Review Symposium: Sebastian Moore's *Jesus Liberator of Desire*," *Horizons* 18 (1991): 102.

Sebastian Moore's concern is to explore the psychological processes involved in conversion. This concern emerges from the conviction that the failure to mediate religious meaning in the contemporary world is primarily a failure to mediate religious meaning in meaningful psychological terms. He explains:

> It seems to me that a primary theological need in our time is for the psychological to mediate the transcendent. Until this comes about, the psychological dimension remains subjective, the transcendent dimension extrinsic. The perennial vigor of Christianity stems from a dangerous memory, of the experience of a group of people being brought to a crisis whose issue was such a freedom in face of our mortality as can only come from the transcendent ground of being. The psychological mediation of the transcendent is *remembered*. . . . To be awakened at this level is to have one's answer to the common view that the Christian myth has lost its power.[3]

Moore's aim is thus not a systematic statement on trinitarian theology, but rather to mediate faith to contemporary consciousness in psychological terms, in order to facilitate the process of conversion in the contemporary context. Motivated by this concern, he aims to identify, at the level of "felt meaning" in human subjectivity, the psychological transformation of the individual that occurs in the event of religious conversion. He recognizes that an extraordinary irruption of new meaning takes place in the believer's consciousness in the process of conversion, just as demonstrably occurred for the very first Christians. Seeking "a full psychological appropriation of the story of Jesus,"[4] he turns his attention to the experience of the very first Christians, whose lives were clearly radically transformed through their experience of the life, death, and resurrection of Jesus. Moore then attempts an imaginative reconstruction of the psychologically and spiritually revolutionary experience that so transformed them. In this way, Moore develops a theological construct in which to retell the original story of Jesus "no longer in terms of myths, no longer in terms of its rational implications, no longer in terms of different human experiences, but as the story of the real self in all people."[5]

Given the scant information in regard to the experience of Jesus' disciples,

---

3. Sebastian Moore, *Jesus the Liberator of Desire* (New York: Crossroad, 1989), x.
4. Sebastian Moore, *The Fire and the Rose Are One* (London: Darton, Longman & Todd, 1980), xiii.
5. Ibid., 4.

however, this is a highly speculative and consequently problematic exercise. Moore is aware of this criticism of his project, but avers: "I have dared to surmise how the human psyche, at the beginning of our era, was shocked into a bliss of which God alone could be the author and from which, thank God, it will never recover."[6] In reconstructing the disciples' experience of Jesus' death and resurrection, Moore's aim is to ground theology in the world of human interiority and subjectivity, and thus to meet the concerns, sensibilities, and exigences of contemporary consciousness, by describing the process by which Jesus' story transforms our personal story, yours and mine. For theology, Moore explains, "is the making-contemporary of the drama of Jesus as the transforming of my story, and being able to speak coherently about this transformation. For the great story is essentially the smaller-story transformer. That is how it is great."[7]

Moore reminds us that Jesus' disciples were strict monotheists. Clearly, a remarkably dramatic change of consciousness led them to proclaim that Jesus was Lord and God. Moore seeks to describe that dramatic change of consciousness, that "grassroots" experience of conversion, that took place in the disciples, in the course of Jesus' paschal mystery, from which issued that astonishing proclamation—Jesus is Lord. It is this grassroots experience that ultimately provided the ground and the framework for the development of the doctrine of the Trinity in the Christian tradition. It is that grassroots experience of the disciples that Moore seeks to describe in psychological terms. As Moore explains:

> We talk about the Trinity as though it were from the start a highly recondite doctrine for which we have to seek analogies at the human level. Actually, it is given to us from the start at the human level, in a form that already contains the clue for thinking about it in itself. . . . The Passion, Death and Resurrection of Jesus is the estuary in which this river branches out into the Trinitarian mystery of Jesus "at the right hand" of the Father, the Father dependent for his manifest meaning on Jesus, the Spirit the abundance of this to-each-other-ness of Father and Son "poured out in our hearts". The pedagogy of the Trinitarian mystery is perfect. Jesus in person carries us over from its human articulation . . . into the fullness of the economy of Father, Son and Spirit.[8]

6. Ibid., 108.

7. Sebastian Moore, "Four Steps towards Making Sense of Theology," *Downside Review* 111 (1993): 88. The reader will notice the influence on Moore of both C. G. Jung and, especially, Bernard Lonergan.

8. Ibid., 79.

Resurrection Shock Waves

Moore situates his reconstruction of the disciples' paschal experience in terms of the experience of desire.[9] Moore even goes so far as to define the human person in terms of desire, a desire to be oneself for another, and ultimately a desire for God. Indeed, we could describe Sebastian Moore's work in terms of a theology of desire. In regard to the disciples, Moore describes the transformation of their consciousness in terms of three stages of desire: awakening, desolation, and transformation of desire. They first experience the awakening of desire. Their time with Jesus in Galilee is a time of joy, bliss, and ecstasy; it is a springtime. In their experience of being with him, they experience a new sense of self, a sense of self that is unburdened by guilt and unworthiness, and a new sense of God, not as judgmental or jealous but as loving presence. Then, with Jesus' hideous death, they experience utter desolation and despair. With the death of the one who awakened their desire, they too experience a kind of death. The desire that had been awakened by him now experiences a mortal crisis. The disciples feel themselves to be as good as dead—such is the depth of their psychological experience of desolation, despondency, and dispiritedness. They also experience what seems like the death of God, for the sense of God awakened by Jesus dies with him. In this stage of spiritual collapse and utter desolation of their desire, they experience a despair that only God can dispel. These stages of awakening of their desire and then of its desolation effectively prepare and make room for the transformation and liberation of their desire, which occurs with Jesus' appearance to them as risen Lord.

Imagine yourself in the disciples' shoes! Imagine the joy of being with Jesus in Galilee—his compassion, his hospitality, his wisdom, the warmth of his presence. The world is a different place in his presence and through his eyes. My sense of self and my sense of God are different when I am with Jesus. Next imagine first the terror, then the shame and confusion, followed by the utter desolation that comes with his arrest, torture, and public execution. Imagine huddling in the room with the doors closed in fear and dread of one's own arrest and execution. Imagine the shame in having left him to his plight and deserted him. Imagine then the shock of his appearance, alive and bearing the marks of his death. Think of Peter, having three times denied his connection with Jesus, looking into the face of the risen Jesus in that first moment of his

---

9. See, e.g., J. Daurio, "Toward a Theology of Desire: The Existential Hermeneutic in the Soteriology of Sebastian Moore," *Downside Review* 106 (1988): 195.

appearance to them. Imagine the shame Peter feels. And hear Jesus' first words to them, words of love and forgiveness: "Peace be with you" (John 20:20). This effort to imagine the psychological stages through which the first disciples were plunged in their experience of Jesus' paschal mystery is part of that "psychological workout" that Moore wants you, the reader, to undertake. He wants you to get right down to the grass roots of their experience, and then of your own. Much more than mere reading of the text is required!

Moore then describes the radical change in the disciples' religious consciousness as a result of their encounter with the risen Jesus in terms of "resurrection shock waves." The first resurrection shock wave erupts with the appearance of the risen Jesus and the disciples' spontaneous confession that Jesus is Lord and God. He has, after all, done what only God can do. He is risen from the dead. Consider, for example, the experience of Thomas, as presented in John 20. Thomas exclaims: "My Lord and my God!" Note too that John's Gospel records Jesus' first words to them: "Peace be with you" (John 20:26). In this first resurrection shock wave, the disciples recognize that Jesus is God. Moore therefore describes the change in religious consciousness as a result of this first shock wave as "the displacement of divinity to Jesus."

The second resurrection shock wave in their consciousness comes with the experience and recognition of another divine one, the one whom Jesus himself called Abba/Father, as the one who is the author of this great event, this sending of Jesus to us, for us and for our salvation. Moore identifies what he calls "the extension of divinity to the Father" in this second resurrection shock wave. The disciples, albeit strict monotheists, recognize that divinity resides in both Jesus *and* the Father. Jesus is God and the one whom he called Abba/Father is God. Third, there occurs another resurrection shock wave: the experience of the presence of God as Spirit, mysteriously in their midst, animating and inspiring the community, Spirit of Jesus, Spirit of love, Spirit of unity. In this stage, the disciples recognize the experience of a third center of God-consciousness, a consciousness of the one who is, in person, the "cyclic life-flow" between Father and Son, the one who is, in person, the unity of the Father and Son. Moore describes this shock wave in terms of a further extension of divinity to this third one, the Spirit. The Spirit also is God. As Moore explains:

> With this, the pattern becomes cyclic, a system, a flow of life between Father and Son through the Spirit. The three stages of shock-waves of the Resurrection encounter are thus these: displacement, extension, cyclic life-flow. . . . Thus the matrix of the images of the divine persons is the "infinite connection" as it undergoes the transformation of the encounter with

the risen Jesus. The pre-religious concentration of divine energy takes, under the pressure of this encounter, the shape of Father, Son and Spirit.[10]

In this psychological reconstruction of the disciples' experience of Jesus' paschal mystery, Moore thus articulates three postresurrection shock waves, three radically transforming irruptions of God-consciousness in the disciples' consciousness, and the concomitant emergence of a trinitarian pattern in their God-consciousness. Larry Hurtado's magnificent study *Lord Jesus Christ: Devotion to Jesus in Earliest Christianity*, which traces the evidence of this extraordinary change in God-consciousness in the early Christian movement by tracking the development of devotion to Jesus in Christian worship from its beginnings, as attested in our earliest written witnesses (ca. 30-170), in fact demonstrates some striking parallels with Moore's reconstruction of originating experience that led to the proclamation that Jesus is Lord and that the one God was three, Father, Son, and Holy Spirit.[11]

The Trinity as "Dogmatized Mystical Experience"

By reconstructing the emergence of a new religious consciousness of the disciples, a new God-consciousness, on the basis of their felt experience of the resurrection encounter, Moore identifies the process by which the disciples' psyches were radically transformed. He also recognizes that their new religious consciousness would eventually be brought to the bar of logic, as the early Christian texts attest. Questions would inevitably be asked, a range of possible interpretations presented, and clarification sought as to what this threefold God-consciousness really meant. The originating experience would thus eventually be pressed into expression as dogma. In other words, that originating revolutionary mystical experience of this new God-consciousness would eventually be dogmatized. In fact, some three hundred years later, at the Council of Nicaea (325) and the Council of Constantinople (381), it would be articulated in terms of the doctrine of the Trinity. But then, as always, no matter how awkward or confounding, as indeed it proved to be, the bottom line was that Jesus had done what only God could do and so had to be God. As Moore explains: "The bottom line of Nicaea was that Jesus had done for us what only God could do, had given us what only God could give, and therefore had to be God, whatever the awesome problems created by

10. Moore, *Fire and the Rose Are One*, 83-84.

11. See Anne Hunt, "The Emergence of Devotion to Jesus in the Early Church: The Grass-Roots Derivation of the Trinity," *Australian EJournal of Theology*, Issue 4, 2005. http://dlibrary.acu.edu.au/research/theology/ejournal/.

such an equation in the intellectual world."[12] In Moore's distinctly psychological frame of reference, with its focus on the disciples themselves and their experience of the irruption of new meaning in their consciousness, the mystery of the Trinity thus emerges as "dogmatised mystical experience."[13] What Moore would have us clearly understand here is that the doctrine of the Trinity is grounded in that initial psychologically revolutionary experience of Jesus' paschal mystery that so radically transformed the disciples.

The paschal mystery thus emerges in Moore's exploration as the psychological pattern through which the disciples' consciousness is utterly transformed. An exploration of the origin of trinitarian belief in the disciples' consciousness thus leads Moore into the mystery of our own self-awareness and interiority, the process of conversion, and our own paschal mystery. To those who would dismiss his work as mere spirituality, Moore retorts: "I wish people wouldn't call this stuff spiritual theology. It is a somewhat gauche attempt to do real theology in a world whose intellectual climate is still divorced from feeling."[14] Moore seeks precisely to heal the rift between the existential and the theoretical in theology, wherein lies that very failure to mediate religious meaning to the contemporary world in meaningful psychological terms. In more recent writings, he continues to pursue the psychological mediation of the meaning of the Christian doctrine of the Trinity.[15]

We turn now to take a different perspective on the interconnection of the paschal mystery and the mystery of the Trinity. Sebastian Moore has explored the connection from the perspective of human consciousness. François-Xavier Durrwell, like Hans Urs von Balthasar and Jürgen Moltmann, approaches it in order to delve more deeply into the trinitarian mystery of God.

FRANÇOIS-XAVIER DURRWELL AND THE MYSTERY OF THE RESURRECTION

In order to situate and to appreciate Durrwell's contribution, we must first consider the theological context in which Durrwell's focus on the theological significance of the resurrection emerged. Following Anselm's understanding of redemption in terms of notions of satisfaction and the divine demand for

12. Moore, *Fire and the Rose Are One*, 91.
13. Sebastian Moore, *The Inner Loneliness* (London: Darton, Longman & Todd, 1982), 103-9.
14. Moore, "Four Steps towards Making Sense of Theology," 81.
15. See especially Sebastian Moore, "Are We Getting the Trinity Right?" *Downside Review* 117 (1999): 59-72; idem, "'And There is Only One Dance': Reflections on the Trinity," *Downside Review* 119 (2001): 269-96.

justice, the mystery of redemption was traditionally understood in essentially ontological juridical terms.[16] From this perspective, it was the merit of Jesus' life and death, as distinct from his resurrection, that provided the necessary satisfaction and reparation to the infinite offense to God that was made by human sin. The resurrection was consequently effectively relegated to the realm of apologetics, as proof of Jesus' divinity, validation of his identity, a bolster to credibility, even a kind of addendum rather than being substantially related to the mystery of our redemption. It was recognized neither as itself redemptive per se—that was achieved in Jesus' life and death—nor as revelatory of the divine being. As a consequence of this juridical approach to the mystery of redemption, consideration of the resurrection was in effect separated from consideration of the life and death of Jesus. Death and resurrection were not recognized and treated as complementary aspects of the one paschal mystery. Nor were the death and resurrection recognized as revelatory of the being of God per se.

One of the fruits of the blossoming of biblical scholarship in recent decades has been a reconsideration of the resurrection as presented in the New Testament.[17] Renewed attention to the biblical witness has shown that this apologetic approach to the mystery of the resurrection is not in close accord with the New Testament witness. In the New Testament, satisfaction theories are by no means prominent, and the resurrection is no mere addendum or apologetic proof. As Durrwell observes, Scripture speaks of communion and of the resurrection as *parousia*, the coming of the Lord that permits this communion.[18] Jesus' resurrection lies at the core of Christian faith. As St. Paul says: Christ "was put to death for our trespasses and raised for our justification" (Rom. 4:25) and "if Christ has not been raised, then our preaching is in vain and your faith is in vain" (1 Cor. 15:14). In other words, it is in the resurrection, not just in the life and death of Jesus, that our salvation is achieved. The resurrection is no mere payment in satisfaction of a debt, but mystery of utmost redemptive significance and promise of our entry into the divine communion. There in the New Testament, the resurrection, and the whole paschal mystery of Jesus' passing over, emerges as an event that is trinitarian in its origin, its unfolding and its goal. Moreover, the mystery of resurrection as attested in the New Testament is replete with eschatological

16. Thanks to Harvey Egan SJ who commented that justice in that period was not understood as the extrinsic legalism that it is in our age, but rather as an ontological and metaphysical category, having everything to do with being and existence.

17. For an outstanding recent study, see N. T. Wright, *Christian Origins and the Question of God,* vol. 3, *The Resurrection of the Son of God* (London: SPCK, 2003).

18. F.-X. Durrwell, "Mystère pascal et Parousie: L'importance sotériologique de la présence du Christ," *Nouvelle Revue Théologique* 95 (1973): 253-78, esp. 268-70.

meaning. Indeed, Durrwell suggests that it was a failure to appreciate the distinctly eschatological dimension of the resurrection that allowed for the development of the satisfaction theories of redemption and, moreover, the dearth of theology in regard to the Holy Spirit.

The Resurrection as Eschatological Plenitude and Permanent Actuality

It is in this theological context that François Durrwell's work emerged, shedding new light on the resurrection in particular and on the paschal mystery, and focusing attention on its properly theological significance. Anticipating Vatican II's rediscovery of the paschal mystery (SC 5, 6, 61, 104, 106; GS 22, 38, 52; OT 8), Durrwell recognized that Jesus' death and resurrection constitute essentially complementary dimensions of the one mystery, "two aspects of the one Paschal Mystery."[19] Durrwell's *La Résurrection de Jésus, mystère de salut: Étude biblique* was published in 1960.[20] There Durrwell considered the biblical texts that deal with the resurrection of Jesus Christ. As he explained, his aim was a thoroughly biblical approach, guided by the texts themselves, unencumbered by preconceived philosophical or juridical notions:

> My wish was to let myself be wholly guided by them [Sacred Scriptures], in the Church's faith and free from all preconceived systems. Whereas theology usually reasons about God according to concepts of essence or nature, a legacy of Greek philosophy, or according to juridical concepts on questions about redemption, the Scriptures have taught us to favour, in all reflection on God and salvation, the mysterious reality of *the person.* Just as faith is an encounter with Someone, theology is research on the part of the intellect into a mystery that is personal.[21]

Fundamental to Durrwell's understanding of the resurrection, based on his study of the New Testament texts, is what he describes as its eschatological

19. F.-X. Durrwell, *L'Ésprit du Père et du Fils,* Maranatha 18 (Paris: Médiaspaul, 1989), 58.

20. F.-X. Durrwell, *The Resurrection: A Biblical Study*, trans. Rosemary Sheed (New York: Sheed & Ward, 1960). Durrwell has been steadfast in his exploration of the significance of the resurrection throughout his life. See his recent work *Christ Our Passover: The Indispensable Role of Resurrection in Our Salvation*, trans. John F. Craghan (Liguori, Mo.: Liguori, 2004), wherein Durrwell explains that his goal is "to bring together the elements scattered in those works [which followed the publication of *The Resurrection* and treated the same subject], to bundle the sheaves, and make of them 'the evening offering'" (p. xiii).

21. F.-X. Durrwell, original French edition, *L'Ésprit Saint de Dieu* (Paris: Éditions du Cerf, 1983); Eng. trans., *Holy Spirit of God: An Essay in Biblical Theology*, trans. Benedict Davies (London: Geoffrey Chapman, 1986), viii.

plenitude and its permanent actuality. Durrwell draws our attention to the reality that, from the moment of the resurrection, Jesus is established in the fullness, plenitude and perfection of glory. In other words, from the moment of the resurrection, Jesus is raised once and for always in that moment (the permanent actuality of the resurrection), and he is raised to the fullness of glory of his divine sonship (the eschatological plenitude of the resurrection). Logically and theologically, nothing can be added to that fullness and plenitude to which Jesus is raised, for nothing can be added to perfection, and nothing can be added to plenitude. In that sense, as Durrwell expresses it, the resurrection, in Jesus, knows no tomorrow.[22] As he explains: "We must take it that Christ will never grow any older than he was at the Resurrection, that his life remains new, that his body, new-born in the Spirit, never grows beyond the moment of his Easter birth and therefore that the Father's action in raising Christ continues eternally in its single moment."[23] The risen Christ remains forever in the eternal (that is, ever present) actuality of the one single eternal moment of this plenitude and perfection.[24] As the Letter to the Hebrews says: "Jesus Christ is the same yesterday and today and forever" (Heb. 13:8). In this sense, the resurrection remains ever present and ever actual. Durrwell would therefore also persuade us that the resurrection itself is a permanent and eternal divine action, enacted in the realm of creation.

The Resurrection as Enactment in Creation of the Inner-trinitarian Begetting of the Son by the Father

Durrwell presses further still and recognizes that the resurrection enacts, in the realm of creation, the inner-trinitarian begetting of the Son by the Father, the eternal generation, for the whole being of Christ is raised to the glory of sonship:

> The Resurrection brought Christ wholly to birth in the life of the Son, extending to his whole being the glory of his eternal generation. And in that birth, there is no "tomorrow." Alongside our ancestor Adam, the old man, who continues to decay within us (2 Cor. iv. 16), here is the young Adam, the new man, Son of God, in the everlasting newness of his sonship.[25]

22. Durrwell, *Resurrection*, 131.
23. Ibid., 130.
24. F.-X. Durrwell, "Liminaire: La Pâque du Christ selon l'Écriture," in *La Pâque du Christ, Mystère de Salut: Mélanges en l'Honneur du Père Durrwell* (Paris: Éditions du Cerf, 1982), 13.
25. Durrwell, *Resurrection*, 131.

Durrwell thus understands that the resurrection corresponds to the divine generation by the Father of the beloved Son. In other words, the resurrecting act of the Father is the enactment of the divine begetting. It corresponds to the Father's generation of the Son in the inner-trinitarian mystery of God. This means that trinitarian being and relationality are not only revealed but also enacted in creation in the resurrection of Jesus Christ. It means that, in the resurrection of the incarnate Son, the eternal begetting of the divine Son is accomplished within the realm of creation. The eternal trinitarian movement of God *ad intra* is thus realized *ad extra*. In other words, God enacts in creation what God is eternally in the mystery of the Trinity: the Father who begets the Son in the love of the Holy Spirit.

Of utterly crucial importance to this understanding of the mystery of the resurrection as the enactment of the divine begetting is that it is Jesus, the incarnate Son, in his whole being, who is risen, risen in his humanity as well as his divinity. As Durrwell explains:

> Then the Father took him to himself, and introducing him totally into the secret of his divine being, into that embrace which confers sonship, he abolished in him the "condition of a slave" and brought his whole, once mortal, humanity into the eternal origins of the life of sonship, into the instant of divine generation. He generated him as Son of God in his entire being, saying in the act of glorifying him: "Thou art my Son, this day have I begotten thee."[26]

Precisely here is the mystery of our salvation constituted: that God, in the resurrection, takes Jesus, in his humanity, into the fullness of the eternal begetting of the Son. Herein lies the mystery that, as we confess in the creed, is "for us and for our salvation," for Jesus' human being is raised into the permanent actuality of the resurrection, the eternal moment of his glory. As Durrwell observes: "The whole of his human being is woven, by the Spirit, into his eternal filial origin."[27] His whole being, human and divine, enters into and is henceforth interior to the trinitarian mystery where God engenders his Son. That Jesus, in his humanity, is taken into the mystery of the Trinity, means that we, in our humanity, in union with Christ are incorporated into the same divine generation. Raised with him, we too are born of God in the Holy Spirit, and share fully in the divine birth that is Christ's.[28]

26. F.-X. Durrwell, *In the Redeeming Christ*, trans. Rosemary Sheed (London: Sheed & Ward, 1963), 329.

27. Durrwell, *Holy Spirit of God*, 43.

28. See, e.g., Durrwell, *In the Redeeming Christ*, 328-36.

Moreover, not just humankind but all creation is involved in this divine begetting. In communion with him, all creation enters into the trinitarian mystery wherein God begets his Son. Creation, the whole cosmos, enters into the eternal begetting of Christ. Through the resurrection, the whole universe is drawn into the trinitarian mystery of God. As Durrwell explains: "In Christ who inhabits the Trinity, this creation is 'within' God; at its height and in its roots, it enters into the eternal begetting of Christ."[29]

This, in Durrwell's theology, is salvation. It is that, in Christ, all creation becomes filial, entering into the mystery of the eternal generation of the Son. Our salvation is not the distribution of merits or the redemption of a debt but our entry into the mystery of Jesus as Son and, through him, into the mystery of the Trinity. Salvation is to be incorporated into his filial being. Through the Father and in the Spirit, Jesus himself, in person, constitutes the mystery of our salvation. Salvation is to be raised with him into the mystery of his resurrection. It is birth, in him, into the trinitarian communion. It is the re-creation and the consummation of all creation, in him. As Durrwell explains: "The resurrection is the synthesis and the climax of creation, beyond which one cannot go, in the permanent today of the Easter birth of Christ (cf. Acts 13:33). *Henceforth the eternal begetting of the Son in the Spirit is immanent within the world*: the world is steeped, at this its own climax, in the eternal trinitarian movement."[30]

We see then how, in Durrwell's work, Jesus' death is connected with the resurrection in the one saving paschal mystery, and the paschal mystery is connected with the Trinity, as its source and goal. The paschal mystery, as the revelation of the Trinity *ad extra*, then serves as analogy, properly speaking, for the Trinity *ad intra*. Notice too that soteriology (the mystery of salvation) is inextricably connected with the Trinity: not only humankind but all creation is incorporated in Christ, and, with him, enters into the glory of filial being, in the trinitarian communion.

Durrwell is acutely conscious that, in the mystery of the resurrection, the stigmata of Jesus' suffering and death remain. For Durrwell, this powerfully symbolizes that death and resurrection are inextricably related and that both enter into the eternal begetting of Jesus. Indeed, Durrwell does not tire in reminding us that the risen Lord is forever the Slain Lamb,[31] "the Lamb that

29. Durrwell, *Holy Spirit of God*, 140; see also *Resurrection*, 290-93.

30. Durrwell, *Holy Spirit of God*, 131. "Salvation history has progressed to the rhythm of God's mystery in the world. It reaches its climax in Christ's passover, when the mystery becomes immanent in creation as it has ever been in eternity" (ibid., 74).

31. This powerful image recurs frequently in Durrwell's theology. He stresses: "He is not only like a lamb, He is the Lamb." See F.-X. Durrwell, "Lamb of God," in *New Catholic Encyclopedia*, 2nd ed., ed. Berard Mathaler (Detroit: Thomson/Gale, in association with the Catholic University of Amer-

was slaughtered, to receive power and wealth and wisdom and might and honor and glory and blessing" (Rev. 5:12). The very body of the risen Lord tangibly bears witness to the unity of death and resurrection in the one paschal mystery. Death emerges not as means of reparation or redemption of a debt but as the necessary passage or passover to resurrection and to life in communion with the triune God.

Durrwell's exploration of the resurrection as the mystery of our salvation results in a thoroughly trinitarian theology. Moreover, the role and person of the Holy Spirit emerge much more clearly when approached in this way.[32] Indeed, based on Durrwell's understanding of the resurrection as *the* eschatological event—for in it the plenitude of glory and power is accorded to Christ—the Holy Spirit emerges in Durrwell's theology as *the* eschatological gift,[33] a point that comes to prominence in the work of Wolfhart Pannenberg.[34]

CONCLUSION

Sebastian Moore and François-Xavier Durrwell, from the perspective of trinitarian faith, explore two levels of meaning in the paschal mystery. One concerns the mystery of human person; here the paschal mystery emerges as the dynamic by means of which our consciousness is radically transformed and we enter into a trinitarian God-consciousness and ultimately into the trinitarian communion. The other concerns the trinitarian mystery itself; here the paschal mystery serves as analogy of trinitarian being. The paschal mystery thus reveals both the means and the meaning of salvation (our redemption) and the trinitarian reality of God who saves (revelation of the triune God). The connection between the two levels of meaning and between the Trinity and the paschal mystery is ultimately grounded in the very person of Jesus, as the incarnate Son who is fully human and divine.

In terms of the divine being, the paschal mystery emerges as the paradigmatic image in creation of trinitarian life. It is the projection, in the realm of creation, of the eternal trinitarian exchange of life and love, whereby the three

---

ica, 2003). For Hans Urs von Balthasar, the image of the risen Christ as the Slain Lamb is highly significant.

32. Durrwell, *L'Ésprit du Père et du Fils*; see also idem, "Pour une Christologie selon l'Ésprit Saint," *Nouvelle Revue Théologique* 114 (1992): 653-77. For a discussion of Durrwell's theology of the Holy Spirit, see Gérard Remy, "Une Théologie pascale de l'Ésprit Saint," *Nouvelle Revue Théologique* 112 (1990): 731-41. See also Hunt, *Trinity and the Paschal Mystery*, 20-28.

33. Durrwell, *Resurrection*, 78-105.

34. Wolfhart Pannenberg, *Systematic Theology*, vol. 3, trans. Geoffrey W. Bromiley (Grand Rapids: Wm. B. Eerdmans, 1994), 1-7.

divine persons inhere in one another in the inner-trinitarian mystery of the unity of God. It expresses the eternal trinitarian exchange, thus allowing us to glean the trinitarian processions in the inner-trinitarian being of God. In this sense, Jesus in his paschal mystery is "icon" of the Trinity, image of trinitarian life. The paschal mystery of his death and resurrection signifies something that is true of God's very being; it is properly revelatory of the interior modality of trinitarian being.

In terms of human being, the paschal mystery of Jesus Christ reveals that entry into communion with God necessarily passes through a stage of death. It shows that the transfiguration of our existence into the new life of the resurrection requires a real renunciation of our this-worldly existence, a radical surrender and transcendence of the self. Physical death is the ultimate expression of this radical surrender. The paschal mystery reveals that this transcendence of self in radical other-regarding relationality is our ultimate vocation and destiny: we are invited to it and, through it, we enter into the life of the trinitarian communion. The paschal mystery thus discloses that humanity, the world—indeed all creation—finds its meaning, its destiny, and its salvation in radical transfiguration and entry into the trinitarian exchange.

FOR FURTHER READING

Durrwell, François-Xavier. *Christ Our Passover: The Indispensable Role of Resurrection in Our Salvation*. Translated by John F. Craghan. Liguori, Mo.: Liguori, 2004.

———. *Holy Spirit of God: An Essay in Biblical Theology*. Translated by Benedict Davies. London: Geoffrey Chapman, 1986.

———. *The Resurrection: A Biblical Study*. With an introduction by Charles Davis. Translated by Rosemary Sheed. London: Sheed & Ward, 1960.

———. *The Spirit of the Father and of the Son: Theological and Ecumenical Perspectives*. Translated by Robert Nowell. Middlegreen; Slough, UK: St. Paul, 1990.

Hunt, Anne. "Psychological Analogy and the Paschal Mystery in Trinitarian Theology." *Theological Studies* 59 (1998): 197-218.

———. *The Trinity and the Paschal Mystery: A Development in Recent Catholic Theology*. New Theology Studies 5. Collegeville, Minn.: Liturgical Press, 1997.

Hurtado, Larry W. *Lord Jesus Christ: Devotion to Jesus in Earliest Christianity*. Grand Rapids: Wm. B. Eerdmans, 2003.

McDade, John. "The Trinity and the Paschal Mystery." *Heythrop Journal* 29 (1988): 175-191.

Moore, Sebastian. "'And There Is Only One Dance': Reflections on the Trinity." *Downside Review* 119 (2001): 269-96.

———. "Are We Getting the Trinity Right?" *Downside Review* 117 (1999): 59-72.

———. *The Fire and the Rose Are One*. London: Darton, Longman and Todd, 1980.
———. *Jesus the Liberator of Desire*. New York: Crossroad, 1989.
Wright, N. T. *The Resurrection of the Son of God.* Christian Origins and the Question of God 3. London: SPCK, 2003.

5

Trinity and Creation, Ecology and Evolution

For from the greatness and beauty of created things comes a corresponding perception of their Creator. (Wis. 13:5)

MODERN SCIENTIFIC COSMOLOGY tells us that the universe began from the Big Bang some ten to fifteen billion years ago and that communities of bacteria were well developed more than three billion years ago. Scientific evidence also demonstrates that life on earth has evolved and that it continues to evolve in a movement toward ever-increasing differentiation and complexity of life forms. Indeed, as Jesuit astronomer William Stoeger observes, "material reality is on every level more vast, more intricate in its structure and development, more amazing in its evolution, in its variety flowing from fundamental levels of unity, and in its balance of functions, than we could have imagined without the contributions of the sciences."[1] Christian theology, on the other hand, describes creation as the free and gracious act of the Father, through the Son in the Holy Spirit,[2] the three divine persons together constituting, as one principle, the one omnipotent creator. While Christian theology understands the world as the creation of the triune God, the very plausibility and integrity of a Christian theology of creation surely demand that it attend to—and indeed engage in dialogue with—the physical and biological sciences and their explanations of the origin of the cosmos and its ongoing natural and cosmic processes. The truth that abides in the Christian understanding of God as Trinity must surely accommodate and sit

1. William R. Stoeger, "Contemporary Cosmology and Its Implications for the Science-Religion Dialogue," in *Physics, Philosophy, and Theology: A Common Quest for Understanding*, ed. Robert John Russell et al., 3rd ed. (Vatican City: Vatican Observatory Foundation, 1997), 240. This is a most helpful resource for further study of the connection between science and theology.

2. Athanasius writes, for example, "There is then a Triad, holy and complete, confessed to be God in Father, Son and Holy Spirit . . . not composed of one that creates and one that is originated, but all creative; and it is consistent and in nature indivisible, and its activity is one. The Father does all things through the Word in the Holy Spirit" (*Letter to Serapion* 1.28, in *The Letters of Saint Athanasius Concerning the Holy Spirit*, trans. C. R. B. Shapland [New York: Philosophical Library, 1951], 134-35).

coherently with other approximations to the truth, as approached from other areas of human endeavor, including the sciences. The strategy of interconnection is not simply an intra-theological strategy, confined only to the realm of theology, but necessarily includes and embraces all areas of the human search for meaning and truth.

It was Charles Darwin (1809-1882), author of *On the Origin of Species by Means of Natural Selection*, first published in 1859, who proposed the now generally accepted theory of evolution and the notion of natural selection. As we shall see in our study, the theory of evolution, while initially greeted with suspicion, has in fact provided Christian theology with the opportunity to see God's ongoing creative and providential activity not merely in terms of the preservation of a fixed order but rather in terms of the constant bringing forth of new forms of life. Indeed, this is as Darwin himself perceived the situation, concluding *On the Origin of Species: By Means of Natural Selection* with the words: "There is grandeur in this view of life, with its several powers having been originally breathed by the Creator into a few forms or into one; and that, whilst this planet has gone cycling on according to the fixed law of gravity, from so simple a beginning endless forms most beautiful and most wonderful have been and are being evolved."[3] As John Haught, a Roman Catholic theologian who currently specializes in theological issues relating to science, cosmology, ecology, and evolution, observes: "Darwin has gifted us with an account of life whose depth, beauty, and pathos—when seen in the context of the larger cosmic experience of evolution—expose us afresh to the raw reality of the sacred and to a resoundingly meaningful universe."[4] Our goal in this chapter is to explore the gift to which Haught so evocatively refers, by means of an exploration of the connection between the Trinity and creation, including current issues in relation to ecology and evolution.

THE CLASSICAL THEOLOGY OF CREATION: THE WORK OF THE TRINITY *AD EXTRA* IS ONE

Classical Christian doctrine, based on the scriptural narratives concerning the earth's origin and that of its creatures in the book of Genesis, affirms that the whole cosmos has its origins in an utterly free and gracious act of God. It insists that it was not by any *necessity* of God's nature that God created the

3. Charles Darwin, *On the Origin of Species: By Means of Natural Selection* (1859; reprint, Cambridge, Mass.: Harvard University Press, 1964), 243.

4. John Haught, *God after Darwin: A Theology of Evolution* (Boulder, Colo.: Westview Press, 2000), 2.

world. This means that, on the one hand, the world is utterly contingent and that it might not have existed. On the other hand, it means that God's existence would not have been lacking, nor the divine being diminished in any way at all, had God not created the world. Creation adds nothing, classically speaking, to the perfection of the divine being. We should note however, as Wolfhart Pannenberg points out, that when Christian theology insists that there was no necessity or need on God's part to create the world, this is in fact more a statement about the world and its radical contingency than God's relationship to the world.[5] The vital point is that the contingency of the world, of all creation, is grounded in the omnipotent freedom of God.

As the utterly free and gracious act of God, the very existence of creation—and, moreover, its ongoing existence and indeed its consummation—is the expression of divine goodness and love. In Dante's words, it is love "that moves the sun and the other stars."[6] The mystery of creation is a mystery of love. The logic of creation is the logic of love. Graciously and generously loved into existence, creation and its ongoing continued existence are pure gift. As Pannenberg explains:

> The contingency of the world as a whole and of all individual events, things, and beings has its basis in the omnipotent freedom of the divine creating. Precisely by this freedom of its origin, that things are or are not becomes an expression of divine love. God had only one reason to create a world, the reason that is proclaimed in the fact of creation itself, namely that God graciously confers existence on creatures, an existence alongside his own divine being and in distinction from him. Part of this creating is the continuity of creaturely existence. Only as it continues to be does creaturely existence acquire the independence of its own being distinct from God's. We see here the intention of the Creator which is inseparably connected with the act of creation and which has the existence of creatures as its goal.[7]

The theological notion of creation *ex nihilo* or "creation out of nothing" (2 Macc. 7:28; Rom. 4:17; Heb. 11:3) was a notion foreign to Greek thought. It also served to express the unlimited freedom of the divine action in creation. "Creation out of nothing" means that the world and the matter of

5. Wolfhart Pannenberg, *Systematic Theology*, vol. 2, trans. Geoffrey W. Bromiley (Grand Rapids: Wm. B. Eerdmans, 1994), 9.

6. Dante Alighieri, "Paradise," in *The Divine Comedy*, trans. Charles Eliot Norton (Chicago: William Benton, 1952), canto 33, line 142, p. 156.

7. Pannenberg, *Systematic Theology*, 2:20.

which it consists did not exist in any form at all before it existed. It was from the free will and act of God and, literally, nothing else, that creation came into existence. Creation *ex nihilo* implies an ultimate temporal beginning (t = 0) of the cosmos. It also means that there is nothing that is not God's creation, nothing that does not owe its existence to the Creator God. It was God and God alone who brought forth all things, out of nothing, and who sustains their being. Creation *ex nihilo* thus also powerfully attests to creation *ex amore*, creation out of divine love. As Arthur Peacocke, an Anglican theologian with particular interest in the relation of the sciences to theology, explains: "The principal stress in the Judeo-Christian doctrine of creation . . . is of the dependence and contingency of all entities, and events, other than God himself; it is about a personal relationship between God and the world and not about the beginning of the Earth, or the whole universe, at a point in time."[8]

Although the cosmos results from the utterly free act of God, its creation was not an expression of divine whim or caprice. Scriptures attest to a belief in God who sustains God's creatures, who is steadfast in loving care, and who indeed promises eschatological consummation. That God's creative will constantly sustains and preserves the world negates any notion of whim or caprice. Furthermore, that sustaining and preserving of the world express God's *ongoing* creative action (*creatio continua,* continuing creation)[9] in the world. Creation is thus not just the act of *beginning* of the world but the *continuation* of creaturely existence. In other words, the creation of the universe is but the first stage in a gracious economy of divine action in relation to the world. A trinitarian theology of creation therefore concerns not only the world's beginning, but also its preservation. Moreover, as Pannenberg points out, its preservation concerns not just an unchanging conservation, but continued and continuing creation, a constantly new creative fashioning that goes beyond what was originally given existence and the creation of new forms of being.[10] God's creative action thus embraces the whole cosmic process, including the increasing differentiation and complexity in the evolution of life. Indeed, Pannenberg notes: "The element of contingency in the ongoing process of nature has become the mark of the creative activity of

8. Arthur R. Peacocke, *Creation and the World of Science,* The Bampton Lectures 1978 (Oxford: Clarendon Press, 1979), 78.

9. Note that Aquinas did not use the expression *creatio continua.* In terms of continued existence, Aquinas speaks in terms of *duratio* and, in regard to continuing sustaining creative activity, Aquinas speaks in terms of *conservatio.* See *STh* I, q. 45, a. 4; I, q. 8, a. 1; and I, q. 104, aa. 1-2. See the explanatory comment at *STh* I, q. 46, a. 3 in the Blackfriars edition.

10. Wolfhart Pannenberg, *An Introduction to Systematic Theology* (Grand Rapids: Wm. B. Eerdmans, 1991) 40-41; also idem, *Systematic Theology,* 2:34.

God in the history of the universe."[11] We shall return to this notion when we consider evolution later in this chapter.

The Christian tradition rejected the notion that the cosmos is eternal. Any notion that matter was eternal was rejected. While the *act* of creation, which spans the entire temporal process, is eternal, as the eternal act of the eternal God, the created universe itself is not eternal. The Fourth Lateran Council in 1215 defined that the world had a temporal beginning.[12] The world's existence is thus not like the existence of the eternal Son, who exists for eternity with the Father and the Holy Spirit. It does not proceed by way of generation, as does the Son. Similarly Augustine rejected the notion that the act of creation is an act *in* time. Concerned to protect the immutability of God, he proposed that time itself had its origin in God's creative act and that the world was created not *in* time, but *with* time (*non est mundus factus in tempore, sed cum tempore*) (*City of God* 11.6).[13] In other words, time itself came into existence with the creation of the universe. Creation and time are, in this sense, contemporaneous.

Western theology, following Athanasius, the Cappadocians, Augustine, and Aquinas held strongly to the notion of the unity and indivisibility of the divine action in all the works of the Trinity in the economy.[14] Hence the classical trinitarian understanding found expression in the axiom: "The works of the Trinity *ad extra* are indivisible" (*opera trinitatis ad extra indivisa sunt*). The Fourth Lateran Council in 1215 declared that the divine substance, essence or nature is the sole principle of the universe (*sola universarum principium*).[15] Thomas Aquinas taught that "the creative power of God is common to the whole Trinity, for it pertains to the unity of nature and prescinds from the distinction of Persons" (*STh* I, q. 32, a. 1). The Council of Florence in the fifteenth century, following Augustine's reasoning (*De Trinitate* 5.14, 15), declared that, just as the Father and Son are not two principles but one prin-

11. Pannenberg, *Introduction*, 41.

12. DS 800; ND 19.

13. In *Nicene and Post-Nicene Fathers*, 1st series, 2:208.

14. See, e.g., Athanasius, *Four Discourses against the Arians* 2.41; 3.12, 15, in *Nicene and Post-Nicene Fathers*, 4:370, 400, 402; Gregory of Nyssa, *On Not Three Gods*, in *Nicene and Post-Nicene Fathers*, 2nd series, 5:331-36, esp. 334; Augustine, *Letter* 174.17, in *Nicene and Post-Nicene Fathers*, 1st series, 1:520; see also Augustine, *De Trinitate* 1.7; 2.3, 9; 5.15; Aquinas, *STh* I, q. 45, a. 6, ad 1.

See DS 535; ND 630; also DS 171; ND 306/19; and DS 531; ND 315; and DS 1331; ND 326. With reference to the notions of *ad intra* and *ad extra*, of "inside" and "outside" God, William Hill comments helpfully: "'Inside' and 'outside' here are, of course, metaphors. Indeed, the deepest implication of St Thomas' understanding of the reality of the finite order is that it exists only 'in' God; in the creative act, God empties himself out kenotically, as it were, making room 'within' himself for the non-divine" (William J. Hill, *The Three-Personed God: The Trinity as a Mystery of Salvation* [Washington, D.C.: Catholic University of America Press, 1982], 76 n. 53).

15. DS 804; ND 318.

ciple of the Spirit, so the Father, Son, and Spirit are not three principles but a single principle of creation (*non tria principia creaturae, sed unum principium*).[16]

That the divine persons act in inseparable unity in their actions *ad extra* in regard to the world means that creation, in and of itself, does not directly reveal the trinitarian mystery. Indeed, Christian theology traditionally holds that the trinitarian mystery is derivable neither from the natural world nor from reason, but is rather given in the revelation of Jesus Christ. Classical trinitarian theology understands that it is the mutual relations of the divine persons relative to one another in the Trinity *ad intra* that ground the personal distinctions between Father, Son and Holy Spirit and that everything is one where there is no opposition of relationship (*omnia sunt unum ubi non obviat relationis oppositio*).[17] On the basis of the inner-trinitarian relations—the Father as unbegotten origin, the Son as Begotten by the Father, and the Holy Spirit as proceeding from the Father (through the Son)—the strategy of appropriation allows for the common work of the undivided three, while not formally or technically proper to any one of them, to be appropriated to one of the divine persons, because of its greater likeness to one person rather than to another. In this way, the work of creation is traditionally appropriated to the Father, while reconciliation is appropriated to the Son and consummation to the Holy Spirit (Aquinas, *STh* I, q. 39, aa. 7-8).

The problem, however, is that this classical approach to a theology of creation, with its heavy stress on the undivided unity of action of the Godhead in all the works of God *ad extra*, as a necessary corollary to the unity of divine substance or nature, tends to leave our faith in God as Trinity somewhat lacking in depth and substance. The divine persons in their distinctiveness, from this perspective, remain effectively shrouded behind the heavy veil that is the argument concerning the divine unity, as the very use of the strategy of appropriation attests. The strategy itself effectively emerges as a somewhat strained attempt to reinvest our trinitarian faith with meaningful existential reference.

Admittedly, St. Thomas had a much more nuanced understanding of the distinctive roles of the divine persons in the work of creation, compared to the tradition that later developed.[18] Recognizing that the Creator of the cosmos is not an impersonal but the tripersonal God, Aquinas argued that, though

16. DS 1331; ND 326.

17. DS 1330; ND 325. Neuner and Dupuis note that this fundamental principle of trinitarian theology seems to have been enunciated first by Anselm in *De Processione Spiritus Sancti* 1.

18. For a most helpful exposition of Aquinas's teaching regarding the trinitarian dimension of the divine creative activity, see Gilles Emery, *Trinity in Aquinas*, with a foreword by Jean-Pierre Torrell (Ypsilanti, Mich.: Sapientia Press, 2003), esp. 33-70, 171-75. Emery explains that Aquinas presents "a theology which is profoundly characterized by the Trinitarian dimension of creation and of the history of salvation" (p. 70).

the creative power is common to the Three, it does not belong to them without order or personal distinction. As Aquinas explains:

> Creation is God's action by reason of his existence, which is his very nature, and this is common to the three Persons. So that creative action is not peculiar to any one Person, but is common to the whole Trinity. Still, the causality concerning the creation of things answers to the respective meaning of the coming forth each Person implies. For, as was shown when we were discussing God's knowledge and willing, God is the cause of things through his mind and will, like an artist of works of art. An artist works through an idea conceived in his mind and through love in his will bent on something. In like manner God the Father wrought the creatures through his Word, the Son, and through his Love, the Holy Ghost. (*STh* I, q. 45, a. 6)[19]

The Father creates everything through his Word and his Spirit. The immanent processions—the generation of the Word and the spiration of the Spirit—are the exemplary cause, as well as final cause, of creation and the processions of things (Aquinas, *STh* I, q. 45, a. 6, ad 1). In other words, the Wisdom of the Son and the Goodness of the Holy Spirit are the exemplars of created wisdom and goodness.

> As the divine nature, while common to all three Persons, is theirs according to a certain precedence, in that the Son receives it from the Father, and the Holy Ghost from them both, so it is with creative power, for it is common to them all; all the same the Son has it from the Father, and the Holy Ghost from them both. Hence to be Creator is attributed to the Father as to one not having the power from another. Of the Son we profess that through him all things were made, for while yet not having this power yet from himself, for the proposition "through" in ordinary usage customarily denotes an intermediate cause, or a principle from a principle. Then of the Holy Ghost, who possesses the power from both, we profess that he guides and quickens all things created by the Father through the Son. (*STh* I, q. 45, a. 6, ad 2)

Alas, however, this subtly nuanced understanding of the eternal processions as the cause of all creation was submerged and effectively lost under the weight of a rather bland interpretation of creation as the work *ad extra* of the undivided undifferentiated Trinity. The resulting theology of creation cer-

---

19. The reader will recall that Bonaventure also refers to God as an artist.

tainly attributed creation to the triune God, but effectively divested the act of creation itself of any distinction between the divine persons.

CONTEMPORARY APPROACHES REGARDING THE TRINITY'S ROLE IN CREATION

Recent attempts to construct a theology of creation seek to affirm more explicitly the distinct individual roles of the divine persons in the one trinitarian act of creation and to reinvest more expressly trinitarian meaning in our understanding of creation. From the Lutheran tradition, Wolfhart Pannenberg, professor of systematic theology at University of Munich until his retirement in 1994, is undoubtedly one of the greatest systematic theologians of our time. He offers a remarkable example of a theology of creation and indeed a systematic theology that is constructed in explicitly and consistently trinitarian terms.[20] He situates his theology of creation in terms of the divine freedom in the act of creation and the mutuality of the divine persons. He describes the role of the Father as the origin of creatures in their contingency, granting them existence, caring for them, and making possible their continued life and independence.[21] He recognizes that the very multiplicity of forms in creation expresses the inexhaustible wealth of God's creative power.[22]

Pannenberg stresses that the goodness of the Father, as Creator, by which he grants and upholds the existence of his creatures, is no different from the love with which the Father from all eternity loves the Son.[23] While the Son is the primary object of the Father's love, the Father's love for his creatures is not in competition with the love with which he loves the Son from all eternity. Rather, the Father's love is always mediated through the Son. Indeed, in loving all the creatures in creation, each manifesting the eternal Son in its own distinctive way, the Father loves the Son.

Pannenberg focuses attention on the Son as the origin of the principle of otherness and distinction and hence as the origin of the different creatures in their specific distinctiveness.[24] He recognizes the Son as origin of all that dif-

20. Wolfhart Pannenberg, *Systematic Theology*, 3 vols., trans. Geoffrey W. Bromiley (Grand Rapids: Wm. B. Eerdmans, 1991-98). For a theology of creation, see esp. 2:20-35; also idem, *Introduction*, 37-52.

21. Pannenberg, *Systematic Theology*, 2:21.

22. Ibid., 115.

23. St. Thomas too had recognized that "the power to generate (the Son) and the power to create is a single, identical power, if we consider the power in itself, but these powers differ according to their diverse relations to diverse acts" (*De Potentia* q. 2, a. 6, in *Quaestiones Disputatae: Accedit liber De ente et essentia* [Paris: In libraries Consociationis Sancti Pauli, Barri-Ducis, 1883]). See also Aquinas *STh* I, q. 45, a. 6, as noted above.

24. See Pannenberg, *Systematic Theology*, 2:22ff.

fers from the Father and of the independence of creatures in relation to the Father. In other words, it is the Son's otherness, distinctness, and independence, so to speak, that ground the otherness, distinctness, and independence of creatures and the very possibility of creation and of all creatures, of all that is not God. Moreover, the bringing forth of creatures reaches its fulfillment, as the goal of God's creative action, in the creatures' continued independent and distinct existence.

The classical theological tradition explained the participation of the eternal Son in the act of creation through the notion of Logos, wherein the Logos corresponds to the divine intellect, which contains within itself the images or ideas of things from all eternity. Pannenberg, with an understanding of God's ongoing creative action in mind, suggests that the function of the Logos be understood and reconceived in a more dynamic form, in terms of generating ever new creatures and the web of relationships between them.[25] Pannenberg argues that the Son is not only the principle of self-distinction for the creatures in creation but also the principle of order and interrelation among them. Here too the Son is Logos of creation, as Pannenberg explains:

> As in the innertrinitarian life of God the self-distinction of the Son from the Father is the condition of his unity with the Father through the Spirit, so creatures are related to their Creator by their distinction from God and to one another by their distinctions from one another.[26]

Pannenberg argues that the preservation of creatures is especially related to the work of the Son through the order of the creaturely world and the mutual relations of creatures of different forms.[27] Pannenberg thus proposes that the Son, as Logos, is both the principle of the plurality of creatures in the world and the principle of its order, whereby all phenomena, in all their variety, are related to one another. Through the Son, as Logos of creation, everything acquires its form and place in the order of creation.

Pannenberg argues, however, that the role of the Son in creation is inextricably linked at every point to the role of the Holy Spirit, who is the life-giving principle to which all creatures owe life, movement, and activity (Gen. 2:7).[28] As Pannenberg explains:

---

25. Pannenberg, *Introduction*, 42.

26. Pannenberg, *Systematic Theology*, 2:31. Interestingly, Denis Edwards notes that "Pannenberg uses a great deal of Father-Son language even though the logic of his argument depends upon the theology of Wisdom and Word" (Denis Edwards, "The Ecological Significance of God Language," *Theological Studies* 60 [1999]: 720 n. 37).

27. Pannenberg, *Systematic Theology*, 2:32.

28. Ibid., 76.

> In his linkage with the Spirit the Son acts in creation as the principle not merely of the distinction of the creatures but also of their interrelation in the order of creation. In this sense, too, he is the Logos of creation. He gathers the creatures into the order that is posited by their distinctions and relations and brings them together through himself (Eph. 1:10) for participation in his fellowship with the Father. But this takes place only through the Spirit, for the creative work of the Son is linked at every point to that of the Spirit.[29]

So, while the Son has a mediatorial role in creation (Heb. 1:2; John 1:3), that role is conducted in the power of the Holy Spirit, whom Pannenberg describes as "the supreme field of power that pervades all of creation."[30] The Holy Spirit mediates the work of the Logos in creation, and also in the incarnation. As Pannenberg observes: "The incarnation is simply the theologically highest instance of creation, the perfect realization of the Logos in the singularity of an individual creaturely form."[31]

In Pannenberg's theology of creation, the Spirit's work, although closely related to that of the Son, is uniquely the Spirit's own. While the independence and otherness of creatures relative to God is grounded in the self-distinction of the Son, the Spirit emerges as the principle of the creative presence of the transcendent God with God's creatures and, at the same time, the medium of their participation in the divine life and in life itself. We noted above that the Son is not only the principle of self-distinction but also the principle of interrelation among creatures. It is through the Spirit, however, that all creatures, in their distinctiveness, are brought together in unity in Christ to participate in the divine life. Self-distinction is a condition of fellowship; and fellowship requires self-distinction. Again, Pannenberg stresses that the roles of the Son and the Spirit are indissolubly related. As Irenaeus described it, God works with his two hands, Son and Spirit (*Against Heresies* 4.20.1).[32]

Pannenberg holds to the classical axiom that the divine work in creation is the one work of the one God. "In all its forms the activity of the Trinitarian

---

29. Ibid., 32.

30. Pannenberg, *Introduction*, 46ff.; and *Systematic Theology*, 2:79ff. See also Wolfhart Pannenberg, "The Doctrine of Creation and Modern Science," in *Toward a Theology of Nature: Essays on Science and Faith*, ed. Ted Peters (Louisville: Westminster John Knox, 1993), 29-49. For a discussion of Pannenberg's notion of the "field structure of the cosmic activity of the Holy Spirit" from a physicist's viewpoint, see Lawrence W. Fagg, *Electromagnetism and the Sacred: At the Frontier of Spirit and Matter* (New York: Continuum, 1999); idem, "Sacred Indwelling and the Electromagnetic Undercurrent in Nature: A Physicist's Perspective," *Zygon* 37, no. 2 (June 2002): 473-90.

31. Pannenberg, *Systematic Theology*, 2:114.

32. In *The Ante-Nicene Fathers*, 1:487.

God in creation is an activity of the Father by the Son and Spirit, an activity of the Son in obedience to the Father, and the glorifying of both in the consummation of their work by the Spirit."[33] He is critical of the notion of relations of origin, in the traditional sense, as simplistic, and argues instead that the relations be understood in terms of mutual self-distinction.[34] He proposes that each divine person is active in its own distinct way, as "direct subjects of the divine action,"[35] in unity with the others: "If the trinitarian relations among Father, Son, and Spirit have the form of mutual self-distinction, they must be understood not merely as different modes of being of the one divine subject but as living realizations of separate centers of action."[36] Pannenberg explains:

> The three persons of Father, Son and Spirit are primarily the subject of the divine action. By their cooperation the action takes form as that of the one God. . . . The action of Father, Son, and Spirit in the world is thus ascribed not merely to the three persons of the Trinity but also to the one divine essence. Only for this reason can we ascribe to God the qualities of his being on the basis of his action in the world. The one God is thus the acting God, the subject of his action. But this being as subject is not a fourth in God alongside the three persons of Father, Son, and Spirit. It does not precede the persons and find development in the trinitarian differentiation. It expresses their living fellowship in action toward the world.[37]

TRINITY AND ECOLOGY: AN ECO-TRINITARIAN THEOLOGY

We turn now to Denis Edwards, who takes up the question of ecology in relation to trinitarian theology, in response to the current ecological crisis and the newly emerging ecological consciousness. Edwards recognizes that theology meets ecology precisely at that point where it shows that reality is relational at its most fundamental level, thereby supporting and dovetailing with the relational and communal ecological worldview. Like Pannenberg,

---

33. Pannenberg, *Systematic Theology,* 3:1.
34. See ibid., 1:319-27.
35. Ibid., 1:383.
36. Ibid., 1:319. Pannenberg adds: "Whether we must also view these centers of action as centers of consciousness depends on whether and in what sense we can apply the idea of consciousness, which derives from human experience, to the divine life."
37. Ibid., 1:388-89.

Edwards presses to an understanding of creation as the work of the united but *differentiated* Trinity, with each divine person having a unique role that is strictly proper (and not just appropriated) to that particular person. Creation, he argues, "is the action of the whole Trinity, but it needs to be seen as involving the distinct roles of the Trinitarian Persons, which are not only 'appropriated' to them, but 'proper' to them."[38]

Edwards turns to the theology of Richard of St. Victor (d. 1173) for a communal trinitarian theology. Readers will recall from our overview of the development of trinitarian theology that Richard of St. Victor develops a trinitarian model of mutual love, based on his reflections on charity, as the supreme form of the good, which, by its very nature, seeks to share itself with another. This reflection on charity serves to provide Richard of St. Victor with the basis for demonstrating that there must be a plurality of persons in the Godhead. The perfection of love, he recognizes, requires not just love (*dilectio*) on both sides but shared love (*condilectio*), that love that exists when a third person is loved by two persons harmoniously.

Edwards also turns to St. Bonaventure (ca. 1221-1274), who, following Richard of St. Victor and, even more importantly, the Christocentric spirituality of St. Francis of Assisi, founder of the Order of Franciscans, constructs a dynamic model of the Trinity that is also expressly based on the concept of the good, but from the perspective, as expressed by Pseudo-Dionysius, that the good is by its very nature self-diffusive, freely giving of itself to another (*bonum diffusivum sui*).[39] Since goodness is the preeminent attribute of God, and goodness is naturally self-diffusive, God is necessarily self-communicative. For Bonaventure, this Dionysian focus on the good provides the metaphysical basis for the first emanation in God (the Son/Word), as a natural emanation (i.e., by way of nature), which necessarily flows from the dynamics of the divine nature as good. Bonaventure turns to Richard of St. Victor's emphasis on love as the supreme form of the good to understand the emanation of the Spirit as a free and generous self-communication by way of love (or will). So, for Bonaventure, the first procession emanates from the divine nature precisely as the good and its diffusiveness, while the second emanates from the free self-communication of the divine love.

Bonaventure's doctrine of creation continues along these same lines, based on an understanding of the divine goodness as the primary principle. In this

38. Denis Edwards, *Jesus the Wisdom of God: An Ecological Theology,* Ecology and Justice (Maryknoll, N.Y.: Orbis Books, 1995), 118.

39. For a helpful discussion of Bonaventure's metaphysics, see Ilia Delio, "Bonaventure's Metaphysics of the Good," *Theological Studies* 60 (1999): 228-46.

way, Bonaventure arrives at an understanding of creation as the self-expression *ad extra* of the divine goodness, the free self-expression of an ecstatic and fecund God. Concomitantly, the self-expressiveness of God *ad extra* reflects the self-expressiveness of God *ad intra*, God who is Trinity.[40] Bonaventure thus understands that, as source of all, the Trinity leaves its imprint or stamp on everything, on all creation. Correspondingly, all reality is stamped with the Trinity, at every level. The whole world is thus a symbol of the Trinity, emanating from its trinitarian exemplar and reflecting the trinitarian order at various levels and degrees. As Bonaventure explains:

> The creation of the world is a kind of a book in which the Trinity shines forth, is represented and found as the fabricator of the universe in three modes of expression, namely, in the modes of vestige, image, and similitude, such that the reason for the vestige is found in all creatures, the reason for the image in intelligent creatures or rational spirits alone, and the reason for similitude in the Godlike only. Hence, as if by certain steplike levels, the human intellect is born to ascend by gradations to the supreme principle, which is God. (*Breviloquium* 2.12.1)[41]

Edwards argues that Bonaventure would thus persuade us that *every* creature is like a word of revelation in the book that is creation, at very least a vestige representing the Trinity, even if in but a distant and unclear way. Intellectual creatures, as images of the Trinity, reflect their trinitarian maker in a still closer and more distinct way, while the rational spirit that is conformed to God through grace provides that likeness or similitude that is the most intense reflection of the Trinity. What is striking here, from Edwards's theological perspective, is that all creatures have value *in themselves*, intrinsic value, because they exist as modes of divine self-expression and presence, and not just in relation to their value to human beings. Each is the self-expression, symbol and sacrament of the triune God. As Edwards explains:

> This means that the rain forest of the Amazon is to be understood as the self-expression of the divine Trinity. It is a sacrament of God's presence. Its vitality and exuberance spring from the immanent presence of the Spirit,

---

40. Edwards notes that Pannenberg makes no reference to Bonaventure and suggests that Pannenberg's concept of otherness and self-distinction, grounded in the person of the Son, would be fruitfully complemented by Bonaventure's notion of likeness and of creation as the divine self-expression of goodness. Then, Edwards argues, the Wisdom of God is reflected both in the principle of self-distinction (Pannenberg) and in the principle of God's self-expression (Bonaventure) so that each creature expresses not only the otherness and self-distinction but also the divine goodness and bounty. See Denis Edwards, "The Ecological Significance of God Language," *Theological Studies* 60 (1999): 721.

41. Trans. Erwin Esser Nemmers (London: B. Herder, 1947), 76.

> the giver of life. They express the trinitarian love of life. The rain forest, in its form, function and beauty as a harmonious biotic community is the work of art of divine Wisdom. The species of plants and animals which are being destroyed forever are modes of God's self-communication and presence.[42]

A theology and an ethic of the intrinsic value of all creatures, together with a respect for the unique dignity of the human person, thus emerge.[43] Moreover, the very *diversity* of living creatures itself emerges as the self-expression of divine fruitfulness. In this way, Edwards's theology meets the concerns of the modern ecological movement and urges us to a profound respect and reverence not just for life or for individual animals or plants but for the very diversity of living systems and interacting ecosystems, and to the ecologically responsible praxis and what we might call the ecojustice that such a theology necessarily demands.

TRINITY AND EVOLUTION: CHARLES DARWIN'S "GIFT TO THEOLOGY"

Denis Edwards also takes up the question of the connection between trinitarian theology and evolution. While the theory of evolution was initially rejected as irreconcilable with the biblical account of creation, the Roman Catholic Church never actually condemned the theory and left the hypothesis open to scientific investigation, although it did categorically condemn the notion of the evolution of the *soul*, insisting that the soul is immediately created by God.[44] It is now widely accepted that the theory of evolution and Christian faith in creation are not necessarily contradictory. As proposed by Charles Darwin, evolution occurs by way of the process of natural selection, whereby those variations and adaptations which spontaneously emerge in a species and which are useful in terms of survival and reproduction are preserved, while those that are unhelpful are eradicated. Some aspects of the evo-

42. Edwards, *Jesus the Wisdom of God,* 117.

43. Ibid., 153-71.

44. See Pius XII, *Humani Generis,* DS 3896; ND 419. See also John Paul II's Address to the Pontifical Academy of Sciences in 1996 (ND 436-39). Pierre Teilhard de Chardin (1881-1955), Jesuit priest-theologian and geologist-paleontologist, argued in *The Phenomenology of Man* for the notion of a divine creativity immanent in the whole natural order, with Christ as creation's fulfillment, the culmination of the cosmic evolutionary process. For a useful introduction to Teilhard's contribution, see *Teilhard in the 21st Century: The Emerging Spirit of Earth,* ed. Arthur Fabel and Donald St. John (Maryknoll, N.Y.: Orbis Books, 2003). See also the Web site of The Forum on Religion and Ecology at http://www.environment.harvard.edu/religion for current discussions on the theology-creation-ecology nexus.

lutionary process are, however, even to the modern Christian mind, particularly challenging, even deeply disturbing. Consider, for example, the remarkable waste of life, the costliness of the process, and what seems like the tragedy and even pathos it involves. Given the interplay of random chance and natural selection that is integral to the evolutionary process, the process itself seems capricious, violent, and cruel—some would even speak of the problem of evil.[45] In at least some respects, the reality of evolution, replete as it seems to be with suffering, pain, death, and the extinction of entire species, seems to contradict the Christian notion of a loving, caring, compassionate Creator God and indeed to raise questions of theodicy. As we noted above, John Haught argues, however, that Darwin's "gift to theology" is to "challenge religious thought to recapture the tragic aspects of divine creativity. Evolutionary science compels theology to reclaim features of religious faith that are all too easily smothered by the deadening disguise of order and design."[46]

Here, too, Edwards turns to a trinitarian understanding of God, inspired by the medieval theologians Richard of St. Victor and Bonaventure, to ground a trinitarian theology of creation that accommodates and respects a modern evolutionary worldview. Here, as in regard to ecological issues, their trinitarian visions provide Edwards with a basis for a theological understanding of the universe as fundamentally relational and for life on earth as an interrelational biological community, which is dependent on God, who, in Godself, is constituted as persons in mutual relations of love. In the context of evolution, Edwards argues for an understanding of "a self-limiting God," a God who, in loving finite creatures, freely accepts limits to the divine power, the kinds of limits that are intrinsic to loving relationships.[47] In contrast to the classical theological approach, which understands that God has no real relation (but only a logical relation [See Aquinas, *STh* I, q. 13, a. 7; 1, q. 45, a. 3, ad 1]) to the world and that God's being does not depend in any way on creation, Edwards argues that the perfection of interpersonal love necessarily involves a certain vulnerability and that, as a God of mutual relations, God, out of love, accepts a self-limiting of divine power in relation to the world and its creatures and indeed its processes. As Edwards explains:

> The divine act of creation is an act of love, by which the trinitarian persons freely make space for creation, and freely accept the limits of the

---

45. Jürgen Moltmann, for example, refers to the "victims" and to the "ambiguities" of evolution. See *The Way of Jesus Christ: Christology in Messianic Dimensions* (London: SCM, 1990), 303.

46. Haught, *God after Darwin*, 5.

47. See Denis Edwards, *The God of Evolution: A Trinitarian Theology* (New York: Paulist Press, 1999), 36ff.

> process. God respects the integrity of nature, its processes and its laws. And in creating and relating with human creatures, God freely accepts the vulnerability of interpersonal love, and enters into love with a divine capacity of self-giving love. God accept the limits of physical processes and of human freedom.[48]

It is this same notion of a self-limiting God who respects the integrity of creation and its processes that Edwards brings to considerations regarding the process of natural selection and evolution. Edwards argues:

> The God of natural selection is the liberating, healing and inclusive God of Jesus. This suggests a God who freely accepts the limits of the process of emergence, a God who creates through the losses and gains of evolutionary history. It suggests a God engaged with creation, a God who respects the process, who suffers with creation, a God whose ongoing action is adventurously creative in and through the unfolding of evolutionary history.[49]

From this perspective, the theory of natural selection and of the evolutionary process is not opposed to a theology of creation, Edwards argues. A theology of creation can accommodate a notion of God who creates in and through natural processes. As Arthur Peacocke explains, God is recognized as "an Improvisor of unsurpassed ingenuity."[50] The randomness that is inherent in spontaneous genetic mutation, as science understands it, allows for a theological understanding of God's ongoing creative and providential activity in the world, in an open-ended rather than predetermined way, by means of the potentialities intrinsic in that very randomness. A theology of creation acknowledges that purposeful and fruitful divine action occurs precisely in and through the randomness and contingency of the natural process of mutation, as well as through the "lawfulness" of physical and biological processes and the process of natural selection.

God as Creator is thus understood in terms of initial conditions and natural laws, as a result of which the universe exists and continues to unfold, together with God's ongoing creative activity, which enables the evolutionary process, without interruption or interference in the natural processes. The

---

48. Denis Edwards, "Evolution and the God of Mutual Friendship," *Pacifica* 10 (1997): 196. Thomas Weinandy also argues this case persuasively in *Does God Change? The Word's Becoming in the Incarnation* (Still River, Mass.: St. Bede's Publications, 1985), esp. 113-46.

49. Edwards, "Evolution and the God of Mutual Friendship," 196-97.

50. Arthur Peacocke, *Intimations of Reality: Critical Realism in Science and Religion* (Notre Dame: University of Notre Dame Press, 1984), 73.

natural processes do not thwart God's processes. Rather, God acts *through* natural processes, respecting their autonomy and integrity, in what emerges as the one continuous act of ongoing creation. In other words, God creates in and through, not in spite of, the evolutionary process.

In terms of the involvement of the divine persons in the evolutionary process, Edwards attends in particular to the question of the distinctive role of the Holy Spirit. Edwards assumes the role of the Father as Fountain of Fullness (*fontalis plenitudo*), to use Bonaventure's expression, as ultimate source of all life and goodness, and the role of the Son as exemplar of the unique identity of each creature. Here Edwards focuses on the creedal description of the Holy Spirit as Life-Giver (*Zoopoion*), in the work of creation and its renewal, but also, and in particular, in the process of biological evolution. Edwards thus arrives at the notion of the Holy Spirit as "the power of becoming in evolutionary history."[51] As Edwards explains:

> In an evolutionary framework, I would suggest that it is the life-giving and completing Spirit who is the power that enables creatures to transcend themselves. It is the Life-Giver who enables the movement of the unfolding of the early universe from the Big Bang, the beginning of nuclear processes in stars, the formation of our planetary system, the emergence of life on Earth, and the evolution of self-conscious human beings. . . . The Spirit of God is the Life-Giver, the power of becoming, who enables the unfolding of the universe and the evolution of life on Earth.[52]

Edwards insists that this is indeed the distinctly proper, not just appropriated, role of the Holy Spirit. It is the *proper* role of the Spirit because, Edwards argues, the Spirit *qua* Spirit is the person who is the *ecstatic one.* Readers will recall that, in Richard of St. Victor's trinitarian theology, the Holy Spirit (*condilectus*) represents the ecstasy, dynamism and abundance of divine love within the trinitarian communion. In creation, concomitantly, it is the Holy Spirit whose role it is to be the free and dynamic overflow (*ekstasis*) of divine love to all creation, going beyond the divine communion to what is not divine, and bringing what is not divine into relation with the divine persons. As Edwards explains: "The Spirit is the ecstatic gift of divine communion with creatures, whereby each creature exists, and whereby each creature is caught up with the dynamism of the trinitarian *perichōrēsis.*" As gift of love and of communion, the Spirit, Edwards reiterates, "is God's *ecstasy* directed toward what is God's *other*, the creature."[53]

---

51. Edwards, *God of Evolution*, 88ff.
52. Ibid., 90-91.
53. Ibid., 95-96.

Edwards, aware of feminist concerns in regard to Father-Son imagery, concludes that a theology of creation needs to go beyond categories of Father and Son and incorporate the possibilities afforded by concepts of Wisdom, Word, Image, and Reflection, thereby prompting a reconsideration of the psychological analogy. He explains: "It will be necessary to understand divine generativity not only by analogy with the human experience of begetting offspring, but also by analogy with the human experience of self-expression in the other and self-communication to the other."[54]

CONCLUSION

The classical trinitarian axiom, *"opera trinitatis ad extra indivisa sunt"* (the works of the Trinity are indivisible), tended to evacuate trinitarian theology and the theology of creation, despite the strategy of appropriation, of personal distinction between the divine persons and hence of trinitarian meaning, and, indeed, to attenuate a sense of the distinctly trinitarian presence in creation. In this chapter we have explored how Wolfhart Pannenberg and Denis Edwards attempt to articulate the mystery of creation, its ecology, and its evolution in more explicitly trinitarian terms. Each holds that the driving force of the process of creation and its evolution is God's love. Both Edwards and Pannenberg also press to an understanding of the triune God, whose divine creative love lets things be and lets the cosmos participate in its own creation. As John Haught comments, in a similar vein, with what is not an entirely consoling notion for those who suffer individually and collectively in the process:

> Since divine creative love has the character of letting things be, we should not be too surprised at evolution's strange and erratic pathways. The long struggle of the universe to arrive at life, consciousness and culture is consonant with faith's conviction that love never forces but always allows for the play of freedom, risk and adventure. Love even gives the beloved a share in the creative process.[55]

Trinitarian theology thus meets and accommodates contemporary ecological science and its understanding of the biosphere as an intricately interconnected and dynamic web of relationships, and evolutionary science and its

54. Edwards, "Ecological Significance of God Language," 722.

55. John Haught, "Does Evolution Rule Out God's Existence?" in *An Evolving Dialogue: Scientific, Historical, Philosophical and Theological Perspectives on Evolution* (Washington, D.C.: American Association for the Advancement of Science, 1998), 348.

understanding of the processes of natural selection. An understanding of the cosmos and everything in it as reflecting its triune Creator and an appreciation that each and every thing in creation is a unique reflection of its triune Maker dovetails with contemporary ecological consciousness and concerns and provides a theological grounding for an explicitly custodial attitude to our human responsibility for the management and stewardship of creation. Similarly, a more nuanced theological understanding of creation itself as an ongoing affair, reflecting, albeit in a dim way, the eternal generation of the Son and the procession of the Holy Spirit, dovetails with the modern science of evolution. Attuned to the insights of evolutionary theory, a theology of creation attends to what God has created, is creating, and will create and offers an expanded horizon within which to appreciate the mystery of creation, wherein God allows the universe to participate in its own creation. Christian hope is also prompted to envisage a future that involves and embraces not just humankind but the whole cosmos and the evolution of life within it, a notion that also fits comfortably with biblical eschatology. In this way, as Haught recognizes, evolutionary science offers theology the opportunity to "enlarge upon the ancient religious intuition—expressed so movingly by St. Paul—that the *entirety* of creation 'groans' for ultimate fulfilment. After Darwin we may speak more assuredly than ever about the inseparability of cosmic and human destiny."[56]

Both Pannenberg and Edwards, in their sustained efforts to reinvest a theology of creation with trinitarian meaning, press toward an understanding of "proper" roles of the divine persons in the work of creation, as distinct from the "appropriated" roles, as classical theology understands them.[57] The degree to which the argument for "proper" roles in creation is ultimately logically and theologically coherent is open to question, however. For example, "proper" roles in the realm of creation would imply that creation itself, as distinct from special revelation, would allow the discernment of the mystery of the Trinity. Similarly, a coherent account of the divine unity, on the basis of "proper" roles, is problematic. Here Neil Ormerod offers a helpful explication of the dilemma, in terms of Bernard Lonergan's notion of the various functions of meaning. Ormerod argues:

> Edwards' argument can be read as employing an effective function of meaning, which may motivate a Christian community to greater ecological concern. This is a valid and valuable project in light of criticism levelled

56. Haught, *God after Darwin*, 38.
57. See Thomas Aquinas's account in *STh* I, q. 45, a. 6.

> at Christians for their neglect of environmental concerns. However, this effective role is also self-limiting. The effective function of meaning is "effective" within a Christian community because it elicits Trinitarian faith, but not effective beyond it.[58]

In other words, Edwards and the classical theology he seeks to render more meaningfully are addressing different functions of meaning of Christian faith. Edwards, from this perspective, is more concerned for felt meaning and existential relevance in the mediation of Christian faith; he is not primarily concerned with cognitive meaning and its logical and theoretical refinements.

Setting aside such theological issues that await resolution, what is perhaps most exciting of all in our explorations concerning the Trinity–creation nexus is that science itself emerges as a source and resource, and indeed as nexus for interconnection for theology with quantum theory, chaos theory, and evolutionary biology, for example, opening up all kinds of new possibilities for theology that have not yet been realized. Science and theology do not speak separate and untranslatable languages, nor does scientific knowledge jeopardize our sense of the divine mystery. Here as John Haught comments:

> The mystery-oriented mission of theology in no way conflicts with science's effort to unfold—at its own level and according to its own distinctive method—the boundless secrets of nature. A wholesome expansion of our sense of divine mystery can exist in complete harmony with the scientific disclosure of previously hidden aspects of nature. And irrespective of continuing developments in Darwinian science's grasp of life's hitherto unmanifested intricacies, we can trust that there abides in the depths of the universe a forever fresh wellspring of novelty, unthreatened by the ongoing accumulation of scientific knowledge. It is to this faithful source of endlessly *novel* forms of life that a theology of evolution points, and to which the word "God" most appropriately refers.[59]

Indeed, Pope John Paul II observes that theology, precisely as faith seeking understanding, "must be in vital interchange today with science just as it always has been with philosophy and other forms of learning." Moreover, he adds:

> Theology will have to call on the findings of science to one degree or another as it pursues its primary concern for the human person, the

---

58. Neil Ormerod, *Trinity: Retrieving the Western Tradition*, forthcoming title.
59. Haught, *God after Darwin*, 8-9.

> reaches of freedom, the possibilities of Christian community, the nature of belief and the intelligibility of nature and history. The vitality and significance of theology for humanity will in a profound way be reflected in its ability to incorporate these findings.[60]

New developments in science—for example, in genetic engineering—will no doubt continue to challenge theology. It is not, as His Holiness points out, that theology indifferently incorporates each new scientific theology, but rather that it takes them seriously, seeks to understand them, regards them as potentially valuable resources for theology, and tests them for their value in illuminating the various areas that are theology's concern.

FOR FURTHER READING

Edwards, Denis. "The Discovery of Chaos and the Retrieval of the Trinity." In *Chaos and Complexity: Scientific Perspectives on Divine Action*, edited by R. J. Russell, N. Murphy, and A. R. Peacocke, 157-75. Vatican City State: Vatican Observatory Publications, 1995; Berkeley: Center for Theology, 1995.

———. *The God of Evolution: A Trinitarian Theology.* New York: Paulist Press, 1999.

———. *Jesus the Wisdom of God: An Ecological Theology*. Ecology and Justice. Maryknoll, N.Y.: Orbis Books; Homebush, NSW: St Paul's, 1995.

Emery, Gilles. *Trinity in Aquinas.* With a foreword by Jean-Pierre Torrell. Ypsilanti, Mich.: Sapientia Press, 2003.

Haught, John. *God after Darwin: A Theology of Evolution*. Boulder, Colo.: Westview Press, 2000.

Hayes, Zachary. *The Gift of Being: A Theology of Creation*. New Theology Series 10. Collegeville, Minn.: Liturgical Press, A Michael Glazier Book, 2001.

Johnson, Elizabeth A. "Does God Play Dice? Divine Providence and Chance." *Theological Studies* 56 (1996): 3-18.

Kelly, Anthony. *An Expanding Theology: Faith in a World of Connections.* Newtown, NSW: E. J. Dwyer, 1993.

McDonagh, Sean. *Greening the Christian Millennium*. Dublin: Dominican Publications, 1999.

McFague, Sally. *Models of God: Theology for an Ecological, Nuclear Age.* Minneapolis: Fortress Press, 1987.

Pannenberg, Wolfhart. *Systematic Theology*. 3 volumes. Translated by Geoffrey W. Bromiley. Grand Rapids: Wm. B. Eerdmans, 1991-98. For a theology of creation, see esp. 2:20-35, 76-115.

---

60. Message of Pope John Paul II, in *Physics, Philosophy and Theology* (see n. 1 above), M10.

Peacocke, Arthur. *Paths from Science towards God: The End of All Our Exploring.* Oxford: OneWorld Publications, 2001.

———. *Theology for a Scientific Age: Being and Becoming—Natural, Divine, and Human.* Minneapolis: Fortress Press, 1993.

Powell, Samuel M. *Participating in God: Creation and Trinity.* Minneapolis: Fortress Press, 2003.

Ruse, Michael. *Can a Darwinian Be a Christian*? New York: Cambridge University Press, 2001.

Wiseman, James A. *Theology and Modern Science: Quest for Coherence.* New York: Continuum, 2002.

6

Trinity and Church

May they all be one.
Father, may they be one in us, as you are in me and I am in you, so that the world may believe it was you who sent me. (John 17:21)

AMONG A RANGE OF NOTIONS by which to speak of the reality of the church, such as the body of Christ, or people of God, that of "communion" (Latin *communio*; Greek *koinōnia*) has, from the beginning, been central to the church's understanding of itself and indeed of salvation. As Jean-Marie R. Tillard explains: "If we had to sum up in one word the real context of Salvation, as much individual as collective, announced in the Gospel of God, we would use, following many of the Fathers, *communion*, the word which sums up Acts. In biblical thought, as it is understood in the first centuries, Salvation is called *communion*."[1] The church, as the early tradition understands it, is a *communio fidelium,* a community of believers, baptized "in the name of the Father, and of the Son, and of the Holy Spirit" into the paschal mystery of Christ's death and resurrection, nourished by his body and blood in the Eucharist, and animated by his Spirit, who dwells in our hearts. It is a communion of gifts and services that derive from the indwelling of the Holy Spirit in each person: "Now there are varieties of gifts, but the same Spirit; and there are varieties of service, but the same Lord; and there are varieties of working, but it is the same God who inspires them all in every one" (1 Cor. 12:4-6). It is a communion of local churches, a communion of communions.[2]

The gradually emerging consciousness of the triune nature of God developed in tandem with the growing awareness of the trinitarian character of the church itself. As the Letter to the Ephesians explains: "There is one body and one Spirit, just as you were called to the one hope that belongs to your call, one Lord, one faith, one baptism, one God and Father of us all, who is above

1. Jean-Marie-Roger Tillard, *Church of Churches: The Ecclesiology of Communion,* trans. R. C. De Peaux (Collegeville, Minn.: Liturgical Press, A Michael Glazier Book, 1992), 17.

2. For a classic study of the early church, as reflected in the New Testament, see Rudolf Schnackenburg, *The Church in the New Testament*, trans. W. J. O'Hara (London: Burns & Oates, 1974).

all and through all and in all" (Eph. 4:4). The unity of the church is grounded in the Trinity, with baptism "in the name of the Father, and of the Son, and of the Holy Spirit" introducing the human person into the ecclesial communion (in what we might call the horizontal dimension of communion) but also into the trinitarian communion of Father, Son, and Holy Spirit (what we might refer to as the vertical dimension of communion).

Our aim in this chapter is to examine and explore the mystery of the church from a distinctly trinitarian perspective. Our faith in God who is Trinity, a communion of life and love, revealed to us in the life, death, and resurrection of Jesus Christ, surely has profound ramifications for the way in which we understand the nature and the structure of the church.

CLASSICAL APPROACHES TO ECCLESIOLOGY

Although there are some early defined statements in regard to the church, ecclesiology as such (theology of church) formally emerged fairly late on the dogmatic horizon. The reality of the church, built upon the foundation of the apostles, is presumed rather than articulated as a matter of doctrine or treatise in the patristic era and the Middle Ages. In the early centuries, as we have noted, the church is understood primarily in terms of the communion of the baptized. The Eucharist is the *sacramentum ecclesiae*, the sacrament of the church, effecting and manifesting that communion.[3] Everything, including the evolving hierarchical structure, exists to serve the communion. Thomas Aquinas does not treat the church as a separate systematic treatise. Indeed, not a single question in the *Summa Theologiae* explicitly addresses the topic of the church, although Thomas does address matters in regard to it at various and numerous points in his writings.[4] His theology of church as *congregatio fidelium* emerges as a corollary of his theology of grace.[5] Thomas teaches that

---

3. See, e.g., Jean-Marie-Roger Tillard, *Flesh of the Church, Flesh of Christ: At the Sources of the Ecclesiology of Communion,* trans. Madeleine M. Beaumont (Collegeville, Minn.: Liturgical Press, 2001), 33-82.

4. Yves Congar suggests that "Aquinas acted deliberately when he wrote no separate treatise on the Church," surmising that Aquinas was thus more free to develop his thought as he wished, without being bound or determined by considerations of systematic construction. See Yves Congar, "The Idea of the Church in St Thomas Aquinas," in *The Mystery of the Church: Studies by Yves Congar*, 2nd rev. ed. (Baltimore: Helicon Press, 1965), 53-74, esp. 54-55, 73. Congar also notes (p. 57) that Aquinas's notion of church is profoundly ethical as well as spiritual, and that the entire *Secunda Pars* of the *Summa Theologiae*, wherein Aquinas treats the economy of return toward God, with the Holy Spirit as mover and agent of this movement and return, is effectively ecclesiology. For a discussion of Thomas's understanding of church in terms of his spirituality, see also Jean-Pierre Torrell, *Saint Thomas Aquinas,* vol. 2, *Spiritual Master,* trans. Robert Royal (Washington, D.C.: Catholic University of America Press, 2003), 125-52, 175-99, 291-96.

5. Jean-Pierre Torrell comments that *congregatio fidelium* is probably Thomas's favorite definition of the church (see *Saint Thomas Aquinas,* 2:198).

the Holy Spirit animates and unites the ecclesial community in the body of Christ, with Christ as its head, and that, as the mystery of Christ, the church is a participation in the mystery of the Trinity, effecting the paschal mystery of Jesus Christ in us, through the power of the Holy Spirit. But it is really not until the fourteenth century that we find what we might describe as properly systematic theological treatises on the nature, mission, and structure of the church.

One ecclesiological issue in particular dominated in the early centuries of the church—the unity of the church. Unity was initially a highly practical, not an abstract or theoretical, notion; it was bound up with the faith, prayers, and activities of the church. In the face of the threats of heresy and schism from within, and hostility and persecution from without, unity became an acutely pressing issue. Cyprian, for example, devotes a special study to the issue of church unity (*On the Unity of the Church*). On the one hand, he describes the church as "a people united in one in the unity of the Father, and of the Son and of the Holy Spirit" (*On the Lord's Prayer* 4.23). He emphasizes, on the other hand, that "there is one God, and one Christ, and one hope, and one faith, and one Church, and one baptism ordained only in the one Church" (*Letter* 73.11). Cyprian also famously asserts that "the bishop is in the church and the church in the bishop" (*Letter* 68.8).[6] The letters of Ignatius of Antioch also evince a concern regarding division within the church and for the development of church order. Ignatius teaches that the preservation of unity is a task of the bishop (*Letter to the Smyrnaeans* 8).[7] Tertullian draws a correspondence between the ecclesial and trinitarian three, and, with an allusion to Matthew 18:20 ("For where two or three are gathered in my name, I am there among them")[8] writes:

> For the very Church itself is, properly and principally, the Spirit Himself, in whom is the Trinity of the One Divinity—Father, Son and Holy Spirit. (The Spirit) combines that Church which the Lord has made to consist in "three." And thus, from that time forward, every number (of persons) who

6. For Cyprian's writings, see *Ante-Nicene Fathers*, vol. 5: Treatise 1, *On the Unity of the Church*, pp. 421-29; Treatise IV, *On the Lord's Prayer*, p. 454; *Letter* 73.11, p. 389; *Letter* 68.8, pp. 374-75.

7. In *Early Christian Fathers*, trans. and ed. Cyril C. Richardson (New York: Collier Books, Macmillan, 1970), 115. Note also the reference to "catholic church" in this section of this letter. In his *Letter to the Ephesians* 4.1, Ignatius takes up musical imagery when speaking of unity with the bishop: "Consequently it is right for you to run together with the purpose of the bishop . . . attuned to the bishop like strings to a cithara . . . [wherein] Jesus Christ is sung." See also Ignatius, *Letter to the Magnesians* 6 and 7, in *Early Christian Fathers*, 95-96, and Ignatius, *Letter to the Philadelphians* 8, in *Early Christian Fathers*, 110.

8. This biblical reference also figures in Miroslav Volf's thinking, with strong resonances with the Free Church tradition and its understanding of the role of individual confessing Christians.

may have combined together into this faith is accounted "a Church," from the Author and Consecrator (of the Church). (*On Modesty* 21)[9]

Other ecclesiological questions regarding membership in the church as a requirement for salvation—particularly in regard to schismatics who left the church—and regarding apostolic succession, the episcopate, catholicity, and the validity of the sacraments as independent of the personal holiness of the minister of the sacrament also emerged in those early centuries.

The idea of the papacy emerged very gradually.[10] As early as the third to fifth century, the bishops of Rome asserted their authority as the bishops of the church, successors of the apostle Peter.[11] Leo I (440-461) claimed primacy, a universal and supreme authority, on the basis of apostolic succession from the apostle Peter, appealing to Matthew 16:13-17, Luke 22:31-32, and John 21:15-19. Pope Leo's Tome had great influence and was accorded special significance at the Council of Chalcedon in 451 in its determination regarding the prevailing christological controversy. Pope Damasus (366-384) had the title *Pontifex Maximus* (literally, "the supreme bridge-builder"), a title of the Roman emperor, bestowed on him by Emperor Gratian. Leo I thereafter appropriated it as a permanent papal title. The Gregorian reforms (Pope Gregory VII, 1073-1085) further reinforced the role and preeminence of the papacy and of the authority of the Church of Rome, not only within the church but also in relation to the state, which effectively resulted in a monarchical power of its own. With the rise of papal influence, the authority to convene a council passed from emperor to pope around the eleventh century. It was also Gregory VII who restricted the title *papa* (father or pope) to the bishop of Rome. The process culminated symbolically in the wearing of the papal tiara, for example, by Boniface VIII (1294-1303), with the tiara symbolizing the spiritual and temporal power of the pope.[12] The primacy of the papacy was affirmed at the Second Council of Lyons (1274) and again at the Council of Florence (1431-1439).[13]

Despite the increasing centralization of authority in the papacy, however, countervailing forces that represented a more collegial form of ecclesial gov-

---

9. In *Ante-Nicene Fathers,* 4:99-100.

10. For a helpful survey of the history of the papacy, see Richard McBrien, "The Papacy," in *The Gift of the Church: A Textbook on Ecclesiology*, ed. Peter Phan (Collegeville, Minn.: Liturgical Press, A Michael Glazier Book, 2000), 315-36.

11. For example, Innocent I; see DS 217; ND 801.

12. Paul VI was the last pope to wear the papal tiara. John Paul I (1978) abandoned the practice, choosing instead to receive the pallium, as a sign of the pastoral nature of the papal office. John Paul I described his first papal Mass as the inauguration of his ministry as supreme pastor, rather than as a coronation. He also abandoned the use of the titles Vicar of Christ, and Supreme Pontiff.

13. For Lyons, see ND 803; for Florence, DS 1307; ND 809.

ernment also existed. Bishops met in councils to confer about the issues that confronted them, such as controversies over doctrine, heresies, lapsed Christians, and various matters of governance and discipline. Interestingly, the Council of Constance (1414-1418), in its decree *Haec Sancta,* stated that an ecumenical council receives its power straight from Christ and not from the pope, and so has a superior authority to that of the pope alone. It also decreed that councils be summoned at regular intervals as a counterbalance to papal absolutism and to foster and regulate reform.[14]

The Great Schism between the East and West in the eleventh century, with the severing of relations between the pope and the patriarch of Constantinople in 1054, resulted from a range of theological, political, and cultural tensions, including the controversy over the unilateral insertion by the Western church of the word *filioque* ("and the Son" in regard to the procession of the Holy Spirit) into the Nicene-Constantinopolitan Creed that had been determined at the ecumenical council of 381. This situation precipitated a crisis of ecclesiastical authority. Tension between secular and ecclesiastical powers in the Middle Ages also prompted new questions concerning the nature of the church.[15] Meanwhile corruption and the abuse of power and wealth prompted a measure of anti-ecclesial protest, which was later to erupt in the sixteenth century in the Protestant Reformation and its challenge to the ecclesial system, particularly in regard to the primacy of the pope, the authority of bishops and priests, the magisterium, and the sacraments. In response to the Reformation, however, the Council of Trent (1545-1563), while instituting a number of reforms, confirmed the hierarchical structure of the church.

A surge of interest in ecclesiology emerged in the twentieth century, both in Roman Catholic and in wider Christian circles. To some extent, this was prepared by Vatican I (1869-1870), which embarked on the preparation of a declaration on the nature of the church, in what was effectively the first such comprehensive attempt in the history of the church. Unfortunately, because the council was terminated prematurely by the Franco-Prussian War and the invasion of the Papal States, its planned declaration on the church, *Pastor Aeternus* (Constitution on the Church of Christ), was not completed. Of the proposed fifteen chapters, only four chapters—those dealing with questions of the jurisdictional primacy and infallibility of the pope—were enacted. The chapters treating the wider context of the church, the bishops, and members

14. ND 806.

15. See Boniface VIII, *Unam Sanctam,* which concludes with the declaration that submission to the Roman pontiff is necessary for salvation (DS 870; ND 804). The bull asserts that the pope is head of the Mystical Body, since Christ and the pope form the one head.

of the church were left in abeyance, resulting in a somewhat distorted view of the church. In the absence of the larger ecclesiological context, and without a corresponding theology of the episcopacy, the document conveyed a rather one-sided juridical emphasis on central authority, with the role of the pope seemingly set apart from the episcopal college.[16]

In 1943, in an encyclical on the Mystical Body entitled *Mystici Corporis*, Pope Pius XII treated the relationship of the church to Christ and to the Holy Spirit and emphasized the structure of the church as both human and divine. Pius XII combined notions of the church as the spiritual charismatic community of grace and as institutional, hierarchically ordered society in the image of the church as the Mystical Body of Christ.[17] Though this imagery was intended to balance a heavily hierarchical notion of church, a strongly institutional approach to the church nevertheless prevailed until Vatican II. The image of the church as the Body of Christ—at least to some degree—served to bolster even further the institutional dimension of the church—as divinely ordained and unalterable.

In 1964, in his first encyclical, *Ecclesiam Suam*, Pope Paul VI announced that the church was "the principal object of attention of the Second Vatican Ecumenical Council" (§31). The Dogmatic Constitution on the Church, *Lumen Gentium*, is in fact one of only two dogmatic constitutions that issued from Vatican II (1962-1965). Inspired to return to the sources—Scripture, patristic writings, liturgy, and the tradition of the church—the council articulated its ecclesiology in terms of the missions of the Son and Holy Spirit (LG 14; AG 2-4; NA 2), an understanding of the church as mystery, "a people made one by the unity of the Father, the Son and the holy Spirit" (LG 4) and as sacrament "of communion with God and of the unity of the entire human race" (LG 1, 5; SC 5),[18] indeed universal sacrament of salvation (LG 48; GS 45). It invoked notions of the church as the body of Christ (LG 3, 7),[19] the pilgrim people of God (LG 9-17), and community of faith (LG 4, 8). A new understanding of fellowship, subsidiarity,[20] collegiality, and what effectively amounted to a "communion ecclesiology" emerged. Indeed, Joseph Cardinal Ratzinger described this "ecclesiology of communion" (or

16. DS 3050-74; ND 818-39.

17. DS 3801-8; ND 847-53.

18. The Council's use of this image is more nuanced than that of Pius XII's *Mystici Corporus*. See also LG 7.

19. Cf. Pius XII, *Mystici Corporis* (1943), as noted above.

20. The principle of "subsidiarity" refers to the exercise of authority at the lowest local level possible. It means not transferring to the larger and higher level of an organization those functions that can be performed at the lower subordinate level. See *New Catholic Encyclopedia*, 2nd ed. (Detroit: Thomson/Gale in association with the Catholic University of America, 2003), s.v. "subsidiarity."

eucharistic ecclesiology) as "the real core of Vatican II's teaching on the Church, the novel and at the same time the original element in what this Council wanted to give us," [21] while Avery Dulles has noted that *Lumen Gentium* "probably deserves to be called the most imposing achievement of Vatican II."[22] Pope John Paul II himself, in his encyclical *Ecclesia de Eucharistia* (§34), reiterated the words of the Extraordinary Assembly of the Synod of Bishops in 1985 and acknowledged that "communion" is "the central and fundamental idea of the documents of the Second Vatican Council." *Lumen Gentium* and the ecclesiology it expressed were indeed a momentous development.

LEONARDO BOFF: THE TRINITY AS OUR SOCIAL PROGRAM

Drawing an explicit connection between the church and the Trinity, *Lumen Gentium* describes salvation history in trinitarian terms (§§2-4), and *Gaudium et Spes,* the Pastoral Constitution on the Church in the Modern World, presents the life of the Trinity as model for and source of interpersonal relations in human society: "The Lord Jesus, when praying to the Father 'that they may all be one . . . even as we are one' (Jn 17:21-22) . . . [implied] that there is a certain similarity between the union existing among the divine persons and the union of God's children in truth and love" (§24). Inspired by Vatican II, Latin American Catholic theologian Leonardo Boff proceeded to articulate a distinctly trinitarian ecclesiology. Boff is concerned to answer such questions as: How is the Trinity good news? What is the evangelical dimension of trinitarian revelation? How does our faith in the Trinity inspire and motivate us to live our lives in a fuller and freer and more Christian way? How do we, as individuals and as church, become "a sacrament of the holy Trinity"? (LG 48; GS 45).[23]

---

21. Joseph Ratzinger, *Church, Ecumenism and Politics: New Essays in Ecclesiology*, trans. R. Nowell (New York: Crossroad, 1988), 17. By "communion ecclesiology," we refer in essence to an ecclesiology which recognizes that, while institutional structures are necessary, the ultimate raison-d'être for the church lies in the relationships among human persons with God through Christ and the Holy Spirit. It focuses on those relationships in order to understand the church and eschews an overly juridical approach. For a brief critique of communion ecclesiology in favor of a *missio* ecclesiology, see Neil Ormerod, "The Structure of a Systematic Ecclesiology," *Theological Studies* 63 (2002): 3-30, esp. 27-29.

22. Avery Dulles, "Introduction to the Dogmatic Constitution on the Church," in *The Documents of Vatican* II, ed. Walter Abbott (London: Geoffrey Chapman, 1967), 13.

23. See Leonardo Boff, *Trinity and Society*, trans. Paul Burns, Liberation and Theology 2 (Maryknoll, N.Y.: Orbis Books, 1988); idem, "Trinity," in *Mysterium Liberationis: Fundamental Concepts of Liberation Theology*, ed. Ignacio Ellacuría and Jon Sobrino (Maryknoll, N.Y.: Orbis Books, 1993), 389-404.

Boff argues that, since Christian faith recognizes that the Trinity, the divine communion of three distinct persons, equal in dignity and existing in the reciprocity of love and life, is the prototype of everything else, then the ecclesial community in its visible social reality should model the Trinity through an egalitarian and communitarian organization. The Trinity, Boff insists, means more than just our entry into the divine life in the *next* life, created as we are for communion with God. Boff argues that the Trinity is the model in *this* life for our society in general and our Church in particular. Here, he insists, is the evangelical dimension, the good news that is inherent in our trinitarian faith. The Trinity effectively constitutes a social project, a project to be accomplished in *this* life. "The Trinity is our social program."[24] In other words, the Trinity serves as inspiration and model for our social structures and relationships, motivating and indeed demanding structures that are characterized by participation, inclusion, equality, and respect for differences.

The social model of the Trinity provides the launch pad from which Boff embarks on a critique of society in general and the church in particular. He observes that a hierarchical conception of the Roman Catholic Church prevails, with centralized exercise of sacred power in the clerical corps concentrated in the figure of the pope, and a rather authoritarian manner of leadership of the laity, involving little participation and reflecting a monarchical conception of power. This hierarchical structure is not consistent with our faith in a trinitarian God, Boff argues. It is more consistent with a monotheistic conception of God, wherein God is the pinnacle of the pyramid, a notion that serves to legitimate a correspondingly pyramidal structure in earthly organization.

A consideration of the trinitarian communion ought to prevent the concentration of power and open the way for broad egalitarian participation on the part of all, Boff argues. He returns to the scriptural sources and the sense in the early church that the church is a community of believers, each member bearing his/her own gifts and talents, to be exercised for the benefit of all. Boff explains: "To the extent that anyone creates communion, that person becomes a sacrament of the holy Trinity.... In this fashion the whole Church is transformed into a sign of the Trinity; after all, now it lives the essence of the holy Trinity itself, which is communion."[25]

---

24. Boff, "Trinity," 392. Miroslav Volf notes that it was Nicholas Fedorov, "an erudite friend of such great Russian intellectuals as Leo Tolstoy, Vladimir Solovyov, and Fyodor Dostoyevsky," who first formulated this expression ("'The Trinity Is Our Social Program': The Doctrine of the Trinity and the Shape of Social Engagement," *Modern Theology* 14 [1998]: 403).

25. Boff, "Trinity," 392.

We have already noted that the unity of the church was a vital concern in the early church and that a rather monolithic monotheistic understanding of the unity of the church emerged, reflected as we saw above in the writings of Cyprian and centuries later in the declaration of Vatican I. But, in contrast to any juridical or bureaucratic understanding of unity, Boff explains:

> The unity of the church does not consist in a bureaucratic uniformity, but in a perichoresis among all the faithful, in the service of others (mission). This unity is built around three main axes: faith; worship; and organization for inner cohesion, mutual love and mission. . . . These axes are not three parts of the church, but the one and only church developing in these three specific aspects of its historical embodiment. . . . The unity of the Trinity, which is always the unity of the three divine Persons, is reflected in the unity of the many who make up one community. . . . [The church] becomes "the body of the Three" not by merely existing as a church and calling itself such, but through its continual efforts to become a community of faith, celebration and service.[26]

Boff's considerations regarding the communion of the three distinct beings of the Trinity result in a critical attitude to personhood, community, society, and the church. Being a person means acting in a web of mutual relationships. Being a community means acting in a web of mutual relationships that are participatory and inclusive, not hierarchical or elitist. Being a society means respecting differences; it means mutual giving and receiving; it means fellowship, equality, and openness to personal and group expression. Although critical of society and the church, to the degree that they do not model these trinitarian values, Boff stresses that the trinitarian communion is more a source of inspiration than of criticism. As he explains:

> The solar mystery of perichoretic communion in the Trinity sheds light on the lunar mystery of the church. . . . Just as there is a trinitarian *koinōnia*, so there is ecclesial *koinōnia*. The main definition of the church is this: the community of the faithful in communion with the Father, through the incarnate Son, in the Holy Spirit, and in communion with each other and with their leaders.[27]

Boff argues that episcopal collegiality, wherein the many bishops in the church form the one episcopal body, finds its best theological basis in the

---

26. Boff, *Trinity and Society*, 106-7.
27. Ibid., 153.

communion of the Trinity. Boff's intention is not to question the primacy that belongs to the papacy, but rather to situate it in its proper place, within the church community of the faithful, not above or outside it. Similarly, he argues that, while there are many local churches together, united through the risen Christ and through the Spirit, they make up the one church of God. As Boff comments, albeit rather provocatively:

> The trinitarian vision produces a vision of the church that is more communion than hierarchy, more service than power, more circular than pyramidal, more loving embrace than bending the knee before authority. Such a perichoretic model of the church would submit all ecclesial functions (episcopate, presbyterate, lay ministries, and so on) to the imperative of communion and participation by all in everything that concerns the good of all.[28]

Boff underscores the vital role in the church of the Spirit, who acts through the sacraments, especially confirmation and Eucharist.

> The church is the sacrament of Christ and also that of the Holy Spirit. . . . The church stands on these two columns: the incarnate Son and the Spirit poured out on all humanity, but particularly the church. A church without charisms, without legitimate space given to the Spirit, without the vigour and strength that give it youth and a spirit of inquiry, is not a church in the image of the Trinity, the true church of God.[29]

We see, then, that Boff brings to his ecclesiology a strong and explicitly trinitarian understanding of the church as the people of God, communion of the faithful. He underscores the relational dimension of the church, and he stresses the explicit connection between ecclesial communion and action for social justice. He would persuade us that, in precisely this way, in action for justice, the church is "sacrament of the Trinity."

Unfortunately, we cannot leave our discussion of Boff's ecclesiology without some reference to the Sacred Congregation for the Doctrine of the Faith, which, in 1985, strongly criticized various aspects of his ecclesiology, as stated in his book *Church, Charism and Power*, which the Vatican Congregation of the Faith described as "a danger to church doctrine."[30] Boff was silenced for

---

28. Ibid., 154.
29. Ibid., 209.
30. See "Doctrinal Congregation Criticizes Brazilian Theologian's Book," *Origins* 14 (April 4, 1985): 683-87. See Dennis M. Doyle's discussion of the critique in *Communion Ecclesiology: Vision and Versions* (Maryknoll, N.Y.: Orbis Books, 2000), 131-35.

a year in 1985 and again in 1991. He writes of the suffering he endured in the process. He resigned from the priesthood in 1992 and continues to work for liberation in Latin America.

MIROSLAV VOLF: LIMITS INHERENT IN THE NOTION THAT THE TRINITY IS OUR SOCIAL PROGRAM

Protestant and Free Church theologian Miroslav Volf also brings an explicitly trinitarian view to his understanding of the church, together with a Free Church Protestant perspective (under which name Volf includes a variety of denominations including Baptists, Congregationalists, Quakers, and Pentecostals), with its very strong emphasis on the role of *individual* confessing Christians. In his ground-breaking book *After Our Likeness: The Church as the Image of the Trinity*, Volf explains that his intention "is to make a contribution to the trinitarian reshaping of Free Church ecclesiology," in which, he explains, the theological grounding of the Church has been christological rather then trinitarian. The purpose of this book, Volf explains, "is to counter the tendencies toward individualism in Protestant ecclesiology" and "to spell out a vision of the church as an image of the triune God."[31]

Volf is critical of the notion of the Trinity as our social program. He notes that "the thesis that the ecclesial community should correspond to the trinitarian communion enjoys the status of an almost self-evident proposition."[32] This all-too-readily invoked proposition leads to vague platitudes, he observes, such as "unity-in-diversity." But the divine perichoresis, the notion traditionally used to express the mystery of the divine unity, cannot serve as a model of intra-ecclesial unity, Volf insists. Strictly speaking, there can be no correspondence at the human level to the interiority of the divine persons, because human persons simply cannot be internal to one another in the way that the divine persons are, and so their unity cannot be conceived in a perichoretic fashion. Volf reminds us that the unity of the church is instead grounded—and continually sustained—in the interiority of the Spirit.[33] As he explains:

> It is not the mutual perichoresis of human beings, but rather the indwelling of the Spirit common to everyone that makes the church into

31. Miroslav Volf, *After Our Likeness: The Church as the Image of the Trinity* (Grand Rapids/Cambridge: Wm. B. Eerdmans, 1998), 197, 2.

32. Ibid., 191.

33. For a discussion of recent contributions to Free Church ecclesiology, including that of Volf, see Frank Rees, "Trinity and Church: Contributions from the Free Church Tradition," *Pacifica* 3, no. 17 (2004): 251-67.

> a communion corresponding to the Trinity, a communion in which personhood and sociality are equiprimal. Just as God constitutes human beings through their social and natural relations as independent persons, so also does the Holy Spirit indwelling them constitute them through ecclesial relations as an intimate communion of independent persons. As such, they correspond to the unity of the triune God, and as such they are instantiations of the *one* church.[34]

Even more seriously, Volf argues, the proposition that "the Trinity is our social program" takes no account of the inherent limits to the correspondence between the realities of the Trinity and human community. Volf thus brings a salutary note of caution to too-ready an appropriation of the notion that "the Trinity is our social program." He seeks to draw attention to the limits of the analogy and the correspondences it assumes. As he sees it, "the question is not whether the Trinity should serve as a model for human community; the question is rather in which respects and to what extent it should do so."[35]

Before highlighting what he sees as the two basic limits to the correspondence between human and divine being, Volf argues that to insist that social relations should reflect the trinitarian relations is to fail to take into account that God is God and that we are not God, and that we cannot simply imitate God. An understanding of the Trinity as the model for human community must respect our creaturely difference from God, he insists. Nevertheless, theology maintains that the human person is made in the image of God (Gen. 1:26) and that it is our human vocation to be fashioned in the image of God. Volf observes, for example, that Jesus' prayer to his Father—"May they all be one. Father, may they be one in us, as you are in me and I am in you, so that the world may believe it was you who sent me" (John 17:21)—presupposes communion with the triune God, mediated through faith and baptism, and looks to its eschatological consummation.[36] The correspondence between the ecclesial and the trinitarian communion is thus soteriologically grounded. An understanding of the analogy must therefore also take into account that our most proper human calling is to be conformed to God.[37]

Volf also reminds us that our notions of the triune God are but notions of God, who dwells "in unapproachable light" (1 Tim. 6:16). God's triune nature

34. Volf, *After Our Likeness,* 213. Volf also notes that, similarly, the divine perichoresis cannot serve as a model of inter-ecclesial unity.

35. Volf, "Trinity Is Our Social Program," 405.

36. Volf, *After Our Likeness,* 195.

37. Ibid., 192.

forever remains a mystery to us, which we can worship but not in the end imitate. The social model of the Trinity is just that, a model, a way of approach to the mystery that remains forever unfathomable mystery to our limited creaturely understanding. As the Fourth Lateran Council in 1215 definitively expressed it: in our necessary but necessarily limited language about God, there is an ever greater dissimilarity than similarity between Creator and creature.[38]

Volf then enunciates two basic limits to the proposition that the human ecclesial community should be modeled on the Trinity. First, given that the human being is not divine and is ontologically separated by a vast divide from the Godhead, and also given our necessarily limited understanding of God, such trinitarian notions as person, relation, and perichoresis can be applied to our understanding of human existence and community only in a strictly analogical—not a univocal—sense. In other words, the meaning of "person" and "communion" as used in reference to the doctrine of the Trinity is not identical with the meaning of "person" and "communion" in ecclesiology. We use the terms analogously, always recognizing both a similarity and an ever-greater dissimilarity. Hence, Volf explains, one of the two basic limits to the proposition that the human ecclesial community should be modeled on the Trinity is that human beings, created by God, can only correspond to the uncreated God in a *creaturely* way.

Second, Volf argues, a creaturely imaging of God is necessarily limited, because human being is marred by sin, evil, and transitoriness. As human beings, we are sojourners. The church is a sojourning people, on the way from baptism to the eschatological new creation and communion, which is our destiny. Volf therefore suggests that a second basic limit to the proposition that the human ecclesial community should be modeled on the Trinity is that human beings can correspond to the triune God only in *historically* appropriate ways, *within the conditions of history*.

Given an acknowledgment of these two intrinsic limits to human correspondence to the divine image, between human community and the communion that is the Trinity, Volf agrees with the basic insight that, in an important sense, the doctrine of the Trinity does indeed entail "a social program,"[39] though Volf prefers the notion of "social vision" rather than "social program." "Program," he explains, connotes a plan or system of action to be taken in regard to the achievement of some goal. But the doctrine of the

38. "For between Creator and creature no similitude can be expressed without implying a greater dissimilitude" (DS 806; ND 320).

39. Volf, "Trinity Is Our Social Program," 406.

Trinity does not constitute a "program" in this way. Rather, Volf proposes, it provides "the contours of the ultimate normative end toward which all social programs should strive."[40] Hence his preference for the expression "social vision."

Volf proceeds to shape the implications of the doctrine of the Trinity for an understanding of the social self and of the relations that constitute the self and that the self in turn shapes. He recalls that, at the trinitarian level, "unity is constituted through perfect love, which is the very nature of God and through which the divine persons exist in one another." He suggests that "the relations between persons in the church must reflect the mutual *love* of the divine persons."[41] Volf turns to reflect on the notion of personal identity in relation to the notion of perichoresis. He notes that, even though the divine persons are personally interior to one another, they do not cease to be distinct from one another. Their interpenetration presupposes their distinction, without dissolution or obliteration of the self. Nor is their identity self-enclosed. In the Trinity, the personal identities of the divine persons are shaped through twofold relationships to the other two divine persons. The self is thus shaped and enriched by making space for the other and by giving space to the other. Volf considers that this complex and dynamic notion of identity that is in this way inscribed in the doctrine of the Trinity speaks powerfully to contemporary debates about identity.

Volf also attends to the notion of self-donation, which is embedded in the notion of perichoresis. What does it mean, Volf asks, for human beings to image the self-giving God? This question relates to the notion of identity and the fluidity of boundaries within which identity is maintained. Here Volf insists that to propose a social knowledge based on the doctrine of the Trinity is not so much to "project" or "represent" the Triune God but, above all, to renarrate the history of the cross.[42] As he explains: "But we are called to imitate the earthly love of that same Trinity that led to the passion of the cross because it was from the start a passion for those caught in the snares of nonlove and seduced by injustice, deceit, and violence." It is God's passion for the salvation of the world that should ground our understanding of social practice modeled on the Trinity, Volf argues. "The Trinity as our social vision" means that our "social practices image the Triune God's coming down in self-emptying passion in order to take human beings into their perfect cycle of exchanges in which they give themselves to each other and receive themselves

40. Ibid.

41. Volf, *After Our Likeness,* 219, 195.

42. Here Volf's thought is reminiscent of Jürgen Moltmann's theology of the cross.

back ever anew in love."[43] Volf explores what this means in the very practical terms of relationships, community, and reconciliation in his book *Exclusion and Embrace: A Theological Exploration of Identity, Otherness and Reconciliation*.[44]

THE LOCAL CHURCH AND THE UNIVERSAL CHURCH

Volf extends his exploration of the analogy between human community and trinitarian communion to the often vexed question—vexed because of its ramifications in regard to church authority, papal primacy, collegiality, inculturation, and ecumenism—of the relationship between the universal and the local church (i.e., the church as a whole and each particular church).[45] Here the nonhierarchical nature of the divine community, together with an understanding of church as constituted by faithful receptivity to the Spirit's witness to Christ, serves as the basis of critique of hierarchical structures within the church and in particular with regard to the exercise of decision making and authority. On these issues, Volf enters into conversation with Orthodox theologian and metropolitan of Pergamon John Zizioulas and Roman Catholic cardinal Joseph Ratzinger. We will also engage the reflections of Jean-Marie-Roger Tillard in this discussion of the relationship between trinitarian doctrine and ecclesiology.

In regard to the question of the relationship between the local church and the universal church, Zizioulas, author of the remarkably influential *Being as Communion: Studies in Personhood and the Church*,[46] observes that "Roman Catholic ecclesiology before Vatican II . . . tended to identify the 'catholic Church' with the 'universal Church' . . . thus considering the local Church as simply a 'part' of the Church," a tendency which Zizioulas traces back to Augustine. Zizioulas also notes, however, that, "in certain Protestant churches, the local Church . . . retains priority and almost exhausts the con-

---

43. Volf, "Trinity Is Our Social Program," 415, 417, 419.

44. Nashville: Abingdon, 1996. See also *Practicing Theology: Beliefs and Practice in Christian Life*, ed. Miroslav Volf and Dorothy C. Bass (Grand Rapids: Wm. B. Eerdmans, 2002).

45. Susan K. Wood notes the lack of clarity in the use of the terminology of "local church" and "particular church" (see her "The Church as Communion," in *Gift of the Church*, 163-64). John D. Zizioulas also notes that the meaning of the terms is not clear; see *Being as Communion: Studies in Personhood and the Church* (Crestwood, N.Y.: St. Vladimir's Seminary Press, 1985), 25. So too did Joseph Cardinal Ratzinger call for more clarification of the terms; see *Principles of Catholic Theology* (San Francisco: Ignatius Press, 1987), 308.

46. See n. 45 above; see also John D. Zizioulas, "The Church as Communion," *St. Vladimir's Theological Quarterly* 38 (1994): 3-16; and idem, *Eucharist, Bishop, Church: The Unity of the Church in the Divine Eucharist and the Bishop during the First Three Centuries*, trans. Elizabeth Theokritoff (Brookline, Mass.: Holy Cross Orthodox Press, 2001).

cept of Church."[47] Zizioulas, like Leonardo Boff, argues that, since the God revealed by Jesus Christ and the Holy Spirit is trinitarian, a theology of the church must be explicitly grounded in the doctrine of the Trinity.[48] Since God's being is relational, the being of the church is relational. The notion of the church as "persons in communion" thus serves to ground Zizioulas's theology. Coming from an Orthodox perspective, Zizioulas conceptualizes the structure of ecclesial relations—at both the local and the universal level—in a consistently trinitarian way, based on a trinitarian theology that accords primacy to the person of the Father, as the font of divinity.

Zizioulas returns to the origins and development of ministerial structures in the early church and observes that there the unity of the church is constituted and realized in the celebration of the Eucharist, over which the bishop presides.[49] In other words, ecclesial communion is there identified as eucharistic communion. Zizioulas thus recognizes an integral connection between Eucharist, church, and bishop (and hence the title of one of his books). The role of the bishop, as presider of the Eucharist, is primarily to effect unity. The bishop is the center of unity of the particular church. Unity is, indeed, the essential ministry of the bishop: the unity of the church is unity in the bishop.[50] Moreover, Zizioulas argues, the bishop represents unity within the local church, but also unity with the universal church. True to Orthodox tradition, Zizioulas holds that "wherever there is the Eucharist there is the Church in its fullness as the Body of Christ,"[51] and stresses the ecclesiality of the local church. In other words, the local church is not simply *part* of the church; rather it is completely identified with the church; it is "one, holy, catholic and apostolic" and it is so "in essence, not by way of metaphor."[52] Similarly the unity of the church is not a *unity of parts,* although Zizioulas also stresses that "a local Church, in order to be not just local but also Church, must be in full communion with the rest of the local Churches of the world."[53]

Zizioulas is wary of juridical institutional notions of church and critical of centralizing universalizing tendencies in the church. It is "in this [fixed and

47. Zizioulas, *Being as Communion*, 25.

48. For a discussion of Zizioulas's ecclesiology, see Doyle, *Communion Ecclesiology*, 151-67; see also Patricia A. Fox, *God as Communion: John Zizioulas, Elizabeth Johnson, and the Retrieval of the Symbol of the Triune God* (Collegeville, Minn.: Liturgical Press, A Michael Glazier Book, 2001), 75-98.

49. Zizioulas, *Eucharist, Bishop, Church;* see esp. 215-63 for a treatment of the relationship between the local and the universal church.

50. The First Ecumenical Council at Nicaea, in its eighth canon, thus declared "that there shall not be two bishops in the same city." See *Nicene and Post-Nicene Fathers,* 14:20.

51. Zizioulas, *Being as Communion,* 247.

52. Zizioulas, *Eucharist, Bishop, Church*, 252.

53. Zizioulas, *Being as Communion,* 257.

permanent center for the expression of ecclesial unity] that Roman Catholic ecclesiology since the First Vatican Council has deviated from the early Church,"[54] he argues. Instead of a permanent center of unity, there is the principle of mutual recognition of each of the local churches, as expressed in the convocation of local synods and the institution of ecumenical councils. Zizioulas insists that those structures of ministry which are aimed at facilitating communion among the local Churches must not become "a superstructure"[55] over the local church. As he explains: "all church structures aiming at facilitating communion between local Churches (e.g. synods, councils of all forms etc.) do possess ecclesiological significance. . . . But they cannot be regarded as forms of *Church*."[56] For Zizioulas, neither Protestant provincialism nor Roman Catholic universalism is justified by the sources of the [patristic] period.[57] It is vitally important, he argues, to keep an adequate balance between the "local church" and the "universal church" that avoids both extremes. Neither the local nor the universal takes precedence or has preeminence; such questions are transcended in the Eucharist, he explains: "it is the eucharist itself which will guide us in this, for, by its nature, it expresses simultaneously both the 'localization' and the 'universalization' of the mystery of the Church, that is the transcendence of both 'localism' and 'universalism.'"[58]

Like Zizioulas, Jean-Marie-Roger Tillard, a Catholic theologian and long-standing member of the Faith and Order Commission of the World Council of Churches, also returns to examine and retrieve the early tradition of the church.[59] In the patristic vision, as Tillard understands it, the Church consists of communities around the world gathered by the Holy Spirit and grounded in the Trinity; it is one, holy, apostolic, and catholic. This is quintessentially expressed at Pentecost, an event that, Tillard argues, "dominates and conditions the vision of the Church which gradually becomes imbedded in the Christian consciousness."[60] There the church is manifestly both universal and local, inculturated from its very inception.[61] For Tillard, the inculturated local churches play a constitutive role in the church; indeed, there is no universal church that exists apart from the local church. Tillard, like Zizioulas, thus affirms that each local church is wholly church, while also

54. Zizioulas, *Eucharist, Bishop, Church*, 253.
55. Zizioulas, *Being as Communion*, 258.
56. Ibid., 259.
57. Zizioulas, *Eucharist, Bishop, Church*, 252.
58. Zizioulas, *Being as Communion*, 25.
59. See especially Tillard, *Church of Churches* (n. 1 above); idem, *Flesh of the Church* (n. 3 above).
60. Tillard, *Church of Churches*, 3.
61. Ibid., 2-45.

affirming that no particular church can be the church in isolation. The nature of the local church is to be in communion with other local churches. Tillard explains that the church, as early tradition understands it, is "Church of Churches"; it is "a communion of communions," "a communion of local Churches, spread throughout the world, each one in itself being a communion of the baptised, gathered together into communities by the Holy Spirit, on the basis of their baptism, for the Eucharistic celebration. This existence as communion constitutes its essence."[62]

Tillard also enlists the image of the church as the body of Christ, the flesh of Christ.[63] Like Zizioulas, Tillard observes that, in the early church, the reality of the church and the celebration of the Eucharist are inextricably linked: the ecclesial communion is the eucharistic communion of the faithful. Indeed, the nature of the church is revealed and realized in the Eucharist. It is in the Eucharist that the church is fully itself.[64] Tillard, like Zizioulas, while acknowledging that the history of the episcopacy cannot be traced in detail in the sources, also observes that the office of the bishop or ordained minister, as presider at the celebration of the Eucharist, serves a vital role as the center of unity in the life of the local church. Tillard's examination of the early tradition leads him to affirm the role of the ministerial priesthood, the episcopacy, and, moreover, of the papacy in the church, while nevertheless arguing for reform.[65]

Despite their differences and their heritages, Zizioulas and Tillard agree on the essential nature of the episcopacy, though Zizioulas, coming from a tradition that emphasizes the ecclesiality of the local church, places a stronger emphasis on the role of the bishop in the *local* church, while Tillard, faithful to a tradition that affirms the role of the primacy of the papacy, places a stronger emphasis on the interrelatedness of the episcopacy *worldwide*. Both agree, however, on the importance of the local church, and on the connection of the local church with the universal church, through the episcopacy.

When Joseph Cardinal Ratzinger was Prefect of the Congregation for the Doctrine of the Faith, he agreed that one can see the universal church as "a communion of Churches,"[66] and that the unity or communion between par-

62. Ibid., 29.

63. Hence the title of his historical study, *Flesh of the Church, Flesh of Christ.*

64. Tillard, *Church of Churches*, 105; see also 24-29.

65. Ibid., 169-210, 256-307; also idem, *Flesh of the Church*, 141-42.

66. See Sacred Congregation for the Doctrine of the Faith, 1992, "Some Aspects of the Church Understood as Communion," §8. English translation as published by the Libreria Editrice Vaticana, in *Catholic International* 3:16 (September 1-30, 1992). See http://www.vatican.va/roman_curia/congregations/cfaith/documents/rc_con_cfaith_doc_28051992_communionis-notio_en.html.

ticular churches in the universal church is rooted in baptism and above all in the Eucharist and the episcopate. Nevertheless, he explicitly argued that the universal church is both "temporally and ontologically prior," over and above and as distinct from every individual particular local church.[67] Ratzinger stressed that the term "communion" is not a univocal concept; it is applied analogically:

> In order to grasp the true meaning of the analogical application of the term *communion* to the particular Churches taken as a whole, one must bear in mind above all that the particular Churches, insofar as they are *"part of the one Church of Christ,"* have a special relationship of *"mutual interiority"* [quoting John Paul II, *Address to the Roman Curia*, December 20, 1990] with the whole, that is, with the universal Church, because in every particular Church *"the one, holy, catholic and apostolic Church of Christ is truly present and active."* For this reason, *"the universal Church cannot be conceived as the sum of the particular Churches, or as a federation of particular Churches."* It is not the result of the communion of the Churches, but, in its essential mystery, it is a reality *ontologically and temporally* prior to every *individual* particular Church.[68]

Here it seems that a trinitarian theology that focuses more strongly on the divine substance, as distinct from the communion of three divine subjects, undergirds an ecclesiology that accords priority to the universal church (identified with or at least represented by the Church of Rome) in relation to the individual identities of the respective various local churches. Cardinal Walter Kasper, in contradistinction to this view, argues instead for a more perichoretic view of the relationship between the local and the universal church:

> The universal church certainly does not come into being through any subsequent union, addition and confederation of individual churches, yet the individual churches are, with equal certainty, never merely a subsequent administrative partition of the universal church in individual provinces or departments. The universal church and the individual church are mutually inclusive. They dwell within one another mutually. That is why it is part of the essential structure of the church to have two focuses, like the two focuses of an ellipse: *iure divino*, it is both papal and episcopal.[69]

---

67. Ibid., §9.
68. Ibid.
69. Walter Kasper, *Theology and Church*, trans. Margaret Kohl (London: SCM Press, 1989), 160; see also idem, "The Universal Church and the Local Church: A Friendly Rejoinder" in *Leadership in the Church: How Traditional Roles Can Serve the Christian Community Today,* trans. Brian McNeil

In contrast to the patristic vision, which both Tillard and Zizioulas describe, a vision that is effectively expressed in terms of a theology of communion, wherein the full mystery of the one church is realized in a communion of the many local churches, the governance of the church from this more universalistic perspective is conceived in terms of central administration, a hierarchical order under the authority of the papacy, and a more monarchical than collegial model of operation. In this ecclesiology, the one divine nature acting externally as one (*opera trinitatis ad extra indivisa sunt*) corresponds to the one church, constituted as one person, in Christ. The "one" (not the "three") is structurally decisive—the one divine nature, the one Christ, the one pope, the one bishop—and results in, and effectively legitimates, a strongly hierarchical structuring of the church. While Ratzinger argues that the nature of ecclesial unity is trinitarian, since God is trinitarian, and that "the Church's action and behaviour must correspond to the 'we' of God by following the pattern of this relationship,"[70] the principle of unity and structure that he propounds is effectively monistic.[71]

But Volf, here in accord with Boff, contends that a trinitarian model demands that the structure of the church cannot be conceived by way of "the one." Indeed, Volf also suggests a trinitarianization of the role of the pope's office, whereby the role is exercised collegially.[72] Moreover, Volf insists:

> Conceiving the structure of the church in a consistently trinitarian fashion means conceiving not only the institution of office as such, but also the *entire (local) church* itself in correspondence to the Trinity. . . . The symmetrical reciprocity of the relations of the trinitarian persons finds its correspondence in the image of the church in which *all* members serve one

(New York: Crossroad, 2003), 158-75. For discussion of the Ratzinger/Kasper debate on the relationship between the local and the universal church, particularly in regard to the question of ontological and temporal priority of the universal church, see Kilian McDonnell, "The Ratzinger/Kasper Debate: The Universal Church and the Local Churches," *Theological Studies* 63 (2002): 227-50. McDonnell concludes: "The key to the debate seems to be the simultaneity of the universal Church and local churches, and their perichoretic relationship, one of mutual inclusion, reciprocity" (p. 247). See also Ralph Del Colle, "Communion and the Trinity: The Free Church Ecclesiology of Miroslav Volf—A Catholic Response," *Pneuma* 22 (2000): 303-27.

70. Ratzinger, *Church, Ecumenism and Politics,* 31.

71. Interestingly, Ratzinger himself notes elsewhere that "until now, one might have said more or less correctly that, by comparison, Protestant ecclesiology places too little emphasis on the universal Church and too much on the community, whereas Catholic ecclesiology places too little emphasis on the local church and too much on the universal Church" (*Principles of Catholic Theology,* 305).

72. Volf, *After Our Likeness,* 217. See also Miroslav Volf, "Trinity, Unity, Primacy: On the Trinitarian Nature of Ecclesial Unity and Its Implications for the Question of Primacy" in *Petrine Ministry and the Unity of the Church: "Toward a Patient and Fraternal Dialogue": A Symposium Celebrating the 100th Anniversary of the Foundation of the Society of the Atonement, Rome, December 4-6, 1997,* ed. James F. Puglisi (Collegeville, Minn.: Liturgical Press, A Michael Glazier Book, 1999), 171-84.

> another with their specific gifts of the Spirit in imitation of the Lord and through the power of the Father. Like the divine persons, they all stand in a relation of mutual giving and receiving.[73]

Volf, in contradistinction to the position of Cardinal Ratzinger, places strong emphasis on the local church, as does the Free Church tradition. Volf argues that hierarchical arrangements are not essential structures of the church. Its identity and authority resides not in the institution of office but in the faith of its people.[74] Volf is also critical of both Zizioulas and Ratzinger (and by implication Tillard) on the grounds that they ultimately give too little emphasis in their ecclesiologies to the importance of the faith and commitment of the individual.[75] In terms of explicitly trinitarian correspondences, Volf expressly rejects any notion of the correspondence "divine nature–universal Church" and "divine persons–local churches." Volf instead proposes that the trinitarian correspondence applies to the *relationships* between the divine persons and those between local churches.

Theologically and practically, the challenge is to hold the demands of genuine unity and authentic diversity in the church in creative tension. There is after all no universal church, apart from that expressed and realized in local churches. As Vatican II affirms, it is only in and out of the particular churches that the one and single catholic church exists (LG 23). Similarly, there are no local churches apart from those composed of individual believers. More important still, the church exists as church, not as a being in itself or for itself, but as a being from and toward God, engaged with and participating in the life of the Trinity, and a being for the world, which God so loved . . .

CONCLUSION

We see that a common basis in trinitarian theology, in this case the social model of the Trinity, does not yield a consensus of views on issues regarding the practicalities of church order and structure. Our brief survey demonstrates that the interpretations of the ecclesiological ramifications of trinitarian theology differ markedly in terms of the relative importance accorded to the individual believer, the individual local church, and the universal church.

---

73. Volf, *After Our Likeness,* 218-19.

74. See ibid., 145-54.

75. Ibid., 181-89. Volf speaks, for example, of "catholicity" in terms of the individual Christian. Each individual confessing Christian, he argues, is "catholic" to the degree that he/she is open to relationship with other Christians who are also "catholic" (ibid., 278-82).

That these applications bear a close correspondence to the ecclesial communities from which the theologians themselves come is indicative of the fact that the Trinity is not the only determining feature that is operative in these ecclesiologies. Admittedly, in the sense that, as we noted earlier in this chapter, baptism in the name of the Trinity introduces the baptized person into the ecclesial and the trinitarian communion, the Trinity is the ultimate determining reality for the church. At the same time, however, ecclesial communities, as for all human communities, are inescapably historically and culturally grounded and conditioned. Each realizes its identity and mission historically. It is this conditioning that we see at play in the ecclesiologies we have examined. We see too that, when unaccompanied by a treatment of the historical and cultural dimensions of ecclesiology, trinitarian ecclesiology effectively functions as an idealist—as distinct from a concrete—ecclesiology, providing visionary principles and ecclesial ideals but not structural details and institutional practicalities. Here, then, we have a salutary reminder to be wary of any appropriation of God language in support of our structures and systems, be they ecclesiastical, political, or social. No less important, the data clearly urge us to ongoing ecumenical dialogue and renewed openness to the breadth and depth of Christian experience in our ecclesiological explorations and our quest for discernment of the truth, justice, and life to which we are called as a Christian community.

FOR FURTHER READING

Benedict XVI [Joseph Cardinal Ratzinger]. *Church, Ecumenism and Politics: New Essays in Ecclesiology.* Translated by Robert Nowell. New York: Crossroad, 1988.

Boff, Leonardo. *Holy Trinity, Perfect Community.* Maryknoll, N.Y.: Orbis Books, 2000.

———. "Trinity." In *Mysterium Liberationis: Fundamental Concepts of Liberation Theology,* edited by Ignacio Ellacuría and Jon Sobrino, 389-404. Maryknoll, N.Y.: Orbis Books, 1993.

———. *Trinity and Society*. Translated by Paul Burns. Liberation and Theology 2. Maryknoll, N.Y.: Orbis Books, 1988.

Doyle, Dennis M. *Communion Ecclesiology: Vision and Versions.* Maryknoll, N.Y.: Orbis Books, 2000.

Fullenback, John. *Church: Community for the Kingdom.* Maryknoll, N.Y.: Orbis Books, 2002.

Kasper, Walter. *Leadership in the Church: How Traditional Roles Can Serve the Christian Community Today.* Translated by Brian McNeil. New York: Crossroad, 2003.

———. *Theology and Church*. Translated by Margaret Kohl. London: SCM Press, 1989.

Phan, Peter, ed. *The Gift of the Church: A Textbook on Ecclesiology*. Collegeville, Minn.: Liturgical Press, A Michael Glazier Book, 2000.

Ratzinger. *See* Benedict XVI.

Tillard, Jean-Marie-Roger. *Church of Churches: The Ecclesiology of Communion*. Translated by R. C. De Peaux. Collegeville, Minn.: Liturgical Press, A Michael Glazier Book,1992.

———. *Flesh of the Church, Flesh of Christ: At the Sources of the Ecclesiology of Communion*. Translated by Madeleine M. Beaumont. Collegeville, Minn.: Liturgical Press, 2001.

Volf, Miroslav. *After Our Likeness: The Church as the Image of the Trinity*. Grand Rapids/Cambridge: Wm. B. Eerdmans, 1998. See especially "Trinity and Church," 191-220.

———. "'The Trinity Is Our Social Program': The Doctrine of the Trinity and the Shape of Social Engagement." *Modern Theology* 14 (1998): 403-19.

———. "Trinity, Unity, Primacy: On the Trinitarian Nature of Ecclesial Unity and Its Implications for the Question of Primacy." In *Petrine Ministry and the Unity of the Church: "Toward a Patient and Fraternal Dialogue": A Symposium Celebrating the 100th Anniversary of the Foundation of the Society of the Atonement, Rome, December 4-6, 1997*, edited by James F. Puglisi, 171-84. Collegeville, Minn.: Liturgical Press, 1999.

Zizioulas, John D. *Being as Communion: Studies in Personhood and the Church*. With a foreword by John Meyendorff. Crestwood, N.Y.: St. Vladimir's Seminary Press, 1985.

———. "The Church as Communion." *St. Vladimir's Theological Quarterly* 38 (1994): 3-16.

———. *Eucharist, Bishop, Church: The Unity of the Church in the Divine Eucharist and the Bishop during the First Three Centuries*. Translated by Elizabeth Theokritoff. Brookline, Mass.: Holy Cross Orthodox Press, 2001.

———. "Primacy in the Church: An Orthodox Approach," in *Petrine Ministry and the Unity of the Church: "Toward a Patient and Fraternal Dialogue": A Symposium Celebrating the 100th Anniversary of the Foundation of the Society of the Atonement, Rome, December 4-6, 1997*, edited by James F. Puglisi, 115-25. Collegeville, Minn.: Liturgical Press, 1999.

7

Trinity and the World Religions

In my Father's house there are many rooms. (John 14:2)

WE LIVE IN A WORLD of manifold religious diversity. Alongside Christianity are the spiritually rich and sophisticated religious thought systems of the great world religions of Judaism, Buddhism, Hinduism, Confucianism, and Islam, each inspiring compelling visions of life's meaning in their followers and ethically authentic lives. Judaism, of course, stands in a very special relationship to Christianity. The question as to how, from a Christian perspective, to understand the place of the other world religions in God's salvific plan has emerged as one of the most pressing and important issues facing the church today, together with associated questions of interfaith dialogue and Christian mission. Not that there is anything particularly new, in recent centuries at least, in the phenomenon of the diversity of cultures and of religions and their truth claims. What is new to Christian theology, however, is an acute consciousness of that plurality and of the imperative for interfaith dialogue. Recent events in our world—where so many disputes and tensions relate to interreligious conflict—throw into stark relief the consequences of the failure or absence of dialogue and motivate us with new urgency to constructive interfaith encounter. It is now all too clear that, as Hans Küng has commented, there will be "no world peace without peace among religions."[1]

Two biblical axioms serve to inform our considerations: First, God's salvific will for all, that "God wishes all to be saved and to come to the full knowledge of the truth" (1 Tim. 2:4); and, second, that "There is no other name by which we are saved" (Acts 4:12), which describes Jesus Christ as unique savior and universal mediator of salvation.[2] How, then, from a Chris-

1. Hans Küng, "Christianity and World Religions: Dialogue with Islam," in *Toward a Universal Theology of Religion*, ed. Leonard Swidler (Maryknoll, N.Y.: Orbis Books, 1987), 194. Küng adds that there will be "no peace among religions without dialogue between the religions, and no dialogue between the religions without accurate knowledge of one another."

2. See also John 1:9 ("the true light, which enlightens everyone"); John 3:17 ("that the world might be saved through him"); John 14:6 ("no one comes to the Father except by me"); Rom. 11:32

tian perspective, are we to regard other religions and their adherents? How may we, as Christians, in fidelity to the Christian tradition and in fidelity to the signs and spirit of our times, understand and articulate the relationship of Christianity to the non-Christian religions in a way that is intellectually reasonable and ethically responsible? How are we to understand the place of the other world religions in God's creative plan and to enter into genuine dialogue? What is the role of the church and of Christian mission? How are we to live responsibly, creatively, constructively, and lovingly in a world of religious diversity? This is our theological quest in this chapter. We seek an adequate and appropriate theology of non-Christian religions, a theology that is expressly grounded in a distinctly trinitarian theology.

EXTRA ECCLESIAM NULLA SALUS: CAN NON-CHRISTIANS BE SAVED?

Even as early as the second century, Christian thinkers such as Justin Martyr and Irenaeus allowed for the possibility of salvation of both Jews and Gentiles who lived *before* the time of Jesus Christ.[3] The prospect of salvation for Jews and Gentiles who lived *after* the time of Jesus Christ, when the Gospel had been preached and the church established, was, however, a very different matter. In particular, the fate of those who left the church, having once been members, emerged as a serious issue.

In the third century, Origen in Alexandria (*Homilies on Joshua* 3.5) and Cyprian in Carthage, North Africa (*Letters* 61.4; 72.21) made reference to the axiom *extra ecclesiam nulla salus* (outside of the church, no salvation).[4] The axiom assumes grievous guilt on the part of those who do not belong to the church (although we should note that the understanding of the notion of "church," in terms of what defines the "church," remains problematic here and indeed throughout the history of interpretation of the axiom). It would appear that the axiom was at this stage directed to those who culpably refused to enter the church or who, as heretics or schismatics, deliberately separated themselves from it.

("that he might have mercy upon all"); Heb. 11:6 ("without faith it is impossible to please him [God]"); and Acts 10 (the story of Cornelius, the pagan centurion).

3. See, e.g., Justin Martyr, *First Apology* 46, in *Early Christian Fathers,* ed. Cyril C. Richardson (New York: Macmillan, 1970), 272.

4. For Cyprian, see *Ante-Nicene Fathers,* 5:358, 384; for Origen, *The Fathers of the Church*, trans. Barbara J. Bruce (Washington, D.C.: Catholic University of America Press, 2002), 50. For excellent descriptions of the history of the axiom, see Francis Sullivan, *Salvation Outside the Church? Tracing the History of the Catholic Response* (Mahwah, N.J.: Paulist Press, 1992); and Jacques Dupuis, *Toward a Christian Theology of Religious Pluralism* (Maryknoll, N.Y.: Orbis Books, 1997), 84-102.

Augustine (354-430) adopted a more rigorous approach and argued that, given the universality of original sin, all non-Christians were denied salvation, as were even infants who died without being baptized (*On Baptism, Against the Donatists* 4.17, 24).[5] While others, for example, Prosper of Aquitaine, maintained a milder position, especially in regard to those who had not had the opportunity to hear the gospel, the axiom—*extra ecclesiam nulla salus*—eventually found its way into papal teaching and official documents. For centuries it symbolized the church's essentially negative stance toward the possibility of salvation outside the church and to the salvific power or efficacy of non-Christian religions. Concomitantly, until relatively recent times, the goal of Christian evangelizing mission was conversion, a goal motivated by the belief that there was little, if any, hope of salvation outside of explicit faith in Jesus Christ and membership in the church.[6]

In later centuries, scholastic theologians also maintained a generally pessimistic view of the possibility of salvation outside the church. Thomas Aquinas, for example, argued that explicit faith in Jesus Christ and participation in the sacraments are necessary for salvation (*STh* II-II, q. 2; III, q. 62, a. 1; III, q. 68, a. 2; III, q. 73, a. 3). Thomas O'Meara notes, however, that, while Aquinas makes five references to the traditional axiom, his usage is intra-ecclesial, in reference to church members who had separated from the church or were considering separation from it. O'Meara notes that in no citation does Aquinas apply the axiom to groups outside of Christendom.[7] Indeed, Aquinas develops the notion of implicit faith and of baptism of desire, be it explicit or implicit, notions that would provide a foundation for further development at a later stage (*STh* II-II, q. 2, a. 5-7; III, q. 68, a. 2; III, q. 69, a. 4, ad 2). Official teachings in this period were, however, apparently unflinching in their insistence on the axiom. The Fourth Lateran Council (1215) cites it.[8] In 1302, Boniface VIII stated not only that outside the church there is neither salvation nor remission of sins, but also that "it is absolutely necessary for the salvation of all human beings that they submit to

5. In *Nicene and Post-Nicene Fathers,* 4:458, 461; see also *A Treatise on the Merits and Forgiveness of Sins, and on the Baptism of Infants,*" in *Nicene and Post-Nicene Fathers,* 5:15-78; and *On Nature and Grace,* in *Nicene and Post-Nicene Fathers,* 5:122.

6. For an excellent survey of the history of Christian mission, see David J. Bosch, *Transforming Mission: Paradigm Shifts in Theology of Mission* (Maryknoll, N.Y.: Orbis Books, 1991).

7. Thomas F. O'Meara, "The Presence of God: Outside Evangelization, Baptism and Church in Thomas Aquinas," in *That Others May Know and Love: Essays in Honor of Zachary Hayes, OFM,* ed. Michael F. Cusato and F. Edward Coughlin (St. Bonaventure, N.Y.: Franciscan Institute, 1997), 102. See O'Meara's chapter for a detailed exploration of Thomas Aquinas's theology regarding questions of the extent of and access to grace for those who, without culpability, have not encountered the ordinary Christian means of salvation (pp. 91-131).

8. DS 802; ND 21.

the Roman Pontiff."[9] In 1442, the Council of Florence, in its Decree for the Copts, affirmed, "[The holy Roman Church] . . . firmly believes, professes and preaches that 'no one remaining outside the Catholic Church, not only pagans' [citing Fulgentius of Ruspe], but also Jews, heretics or schismatics, can become partakers of eternal life; but they will go to the 'eternal fire prepared for the devil and his angels' [Matt. 25:41], unless before the end of their life they are joined (*aggregati*) to it."[10] In 1547, the Council of Trent solemnly affirmed the possibility of "baptism of desire,"[11] although, in the profession of faith of the Council of Trent of 1564, Pope Pius IV referred to "this true Catholic faith, outside of which no one can be saved."[12]

The discovery of the New World in the late fifteenth century prompted the emergence of a greatly expanded worldview that was hitherto virtually unimaginable in Catholic Europe. In this new and immensely larger context, wherein huge numbers of people lived outside of and way beyond the reaches of Christian civilization, the belief that salvation would be denied to the vast numbers of people who had failed to become Christians, through no fault of their own, became increasingly untenable. Here Aquinas's recognition of the possibility of an implicit faith reemerged, allowing for the development of a much more nuanced understanding of the axiom *extra ecclesiam nulla salus*, wherein a desire for faith or an unconscious or implicit faith in Christ suffices for salvation for those who, through no fault of their own, lack explicit faith in Jesus Christ. This more nuanced view was eventually accorded papal approbation and made its way into papal teaching. Pope Pius IX, for example, in 1854 taught that, while it is "held as a matter of faith that outside the apostolic Roman Church no one can be saved . . . it must likewise be held as certain that those who live in ignorance of the true religion, if such ignorance be invincible, are not subject to any guilt in this matter before the eyes of the Lord."[13] The axiom, from this perspective, as it did in the early church, refers to those culpably outside the church.

Pope Pius XII, in a letter to the archbishop of Boston in 1949 in regard to a controversy concerning Leonard Feeney and a narrow interpretation of the axiom, restated the axiom as Catholic dogma, referring to "the infallible dictum which teaches us that outside the Church there is no salvation."[14] The pope, however, immediately added: "But this dogma is to be understood as

9. DS 870, 875; ND 804.
10. DS 1351; ND 810, 1005.
11. DS 1524; ND 1928.
12. DS 1870; ND 38.
13. DS 2865-7; ND 813-4.
14. DS 3866; ND 854.

the Church itself understands it. For the Saviour did not leave it to private judgment to explain what is contained in the deposit of faith, but to the doctrinal authority of the Church." While affirming the traditional axiom, the letter proceeds to explain that actual membership in the church is not required for salvation and that one can be related to it in desire or in longing, even implicitly.[15]

As we have previously noted in our study, Pope John XXIII, in his address to the assembled bishops at the opening of the Second Vatican Council, reminded his confreres: "The substance of the ancient doctrine of the deposit of faith is one thing, and the way in which it is presented is another."[16] Such, indeed, was the spirit of Vatican II (1962-1965). While it affirmed the ancient axiom, it did so in an explicitly qualified sense, stating that "those could not be saved who refuse either to enter the church, or to remain in it, while knowing that it was founded by God through Christ as required for salvation" (LG 14). Indeed, Vatican II pressed forward to a much more optimistic and positive stance in its regard to other religions. First, it affirmed the salvific efficacy of other Christian churches, while maintaining that "the fullness of grace and truth" resides in the Catholic Church:

> Separated churches and communities as such, though we believe they suffer from defects already mentioned, have been by no means deprived of significance and importance in the mystery of salvation. For the Spirit of Christ has not refrained from using them as means of salvation which derive their efficacy from the fullness of grace and truth which has been entrusted to the Catholic Church. (UR 3)

More radically still, Vatican II recognized the possibility of salvation outside of the Christian communities:

> Those who have not yet accepted the Gospel are related to the People of God in various ways.... Those who, through no fault of their own, do not know the Gospel of Christ or his church, but who nevertheless seek God with a sincere heart, and, moved by grace, try in their actions to do his will as they know it through the dictates of their conscience—these too may attain eternal salvation. (LG 16)

With explicit reference to other religions, Vatican II stated:

15. DS 3866-72; ND 854-7.

16. *Acta Apostolicae Sedis* 54 (1962): 792. See also *The Documents of Vatican II*, ed. Walter M. Abbott (London: Geoffrey Chapman, 1967), 715; GS 62.

> The Catholic Church rejects nothing of what is true and holy in these religions. It has a high regard for the manner of life and conduct, the precepts and doctrines which, although differing in many ways from its own teaching, nevertheless often reflect a ray of that truth which enlightens all men and women. (NA 2)

Indeed, the council formally broached the matter of dialogue with other religious believers and, before the council was concluded, Paul VI established a Secretariat for Non-Christians, now the Pontifical Council for Interreligous Dialogue.

While recognizing "rays of truth" (NA 2) and "elements of truth and grace . . . a sort of secret presence of God" (AG 9)[17] in other religions, however, Vatican II made no explicit reference to the question of the salvific efficacy of other religions as such. At no point does the council unambiguously acknowledge other religions as mediators of salvation. The emphasis and concern are rather on the issue of the universal possibility of salvation. In that regard, Vatican II expresses the situation with great clarity, reiterating that "since Christ died for everyone, and since all are in fact called to one and the same destiny, which is divine, we must hold that the Holy Spirit offers to all the possibility of being made partners, in a way known to God, in the paschal mystery" (GS 22).

The expansively inclusivist position in regard to the other religions as expressed in the theology of Vatican II had in fact been prepared for earlier in the century by new thinking that had emerged in relation not just to the possibility of salvation of individual non-Christians and the positive values of those individuals, but also in regard to the religious traditions themselves. Most notable and influential in this respect was the work of Karl Rahner SJ (1904-1984).

Rahner's theology of non-Christian religions arose as a necessary corollary to his theology of grace, which recognized that grace is operative and efficacious in the lives of people who are not Christian. The universality of grace then provided the ground for the possibility of universal salvation. Rahner, following Aquinas, recognized that the human response to the divine offer of salvation could be either explicit or implicit. His notion of "the anonymous Christian" refers precisely to the universal divine self-communication and the universal possibility of human response, even if implicit and unthematized.[18]

---

17. Karl Rahner had used this expression, "elements of truth and grace," in his essay "Christianity and the Non-Christian Religions," in *Theological Investigations,* vol. 5 (New York: Seabury Press, 1966), 115-34.

18. See the following writings by Karl Rahner: "Anonymous Christians," in *Theological Investigations,* vol. 6 (Baltimore: Helicon Press, 1969), 390-98; "Atheism and Implicit Christianity," in *Theo-*

As Rahner explains:

> There must be a Christian theory to account for the fact that every individual who does not in any absolute or ultimate sense act against his own conscience can say in faith, hope, and love, Abba within his own spirit, and is on these grounds in all truth a brother to Christians in God's sight. This is what the theory of the anonymous Christian seeks to say, and, in so far as it is valid, what it implies.[19]

Rahner's notion of the anonymous Christian is, in fact, a sophisticated reformulation of the traditional understanding of the salvation of the non-Christian as expressed by Thomas Aquinas and by Justin Martyr centuries earlier.[20] But Rahner presses further to a theology of non-Christian religions, as another necessary corollary to his theology of grace, and there recognizes that the non-Christian is saved not simply in spite of his/her non-Christian religious convictions but positively through them and through the mediation of non-Christian religions, which are therefore accorded positive salvific significance.[21]

Rahner's theology of the anonymous Christian clearly preserves the absolute claim that historically is fundamental to the Christian tradition—that salvation takes place only in and through the person of Jesus Christ. (The scandal of the particular!) While non-Christian religions can, according to Rahner, be regarded as legitimate and positively salvific, there is no question of admitting the equality of those religions with Christianity, which Rahner understands as the absolute religion, with no other religion of equal weight in salvific significance. There is, in Rahner's theology, no equality between Christianity and non-Christian religions. Christianity remains absolute and normative in this theology of non-Christian religions.[22]

---

logical Investigations, vol. 9 (New York: Seabury Press, 1973), 145-64; "Anonymous and Explicit Faith," in *Theological Investigations,* vol. 16 (London: Darton, Longman & Todd, 1979), 52-59; "Observations on the Problem of the 'Anonymous Christian,'" in *Theological Investigations,* vol. 14 (New York: Seabury Press, 1976), 280-94; "Anonymous Christianity and the Missionary Task of the Church," in *Theological Investigations,* vol. 12 (New York: Seabury Press, 1974), 161-78; "Christianity and the Non-Christian Religions," in *Theological Investigations,* vol. 5 (New York: Seabury Press, 1966), 115-34.

19. Rahner, "Observations on the Problem of the 'Anonymous Christian,'" 294.

20. Consider, for example, the notion of *Logos spermatikos*, in Justin Martyr's *First Apology* 46. "Those who lived in accordance with Reason are Christian, even though they were called godless, such as, among the Greeks, Socrates and Heraclitus, and others like them . . . those who lived by Reason, and those who so live now, are Christians." In *Early Christian Fathers*, trans. and ed. Richardson, 272.

21. Rahner, "Christianity and the Non-Christian Religions," 115-34.

22. See Rahner, "One Mediator and Many Mediations," in *Theological Investigations,* 9:169-204.

Rahner's notion of the anonymous Christian drew strident criticism and proved highly controversial. On the one hand, it was rejected on the grounds that it compromised the proclamation of Christ and the absoluteness of Christianity. It was also criticized for relativizing Christian faith, for undermining the need for explicit Christian faith and making mission redundant. In what sense, it was asked, is this "anonymous faith" genuinely Christian? On the other hand, it was accused of imperialism in its assimilation of non-Christians (subsuming all under the heading of "anonymous Christianity"), of presumptuousness to that effect, of not really taking other religions seriously, and of basic lack of respect for the autonomy of other religions. Given a new sense in modern consciousness of the plurality of cultures and traditions and of cultural, moral, and conceptual relativism, many contemporary theologians questioned whether even an inclusivism as expansive and magnanimous as that of Karl Rahner is an adequate and appropriate response to the plurality of non-Christian religions. In response to his critics, Rahner wrote:

> Non-Christians may think it presumption for the Christian to judge everything which is sound or restored (by being sanctified) to be the fruit in every man of the grace of his Christ, and to interpret it as anonymous Christianity; they may think it presumption for the Christian to regard the non-Christian as a Christian who has not yet come to himself reflectively. But the Christian cannot renounce this "presumption" which is really the source of the greatest humility both for himself and for the Church. For it is a profound admission of the fact that God is greater than man and the Church.[23]

The irony of the situation is that Rahner's theology of the anonymous Christian positively intends to preclude any attitude of superiority or imperialism, for, far from regarding non-Christian religions in a negative fashion, it in fact attends with deep respect to the non-Christian religions, with the attitude that Christians can truly learn from them. The Christian, from this perspective, does not, in interfaith dialogue, confront "a mere non-Christian" but one who can and must be humbly and respectfully regarded as an anonymous Christian, one already touched by God's grace and truth.[24] Mission is not,

23. Rahner, "Christianity and the Non-Christian Religions," 134.

24. Rahner describes the characteristic attitudes or actions that manifest anonymous or implicit Christians as love of neighbor, hope for the future, faith in and openness to life, for each involves the attitude of self-transcendence. See "Anonymous Christians," and "Reflections on the Unity of the Love of Neighbor and Love of God," in *Theological Investigations,* 6:390-98, 231-49.

then, a matter of bringing God to the godless, or grace to the graceless. But neither is the church's missionary effort negated, nor is it rendered superfluous. Rather, such an understanding of the universality of grace prompts a new theology of mission, whereby mission is recognized as serving the incarnational dynamic of grace.[25] Vatican II's Decree on the Church's Missionary Activity (*Ad Gentes*) would indeed later explain the church's mission in terms of the trinitarian mission of the Son and Spirit: "The church on earth is by its very nature missionary, since, according to the plan of the Father, it has its origin in the mission of the Son and the Holy Spirit. This plan flows from 'fountain-like love,' the love of God the Father" (AG 2).[26]

Pope John Paul II refered to the classical axiom and even proposed a new version of interpretation of the axiom, "*without* the church there is no salvation,"[27] thereby shifting the focus of its meaning to the necessity of the existence and mission of the church and away from the individual's membership of the church. Pope John Paul II also taught that interreligious dialogue is "part of the Church's evangelizing mission" (*Redemptoris Missio* 55).[28] As he explains: "dialogue is not in opposition to the mission *ad gentes*; indeed, it has special links with that mission and is one of its expressions" (§55).[29] Dialogue, he writes, "is demanded by deep respect for everything that has been brought about in human beings by the Spirit who blows where he wills" (§56). We note too that, in his call for interreligious dialogue, John Paul II ascribes an explicitly positive role to non-Christian religions in the divine economy of salvation, explaining in the words of Vatican II that "the Church seeks to uncover the 'seeds of the Word,' 'a ray of that truth which enlightens all men'; these are found in individuals and in the religious traditions of mankind" (§56).[30] To speak in this way about the church's evangelizing mis-

25. Rahner, "Anonymous Christians and the Missionary Task of the Church," in *Theological Investigations,* 12:161-78; see also "Observations on the Problem of the 'Anonymous Christian,'" in *Theological Investigations,* 14:280-94.

26. For an excellent treatment of a theology of mission in a trinitarian context, see Stephen B. Bevans and Roger P. Schroeder, *Constants in Context: A Theology of Mission for Today* (Maryknoll, N.Y.: Orbis Books, 2004), 286-304.

27. See *L'Osservatore Romano,* June 1, 1995, 4.

28. See http://www.vatican.va/holy_father/john_paul-ii/encyclicals/; see also Congregation for the Doctrine of the Faith, *Declaration Dominus Iesus: On the Unicity and Salvific Universality of Jesus Christ and the Church* (Vatican City: Liberaria Editrice Vaticana, 2000), English translation in *Origins* (September 14, 2000): 209-19, see §§2, 22. See also http://www.vatican.va/roman_curia/congregations/cfaith/documents/rc_con_cfaith_doc_20000806_dominus-iesus_en.html.

29. Note, however, that the link between dialogue and evangelization, with connotations of dialogue as a strategy for conversion, is problematic from the perspective of a number of our interfaith dialogue partners. For a statement acknowledging the church's mission as dialogue, but not with the goal of conversion, see International Theological Commission, "Christianity and the World Religions," *Origins* 27 (August 14, 1997): 114-17.

30. Note John Paul II's reference here to Vatican II.

sion is to expand the meaning of the term "evangelization" so that it includes dialogue, an expansion of meaning that goes back to Paul VI's programmatic encyclical *Ecclesiam Suam*.

THE PLACE OF OTHER RELIGIONS IN GOD'S CREATIVE PLAN: THE SALVIFIC EFFICACY OF NON-CHRISTIAN RELIGIONS

New theological questions, however, continue to emerge. As we have seen, the current question is no longer whether non-Christians can be saved. The question has become whether non-Christian religions are, per se, vehicles of salvation. What does it mean to say that the Holy Spirit is present and active in other religions? Does it imply, for example, the presence in those non-Christian religions of Trinity, church, Kingdom? How is the "necessity" of the church, to which Vatican II referred (LG 14),[31] to be understood, and does that "necessity" negate the salvific value of other religions? How effective are the "truth and grace" within other religions? Can Christian and Catholic theology affirm that the non-Christian religions traditions have, per se, positive significance as means of salvation? What, then, is the role of the church? What, then, is the function of Christian mission? Some theologians, including Jacques Dupuis SJ, press further still and ask whether religious pluralism is a part of God's creative salvific plan, in principle (*de iure*), not just as a matter of fact (*de facto*).

These new questions regarding non-Christian religions are partly prompted by the keen awareness in modern historical consciousness that no culture is normative or absolute, that all are historically conditioned, necessarily limited, and essentially relative, and that even concepts as fundamental as those of justice and rationality are tradition-constituted and tradition-constitutive.[32] In this context, relativism has become a central issue. In its strongest form, it expresses the notion that concepts such as rationality, truth, reality, right, and good are ultimately relative to a specific conceptual scheme, theoretical framework, culture, or society. It is hardly surprising, in this light, that the question of the relationship of Christianity and its truth claims to other religions and their truth claims emerges anew, given that the central

31. The council, however, does not specify the exact nature of the universal necessity of the church for salvation. John Paul II, in *Redemptoris Missio*, speaks of those people who have no explicit faith in Jesus Christ and no membership in a church in terms of "a mysterious relationship with the church" (§10).

32. Alasdair C. MacIntyre, *Whose Justice? Which Rationality?* (Notre Dame, Ind.: University of Notre Dame Press, 1988).

tenet of Christian faith is that in the particular historical person of Jesus Christ is found the absolute savior and the unique and unsurpassable revelation of the one true God. Here is the scandal of the particular! This is our claim—that there is no other one but Jesus! But in the context of modern understandings of cultural, religious, and moral relativism, it is sorely problematic. The Christian claim is also problematic when one considers, for example, the relatively slight impact to date of Christian missionary activity in Asia, and the unlikely prospect of a high impact in the foreseeable future.

So new questions emerge. It is not just a question of whether non-Christians can be saved. Nor is it just the question of whether non-Christian religions have salvific efficacy. But, more radical still, are the non-Christian religions a part of God's salvific plan for humankind? Do they represent, we might ask, not just the human person's search for God, but God's search for the human person? In regard to this issue, the declaration of the Congregation for the Doctrine of the Faith *Dominus Iesus* (2000) clearly rejects any theory that argues for religious pluralism in principle, describing the church's missionary proclamation as "endangered today by relativistic theories which seek to justify religious pluralism, not only *de facto* but also *de iure (or in principle)*" (§4). But, while rightly rejecting "that mentality of indifferentism" (§22) which is "characterized by a religious relativism which leads to the belief that 'one religion is as good as another'" (*Redemptoris Missio* §36), *Dominus Iesus* assumes that religious pluralism in principle necessarily involves rejection of uniqueness of Jesus Christ as universal savior, the central tenet of our Christian faith. But are the two mutually exclusive? Or is it possible to uphold the salvific efficacy of other religions, as part of triune God's plan for humanity and, at the same time, also maintain the universal and unique significance of Jesus Christ as savior? That is a new and very challenging question.

A TRINITARIAN APPROACH TO A THEOLOGY OF NON-CHRISTIAN RELIGIONS AND INTERFAITH DIALOGUE

We have already noted "the scandal of the particular" of the Christian tenet that Jesus Christ is the absolute and universal savior and, in our search for a Christian theology of religions, there will be no resiling from the claim to his unsurpassable uniqueness. But, encouraged by the words of Pope John XXIII—that the substance of the ancient doctrine of the deposit of faith is one thing, and the way in which it is presented is another[33]—our

33. *Acta Apostolicae Sedis* 54 (1962): 792; GS 62.

exploration leads us to consider new perspectives from which to construct a theology of religions. We shall firstly consider the contribution by Raimon Panikkar, a Catholic theologian who, in many ways in his own life, epitomizes interfaith dialogue and intercultural encounter and who in his theology seeks richer resources in the Christian tradition to enable a more fruitful interfaith encounter. He finds those resources in the Christian understanding of the Trinity.

Raimon Panikkar: The Trinitarian Convergence of Spiritualities

Born in Barcelona in 1918, the son of a Hindu Indian father and a Roman Catholic Spanish mother, Raimon Panikkar (or Raimundo, as previously known) grew up in Spain and was raised in the Catholic faith. After his ordination as a Catholic priest in 1946, he was attached to the diocese of Varanasi in India, where interfaith dialogue became his life's work.[34] Before retiring to a small village in Spain, where he continues to write, he taught in several universities around the world. He is the author of many books, including *The Unknown Christ of Hinduism*, *The Trinity and the Religious Experience of Man*, *The Silence of God: The Answer of the Buddha*, and *The Cosmotheandric Experience: Emerging Religious Consciousness.*[35] Rowan Williams describes Panikkar's book *The Trinity and the Religious Experience of Man* as "one of the best and least read meditations on the Trinity in our century."[36]

Panikkar observes that Logos Christology has been a strong universalizing element in Christianity since the teachings of Paul, John, and Justin Martyr, who engaged it to great effect in his missionary encounter with Greek philosophical thought.[37] Panikkar notes, however, that, while a Logos Christology arguably offers a useful and constructive point of entry for encounter with Judaism and Islam, both of which have a strong sense of the revelation of the *word* of God, the concept of the *logos* is not so helpful or fruitful in

---

34. For an excellent survey and discussion of Panikkar's work, see *The Intercultural Challenge of Raimon Panikkar*, ed. Joseph Prabhu (Maryknoll, N.Y.: Orbis Books, 1996).

35. *The Unknown Christ of Hinduism* (London: Darton, Longman & Todd, 1964, rev. ed., 1981); *The Trinity and the Religious Experience of Man* (Maryknoll, N.Y.: Orbis Books; London: Darton, Longman & Todd , 1973); *The Silence of God: The Anwswer to Buddha* (Maryknoll, N.Y.: Orbis Books, 1989); *The Cosmotheandric Experience: Emerging Religious Consciousness* (Maryknoll, N.Y.: Orbis Books, 1993).

36. Rowan Willliams, *On Christian Theology,* Challenges in Contemporary Theology (Malden, Mass.: Blackwell, 2000), 167-80 ("Trinity and Pluralism"), esp. 167.

37. Consider, for example, the prologue of John's Gospel and, from the Pauline corpus, Col. 1:15-20 and Phil. 2:6-11. The Logos Christology of Justin Martyr is mentioned above.

encounter with Hinduism or Buddhism. Panikkar notes that neither advaitan ("not-two," nondualist) Hinduism, with its concept of the nonduality of self and the Absolute, nor Buddhism, with its notion of nirvana, has a grounding in a concept of *logos,* and indeed they both negate it. Hinduism seems to affirm a notion of nothingness, and the fulfillment of human existence is understood not in terms of dialogue but rather as dissolution into the Absolute, while Buddhism seems to affirm a kind of pantheism, a kind of undifferentiated union as the goal of one's spiritual journey. Buddhist spirituality emphasizes silence, darkness, and negation and resists any attempt to make formulations about ultimate reality, for it understands that the ultimate state of enlightenment is beyond words. The notion of the word or the *logos* thus appears to have no ultimate significance in these spiritualities, and so a *logos* approach to the encounter with these religions is inappropriate and unhelpful, even offensive.

Seeking a more fruitful avenue of encounter, Panikkar suggests the realm of spiritual experience and spirituality as a way of approach to interfaith dialogue, rather than creeds and doctrinal formulations (*logos* constructions).[38] Let us start, he suggests, "by defining any given spirituality, pragmatically and even phenomenologically, as being one typical way of handling the human condition. Next let us put this in *more* religious terms by saying that it represents man's basic attitude *vis-à-vis* his ultimate end."[39] Methodologically, Panikkar thus proposes an approach that relies on subjective personal spiritual experience (faith experience), rather than on a more objectivist theoretical creedal approach (beliefs).

Based on his experience of the world religions in the religiously rich context of Asia, Panikkar recognizes three essentially different forms of spirituality in the world religions, and he relates these to three concepts of the divine: (1) a silent self-emptying apophatic dimension of spirituality, such as is found in the Buddhist experience of nirvana; (2) a personalistic dimension, as is expressed in the spirituality of the person of the Son in Christianity, which has its history in Judaism and Yahweh's revelation to the Jews; and (3) an immanent dimension, which is found in Hinduism and its spirituality of nonduality of the self and the Absolute, and of undifferentiated union with the Absolute. Panikkar then brings an explicitly trinitarian approach to world

---

38. My thanks to Gerard Hall, who noted in conversation with me that Panikkar's emphasis on spiritual-religious experience as the primary category also opens up the possibility of dialogue more broadly with post-Enlightenment philosophy and even postmodern sensibilities (even though Panikkar himself is quite suspicious of postmodernism in its various forms).

39. Panikkar, *Trinity*, 9. Panikkar also notes there that "one religion, in fact, may include several spiritualities, because spirituality is not directly bound up with any dogma or institution. It is rather an attitude of mind which one may ascribe to different religions."

religions and interfaith dialogue, by relating these three different spiritual understandings and spiritualities that he perceives in the world religions to the Christian experience of the three persons of the Trinity. As he explains: "my intention here is not to expound the doctrine of the Trinity; my desire is simply to show how in the light of the Trinity the three forms of spirituality described above can be reconciled."[40]

Panikkar first relates the Christian understanding of the person of the Father in the Trinity to the Hindu sense of the Absolute. He notes that the earliest trinitarian formulas speak not of Father, Son, and Spirit but of God, the Christ, and the Spirit. The Father is the Absolute, the only God, *ho theos*. The Father is the unbegotten, the unoriginate, the one from whom the Son and the Spirit proceed, and the one who is the ultimate source and origin of all creation. The Father is the one whom no one has ever seen, except the Son. Everything that the Father is he gives to his begotten Son. In other words, Panikkar suggests, "we may say: the Absolute, the Father, *is not*. He has no *ex-sistence*, not even that of Being. In the generation of the Son he has, so to speak, given everything. In the Father the apophaticism (the *kenosis* or emptying) of Being is real and total." Here Panikkar suggests that "perhaps the deep intuitions of hinduism and buddhism, which come from a different universe of discourse than the greek, may help us to penetrate further the trinitarian mystery."[41] Panikkar then asks:

> Is it not here truly speaking, in this essential apophatism of the "person" of the Father, in this kenosis of Being at its very source, that the buddhist experience of *nirvāna* and *śūnyatā* (emptiness) should be situated. One is led onwards towards the "absolute goal" and at the end one finds nothing, because there is nothing, not even Being. "God created out of nothing" (*ex nihilo*), certainly, i.e. out of himself (*a Deo*)—a buddhist will say.[42]

From this perspective, any attempt to speak of the Father is effectively a contradiction in terms. Rather, a profound apophaticism is appropriate in regard to the Father, who is the source of all being and who has no being. It is necessary not to speak, and to be silent. Panikkar adds, "the spirituality of the Father is not even a spirituality. It is like the invisible bedrock, the gentle inspirer, the unnoticed force which sustains, draws and pushes us. God is truly transcendent, infinite."[43] Panikkar thus relates Buddhism and its

40. Ibid., 41.
41. Ibid., 46.
42. Ibid., 46-47.
43. Ibid., 50.

apophatic silence to the Christian experience and understanding of the Father, the Father who himself is silent, who dwells in inaccessible light, and expresses himself through the Son.

Turning to the Son, Panikkar takes a complementary approach. While silence characterizes the Father, speech characterizes the Son. Indeed, Panikkar argues for the unique personhood of the Son:

> Only the Son is Person, if we use the word in its eminent sense and analogically to human persons: neither the Father nor the Spirit is a person. . . . Correctly speaking, then, it is only with the Son that man can have a personal relationship. The God of theism, thus, is the Son; the God with whom one can speak, establish a dialogue, enter into communication, is the divine Person who is in-relation-with, or rather, is the relationship with man and one of the poles of total existence.[44]

Panikkar thus relates Judaism, Islam and Christianity, as religions that claim personal divine revelation in words, as religions of the Word, to the Christian experience of the person of the Son, who mediates between God and humankind and through whom all creation has been made and has its being.

Third, Panikkar treats the spirituality of the Spirit, which, he argues, is quite different from that of the Word. Personalist structures therefore do not apply. Similarly, it is quite different from that of the Father, for, while transcendence characterizes the Father, immanence characterizes the Spirit. Here Panikkar makes the connection between the immanent dimension of the spirituality of advaitan Hinduism with the Christian understanding of Spirit, who is the union of Father and Son and who dwells in our hearts. He recognizes that the spirituality of the Spirit consists in a "consciousness" of the divine immanence and a "realization" that one is enveloped in, known and loved by the mystery of reality. Panikkar explains:

> When one has seen, felt, experienced that God is in all, that all is in God, that nevertheless God is nothing of that which is . . . then one is close to realisation, to the authentic *advaita* experience, which, like all true experience, cannot be communicated or expressed by words, concepts of thoughts.[45]

Here a kind of passivity is appropriate to the spirituality, for faith in the Spirit, Panikkar explains, cannot be formulated; it too is silent: "Its only way

44. Ibid., 52.
45. Ibid., 37.

is silence—the silence of words no doubt but also that of desires, that of action, the silence, finally, of being, of wishing to be, the total silence of the will to be."[46] In this way, then, Panikkar summarizes the spiritualities of the world religions in terms of apophaticism, personalism, and divine immanence and identifies these three essential dimensions of spirituality with the three persons of the Trinity: Father, Son, and Holy Spirit. Here Panikkar identifies both the inspiration and the hope for the meeting of religions that is, he believes, the *kairos* of our time.[47]

Ewert Cousins describes Panikkar's trinitarian theology as "advaitic Trinitarianism, for it developed out of his own inner dialogue with the advaitic tradition of Hinduism, and yet remains, I believe, authentically trinitarian in the full orthodox Christian sense of that term."[48] Cousins thus argues:

> In this sense, then, Panikkar's trinitarian theology merits a distinctly Oriental, and most appropriately, Hindu adjective. From this advaitic perspective, Panikkar views the inner life of God and the panorama of the finite world, highlighting aspects that have remained veiled from classical western theology and philosophy, thus bringing to light newly available links between Eastern and Western thought. It is precisely this advaitic dimension that expands Panikkar's thought to reflect the more comprehensive universal structure of reality which he believes is emerging into human consciousness in our time.[49]

Whatever the ultimate assessment of the merits or limitations of Panikkar's analysis of the world religions and their spiritualities, Panikkar's point, and the point that we want to highlight here, is that, as he explains, "the Trinity, then, may be considered as a junction where the authentic spiritual dimensions of all religions meet."[50] In Panikkar's approach to a theology of religions, the plurality of divine persons in the Trinity is the ultimate foundation for the plurality of world religions. Indeed, in Panikkar's theology of religious pluralism, the Trinity itself *is* the *ontological* foundation for the very existence of religious pluralism.

Most important of all, a trinitarian approach of this kind offers a comprehensive, constructive and hopeful meeting ground for the religions, recognizing their different spiritualities, and without doing violence to their

46. Ibid., 65.
47. Ibid., 55.
48. Ewert Cousins, "Panikkar's Advaitic Trinitarianism," in *The Intercultural Challenge of Raimon Panikkar*, 120.
49. Ibid., 121.
50. Panikkar, *Trinity*, 42.

fundamental intuitions. Panikkar's trinitarian approach to interfaith dialogue offers new possibilities for understanding and appreciating the spiritual insights of other religions in their own right, not just, for example, by way of some kind of theory of "prolongation" or "fulfillment," whereby all religions find their ultimate fulfillment in Christianity. From this trinitarian perspective, he argues, the Christian is able to recognize and respond to the different spiritual traditions and their spiritualties as interrelated dimensions of each other. While finding a point of convergence of the great spiritual traditions in a theology of the Trinity, his approach also recognizes and respects their irreducible differences.[51]

Panikkar stresses that, in being open and responsive to the trinitarian dimensions of other religions, we as Christians are prompted to examine our own tradition more deeply and also to grow in our appreciation of the mystery of the Trinity. In other words, a trinitarian approach to interfaith dialogue, he suggests, leads not only to greater dialogue but also to a deeper self-awareness and understanding on the part of Christians. Panikkar would thus have us understand that Christianity has no monopoly on trinitarian understanding. Indeed, Panikkar would persuade us that ultimately we as Christians have not plumbed the depths of Christian faith in the Trinity unless and until we have entered into encounter with the spiritual experience of Buddhism, Hinduism, Islam, and, of course, Judaism.

Ewert Cousins points out that Panikkar's innovative approach is in keeping with the well-established universalizing tendency in the tradition of Christian theology.[52] Cousins recalls the teaching of Augustine and later Augustinianism, wherein vestiges of the triune Creator of the cosmos are recognized in the physical world, in the human person, and in human interpersonal community. The plurality of world religions fits within this "vestige doctrine" and, Cousins notes, brings it to a new level. Cousins also recounts the trinitarian doctrine of creation of the Greek fathers, whereby creation is recognized as a trinitarian act of the Father, as the primordial cause of all things, through the Son and Spirit. (Recall that Irenaeus said that God works with his two hands, Son and Spirit [*Against Heresies* 4.20.1].[53]) Redemption and sanctification are also recognized as the dynamic trinitarian act of the

51. See Raimon Panikkar, "The Jordan, the Tiber and the Ganges: Three Kairological Moments of Christic Self-Consciousness," in *The Myth of Christian Uniqueness: Toward a Pluralistic Theology of Religions*, ed. John Hick and Paul Knitter (Maryknoll, N.Y.: Orbis Books, 1987), 89-116; here he engages the metaphor of these three sacred rivers to speak about salvation and the plurality of religious traditions.

52. Ewert Cousins, "The Trinity and World Religions," *Journal of Ecumenical Studies* 7 (1970): 476-98; see also idem, "Panikkar's Advaitic Trinitarianism," 119-30.

53. In *Ante-Nicene Fathers*, 1:487.

three persons. Third, Cousins identifies the strategy of appropriation, which emerged in trinitarian theology in the West, whereby, although all essential divine attributes or perfections are possessed by all three persons, certain attributes are associated with or appropriated to individual divine persons by virtue of the inner-trinitarian processions or their roles in salvation history, for example, power to the Father, wisdom to the Son, and love to the Holy Spirit. Cousins concludes that Panikkar's proposal to situate a theology of non-Christian religions in the context of a theology of the Trinity sits comfortably with the tradition of Christian thought whereby everything in creation is seen as coming from and reflecting its trinitarian creator, the Trinity of the divine persons. Panikkar himself presses further: "Just as traditional theology speaks of a *creatio continua*, we could by analogy envision a continuous incarnation, not only in the flesh, but also in the acts and events of all creatures. Every being is a *christophany*."[54]

Panikkar's thought is complex and continues to evolve in a highly creative way that is uniquely his own. The relationship between the Jesus of history and the Christ of faith becomes problematic, however, where he speaks of Christ as not limited to the historical person of Jesus.[55] At this point, his thought stands in real tension with the central tenet of Christian faith that understands that the historical Jesus *is* the Christ of faith. Given the necessarily limited scope of our exploration here, we shall simply advert to the fact that there are some problematic areas in his theology and leave an exploration of his contribution at this point.[56] To bring our brief explorations of Panikkar's contribution to a conclusion, it is fair and indeed important to say, however, that Panikkar's trinitarian approach to a theology of other religions and to interfaith dialogue positively allows for religious pluralism by grounding the patterns of religious experience in their plurality and yet affirming a deeper unity in that diversity, while avoiding the problems of Rahner's notion of the "anonymous Christian." In Panikkar's theology, the Trinity emerges as the comprehensive reality within which to situate and make sense of human spirituality as expressed in the various patterns of religious experience. It is a highly significant contribution to a Christian theology of world religions. As Rowan Williams explains:

> In showing how a certain kind of practical pluralism can be unconditionally faithful to the gospel, and in warning us away from the lust for reli-

---

54. Panikkar, "Jordan, the Tiber and the Ganges," 114.

55. See, e.g., *Unknown Christ of Hinduism;* and "Jordan, the Tiber and the Ganges."

56. For a helpful critique of Panikkar's thought, see Jacques Dupuis, *Jesus Christ at the Encounter of World Religions*, trans. Robert R. Barr, Faith Meets Faith (Maryknoll, N.Y.: Orbis Books, 1991), 183-90.

> gious Grand Theory, Panikkar does an exceptional service to authentic engagement between traditions *in* their particularity, in a way not to be found among programmatic relativists.[57]

Some would reject this trinitarian approach as yet another form of Christian imperialism by which the non-Christian religious traditions are subsumed under the Christian categories of a trinitarian theology, albeit perhaps more subtly than in the case of Rahner's notion of anonymous Christian, in which all are subsumed under Christian christological categories. But again, we make no apology for adopting an explicitly *Christian* perspective. The challenge is to hold to the Christian tenet regarding the uniqueness of Jesus Christ as universal savior while constructing a distinctly Christian theology of religions and for interfaith dialogue that is neither vacuous nor imperialistic.

Jacques Dupuis:
The Enduring Universal Action of the Word and the Spirit

Jacques Dupuis SJ, whose trinitarian Christology we treated earlier, is chiefly concerned to construct a theology of world religions.[58] His works include *Jesus Christ at the Encounter of World Religions, Toward a Christian Theology of Religious Pluralism*, and *Christianity and the Religions: From Confrontation to Dialogue.*[59]

---

57. Willliams, "Trinity and Pluralism," 180.

58. For a brief autobiographical introduction to this central concern in Dupuis' theology, see "My Pilgrimage in Mission," *International Bulletin of Missionary Research* 27 (2003): 168-71.

59. See nn. 4 and 56 above; and *Christianity and the Religions: From Confrontation to Dialogue* (Maryknoll, N.Y.: Orbis Books, 2002). The book *Toward a Christian Theology of Religious Pluralism* led to an investigation by the Vatican Congregation for the Doctrine of the Faith. In the Notification (dated January 24, 2001), Joseph Cardinal Ratzinger, Prefect of the Congregation for the Doctrine of the Faith, states that members of the Congregation "found that his book contained notable ambiguities and difficulties on important doctrinal points, which could lead a reader to erroneous or harmful opinions" (preface; see http://www.natcath.com/NCR_Online/documents/notification.htm). Admittedly, the term "religious pluralism" has unfortunate connotations of relativist pluralist models of religions, such as that proposed by John Hick, wherein all religions are regarded as partial and incomplete interpretations of a transcendent reality, and wherein no religion may legitimately claim to be superior to any other religions. See, e.g., John Hick, *An Interpretation of Religion: The Challenge of Other Religions* (Oxford: Basil Blackwell, 1989). But this kind of theological relativism is not Dupuis' position. In his later book *Christianity and the Religions,* Dupuis moves away from the term "religious pluralism" and describes his theology in terms of "inclusive pluralism" (p. 87). Whatever the term, Dupuis reiterates that he seeks to combine the two fundamental—though apparently contradictory—affirmations: "the universal constitutive character of the Christ event in the order of salvation and the saving significance of the religious traditions in a plurality of principle of the religious traditions within the one manifold plan of God for humankind" (p. 95); idem, "'Christianity and the Religions' Revisited," *Louvain Studies* 28 (2003): 367-68.

We have seen that a critical question in our search for a Christian theology of non-Christian religions and of religious pluralism is how to combine recognition of both Jesus Christ as universal savior and the salvific significance of other religions traditions. How not to put Christian faith in jeopardy in our quest for a Christian theology of non-Christian religions? Christian faith recognizes God's universal self-manifestation and self-gift in the person of Jesus Christ and affirms Jesus Christ as the one unique universal savior whose decisive role in human history is unsurpassable. Vatican II spoke of "seeds of the Word" (AG 11, 15) and of "a ray of that truth which enlightens everyone" (NA 2), which is found in the other religions, but it left unanswered the question of the theological significance of non-Christian religions and their salvific efficacy per se. The question now is whether, and if so how, a Christian theology of religions can recognize other religious traditions as true mediators of the mystery of salvation in Jesus Christ for their members. Can we as Christians recognize those traditions as channels or paths through which the saving grace of God is encountered?

Dupuis explores how "those elements of truth and grace and which are, as it were, a secret presence of God" to which Vatican II referred (AG 9) can be discovered in the other religious traditions. Like Panikkar, he proposes a trinitarian approach to the question, but he adopts a very different perspective. Whereas Panikkar takes the different spiritualities of the world religions as his point of departure, Dupuis takes the history of salvation as the framework within which to consider the question of the plurality of religious traditions. Dupuis would persuade us to consider what he describes as the trinitarian rhythm of God's dealings with humanity throughout the history of creation, as manifested in the active presence of the Word of God throughout history (John 1:1-5, 9) and in the universal dynamic action of the Spirit of God in the world. From the very beginning of creation, Dupuis argues, God has revealed Godself to humankind, through God's Word and God's Spirit. Dupuis thus seeks to attend expressly to the pneumatological as well as the christological dimensions of the history of salvation and their interaction and complementarity, as they bear on the presence of the mystery of salvation in non-Christian religious traditions. Moreover, as we noted above, for Dupuis, the question is not simply whether non-Christian religions have salvific efficacy, but whether non-Christian religions have positive significance as part of God's plan for creation. In other words, is religious pluralism something that exists not just *de facto* (in fact), not just incidentally or accidentally, so to speak, but *de iure* (in principle)?

Dupuis maintains that without question God's self-communication in the person of Jesus Christ is the apex and summit of God's self-revelation in salvation history. In the person of Jesus Christ, in that unique and unsurpassable event, God's divine self-communication reaches its culmination in the history of the cosmos. As the incarnate Son of God, Jesus Christ is constitutive of universal salvation.[60] He is the Savior of the world. He is the fullness of revelation. Therein, Dupuis insists, lie his unique significance and the key for interpreting all salvation history. But Dupuis argues that God's self-revelation in Jesus Christ does not exhaust the divine mystery. So, while Jesus Christ is constitutive of the salvation of all, this does not exclude other saving figures or traditions. Dupuis explains:

> The qualitative fullness—let us say, the intensity—of the revelation in Jesus Christ is no obstacle, even after the historical event, to a continuing divine self-revelation through the prophets and sages of other religious traditions, as, for example, through the prophet Muhammad. That self-revelation has occurred, and continues to occur, in history. No revelation, however, either before or after Christ can either surpass or equal the one vouchsafed in Jesus Christ, the divine Son, incarnate.[61]

Dupuis proceeds to situate a theology of world religions within the broader trinitarian framework of God's gracious dealings with humanity throughout history. God's involvement with humankind throughout history is marked, Dupuis stresses, with a trinitarian rhythm. Dupuis recalls that scriptures attest, in John 1:1-3, that God created all things through God's Word, who throughout history, before as well as after the incarnation, has been "the true light that, by coming into the world, enlightens everyone" (John 1:9). Dupuis notes that the true light here refers not to the Word incarnate but to the Word, who is known in the Jewish scriptures as the Wisdom of God. He therefore maintains that the action of the Word is not constrained by the particularity of the incarnation event and that, similarly, the Holy Spirit is universally present and operative throughout salvation history and is not exhausted or limited by being communicated through the risen Christ. In other words, both the Word and Spirit of God are universally present and active before and after the incar-

60. Readers will recall from the previous chapter on Christology that Dupuis eschews the use of the word "absolute" (since only God is truly "absolute") and prefers to speak of Christ as "universal" and "constitutive." Similarly, in reference to the Christ-event, he prefers "decisive" rather than "definitive." Dupuis does *not* mean, however, that Christ as savior is relative and that there are various other more or less equal saviors and revealers.

61. Jacques Dupuis, *Toward a Christian Theology of Religious Pluralism*, 249-50, also 388. The Notification states: "It must be firmly believed that Jesus Christ is the mediator, the fulfilment and the completion of revelation. It is therefore contrary to the Catholic faith to maintain that revelation in Jesus Christ (or the revelation of Jesus Christ) is limited, incomplete or imperfect" (a. 3).

nation of the Word in the person of Jesus Christ.[62] Unlike Panikkar who, as we have seen, eschews a christological approach to the question of non-Christian religions, Dupuis thus proposes a trinitarian Christology, a Christology grounded in the intra-trinitarian relationships, as an avenue of approach to a Christian theology of religious pluralism. As Dupuis explains:

> A Trinitarian Christology model opens the way for distinct considerations which, though closely interrelated, can nevertheless be clearly distinguished. Divine grace or salvation "bears within itself both a Christological aspect and a pneumatological one" (*Dominum et Vivificantem* 53). . . . This means that God's saving action, which always operates within the framework of a unified plan, is one and at the same time multifaceted. It never prescinds from the Christ-event, in which it finds its highest historical density. Yet the action of the Word of God is not constrained by its historically becoming human in Jesus Christ; nor is the Spirit's work in history limited to its outpouring upon the world by the risen and exalted Christ.[63]

Without denying that Jesus Christ is the apex of the divine self-communication, Dupuis argues that the incarnation, the life, and the paschal mystery of Jesus Christ do not exhaust the revealing and saving power of God. Nor, he insists, is there a question of separating or dividing the action of God's Word from God's Spirit and of constructing a Christology and pneumatology so as to suggest two distinct economies of divine–human relationships for Christians and for the members of other traditions.[64] Dupuis argues that it is rather a matter of distinguishing the two inseparable and intrinsically related aspects of God's saving activity in the economy as complementary aspects of God's plan for salvation and of recognizing the combined action of both God's Word and God's Spirit in salvation history. (The concern remains, however, as to whether Dupuis gives sufficient emphasis to the Spirit as the Spirit of Jesus, the incarnate Word.)

This trinitarian approach then affords Dupuis the possibility of viewing other religious traditions as mediators of God's salvation, mediators of God's saving activity in the economy, through the presence of the Word of God and of the Spirit of God.[65] Having begun with an exploration of the active pres-

---

62. The Notification states: "It is . . . contrary to the Catholic faith . . . to maintain that there is a salvific activity of the Word as such in his divinity, independent of the humanity of the Incarnate Word" (a. 2).

63. Dupuis, *Toward a Christian Theology of Religious Pluralism,* 316. For a more detailed discussion of Dupuis' Christology, see chap. 4 above.

64. Dupuis, *Toward a Christian Theology of Religious Pluralism,* 207.

65. The Notification states: "It is consistent with Catholic doctrine to hold that the seeds of truth and goodness that exist in other religions are a certain participation in truths contained in the revelation of or in Jesus Christ. However, it is erroneous to hold that such elements of truth and goodness, or some of them, do not derive ultimately from the source-mediation of Jesus Christ" (a. 4).

ence of the Word of God in history (John 1:1-5, 9) and recognizing the universal abiding action and presence of the Spirit of God throughout world history, Dupuis proposes a theology of religious pluralism in which the other religions traditions *converge* in God's one creative plan. He argues that it is legitimate to speak of "complementarity and convergence" between Christianity and the religious traditions. From this perspective, other religious traditions emerge as "ways" of salvation, and religious pluralism emerges as not just *de facto* but *de iure*, intended and willed by God.[66]

A trinitarian Christology, Dupuis argues, not only allows a deeper appreciation and a more positive assessment of the richness and complexity of religious pluralism. It enables us to move beyond a narrow ecclesiocentric (church-centered) view of other religions and their adherents, as expressed in that ancient axiom *extra ecclesiam nulla salus*, to what Dupuis describes as a regnocentric (Reign of God, or Kingdom-centered) approach, wherein the Reign of God (for which the church exists and which its mission serves) is the decisive point of reference. The church continues to have a vital role in the accomplishment of the Kingdom: it is the sacrament of the Kingdom, and its mission, including interfaith dialogue, is in the service of the Kingdom. As Pope John Paul II taught: "the Church is not an end unto herself, since she is ordered towards the kingdom of God of which she is the seed, sign and instrument" (*Redemptoris Missio* 18) Here too, as in Panikkar's theology, interfaith dialogue emerges as mutually enriching.[67] Dupuis explains:

> Christians have something to gain from dialogue. They will benefit in two ways. On the one hand, their own faith will be enriched. Through the experience and testimony of the others, they will be able to discover at greater depth certain aspects, certain dimensions, of the Divine Mystery that they had perceived less clearly and that have been communicated less clearly by the Christian tradition. At the same time, they will gain a purification of their faith. The shock of the encounter will often raise questions, force Christians to revise gratuitous assumptions, and destroy deep-rooted prejudices or overthrow certain overly narrow conceptions or outlooks.[68]

In bringing this part of our exploration to a conclusion, we note that Dupuis, in constructing a theology of religious pluralism, explicitly com-

---

66. The Notification states: "It must be firmly believed that the Church is sign and instrument of salvation for all people. It is contrary to the Catholic faith to consider the different religions of the world as ways of salvation complementary to the Church" (a. 6). Further, "to hold that these religions, considered as such, are ways of salvation, has no foundation in Catholic theology, also because they contain omissions, insufficiencies and errors regarding fundamental truths about God, man and the world" (a. 8).

67. See Dupuis, *Christianity and the Religions*, 232-35.

68. Ibid., 234.

bines the essential Christian tenet of the universal saving significance of Jesus Christ with the conviction that other religious traditions have saving power for their adherents. His theology rests on a distinctly trinitarian understanding of God, wherein each of the divine persons is present and active in its own distinctive way throughout salvation history. Dupuis concludes with the encouragement to interfaith prayer.[69] Such was the spirit of John Paul II's words, at the meeting of Buddhists, Muslims, Jews, Hindus, and representatives of other religious traditions for the World Day of Prayer for Peace at Assisi in 1986: "Every authentic prayer is called forth by the Holy Spirit, who is mysteriously present in the heart of every human person."[70]

Another question arises at this point: On what foundation can this plurality of religions *de iure*, in principle, rest? Dupuis insists that Christian faith in a trinitarian God, the trinitarian plurality of persons, of itself provides no necessary foundation for religious pluralism, nor the evidently plural nature of reality itself. Rather, Dupuis explains:

> It belongs to the overflowing communication of the Triune God to humankind to prolong outside the divine life that plural communication intrinsic to that life itself. That God spoke "in many and various ways" before speaking through his Son (Heb 1:1) is not incidental; nor is the plural character of God's self-manifestation merely a thing of the past. For the decisiveness of the Son's advent in the flesh in Jesus Christ does not cancel the universal presence and action of the Word and the Spirit. Religious pluralism in principle rests on the immensity of a God who is love.[71]

Dupuis thus recognizes that the reality of religious pluralism finds its foundation in the mystery of God who is Love. Therein lies the mystery, as Dupuis would persuade us, a mystery of love. "Religious pluralism in principle"—in other words, a principled religious pluralism—Dupuis argues, "is based on the immensity of God who is Love and communication."[72]

---

69. See Dupuis, *Christianity and the Religions*, chap. 10. While few Vatican II documents advert to the possibility that Catholics themselves might benefit significantly from interfaith dialogue, John Paul II speaks of interreligious dialogue as "a method and means of mutual knowledge and enrichment" (*Redemptoris Missio*, 55).

70. *Interreligious Dialogue: The Official Teaching of the Catholic Church (1963-1995)*, ed. Francesco Gioia (Boston: Pauline Books & Media, 1994), no. 572. This is a most helpful resource for those who wish to study developments in the official teachings on interfaith dialogue.

71. Dupuis, *Toward a Christian Theology of Religious Pluralism*, 387.

72. Dupuis, *Christianity and the Religions*, 254-55.

CONCLUSION

The phenomenon of religious pluralism, so vibrantly manifest in the world's non-Christian religions, surely challenges the Christian imagination to consider the cosmic dimensions—"the breadth and the length and the height and depth" (Eph. 3:18)—of the mystery of God's love for humankind and God's will for the salvation of all. In our search for a Christian theology of non-Christian religions, we have surveyed the thought of two contemporary Catholic theologians, Raimon Panikkar and Jacques Dupuis, each of whom adopts a highly innovative explicitly trinitarian approach to the question. Panikkar adopts a more expressly theocentric (as distinct from christological) approach, while Dupuis, in what he describes as "a religious pluralism in principle,"[73] adopts an explicitly trinitarian christological approach. In each case, we have seen that a trinitarian perspective allows much greater scope within which to construct a theology of world religions.

A trinitarian approach undoubtedly affords Christian theology a much broader and more generous and gracious horizon within which to reconsider questions concerning the other world religions, compared with that afforded by more traditional fulfillment theologies, wherein the world religions find their fulfillment in the mystery of Christ. While certainly challenging the traditional Christian understanding of the mystery of Christ, the result, as Cousins has noted, is remarkably in close accord with the classical vestige doctrine of the Trinity, articulated by Augustine. Stretching beyond the confines of a narrowly Christomonistic and ecclesiocentric approach, a trinitarian imagination and approach to the question of the world religions allow a new openness, a basis for inclusiveness, a respect for diversity, a glimpse of unity, and a more hopeful horizon for genuinely dialogical interfaith encounter, as well as a new appreciation of the trinitarian depths of our own Christian religious experience.[74]

---

73. Ibid., 255.

74. The belief in God as Trinity is, of course, unique to Christianity. Though Judaism and Islam assent to the notion of God's word as spoken by the prophets, the word of God is never simply identified with God, nor is it personalized, and the Christian doctrine of God as Trinity is rejected by both. The notion of incarnation is also unacceptable in Islamic thought. Interfaith dialogue has emerged as a burgeoning field of study in recent years. For helpful discussions of the Christian doctrine of the Trinity in relation to Islam and Judaism, see Claude Geffré, "The One God of Islam and Trinitarian Monotheism," in *God, Experience and Mystery,* ed. Werner Jeanrond and Christoph Theobald with Seán Freyne and Guiseppe Ruggieri (London: SCM Press, 2001), 85-93; Robert L. Fastiggi, "The Incarnation: Muslim Objections and the Christian Response," *The Thomist* 57 (1993): 457-93; *Christianity through Non-Christian Eyes,* ed. Paul J. Griffiths, Faith Meets Faith (Maryknoll, N.Y.: Orbis Books, 1990); Hans Küng, *Christianity and the World Religions: Paths of Dialogue with Islam, Hinduism, and Buddhism,* trans. Peter Heinegg (New York: Doubleday, 1986), esp. 109-30; Michael Barnes, *The-*

FOR FURTHER READING

Cousins, Ewert. "Panikkar's Advaitic Trinitarianism." In *The Intercultural Challenge of Raimon Panikkar,* edited by Joseph Prabhu, 119-30. Maryknoll, N.Y.: Orbis Books, 1996.

———. "The Trinity and World Religions." *Journal of Ecumenical Studies* 7 (1970): 476-98.

Dupuis, Jacques. *Christianity and the Religions: From Confrontation to Dialogue.* Maryknoll, N.Y.: Orbis Books, 2002.

———. "'Christianity and the Religions' Revisited." *Louvain Studies* 28 (2003): 363-83.

———. *Jesus Christ at the Encounter of World Religions.* Translated by Robert R. Barr. Maryknoll, N.Y.: Orbis Books, 1991.

———. *Toward a Christian Theology of Religious Pluralism.* Maryknoll, N.Y.: Orbis Books, 1997.

———. "Trinitarian Christology as a Model for a Theology of Religious Pluralism." In *The Myriad Christ: Plurality and the Quest for Unity in Contemporary Christology.* Edited by T. Merrigan and J. Hears. 83-97. Leuven: Leuven University Press, 2000.

———. "'The Truth Will Make You Free': The Theology of Religious Pluralism Revisited." *Louvain Studies* 24 (1999): 211-63.

Fredericks, James L. *Faith among Faiths: Christian Theology and Non-Christian Religions.* New York/Mahwah, N.J.: Paulist Press, 1999.

Panikkar, Raimon. "The Jordan, the Tiber and the Ganges: Three Kairological Moments of Christic Self-Consciousness." In *The Myth of Christian Uniqueness: Toward a Pluralistic Theology of Religions,* edited by John Hick and Paul Knitter, 89-116. Maryknoll, N.Y.: Orbis Books, 1987.

———. *The Trinity and the Religious Experience of Man.* Maryknoll, N.Y.: Orbis Books; London: Darton, Longman & Todd, 1973.

Sullivan, Francis. *Salvation Outside the Church? Tracing the History of the Catholic Response.* Mahwah, N.J.: Paulist Press, 1992.

---

ology and the Dialogue of Religions, Cambridge Studies in Christian Doctrine (Cambridge: Cambridge University Press, 2002), esp. 205-29; Karl Rahner, "Oneness and Threefoldness of God in Discussion with Islam," *Theological Investigations,* vol. 18, trans. Edward Quinn (London: Darton, Longmann & Todd, 1983), 105-21; Karl Rahner, "Jesus of Nazareth between Jews and Christians," in *The Content of Faith: The Best of Karl Rahner's Theological Writings,* ed. Karl Lehmann and Albert Raffelt, trans. Harvey D. Egan (New York: Crossroad, 1994), 273-77; Karl Rahner and Pinchas Lapide, *Encountering Jesus—Encountering Judaism: A Dialogue,* trans. Davis Perkins (New York: Crossroad, 1987), esp. 30-36. My thanks to Harvey Egan SJ for his helpful comments in this area.

8

Trinity, Grace, and the Moral Life

Therefore be imitators of God as beloved children. And walk in love, as Christ loved us and gave himself up for us. (Eph. 5:1-2)

KARL RAHNER, one of the greatest theologians of the twentieth century, once notably observed that the doctrine of the Trinity is basically irrelevant to people's lives. According to Rahner, "despite their orthodox confession of the Trinity, Christians are, in their practical life, almost mere 'monotheists.' We must be willing to admit that, should the doctrine of the Trinity have to be dropped as false, the major part of religious literature could well remain virtually unchanged."[1] Yet our confession, as Christians, of trinitarian faith is surely incomplete unless it finds tangible and practical expression in the way we live our lives, the choices we make and the stands we take. Surely our faith in God as Trinity has practical—perhaps even radical—consequences for Christian conduct. Just as surely the trinitarian being of God cannot be irrelevant to our moral being. How, then, is trinitarian orthodoxy related to Christian orthopraxis in the real world of family, work, business, and politics, with its social demands, political and economic struggles, and moral dilemmas? This is the essential question that concerns us in this chapter. More specifically, our exploration concerns the ways in which the mystery of the Trinity explicitly informs and enlightens the mystery of our own human being and the way we conduct ourselves. And how does trinitarian faith correlate with the enabling mystery of grace and with its expression in Christian moral conduct? What issues and what principles emerge for the practical demands and the pressing moral questions we face, when moral conduct is approached from an explicitly trinitarian perspective? A more explicitly trinitarian understanding of grace and the Christian moral life is our goal.

Catherine Mowry LaCugna would persuade us that the doctrine of the Trinity is ultimately a very practical doctrine with radical consequences for

1. Karl Rahner, *The Trinity*, trans. Joseph Donceel (London: Burns & Oates, 1970), 10-11.

Christian life. As she explains: "Living faith in the God of Jesus Christ means being formed and transformed by the life of grace of God's economy: becoming persons fully in communion with all; becoming Christ to one another; becoming by the power of the Holy Spirit what God is: love unbounded, glory uncontained."[2] Our trinitarian faith, she argues, inspires and impels us to Christian community and to moral action in transforming the world. It is genuinely constitutive of the Christian moral person. Notice the explicit connection that LaCugna makes here between Trinity, grace, and orthopraxis. It is here indeed that we shall begin our exploration, at the nexus of grace.

The study of orthopraxis, of right actions and right practice in human conduct, properly belongs to the domain of ethics. It involves the task of careful reflection, discernment, and choice in regard to what we, as responsible human subjects, should do in the face of moral dilemmas. The study of ethics becomes moral theology when situated in a distinctly theological context and given a properly theological orientation. Moral theology understands the moral life in terms of the divine origin, form, and finality of human life. Its proper concern is that which supports and fosters the flourishing of human beings, as uniquely created in the image of God, and indeed the flourishing of the cosmos, as the creation of God. It understands moral action and the moral life as the life of grace, directed and enabled by God, and indeed conformed by grace to the divine wisdom and love.

THE CLASSICAL APPROACH TO A THEOLOGY OF GRACE

Grace translates the Latin *gratia* and the Greek *charis* of the Scriptures, where it is primarily a Pauline term, occurring far more frequently in the Pauline corpus (where it features in the greeting at the beginning and in the farewell at the conclusion of almost every letter) than in the rest of the Scriptures. [3] There, in the Scriptures, grace is the gift of God. It is a new life and a new way of being. In early Christian centuries, an understanding of grace was articulated in terms of sharing in the divine nature, re-creation in Christ through the Spirit, forgiveness of sin, and, particularly in the East, deification (*theopoiēsis*), a notion that is fundamentally founded on the incarnation of

2. Catherine Mowry LaCugna, *God for Us: The Trinity and Christian Life* (New York: HarperCollins, 1991), 377.

3. For a helpful introduction to a theology of grace, see Roger Haight, *The Experience and Language of Grace* (New York: Paulist Press, 1979); Stephen J. Duffy, *The Dynamics of Grace: Perspectives in Theological Anthropology*, New Theology Series 3 (Collegeville, Minn.: Liturgical Press, A Michael Glazier Book, 1993).

Christ. As Irenaeus writes: Christ became "what we are, that He might bring us to be even what He is Himself" (*Against Heresies* 5, preface),[4] and as, later, Athanasius, the great defender of Nicene faith, would reiterate: "For He was made man that we might be made God" (*De Incarnatione Verbi Dei* 54).[5]

Grace emerged as a distinct theological theme with Augustine (354-430), largely in response to the conflict with the British monk Pelagius. Pelagius was teaching in Rome in the late fourth and early fifth centuries and raised the perennial question regarding human behavior and the source of good and evil, and the related issues of freedom, sin, and grace. Pelagius taught that human freedom enabled the human person to choose between good and evil and that good deeds merited grace. Human freedom was thus able, according to Pelagius, to decide between good and evil. Augustine, however, rejected Pelagius's optimism in regard to human freedom and autonomy and argued that human freedom was inherently constrained and entangled in a web of sin and that human nature, and with it human freedom, is fundamentally disordered as a consequence of inherited sinfulness (original sin).[6] "Our heart is not in our own power," he argued (*On the Gift of Perseverence* 13).[7] Grace, as he understood it, is primarily a dynamic liberating internal force; it is a delight in the good. It is not merited by good deeds; rather, good deeds are themselves the works of grace.

Augustine, who is acclaimed in the Latin church as Doctor of Grace, indelibly shaped the doctrine of grace in the West for centuries to come. One of Augustine's most frequently cited scriptural references—"God's love has been poured into our hearts through the Holy Spirit who has been given to us" (Rom. 5:5)—expresses the heart of the matter. Augustine recognized grace as the sheer gift of God (*gratia Dei gratuita*), given totally gratuitously to the human person. Grace, Augustine taught, comes to the human person, utterly underserved and by the sheer gratuity and radical initiative of God. For Augustine, it is God's grace that is the ultimate source of self-transcending love in the world, for love of neighbor, and hence of goodness in the world.

Augustine's theology of grace is set in the context of his understanding of

---

4. In *Ante-Nicene Fathers*, 1:526.

5. In *Nicene and Post-Nicene Fathers*, 2nd series, 4:65. See also *Orationes Contra Arianos,* Oratio II, 70, in *Nicene and Post-Nicene Fathers*, 2nd series, 4:386; and *Letter* 60.4, in *Nicene and Post-Nicene Fathers*, 2nd series, 4:576.

6. See Augustine, *On Original Sin,* in *Nicene and Post-Nicene Fathers*, 1st series, 5:237-55.

7. "Non enim est in potestate nostra cor nostrum et nostrae cogitationes," in *Nicene and Post-Nicene Fathers*, 1st series, 5:538. See also Augustine, *Against Julian* 2.8.23, where the text is "non enim in potestate nostra est cor nostrum, et nostrae cogitationes," in *The Fathers of the Church*, vol. 35, trans. Matthew A. Schumacher (Washington, D.C.: Catholic University of America Press, 1957), 84. Here Augustine quotes Ambrose (*De fuga saeculi* 1.1). My thanks to Stephen Duffy and to Raymond Canning for their advice here.

original sin and its effects on human nature, human will and human freedom. The human person, because of inherent sinfulness, is unable to do good without the gift of grace. Grace thus corrects nature; it is healing and enabling. It effects a reordering of human nature—a reordering of will and freedom—thus orienting the human will toward the good and enabling good works, the works of grace, and meritorious acts. In other words, it is grace that enables one to perform virtuous actions and to lead a virtuous life. It is not merited by virtuous deeds; rather, such deeds are made possible by grace. Grace is thus the enabling mystery, the source of, not the reward for, good works. Augustine recalls the words of Scriptures: "What do you have that you did not receive? And if you received it, why do you boast as if it were not a gift?" (1 Cor. 4:7). His understanding of life as guided by grace finds expression in the prayer: "Command what you wish, but give what you command" (*Confessions* 10.29).

Augustine's polemic against Pelagius sparked the centuries-long debate concerning the relation of nature and grace, and his theology of grace effectively established the parameters for the development of medieval theology, setting the foundation for the thirteenth-century distinction between the natural and supernatural orders. Thomas Aquinas and the highly technical language of Scholasticism then determined the Roman Catholic understanding of grace for several centuries to come. For Thomas Aquinas, as for Augustine, grace is primarily an interior reality.[8] But for Thomas, grace is not just sanative or healing of inherently sinful human nature; it is elevating. It is neither simply a remedy nor a medicinal cure for sin, nor the opposite of sin. In other words, grace does not simply restore human nature to what it should be; rather, it adds to nature and builds on it. It effects an ontological elevation of human nature, by conferring a new nature on the human person, which is ordered to a supernatural end. Grace is thus not simply something that is added onto, but rather a change or modification of the human spirit, inhering in the human person, and causing the human person to exist in a new way (Aquinas, *STh* I-II, q. 110, a. 2, ad 3). Augustine's more experientially fashioned notion of grace, which is expressed in terms of cure or healing and as a force in human life, thus yields in Thomas's theology to a more ontologically and teleologically fashioned notion of grace as supernatural elevation of the human person.

By ordering the human person to a supernatural end, as distinct from the

8. For a helpful introduction to Thomas Aquinas's theology of grace, see Aidan Nichols, *Discovering Aquinas: An Introduction to His Life, Work and Influence* (London: Darton, Longman & Todd, 2002). For more detailed discussions of Aquinas's theology, see Donald Juvenal Merriell, *To the Image of the Trinity: A Study in the Development of Aquinas' Teaching* (Toronto: Pontifical Institute of Mediaeval Studies, 1990).

natural end of the human person to which human nature is naturally ordered, grace is not just healing and curing but sanctifying and divinizing. This sanctifying, divinizing role of grace realizes the divine life of God in the human person, our graced growth into the being of God. It effects a real participation in God, in the very nature and goodness of God. Through grace, the human person's mode of being is thus radically changed and elevated into the divine life (Aquinas, *STh* I-II, q. 110, a. 1). The graced human person really possesses God's love and participates in the divine nature. As Thomas explains: "grace is nothing else than a certain shared similitude to the divine nature" (*STh* III, q. 62, a. 1).[9] It is "nothing else than a certain beginning of glory in us" (*STh* II-II, q. 24, a. 3, ad 2).[10] Grace is necessary because the human person, without grace, is naturally teleologically unable to attain the supernatural goal of participation in God, the communion with God in the divine life, to which we are called and destined.

Thomas recognized that the gift of grace is intrinsically related to the missions of the divine persons, which have grace as their "common root" (*STh* I, q. 43, a. 6) Following Augustine, Aquinas taught that the missions are prolongations of the inner-trinitarian processions into the economy. By means of the invisible missions, reaching into creation, the Word of Truth and the Spirit of Love are sent to, communicated to, the human person. Through the divine missions, the Trinity of the three divine persons comes to abide in the human person and enters into the very process of our human self-becoming. In this way, through the gift of grace that is given in and through the divine missions, the human person is drawn into the divine life and communion, and progressively conformed to the Trinity of divine persons, transformed into the likeness of God. Human nature is thus brought to its fulfillment and perfection—hence the adage: *gratia perfecit naturam,* grace perfects nature.[11] Grace does not destroy nature but rather builds on nature and brings it to its perfection. In Thomas's theology of grace, nature and grace are not sealed and separated from each other. Grace is not superimposed on nature; the two are distinct but not separate, just as in the one person of Jesus Christ, the divine and the human natures are distinct but not separate.

The divine self-communication of the triune God thus emerges in Aquinas's theology as the foundation, form, and the goal of grace. Grace then functions as the theological leitmotif and the organizing principle, the unify-

9. Here Aquinas speaks of grace in the context of the sacraments.

10. Here, too, grace perfects nature. Aquinas explains: "Nature is not done away, but perfected by glory" (*STh* II-II, q. 26, a. 13).

11. See *STh* I, q. 1, a. 8, ad 2. Indeed one could argue that Aquinas's use of the psychological analogy is itself illustrative of this central claim that grace perfects nature. For Aquinas's treatment of grace, see *STh* I-II, qq. 109-14.

ing thread, for the Angelic Doctor's *Summa Theologiae*.[12] As Stephen Duffy explains: "The entire sweep of the *Summa* moves toward this goal: the vision of God in Godself and of creation in God, the free participation of humanity in the happiness of its God. Grace is the teleological dynamism in creation."[13] The subtlety of Aquinas's understanding of the distinction, without separation, of grace and nature was, however, lost in what emerged as a dualistic approach to a theology of grace in the standard scholastic manuals, wherein the supernatural order, as a realm that is essentially distinct from and extrinsic to the realm of the natural order, was understood to be remote from and inaccessible to human consciousness and experience. According to the logic of mainstream Scholasticism, grace, as supernatural, by definition exceeds human experience, and therefore grace and the operation of grace do not enter into human consciousness. What human beings experience in this world, from this perspective, is simply nature; grace does not and cannot enter into human consciousness and is extrinsic to human experience. The relationship between grace and nature was thus understood as rather like a double-decker bus or a two-storey building, wherein one section or compartment is juxtaposed on top of another, with one layer hermetically sealed and superimposed above the other, a far cry from Aquinas's understanding. Grace thus came to be understood in terms of a purely entitative (ontic) elevation of human nature, ordering the human person to a supernatural end. This elevation to the *supernatural* order was considered to have no ontological effect on our *human* nature. Given that the *supernatural* order was by definition remote from *natural* human consciousness and experience, grace was assumed to be imperceptible to human consciousness. Its remoteness from human experience also meant that it had little practical significance for Christian life. Similarly, there was no notion, in this radically extrinsicist theology of grace, that grace effected a personal relation between the graced human person and the divine persons of the indwelling Trinity. The reality of the gift of grace was therefore not articulated in a distinctly trinitarian way. Indeed, there was no intrinsic connection in this manual approach between grace and our experience of God's self-communication in Christ and the Holy Spirit.

KARL RAHNER: GRACE AS THE DIVINE SELF-COMMUNICATION

In the twentieth century, in response to the scholastic manual approach to grace, Karl Rahner sought to retrieve and refashion the notion of grace, rein-

12. See Thomas F. O'Meara, "Grace as a Theological Structure in the *Summa Theologiae* of Thomas Aquinas," *Recherches de Théologie ancienne et médiévale* 55 (1988): 130-53.

13. Duffy, *Dynamics of Grace*, 155.

vesting it with explicitly trinitarian meaning and dynamism. Rahner insists that God is not only trinitarian in Godself but also trinitarian in God's self-communication to us in grace. He would thus have us understand that the giver of grace is in fact the gift, the divine self-gift, the divine indwelling. In other words, God's offer of grace is nothing less than the offer of Godself in interpersonal communication with us. Grace is not something; it is Someone—God imparting Godself to us (uncreated grace). It is not just imparted virtue or a created quality (in other words, created grace). It is God given directly as Godself, bringing us to participate in the divine life. Indeed, this divinization is the fulfillment of our humanization; thus it is that grace perfects nature. Rahner thus reestablished the primary meaning of grace in terms of God's presence to and indwelling in the human person, shifting the emphasis from created to uncreated grace. Grace is the divine self-communication. It is God communicating Godself to the human person. A theology of grace is then necessarily articulated in personalist trinitarian terms.

An understanding of grace as God's free, unmerited, and forgiving self-offer to every person as an existential reality—not by nature but by grace of God's universal saving will—lies at the heart of Rahner's theology.[14] Rahner recognized that one of the conditions of the possibility of the offer or gift of grace is that the human person is created in such a way that we are open to and capable of accepting and receiving this gift of the divine self-communication. Indeed, Karl Rahner proposed an understanding of the human person as "openness" to being as such, in other words, orientation to transcendent mystery.[15] As created spirit, the human person is not limited in desiring infinite truth and good, but is open—"naturally," we might say—to God's self-gift, should that be offered, and enabled by grace to accept it. Rahner then locates the experience of grace in the strivings of the human spirit for fulfillment. Grace is experienced, he explains, not as grace per se, but rather in the dynamism of human self-transcendence. The transcendence of the human spirit serves as the vehicle for the operation of grace. In other words, grace is hidden in the strivings of the human spirit for fulfillment and in the stirrings and dynamism of human self-transcendence. Rahner explains:

14. This understanding of grace as God's self-communication, at least as offer and invitation, to every human person, as an innermost constitutive element of his/her very being, is what is described in theology as the "supernatural existential." It means that, by virtue of God's universal saving will, there is no such thing as pure human nature, the offer of God's self-communication having been made to each human person, and constituting a supernatural existential in each person. Nature, for Rahner, is thus "a remainder concept."

15. This understanding of the human person as created in such a way as to be open to the possibility of the offer of God's self-communication is what is described as the "obediential potency." The notion goes back to Augustine. The ultimate expression of human being's obediential potency is, of course, the hypostatic union.

> The initial elements of such a fulfilment are already present: the experience of infinite longings, of radical optimism, of unquenchable discontent, of the torment of the insufficiency of everything attainable, of the radical protest against death, the experience of being confronted with an absolute love precisely where it is lethally incomprehensible and seems to be silent and aloof, the experience of a radical guilt and of a still abiding hope etc. These elements are in fact tributary to that divine force which impels the created spirit—by grace—to an absolute fulfilment. Hence in them grace is experienced *and* the natural being of man. For the essence of man is such that it is experienced where grace is experienced, since grace is only experienced where the spirit naturally is. And vice versa: where spirit is experienced in the actual order of things, it is a supernaturally elevated spirit.[16]

In other words, the strivings of the human spirit are the strivings of our graced nature; their ultimate horizon is God. Nature never exists apart from grace. The supernatural order is therefore neither alien nor remote from human existence and experience. The human person, be he/she Christian or non-Christian, experiences grace—though not as grace per se,[17] for grace is indistinguishable from the stirrings of human transcendentality—in the love, the longings, the hopes, the strivings for truth and goodness, as well as in the emptiness and the loneliness, which accompany a life that is lived in self-transcending love and commitment to love of neighbor. Rahner thus understands that grace works in and through human self-transcendence and, concomitantly, that transcendence is always graced. Nature and grace, though distinct, are inseparable co-inhering constitutive dimensions of our human existence. Grace then does indeed affect our conscious life. It has a perceptible effect on human consciousness. The entitative elevation to the supernatural order, which grace, as the offer of God's self-communication, effects in us, transforms human existence and results in a change in our consciousness, in our awareness of ourselves and of God, even if that awareness remains implicit and unthematized.

We now return to the psychological analogy as a helpful explanatory tool in trinitarian theology, for we shall find that it also proves most helpful in understanding the dynamics of grace in achieving the transformation that grace effects in the human person.

---

16. Karl Rahner, "Nature and Grace," in *Theological Investigations*, vol. 4, trans. Kevin Smyth (London: Darton, Longman & Todd, 1974), 183-84.

17. Rahner stresses that "the possibility of experiencing grace and the possibility of experiencing grace *as* grace are not the same thing." See Karl Rahner, "Concerning the Relationship between Nature and Grace," *Theological Investigations*, vol. 1, trans. Cornelius Ernst (London: Darton, Longman & Todd, 1961), 300.

THE PSYCHOLOGICAL ANALOGY AND THE DYNAMICS OF GRACE

In our earlier brief overview of the historical development of trinitarian theology, we examined the use of the psychological analogy as a way of understanding the trinitarian being of God, and particularly its account of the two inner-trinitarian processions of Word and Spirit within the divine subjectivity. Recall that the psychological analogy, as articulated by Augustine, is grounded in the conviction, attested in Scripture (Gen. 1:26), that the human person is created in the image of God and that it derives from our reflections on our own most intimate experience of the human mind and its acts of intellect and will and of our conscious human selves as seekers of truth and of goodness. Based on this reflection on our experience, the psychological analogy locates an image of the trinitarian God in the human faculties of being, understanding (or knowing), and willing (or loving). By analogy with the human experience of consciousness, the processions of the Word and Spirit in the Trinity are then understood as constituted by acts of understanding and of love within the divine consciousness. The Word is understood to proceed in God by way of intelligence, and the Holy Spirit by way of love. Now the psychological analogy, when grounded in an analysis of human intentionality, allows us to link the Trinity with the intentionality of the moral life, by providing a very strong correlation between the Trinity, grace, and the moral life. Grace is the point of connection and correlation, the nexus, between the Trinity and the moral life. So we return now to the question of grace. What is grace? How does grace affect and transform us? How is grace practically expressed in our lives?

Both Augustine and Thomas Aquinas taught that the missions are prolongations of the inner-trinitarian processions into the economy, that the missions are the processions with a temporal effect. By means of the invisible missions, the Word of Truth and the Spirit of Love are sent to the human person. The Trinity of the three divine persons thus comes to abide in the human person and, in this way, the human person is drawn into the divine life and communion and is progressively conformed to the Trinity of divine persons. It is precisely here that the psychological analogy throws light on the dynamics of grace. The indwelling divine persons dynamically conform the graced human person to the triune God, by conforming the human person's knowing and loving to the divine knowing and loving. Through the gift of grace, the human intellect participates in the divine knowledge and the human will in the divine love. In this way, then, the human person is dynamically engaged in the process of being conformed to the image and likeness of God. Through the gift of grace, we become conformed to the wisdom of the Word and the love of the Spirit. Our self-transcending acts of knowing and loving are progressively conformed to the Trinity of divine persons present to us in grace. This, then, is the transforming gift of grace, transforming because it conforms us to the image of the divine being, its wisdom and love. It is from this participation in the divine life and communion that the life of grace and the virtues of Christian life that ground the moral life ultimately derive.[18]

Assisted by the psychological analogy, we can then understand the way in which the mystery of the Trinity is related to the gift of grace and hence to the life of grace and the moral life of the human person. The psychological analogy, more than any other trinitarian analogy or model, enables us to understand the dynamics of grace in terms of our participation in the very life and being of the triune God. It allows the understanding that, in the order of grace, the human person actively participates in and is dynamically conformed to the understanding of the Word and the love of the Holy Spirit. Through the gift of grace, the human person actively participates in the intelligence of the Word and the love of the Spirit and is dynamically conformed to the divine persons, so that the human person truly becomes image of God, *imago Dei*—indeed, image of the triune God, *Dei Trinitatis*. Thus transformed and conformed, the graced human person, albeit but dimly, understands and loves as God does. Progressively conformed to the image of the triune God, actively participating in the consciousness of God, the graced person thus becomes a living analogue of the Trinity, enabled to understand as God understands and to love as God loves.

The psychological analogy thus affords a view of grace in terms of God's self-communication in grace implanted or infused in the very essence or nature of the human spirit, at the level of the powers of intellect and will by which the human person expresses him/herself in action. Grace, then, is not a possession; it always remains God's gracious gift, the divine self-communication. It is a real sharing in the divine life, the divine life and love of the Trinity. It effects a new mode of personal being, a new personal dynamic, so that the graced person exists in a new way. Indeed, as Aquinas recognized, grace effects a kind of beginning of glory in us. Ultimately, it effects our transformation into the likeness of God and our entry into the divine communion, the deification

18. For a discussion of the likening of the human person to the *imago Dei,* see Michael A. Dauphinais, "Loving the Lord Your God: The Imago Dei in Saint Thomas Aquinas," *The Thomist* 63 (1999): 241-67; A. N. Williams, *The Ground of Union: Deification in Aquinas and Palamas* (New York/Oxford: Oxford University Press, 1999), esp. 65-101; idem, "Deification in the *Summa Theologiae:* A Structural Interpretation," *The Thomist* 61 (1997): 219-55; Merriell, *To the Image of the Trinity;* Francis L. B. Cunningham, *The Divine Indwelling of the Trinity: A Historical-Doctrinal Study of the Theory of St. Thomas Aquinas* (Dubuque, Ia.: Priory Press, 1955).

or divinization that is our destiny. The presence of grace expresses itself in graced actions in our daily lives. Graced action proceeds by way of human choice and by the grace of God moving and empowering human freedom in the exercise of human intellect and will. Here, then, in an understanding of the dynamics of grace in our lives, we can locate the point of connection between trinitarian theology and moral theology and what we might describe as the trinitarian grounding of our moral lives. As moral agents we are dynamically engaged in the process of realizing in ourselves the image of God to which, through grace, we are being conformed. We performatively "image" the understanding and love that is the life of the Trinity and, in this way, we "enact" what we might rightly call "trinitarian morality."[19]

THE COGNITIVE AND AFFECTIVE DIMENSIONS OF THE MORAL LIFE

Working on the basis of the psychological analogy, when transposed in terms of the dynamics of self-transcendence and an analysis of intentionality, Anthony Kelly embarks on an exploration of "a trinitarian moral theology." He too would persuade us that our human activities of intelligence and judgment in the search for and service of truth and self-transcending love in the conduct of our lives provide not only the analogy for understanding the Trinity and for a systematic intelligibility of the gift of grace, but they also provide, through the gift of grace, modes of participation in God's knowing and loving and of our conformation to the image of God who is Trinity.[20]

Kelly proceeds to mine the psychological analogy for its resources in specific regard to moral theology. He argues that the systematic intelligibility of the dynamics of grace, which the psychological analogy affords, also serves to clarify and indeed to sharpen our understanding of the dynamics of moral life and action. The psychological analogy emphasizes both the intelligent and the loving aspects of divine life and, correlatively, of human life and moral action. Kelly observes that this explication of the dual roles of understanding and love, on which the psychological analogy rests, ensures that moral action is neither left devoid of its proper intelligence or affectivity nor extracted from the realm of the universe of meaning and intelligibility. The moral life, as Kelly rightly stresses, is not only affective but also intelligent. Indeed, it is intrinsically intelligible. Moral action necessarily engages both dimensions of

19. Anthony Kelly, "A Trinitarian Moral Theology," *Studia Moralia* 39 (2001): 245-89; see also idem, "A Multidimensional Disclosure: Aspects of Aquinas's Theological Intentionality," *The Thomist* 67 (2003): 335-74.

20. Kelly, "Trinitarian Moral Theology," 271.

our self-transcending lives, the intelligent and the affective. The psychological analogy thus brooks no deintellectualizing of the moral life, or any absolutizing of a notion of love and community without due attention to the demand for the intelligent and meaningful constitution of our moral selves. The psychological analogy, Kelly insists, demands due recognition of and serious attention to meaning and intelligibility, as well as to affectivity and love, as constituent elements of the moral life. The psychological analogy, in other words, alerts us to the truth that the love that is poured out into our hearts through the Holy Spirit (Rom. 5:5) expresses itself intelligently and enacts itself responsibly. It recognizes that love necessarily finds expression in responsible decisions and loving actions and commitments, and that those decisions, actions, and commitments rely on judgments of value, just as the divine love expressed itself and enacted itself in the world in judgments of value, responsible decisions, and loving engagements and commitments in the paschal mystery of Jesus' death, descent, and resurrection.

In the course of its long history, the application and interpretation of the psychological analogy have arguably suffered and have certainly been accused of a certain degree of distortion of an intellectualist kind, whereby the intellect has been given priority over the will, and knowledge priority over love (based on an application to the analogy of the old adage, *nihil amatum nisi praecognitum,* knowledge precedes love, for nothing is loved that is not first known—an adage that the experience of many a mystic would, of course, reverse). But, with that admittedly possible distortion in check, the psychological analogy in fact offers a salutary reminder of the vital role of intelligence in judgments of value to the world of modern moral discourse, which, as Alasdair MacIntyre has observed, is characterized by interminable debates on questions of value and morality, because of a lack of consensus on judgments of value and, moreover, a reluctance to make such judgments.[21] To a world of moral discourse that suffers from a lack of intelligibility and rationality in its deliberations on our moral and social attitudes, commitments, and dilemmas, the psychological analogy, appropriately divested of its medieval metaphysical wrappings and transposed into terms that are meaningful and accessible to contemporary consciousness, offers a vital corrective to the equally serious possibility of a kind of voluntarist distortion, which leaves judgments of value and the concrete demands of responsible decision and loving action dangerously subject to the arbitrariness of individual assessment based on personal interest, whim, desire, or need.[22]

---

21. Alasdair MacIntyre, *After Virtue: A Study in Moral Theology,* 2nd ed. (Notre Dame, Ind.: University of Notre Dame Press, 1984); idem, *Whose Justice? Which Rationality?* (Notre Dame, Ind.: University of Notre Dame Press, 1988).

22. See Anne Hunt, "The Psychological Analogy and the Paschal Mystery in Trinitarian Theol-

GRACE AND THE MORAL LIFE

A strong correlation between the Trinity and the moral life thus emerges, via the psychological analogy and the intelligibility of the dynamics of grace that it affords. In grace, in the invisible missions of Word and Spirit, the divine persons are communicated to and come to abide in the human person. The indwelling Trinity brings about a new mode of existence, because, through the gift of grace, the human person in his/her subjectivity is progressively conformed to the image of the Trinity of divine persons, the divine subjectivity. In this way, the missions of the Word and Spirit effect a graced life to the human person. Moral action is in this way enabled by God, through the gift of grace, which progressively conforms human decision making and action to divine wisdom and love. Moving and transforming us interiorly, grace thus operates not as an extrinsic force but as an intrinsic fundamental source of moral decision making and action. It finds concrete expression in and through the events of human life. Moral action thus emerges as a dynamic participation in what we might call the moral consciousness of the Trinity, or trinitarian morality, so to speak.

The psychological analogy and its explication of the dynamics of grace in terms of conformity with the Trinity of divine persons also assist in our appreciation of the role of virtues in the moral life. We can first understand virtues in terms of modes of action, as habits of grace that enable human persons to move forward toward that special destiny which is theirs, communion with the Trinity. Second, we can understand the gift of grace as a dynamic source of the virtues—not only faith, hope, and love but also the cardinal virtues of justice, prudence, temperance, and fortitude—and of higher modes of action, such as the gifts of the Holy Spirit. Indeed, grace provides the context and ground of those habits of grace and dispositions that are the virtues, those modes of action and those practical judgments that find expression in the very practical demands of a moral life (Aquinas, *STh* II-II, qq. 47-170).

THE SOCIAL MODEL OF THE TRINITY AND THE MORAL LIFE

We see that the psychological analogy, when grounded in the dynamics of self-transcendence and an analysis of internationality, allows for an understanding of the progressive conformation of the human person in the image

ogy," *Theological Studies* 59 (1998): 197-218; see also Anthony Kelly, "The 'Horrible Wrappers' of Aquinas' God," *Pacifica* 9 (1996): 185-203.

of the Trinity, a progressive realization in both understanding and loving in the practice and action of the graced human life. We turn now to the community or social model of the Trinity, which, with its strong emphasis on the personal, relational, and social aspect of being, also provides rich food for thought in terms of a more social understanding and interpretation of the life of grace, Christian orthopraxis, and moral principles. Here Catherine Mowry LaCugna makes a valuable contribution to our study.

With the social or community model of the Trinity foremost in mind, based in the missions of the Son and Spirit as revealed in the economy, but consciously eschewing the psychological analogy, LaCugna argues that "Christian praxis must correspond to what we believe to be true about God: that God is personal, that God is ecstatic and fecund love, that God's very nature is to exist toward and for another. The mystery of existence is the mystery of the commingling of persons, divine and human, in a common life, within a common household."[23] LaCugna explains that trinitarian theology is above all a theology of relationship and a theology of personhood. Indeed, she argues that trinitarian theology could be described, par excellence, as a theology of relationship, which explores the mysteries of love, relationship, personhood, and communion within the framework of God's self-revelation in the person of Christ and the activity of the Spirit. Precisely here, for LaCugna, in the mystery of God as communion, the radical consequences and practical ethical implications for a doctrine of the Trinity emerge. Based on this understanding of the Trinity, the ultimate ground and meaning of being is communion among persons. To be a Christian, she insists, is to participate in the life of God through Jesus Christ by the power of the Holy Spirit and to live a life in God's economy that is appropriate to the mystery of persons in communion. As LaCugna expresses it:

> Living trinitarian faith means living God's life: living from and for God, from and for others. Living trinitarian faith means living as Jesus Christ lived.... Living trinitarian faith means living according to the power and presence of the Holy Spirit. . . . Living trinitarian faith means living together in harmony and communion with every other creature in the common household of God.... Living trinitarian faith means adhering to the gospel of liberation from sin and fractured relationship.[24]

A determinedly social emphasis on the moral life and its imperatives emerges in LaCugna's trinitarian theology. As is the case in the trinitarian

23. LaCugna, *God for Us*, 383.
24. Ibid., 400-401.

theology that engages the psychological analogy, this theological perspective on the mystery of the Trinity also accords great significance to an understanding of the human person as created in the image of God. In this case, however, it is not the intrapersonal dynamic of subjectivity that is seen to constitute the image, but rather that the being of triune God is the mystery of communion of love among persons. While the psychological analogy highlights the vital role of intelligence as well as affectivity in the dynamics in the life of grace and of moral action, and indeed insists on the role of judgments of value in moral deliberation, the social model of the Trinity provides more explicitly interpersonal and social principles for moral action and a Christian moral life.

The moral life, from this perspective, will be characterized by a profound respect for mutuality, relationality, and reciprocity, values derived from the model of community, equality, love, and justice of the trinitarian communion of the three divine persons. It will uphold the essential equality of persons. It will cherish individuality but reject individualism. It will foster inclusiveness, egalitarianism, collaboration, and cooperation. It will reject dualism, and any kind of subordinationism or elitism. It will not brook domination or authoritarianism. It will value participation, inclusion and collegiality. It will respect and defend democratic processes. It will be characterized by a certain self-yielding and deference toward the other, of being not-for-oneself but for-the-other. Concern and responsibility for the welfare of others and a spirit of reconciliation will be its hallmark. It will uphold respect for the other and for the other's freedom, conscience, and dignity. It will champion human rights, human dignity, and human freedom. It will insist on nonviolence and resist aggression. It will strive for freedom and liberation of the other, and neither tolerate nor perpetrate injustice. While respecting difference, it will refuse indifference. It will welcome the other in a spirit of hospitality, openness, sharing, and compassion. It will welcome the stranger, offer refuge to those in need, and oppose all forms of alienation, isolation, and self-centeredness. It will cherish otherness and diversity. It will strive for unity in diversity. It will not confuse unity, which it prizes and which it recognizes as a necessary requirement of communion, with uniformity, which it rejects as a denial and suppression of diversity. Moreover, moral action, inspired by this understanding of the Trinity as a communion of persons, will be characterized by a profound sense of the innate goodness and sanctity of life and of all creation, as the work of its trinitarian Creator. It will not abide the destruction of the environment and its ecosystems, or the exploitation of the earth's resources. It will be motivated by a sense of stewardship and custodianship of creation. It will value and seek to foster communion, as manifest in human community, family, friendship, and collegiality. It will be nurtured by the celebration of the Eucharist as sacramental sign of communion. It will be characterized by faith in God's providence, hope in the future, and love for all creation, a love that "bears all things, believes all things, hopes all things, endures all things" (1 Cor. 13:7), a love that expresses itself in responsible decisions and loving commitments. All this, LaCugna reminds us, because God's *archē*, God's rule, is relational, personal, and shared. It is characterized by personhood, love, and communion, without hierarchy or subordination. Here, she insists, is the non-negotiable truth of our existence and for our moral life. As she explains:

> The trinitarian *archē* of God emerges as the basis of mutuality among persons: rather than the sexist theology of complementarity, or the racist theology of superiority, or the clerical theology of privilege, or the political theology of exploitation, or the patriarchal theology of male dominance and control, the reign of God promises the life of true communion among all human beings and all creatures. Mutuality rooted in communion among persons is a non-negotiable truth about our existence, the highest value and ideal of the Christian life, because for God mutual love among persons is supreme.[25]

The moral life, inspired by this social model of the Trinity, is a life of self-transcending love and communion with others, a life lived as persons toward and for others, as in a common household, the household of God. "Household," LaCugna explains, "is an appropriate metaphor to describe the *communion of persons* where God and creature meet and unite and now exist together as one."[26] Household connotes home, family, friends, hospitality, and openness.

CONCLUSION

Trinitarian faith is in fact potentially powerful in inspiring and motivating the relationships that make for Christian community and the patterns and principles of moral action for transforming the world. The social model of the Trinity has, as LaCugna insists, eminently practical ramifications in terms of how we live our lives and for the practical demands of Christian faith in God who is Trinity. It motivates a strongly communitarian and communal way of

25. Ibid., 399.
26. Ibid., 411.

being in society, the world, and indeed the cosmos, as persons in communion, communion with all creation. As LaCugna explains: "The practical nature of the doctrine of the Trinity does not mean it is a pragmatic principle that furnishes an easy solution to war and violence, or yields the blueprint for a catechetical program, or settles vexing disagreements over the church's public prayer. Rather, the theoretical framework of trinitarian theology yields a wisdom, a discernment, a guide for seeing the 'two hands of God' (Irenaeus) at work in our salvation."[27] It informs our understanding of how we should live our lives and what it is that supports the flourishing of human beings, and of all creation.

On the other hand, the psychological analogy allows for an unparalleled systematic intelligibility of the gift of grace and of the nexus between Trinity, grace, and the moral life. By attending to the twin dynamics of knowing and loving in the inner-trinitarian life and as they come to bear in the gift of grace to the human person, the psychological analogy offers a cogent explication of the progressive conformation of the human person in the image of God who is Trinity, a progressive realization in both understanding and loving that expresses itself in the moral action of the graced human person, manifesting itself in what we might call "trinitarian morality." From this perspective, Christian moral action emerges as a real participation in the moral consciousness of the Trinity itself. The psychological analogy also serves to reinforce the crucial importance of the engagement of both intelligence and affectivity in moral decision making and action.

FOR FURTHER READING

Cunningham, David S. *These Three Are One: The Practice of Trinitarian Theology.* Malden, Mass./Oxford: Blackwell, 1998.

Duffy, Stephen J. *The Dynamics of Grace: Perspectives in Theological Anthropology.* New Theology Series 3. Collegeville, Minn.: Liturgical Press, A Michael Glazier Book, 1993.

Fiddes, Paul S. *Participating in God: A Pastoral Theology of the Trinity.* Louisville: Westminster John Knox Press, 2000.

Haight, Roger. *The Experience and Language of Grace.* New York: Paulist Press, 1979.

Jones, L. Gregory. *Transformed Judgment: Toward a Trinitarian Account of the Moral Life.* Notre Dame, Ind.: University of Notre Dame Press, 1990.

Kelly, Anthony. "A Trinitarian Moral Theology." *Studia Moralia* 39 (2001): 245-89.

LaCugna, Catherine Mowry. *God for Us: The Trinity and Christian Life.* New York: HarperCollins, 1991. See esp. 377-417.

27. Ibid., 379.

Merriell, Donald Juvenal. *To the Image of the Trinity: A Study in the Development of Aquinas' Teaching*. Toronto: Pontifical Institute of Mediaeval Studies, 1990.

Rahner, Karl. *Foundations of Christian Faith: An Introduction to the Idea of Christianity*. Translated by William V. Dych. New York: Crossroad Publishing Company, 1987.

———. *A Rahner Reader*. Edited by Gerald A. McCool. New York: Crossroad, 1987.

———. "Reflections on the Experience of Grace." In *Theological Investigations*, vol. 3. 86-90. London: Darton, Longmann & Todd, 1967.

Webb, Stephen H. *The Gifting God: A Trinitarian Ethics*. Oxford: Oxford University Press, 1996.

Williams, A. N. *The Ground of Union: Deification in Aquinas and Palamas*. New York/Oxford: Oxford University Press, 1999.

9

Trinity, Spirituality, and Worship

God's love has been poured into our hearts through the Holy Spirit who has been given to us. (Rom. 5:5)

TO SPEAK OF CHRISTIAN SPIRITUALITY is to speak at that most basic level of one's lived experience of a distinctly and explicitly Christian way of being in the world that encompasses the full gamut of engagements which together constitute one's being: one's relationships with God, others, self, and the social, political, and economic realms of one's existence.[1] It is more expansive in its scope than morality. Spirituality is not merely an *aspect* of Christian life, nor is it chiefly concerned with some kind of solitary journey toward the attainment of a personal spiritual self-fulfillment. It *is* Christian life, as lived in the very ordinary as well as the extraordinary engagements, events, and conundrums that are part of the unfolding tapestry of everyday life. No dimension of life is excluded from its purview or influence. Christian spirituality ultimately concerns our graced growth in holiness and wholeness.

Our aim in this chapter is to articulate an expressly trinitarian spirituality and its expression in prayer and worship. Given that we believe that we are created in the image of God, the doctrine of the Trinity throws light on our life, on what we are created and called to be, on our sharing with each other and in the divine life, the communion of love that is God. In other words, the doctrine of the Trinity is not just about who God is, but who we are and what we are called to be and become. It concerns all of human reality—its joys and sorrows, its hopes and its fears, its fragility and its nobility, and its ultimate destiny. Christian spirituality is surely intrinsically trinitarian, for it ultimately concerns the invitation to each and every one of us, individually and in community, to participate in the very life of the triune God, through communion

1. For an introduction to the notion of spirituality in the Christian tradition, see Walter Principe, "Spirituality, Christian," in *The New Dictionary of Catholic Spirituality*, ed. Michael Downey (Collegeville, Minn.: Liturgical Press, A Michael Glazier Book, 1993). See also Walter Principe, "Toward Defining Spirituality," *Sciences Religieuses/Studies in Religion* 12 (1983): 121-41.

with the Son in the power of the Holy Spirit, who is love. It is rooted in baptism, "in the name of the Father and of the Son and of the Holy Spirit," and expressed and renewed in celebration of the Eucharist. Its ultimate goal is union with the triune God. It concerns our graced growth in conformity to the person of Christ, entering ever more deeply into participation in the communion that is God, through the gift of the Holy Spirit. As Hans Urs von Balthasar says: "We belong more to God than to ourselves; thus, we are also more in him than in ourselves. Ours is only the way leading to the eternal image of us that he bears within himself."[2] Christian spirituality refers to the daily living out of the longing for and the belonging to God, for which our hearts burn (Luke 24:32).

Michael Downey and Catherine LaCugna unjustly dismiss the works of Augustine and Thomas Aquinas,[3] and indeed other theologians such as Bonaventure, Richard of St. Victor, Jan van Ruusbroec, and Julian of Norwich, whose contributions we briefly surveyed in our overview of the development of trinitarian theology, when they suggest that very few mystical writings in the tradition rely on an explicitly trinitarian symbolism, and that the connection in the Christian tradition between spirituality and the Trinity has not always been very clear.[4] While we do not agree with their reading of the tradition, which is in fact deeply imbued with trinitarian spirituality, albeit admittedly not so strongly in the modern era, we do agree that Christian faith in the mystery of the Trinity inspires our confidence in the conviction that, by the utterly gracious gift of God, we are invited into the life of the Trinity, that our life of grace is a real sharing in the very life of God. This is the fullness of life, the wholeness and the holiness to which we are called, as Herbert McCabe explains:

> The Trinity is what makes the gospel what it is—the kind of good news that it is. . . . Our gospel is not just that we are saved from sin but that we

2. Hans Urs von Balthasar, *The Grain of Wheat: Aphorisms*, trans. E. Leiva-Merikakis (San Francisco: Ignatius Press, 1995), 2.

3. See Jean-Pierre Torrell, *Saint Thomas Aquinas*, vol. 2, *Spiritual Master*, trans. Robert Royal (Washington, D.C.: Catholic University of America Press, 2003), 1-224, for a superb study of the trinitarian spirituality that inspires and informs Thomas Aquinas's theological corpus. See also Edmund Hill's comments on Augustine's profoundly trinitarian spirituality in Hill's introduction to his translation of Augustine's *De Trinitate*, where Hill comments: "the central point . . . is that Augustine is proposing the quest for, or the exploration of, the mystery of the Trinity as a complete program for the Christian spiritual life, a program of conversion and renewal and discovery of self in God and God in self" (Augustine, *The Trinity*, with introduction, translation and notes by Edmund Hill [Brooklyn, N.Y.: New City Press, 1991], 19).

4. Michael Downey and Catherine LaCugna, "Trinitarian Spirituality," in *New Dictionary of Catholic Spirituality*, 969.

> are taken up into the life of God himself . . . to have a share in divinity itself. This indeed is what our doctrine of the Trinity tells us.[5]

TRINITY AND SPIRITUALITY: THE TRINITARIAN GRAMMAR OF CHRISTIAN SPIRITUAL LIFE

In seeking to articulate an explicitly *trinitarian* spirituality, Michael Downey would first have us understand that the doctrine of the Trinity contains what he calls "the rules of grammar" by which we speak meaningfully of God, whose name above all is Love, Love given and giving as gift. He explains: "Grammar has to do with a way of speaking correctly. Rules of grammar set the limits within which creative discourse can take place. Rules of grammar do not guarantee that we will speak the truth, but if we are to speak in a meaningful and coherent way, we must work within the rules of grammar."[6]

Pressing further with his analogy of grammar, Downey then recognizes what he calls "a grammar of gift" in the doctrine of the Trinity, which is consequently fundamental to a trinitarian spirituality.[7] Gift is a key notion in Downey's trinitarian spirituality. As he explains: "A Christian spirituality which is Trinitarian through and through is thus shaped by 'gift' and 'gift/ing,' for the doctrine of the Trinity is a grammar by which Christians try to speak of the ineffable mystery of God's constant, eternal giving as gift."[8] The gift is Love, God's very being, the divine self-gift, given and giving as gift. It is Love that refuses to be anything but love. It is the love of these three, Father, Son, and Holy Spirit, three in the one Love: "the Father as the originator and Pure Source of Love, Jesus Christ the Son as the ongoing and inexhaustible activity of that Love, drawing everything and everyone back to the origin and end of Love in the bonding of Love itself."[9] It is the undying Love poured out for us in the life, death, and resurrection of Jesus, as Downey explains:

> Jesus speaks the very truth of the Giver, Given and Gift/ing which is Love itself. The Life that pours itself forth (Son) from, toward and for the originating Lover (Father) in and through Love (Spirit) is the very Love that

---

5. Herbert McCabe, "Preaching the Trinity," *Priests and People* 14 (2000): 233.

6. Michael Downey, *Altogether Gift: A Trinitarian Spirituality* (Maryknoll, N.Y.: Orbis Books, 2000), 47.

7. Walter Kasper also speaks of the doctrine of the Trinity in terms of grammar: "This doctrine [of the Trinity] is in a sense the summation of the entire Christian mystery of salvation and at the same time, its grammar" (*The God of Jesus Christ*, trans. Matthew J. O'Connell [New York: Crossroad, 1988], 311).

8. Downey, *Altogether Gift,* 14.

9. Ibid., 45.

> endures. He who is Love itself, unto death and into hell, lives. Love lives. Love is loving—a gift still on offer.[10]

The "grammar of gift" serves, as Downey explains, to clarify the language with which we speak of our experience of God as Giver, Given, Gift/ing. "By the Spirit who is Gift/ing, dwelling within our hearts, we behold the mystery of the Trinity in the Incarnate Word, Given, whose life, words, mission, passion, dying, and rising are the very love of the Giver of all life and love."[11] At the same time, the distinctive manner of self-giving varies by virtue of the uniqueness of the relation of Father, Son, and Spirit: Giver, Given, and Gift/ing. "The Father is originating Lover; the Son is the self-expression of Love; the Spirit is the inexhaustible self-giving of Love."[12]

Because gift-giving is always in relation to another and because, grammatically speaking, prepositions express relationship and relationality, Downey proposes that the "grammar of gift" is best expressed in prepositions, such as "through," "with," "in," "to," "for," and "toward." As he explains: "We know it because of the way that God is for us in the grand economy of salvation: Father, Son, and Spirit-toward us, for us, with us, in us as Giver, Given, Gift/ing."[13] Trinitarian spirituality, Downey explains, is thus a way of perceiving the gift of God's love in the mundane, ordinary and routine details of everyday life. It is not that the Trinity is a model for how to live the Christian life, he notes. Rather, as Downey explains, "understanding the grammar of the Trinity helps us to live freely in and from the gift given through the Word and in the Spirit, to speak the Trinitarian mystery with our whole lives."[14] "The grammar of gift" in the doctrine of the Trinity then serves to illumine our understanding of "the grammar of spiritual living." Here the practical implications of trinitarian doctrine for Christian spirituality emerge.

The mystery of the Trinity, to which a trinitarian spirituality is wholly oriented as its source, center and ultimate end, grounds the communion among human persons and indeed their communion with other living things and all creation. A trinitarian spirituality thus implies and impels the journey to ever more complete communion with and between persons both divine and human. Trinitarian spirituality is therefore essentially personal and relational. It is inclusive of everyone and everything, and every human concern. It is characterized by solidarity between and among persons and rightly ordered

10. Ibid., 58-59.
11. Ibid., 55.
12. Ibid., 67.
13. Ibid., 56.
14. Ibid., 103.

relationships, which are characterized by diversity, equality, mutuality, reciprocity, interdependence, charity, and love.[15] As Herbert McCabe points out: "It is because of the doctrine of the Trinity, or the truth that this doctrine expresses, that we can point to the love between people and say quite literally: There is God. *Ubi caritas et amor, Deus ibi est*—'Wherever there is charity and love, there is God' (from the liturgy of Holy Thursday)."[16]

Here too Downey draws on the notion of "the grammar of the Trinity." The term "perichoresis," he reminds us, describes the active, mutual, equal relations, without subordination, between the Father, Son, and Spirit. "If the doctrine of the Trinity not only expresses what and who we think the divine persons are, but also articulates what human persons are called to be and become, then, in trinitarian perspective, human beings are to cultivate, nurture, and sustain the kinds of relationship that are reflective of this *perichoresis*."[17] If we live from a trinitarian spirituality, he argues, then dualisms—such as secular/sacred, and lay/clerical—are essentially untenable, for we see the whole world and everything within it as the locus of the triune God's presence and action. Such dualisms are antithetical to the notion of the trinitarian perichoresis. Rather, a trinitarian spirituality recognizes that all creation is the arena of God's self-giving love, providence, and salvation, that all is embraced by God who is love, through Jesus Christ in the Holy Spirit.

Downey and LaCugna identify the various aspects of the spiritual life in terms of prayer, meditation, contemplation, and asceticism as means of effecting ever-fuller participation in God's triune life, ever-deeper communion with the divine three-in-one Love. Downey explains:

> All bespeak the truth that learning to receive is a lifelong process, never an entirely accomplished fact. The Christian spiritual life entails the ongoing, rigorous discipline of receptivity, of cultivating, nurturing, and sustaining a grateful heart for what is. All is gift, ours to receive, even that which awaits us at the end of the one and only life we have to live—which is given as gift.[18]

---

15. Downey and LaCugna, "Trinitarian Spirituality," 981.

16. McCabe, "Preaching the Trinity," 236.

17. Downey, *Altogether Gift*, 73. Downey here speaks warmly and evocatively about human persons cultivating and sustaining relationships that are reflective of the trinitarian perichoresis. But critical reflection on this notion of reflecting the divine perichoresis quickly raises several serious concerns as to its meaningfulness and coherence. While we can applaud Downey's attempt to express the mystery of the Trinity in meaningful and attractive ways in the contemporary context, we must note a concern that he pays too little attention to the limitations of using the analogy of the *perichoresis* of the persons of the Trinity as a basis for understanding interpersonal human relations, thus putting at risk and ultimately undermining an understanding of the mystery of the trinitarian communion that the notion of perichoresis expresses.

18. Ibid., 129.

Downey stresses, however, that the Christian spiritual life is not only gift but task; it is both gift *and* task.[19] We are invited to participate in the missions of Word and Spirit, through which the world is transformed by Love into a communion in the one Love. As Downey explains: "A Trinitarian spirituality is at once personal and relational, inclusive of every human concern and commitment, giving particular attention to the last, littlest, and least of the earth, to those who are most wounded and weak in the church and in the world."[20] Such a spirituality demands the work of charity and justice. In this way, Christian spirituality necessarily finds expression not just in reception of, but in response to, gift—in attentiveness to and in tending to the needs of others. The task is ultimately one of deification, the notion that was so strong in early Christian understanding, through which we enter into and participate in the very life of God.[21] This indeed is holiness. As Downey writes: "Holiness rests in becoming persons conformed to the image of God in us, being toward and for another, for others and for God. Being holy is being alive in the glory of God that transforms."[22]

PASCHAL DIMENSIONS OF TRINITARIAN SPIRITUALITY

The paschal mystery of trinitarian love offers further insights on the connection between Trinity and spirituality. Here the French theologian Ghislain Lafont offers fruitful reflections for our study. Lafont, in his exploration of the paschal mystery in his book *Peut-on Connaître Dieu en Jésus Christ?*,[23] identifies two levels of meaning in the paschal mystery, one that we can describe as "theological," concerning the trinitarian mystery itself, the other one being what we might describe as "anthropological," concerning the destiny and vocation of the human person. It is the anthropological aspect of the mystery that concerns us here in our exploration of the connection between Trinity and spirituality.

Lafont observes that, from the anthropological perspective, the paschal mystery of Jesus Christ shows that, in Jesus' *choice of divine communion in pref-*

19. Ibid., 112.

20. Ibid., 119.

21. For a helpful discussion of the doctrine of deification, see A. N. Williams, *The Ground of Union: Deification in Aquinas and Palamas* (New York/Oxford: Oxford University Press, 1999); Donald Juvenal Merriell, *To the Image of the Trinity: A Study in the Development of Aquinas' Teaching* (Toronto: Pontifical Institute of Mediaeval Studies, 1990).

22. Downey, *Altogether Gift*, 106.

23. Ghislain Lafont, *Peut-on Connaître Dieu en Jésus Christ?*, Cogitatio Fidei 44 (Paris: Les Éditions du Cerf, 1969), 254-62, 325.

erence to any autonomy of existence, the perfection of being, at the interior of the life of God, lies in communion, as distinct from any autonomy or independence. Consequently, it is communion, not any notion that connotes autonomy, that informs and shapes our understanding of Christian spirituality. Second, the paschal mystery shows that entry into communion with God necessarily passes through a stage of death.[24] It shows that God's self-communication and offer of communion require a renunciation of existence on the part of the human person, a surrender and transcendence of the self, a radical dying to self, and ultimately physical death. Indeed the paschal mystery reveals that the possibility of this total *ekstasis* of self—an "excentration" or "decentering" of self in a radical other-regarding relationality—is our ultimate meaning and vocation: precisely through it, we enter into the life of the trinitarian communion and exchange. A distinctly paschal element, even if somewhat disturbing and unsettling, emerges from Lafont's exploration of trinitarian relationality and divine being, as revealed in the paschal mystery and, correspondingly, for human relationality and spirituality.[25]

The paschal mystery and the analogy it provides for the mystery of the Trinity here afford a somewhat more austere and sobering perspective on human being and action in the world, in relation to God and our response to God's offer of self-communication and communion, and in relation to Christian spirituality. It reinforces the utter importance of the principle of communion, as opposed to any notion of autonomy and independence, which also emerges strongly from the social model of the Trinity. But it also highlights the reality and indeed the necessity of the suffering, the mortification, the death to self that are indelibly and unavoidably part of the paschal mystery, and that are intrinsic to the passage that leads to the fully graced life that is our destiny, life in communion with the triune God.

TRINITY AND PRAYER

Christian spirituality is sustained and cultivated through prayer, that "movement of the attentive human heart to participate in the very life of God, to respond to the myriad ways that God comes in Christ through the power of

24. E.g., ibid., 241, 243.

25. Lafont, in a way that is reminiscent of Jan van Ruusbroec's trinitarian theology and Ruusbroec's understanding of the role of the Holy Spirit as active principle of return, recognizes that reciprocity is inherent in authentic personhood. Lafont argues for the "reflexive construction" of the person, meaning that the person may be understood to "result" from this unceasing reciprocal operation. Lafont then introduces these characteristics—operation, reciprocity, reflexivity—into his reflections on the mystery of the Trinity (*Peut-on*, 268-69).

the Holy Spirit."[26] Prayer, as Downey and LaCugna explain, is "well thought of as awakening to the divine presence in *every* dimension of everyday life."[27] Here also the grammar of the doctrine of the Trinity is illuminative, as Downey explains: "A trinitarian approach to prayer highlights the communal, social, and indeed public character of all prayer."[28] Through communal prayer, a trinitarian spirituality seeks ongoing participation in a communion of persons, both human and divine. Here too the grammatical prepositions serve to express the relations, based on the conviction at the heart of the doctrine of the Trinity that God is with us, for us, in us. Christian life is to the Father, through the Son, in the Spirit. We make the sign of the cross in the name of the Father and of the Son and of the Holy Spirit. We pray to the Father, through the Son, in the Spirit. In our liturgy we pray to the Father, through, with, and in Christ, in the unity of the Holy Spirit. Moreover, when we pray, we pray not just as creatures but as children of God. "For you have received the Spirit of sonship. When we cry, 'Abba! Father!' it is the Spirit himself bearing witness with our spirit that we are children of God" (Rom. 8:15-16). This means that, when we pray, we are not just creatures calling upon our Creator. We are joining in and entering into the eternal dialogue of the Son and Father, in the Holy Spirit; we are, as we say, in the Spirit: our worship is "in Spirit and in truth."[29] That we are taken into the very life of God lies at the very core and center of our faith and our spirituality.

Here also "the grammar of gift" prevails. In prayer, as Downey explains, "I am held in the knowledge that all that I am and all that I have is first and finally gift. Prayer is a way of living with, in, and from that gift. All the time."[30] A trinitarian spirituality here too serves to challenge dualisms, to reject subordination, and to bring new balance to skewed notions of the relationships between, for example, action and contemplation, the sacred and secular, the church and the world, the ordained and the nonordained, the spiritual and the mundane.[31] Indeed, as Downey notes: "All authentic Christian living is properly understood as doxological. That is to say, Christian life itself, when it is an expression of our long and loving desire for God, is an act of prayer and praise and glory. This is true of the whole of life—not just this or that part or piece of it."[32]

---

26. Downey and LaCugna, "Trinitarian Spirituality," 974.
27. Ibid., 977.
28. Ibid., 973.
29. McCabe, "Preaching the Trinity," 235.
30. Downey, *Altogether Gift*, 122.
31. Downey and LaCugna, "Trinitarian Spirituality," 975.
32. Downey, *Altogether Gift*, 121.

The fourth and final section of the *Catechism of the Catholic Church* treats Christian prayer and is arguably the finest section of the *Catechism*.[33] "Prayer and Christian life are inseparable," the Catechism explains, "for they concern the same love and the same renunciation, proceeding from love; the same filial and loving conformity with the Father's plan of love; the same transforming union in the Holy Spirit who conforms us more and more to Christ Jesus; the same love for all men, the love with which Jesus has loved us" (#2745). The *Catechism* concludes with a reflection on the prayer that Jesus taught us, the Our Father. What is particularly striking is that the *Catechism*'s beautiful exposition on the mystery of Christian prayer is thoroughly trinitarian in its approach.

The role of the Holy Spirit emerges with particular vividness and remarkable beauty: "The Holy Spirit, whose anointing permeates our whole being, is the interior Master of Christian prayer. He is the artisan of the living tradition of prayer" (#2672). The Holy Spirit is "the interior Teacher of Christian prayer" (#2681), "the living water 'welling up to eternal life' in the heart that prays" (#2652). The Catechism makes special reference to the singular place of Mary, the Mother of God, in Christian prayer: "In prayer the Holy Spirit unites us to the person of the only Son, in his glorified humanity, through which and in which our filial prayer unites us in the Church with the Mother of Jesus" (#2673). Mary is "the perfect *Orans* (pray-er), a figure of the Church" (#2679). She "has become the mother of all the living" (ibid.). The *Catechism* stresses her unique role: "While Jesus, the only mediator, is the way of our prayer; Mary, his mother and ours, is wholly transparent to him" (#2674). Similarly the saints and the many and varied spiritualties that have developed in the history of the church share in the living tradition of prayer and serve as precious guides for the spiritual life and the practice of prayer. Evoking the vivid imagery of light and its refraction, the *Catechism* explains: "In their rich diversity they are refractions of the one pure light of the Holy Spirit" (#2684).[34]

TRINITY AND LITURGY

Prayer finds its public expression in communal liturgical worship. Worship, Jaroslav Pelikan writes, "is the metabolism of the Christian life."[35] Christian

33. See *Catechism of the Catholic Church,* 2nd ed. (Washington, D.C.: U.S. Catholic Conference, 2000), 613-88; also http://www.vatican.va/archive/catechism/ccc_toc.htm.

34. For a thought-provoking reflection entitled "The Trinity and Prayer," see Herbert McCabe, *God Still Matters*, ed. Brian Davies (London: Continuum, 2002), 54-75.

35. Jaroslav Pelikan, "A Response" to *Sacrosanctum Concilium,* the Constitution on the Sacred Liturgy in *The Documents of Vatican II,* ed. Walter M. Abbott (New York: Corpus Books, 1966), 179.

worship, like Christian spirituality, is necessarily trinitarian. As Walter Kasper explains: "The doctrine of the Trinity is as it were simply the grammar of the doxology. The trinitarian confession is concerned with the 'Glory be to the Father through the Son in the Holy Spirit.'"[36] In fact, Christian faith in the Trinity was first expressed in prayer and worship, long before that faith found expression in dogma. Readers will recall that the biblical testimony to the experience of the threeness of God is probably more liturgical than confessional. Indeed, worship serves to express the *lex orandi* (the law of praying) of the Christian community, and as such effectively functions as a custodian, so to speak, of Christian faith and revelation, and as guide in and criterion for the discernment of the *lex credendi* (the law of believing) of the church, as has been evident at a number of significant points in the tradition.[37] For example, in the fourth-century debates concerning the question of the divinity of the Holy Spirit, Gregory of Nazianzus, the Minstrel of the Holy Trinity,[38] following the Council of Nicaea (325) and leading up to the resolution of the issue at the Council of Constantinople in 381, argued for the full divinity of the Holy Spirit on the grounds of the practice of Christian prayer and worship: "If he [the Holy Spirit] is not to be worshiped, how can He deify me by Baptism? But if He is to be worshiped, surely He is an Object of adoration, and if an Object of adoration He must be God" (*Fifth Theological Oration: On the Holy Spirit,* Oratio 32.28).[39] In other words, the fact that the Holy Spirit was being invoked, along with the Father and the Son, in baptism and in liturgy, served as irrefutable proof of the Holy Spirit's full divinity, on which the Council of Constantinople duly elaborated: the *lex orandi* thus informed and determined the *lex credendi.*

An explicitly trinitarian Christian spirituality is necessarily ecclesial and sacramental, given the profoundly relational character of divine being. Our sharing in the mission of Jesus Christ and the Holy Spirit necessarily expresses itself in a community of discipleship, which is realized and celebrated in word and sacrament, in communal worship (*leitourgia*). It is in liturgy that our theology and our spirituality find their fullest and most explicit expression. Indeed, as Don Saliers expresses it, not only are prayer and the liturgical life of the church indispensable to Christian theological reflection, but worship *is* theology. As he explains: "the continuing worship of God in the assembly *is* a

36. Kasper, *God of Jesus Christ*, 304.

37. It is Prosper of Aquitaine who is reputed to have coined the principle: *lex orandi, lex credendi* (the law of praying is the law of believing). For use of the principle of *lex orandi, lex credendi,* see Geoffrey Wainwright, *Doxology: The Praise of God in Worship, Doctrine and Life* (London: Epworth Press, 1982), 218-83.

38. Boris Bobrinskoy, *The Mystery of the Trinity: Trinitarian Experience and Vision in the Biblical and Patristic Tradition* (Crestwood, N.Y.: St. Vladimir's Seminary Press, 1999), 153-55.

39. In *Nicene and Post-Nicene Fathers*, 7:327.

form of theology. . . . Worship in all its social-cultural idioms is a *theological* act."[40] Moreover, liturgy is no mere authority or *locus theologicus*; it grounds theology, as Alexander Schmemann explains:

> The formula *lex orandi est lex credendi* means nothing else than that theology is *possible* only with the Church, i.e. as a fruit of this new life in Christ, granted in the sacramental *leitourgia*, as a witness to the eschatological fullness of the Church, as in other terms, a participation in this *leitourgia*. . . . Liturgical tradition is not an "authority" or a *locus theologicus*; it is the ontological condition of theology, of the proper understanding of *kerygma*, of the Word of God, because it is in the Church, of which the *leitourgia* is the expression and the life, that the sources of theology are functioning as precisely "sources."[41]

Boris Bobrinskoy also stresses the properly theological significance of liturgy per se:

> The liturgy is filled with theology; not only do the liturgical texts, the prayers, the hymns, the litanies, the readings, the preaching reflect the rich theological doctrine and express the faith of the Church, but the *liturgical action itself*, the ritual and symbolic celebration express a theological reality, through the sacramental gestures and the action of the assembly. They manifest on the one hand, the presence of God, the ecclesial foretaste of the trinitarian kingdom . . . and they signify, on the other hand, the doxological attitude, that of praise, of the Church before the presence of God.[42]

Liturgy, then, is no mere optional extra in regard to Christian spirituality and theology. It is indeed the indispensable condition of its possibility.

THE EUCHARIST AND THE TRINITY

The Eucharist in particular provides a vital context for the expression and confession of our faith in the Trinity. Here we are immersed, as in a fountain

---

40. Don E. Saliers, *Worship as Theology: Foretaste of Glory Divine* (Nashville: Abingdon Press, 1984), 15. While some might rightly express concern that theology becomes almost anything in this kind of approach, such reservations are not true of Saliers's work, I suggest. On another note, Saliers makes a helpful distinction between worship and liturgy. Worship, he explains, "suggests a vital activity that is a whole form of life," whereas liturgy "can, though it need not, be taken to refer narrowly to what is on paper in the books, or simply to the historically received and authorized rites" (p. 16).

41. *Liturgy and Tradition: Theological Reflections of Alexander Schmemann,* ed. Thomas Fisch (Crestwood, N.Y.: St. Vladimir's Seminary Press, 1990), 18. The term *leitourgia*, Schmemann argues, is much more comprehensive and adequate than "worship" or "cult" (p. 39).

42. Bobrinskoy, *Mystery of the Trinity*, 147.

wherein "we live and move and have our being" (Acts 17:28), in the mystery of the Trinity. As the Munich Statement that resulted from Orthodox and Roman Catholic dialogue regarding the Eucharist states:

> Taken as a whole, the eucharistic celebration makes present the Trinitarian mystery of the Church. In it one passes from hearing the Word, culminating in the proclamation of the gospel—the apostolic announcing of the word made flesh—to the thanksgiving offered to the Father and to the memorial of the sacrifice and to communion in it thanks to the prayer of *epiclesis* uttered in faith. For the *epiclesis* is not merely an invocation for the sacramental transforming of the bread and cup. It is also prayer for the full effect of the communing of all in the mystery revealed in the Son.[43]

Since the very early church, indeed, the Eucharist has been understood and celebrated in the light of the mystery of the Trinity.[44] Justin Martyr, for example, around A.D. 150, describes the eucharistic prayer: "the [presider] taking [the bread and wine], sends up praise and glory to the Father of all the universe through the name of the Son and of the Holy Spirit, and offers thanksgiving at some length that we have been deemed worthy to receive these things from him" (*First Apology* 65).[45] The *Apostolic Tradition* provides what is arguably the earliest surviving specimen of a eucharistic prayer:[46] "We render thanks to you, O God, through your beloved child Jesus Christ, whom in the last times you sent to us as a saviour and redeemer and angel of your will . . . he was made flesh and was manifested as your Son being born of the Holy Spirit and the Virgin."[47] In the fourth century, in what is reputedly the first treatise on the Trinity in Christian history, Hilary of Poitiers, "the Athanasius of the West," writes of the mystery of the eucharistic communion and its link with the Trinity (*Trinity* 8.13-17).[48]

---

43. Joint Commission for Theological Dialogue between the Roman Catholic Church and the Orthodox Church: Second Plenary Meeting, Munich, June 30 to July 6, 1982, "The Mystery of the Church and of the Eucharist in the Light of the Mystery of the Holy Trinity," *One in Christ* 19 (1983): 188-97, a. 6.

44. For a helpful introduction to the eucharistic prayers in Christian worship, see *Prayers of the Eucharist: Early and Reformed*, ed. R. C. D. Jasper and G. J. Cumin, 3rd ed. (New York: Pueblo, 1987).

45. In *Early Christian Fathers*, trans and ed. Cyril C. Richardson (New York: Collier Books, Macmillan, 1970), 286.

46. For a discussion of the *Apostolic Tradition*, the authorship of which has traditionally been ascribed to Hippolytus, see John F. Baldovin, "Hippolytus and the *Apostolic Tradition*: Recent Research and Commentary," *Theological Studies* 64 (2003): 520-42.

47. See *Prayers of the Eucharist*, 35.

48. In *Nicene and Post-Nicene Fathers*, 9:141-42. For comment on Hilary of Poitiers' thought, see Bobrinskoy, *Mystery of the Trinity*, 228-33; also Michael Figura, "Church and Eucharist in the Light of the Trinitarian Mystery," trans. David L. Schindler, *Communio* 27 (2000): 217-39, esp. 230-33.

The eucharistic liturgy (or the Mass as it is more commonly called in the West) is profoundly trinitarian, in its structure and expression, as well as in its history. The entire liturgy is first encompassed in a eucharistic-trinitarian *inclusio,* with the trinitarian invitation in the form of the sign of the cross—"In the name of the Father, and of the Son, and of the Holy Spirit"—at the outset, and the trinitarian blessing together with the sign of the cross at the conclusion—"May almighty God bless you, the Father, the Son, and the Holy Spirit." The triumphant hymn of praise, the *Gloria*, takes up the trinitarian opening note and rises to a trinitarian hymn of praise. The Liturgy of the Word prepares for the Liturgy of the Eucharist, where the eucharistic prayer, celebrating the history of salvation, is fashioned along explicitly trinitarian lines. The liturgy culminates in the eucharistic prayer, a prayer of thanksgiving and sanctification. While the eucharistic prayer is essentially addressed to the Father, as the one to whom the church addresses its thanksgiving (Eucharist), the prayer unfolds with strong christological and pneumatological tones, each echoing the other.[49] The whole liturgy is a celebration of the Trinity, in which the uniqueness and specificity of the divine persons are articulated and celebrated.

The trinitarian rhythm of the liturgy unfolds in three stages: (1) eucharistia (thanksgiving), (2) anamnesis (remembrance), and (3) epiclesis (invocation).

1. *Eucharistia (thanksgiving).* The Eucharist is a sacrifice of praise and thanksgiving to God for all that God has done in creation, redemption, and sanctification, for us and for our salvation. The prayer of praise and thanksgiving is addressed to the Father, whom Jesus taught us to call "Our Father." We pray in the Eucharistic Prayer III, for example: "Father, you are holy indeed, and all creation rightly gives you thanks and praise. All life, all holiness comes from you through your Son, Jesus Christ our Lord, by the working of the Holy Spirit." The great song of acclamation and adoration—"Holy, Holy, Holy Lord, God of power and might, heaven and earth are full of your glory, Hosannah in the highest"—also resonates with trinitarian overtones and indeed brings them to a crescendo.

2. *Anamnesis (remembrance).* The Eucharist is also a commemoration or a "memorial" of the death, resurrection, and glorification of our Lord Jesus Christ, who was crucified and who rose and ascended into heaven, and who becomes present to us in the eucharistic gifts of bread and wine, which

49. For detailed discussion of the history and structure of the Eucharist, see Enrico Mazza, *The Eucharistic Prayers of the Roman Rite*, trans. Matthew J. O'Connell (New York: Pueblo, 1985); idem, The *Celebration of the Eucharist: The Origin of the Rite and the Development of Its Interpretation*, trans. Matthew J. O'Connell (Collegeville, Minn.: Liturgical Press, 1999).

become his body and blood. It is our sacramental calling to mind, our anamnesis, of Christ Jesus. We pray (in Eucharistic Prayer III): "Father, calling to mind the death your Son endured for our salvation, his glorious resurrection and ascension into heaven, and ready to greet him when he comes again, we offer in thanksgiving this holy and living sacrifice."

3. *Epiclesis (invocation).* In calling on the Holy Spirit, we ask that the bread and wine be made into the body and blood of Jesus Christ, and that believers be transformed into one body and one spirit in Christ. Invoking the creativity of the Spirit, we pray: "We ask you to make them [the bread and wine] holy, by the power of your Spirit, that they may become the body and blood of Our Lord Jesus Christ" (Eucharistic Prayer II). "Grant that we who are nourished by his body and blood may be filled with his Holy Spirit, and become one Body, one Spirit in Christ" (Eucharistic Prayer III). The epiclesis of the Spirit is addressed to the Father. Its object is the transformation of the bread and wine and indeed of ourselves into the sacred body and blood of Jesus Christ.

The eucharistic epiclesis effectively culminates in the invocation of the Father as Our Father. The Our Father rightly follows the eucharistic epiclesis, for it is in the Spirit that we call the Father "Our Father, Abba": "God has sent the Spirit of his Son into our hearts, crying 'Abba, Father'" (Gal. 4:6). Bobrinskoy notes that "the 'Our Father' is, together with communion, the high point of the eucharistic mystery, when the Church is constituted in a filial attitude."[50] In reality, as Bobrinskoy explains:

> The Eucharist of the Church (and the eucharistic Church) is entirely epiclesis-invocation, as it is entirely memorial. These moments cannot be juxtaposed, or, at least, this juxtaposition cannot be hardened, as one cannot harden the juxtaposition Pascha-Pentecost. . . . Just as at the time of the Incarnation of the Word the Holy Spirit does not become incarnate, but penetrates the human nature of the Word from whom He is eternally inseparable, so in the time of the Church the Holy Spirit . . . constitutes the power, the very grace of the memorial and of the presence of Christ in the Church.[51]

Similarly, the ecclesiologist Yves Congar, at the end of his great three-volume work *I Believe in the Holy Spirit*, concludes with a reflection that "the life and activity of the Church can be seen as one long epiclesis."[52]

The reception the Eucharist (Holy Communion) unites us to and in

50. Bobrinskoy, *Mystery of the Trinity*, 167.
51. Ibid., 188-89.
52. Yves Congar, *I Believe in the Holy Spirit*, vol. 3, *The River of the Water of Life (Rev 22:1) Flows in the East and in the West*, trans. David Smith (London: Geoffrey Chapman, 1983), 267-71.

Christ: "Whoever eats my flesh and drinks my blood abides in me and I in him" (John 6:56). The celebration of the Eucharist, the taking of communion, is a participation in the eschatological banquet of the Kingdom; as Thomas Aquinas expressed it so beautifully, it is "pledge of future glory" (SC 47),[53] an anticipation of the eschaton, the end-time, when all creation will be transfigured and transformed by the Holy Spirit, when God will be "all in all" (1 Cor. 15:28).

Finally, the solemn doxology offered at the conclusion of the eucharistic prayer also points to and reinforces the trinitarian context, structure, and rhythm of the liturgy: "Through him [Christ], with him and in him, in the unity of the Holy Spirit, all honour and glory is yours almighty Father for ever and ever." Then, in the concluding rite, following the blessings at the end of the Eucharist, is the instruction: "Let us go in peace to love and serve the Lord. . . . Thanks be to God." Here is the last and indispensable dimension of the Eucharist: mission. Having partaken of the body and blood of Jesus Christ, we enter into the process of divinization, our indwelling in the Son and the Father through the Spirit, and we receive a share in the trinitarian life and trinitarian mission. We are therefore sent out, commissioned to share in the redemptive mission of Word and Spirit in the world.[54] As Peter Henrici points out, the Eucharist is the point of the trinitarian God's inbreaking into this world, and not just symbol but sign of the world's redemption.[55] In all of these ways, then, the eucharistic liturgy clearly reflects and expresses the trinitarian doctrine and the faith of the church. Walter Kasper concludes: "In the eucharist the mutual self-communication and self-giving of the trinitarian persons are sacramentally manifested and become present. If the trinitarian confession is the dogmatic summing up of the whole mystery of salvation, the eucharist is the sacramental summing up of that mystery."[56]

PREACHING THE TRINITY

Following the Feast of Pentecost in the liturgical calendar, the Feast of the Trinity admittedly stands rather oddly in the liturgical year. All other feasts celebrate what God has done rather than what God is. Moreover, belief in the Trinity lies at the heart of every Christian feast and every celebration of the Eucharist. It is not simply one mystery among others. Trinity Sunday is surely

53. Quoting Thomas Aquinas, in antiphon to the Magnificat in the Roman Breviary, Feast of Corpus Christi, Second Vespers.

54. See Christopher Cocksworth, *Holy, Holy, Holy: Worshipping the Trinitarian God* (London: Darton, Longman & Todd, 1997), 201-17, for a reflection on Trinity, worship, and mission.

55. Peter Henrici, "Trinity and Eucharist," *Communio* 27 (2000): 211-16.

56. Walter Kasper, *Theology and Church*, trans. Margaret Kohl (London: SCM Press, 1989), 190.

one time in the year when it would seem appropriate to preach about the Trinity. But, how seldom homilies are devoted to this central mystery of our faith as Christians. A priest friend once recalled that when he was a seminarian, after intense study of trinitarian theology, his learned lecturer advised the students not to speak on the topic of the Trinity for more than three minutes, for fear of speaking heresy! A Cistercian tractate of 1230 on the Feast of the Trinity instructed the community that on this day the abbot was to celebrate the Mass solemnly in community, that there were to be three lamps on the altar, and that there was to be no sermon on so complex a matter![57] Even the great St. Augustine, when introducing *De Trinitate*, noted the extreme danger and difficulty involved in regard to matters trinitarian: "For nowhere else is a mistake more dangerous, or the search more laborious," he noted, also commenting that nowhere was "discovery more advantageous" (1.5). The prospect of danger and of labor, it would seem, has resulted in a real reticence and reluctance to speak of this great mystery of our faith.

Yet preaching the Trinity is important in fostering and deepening a personal appropriation of the mystery of the Trinity. By way of assistance, we can take inspiration from the trinitarian reflections of the mystics or the homilies of great contemporary theologians.[58] The point, as Owen Cummings suggests, is that: "If we tried to make our preaching and teaching more carefully trinitarian, then we might move to a more pervasive and perduring appropriation of the Trinity as the shape of our liturgy and of our lives."[59] Preaching affords the precious opportunity to develop our sense of prayer, liturgy, and our spirituality in more consciously and explicitly trinitarian ways.[60]

CONCLUSION

A spirituality that is attuned to our trinitarian faith will mine the boundless depths of our faith that God is Trinity, a communion of three divine persons in the one God. It will be attuned to an understanding of our very being as

57. *Statuta capitulorum generalium ordinis Cisterciensis ab anno 1116 ad annum 1786,* ed. J. Canivez, 8 vols. (Louvain, 1933-41), 2:1230.1, 84. I thank Michael Casey OCSO of Tarrawarra Abbey for his assistance with this reference.

58. See, e.g., Hans Urs von Balthasar, *You Crown the Year with Your Goodness: Sermons Through the Liturgical Year* (San Francisco: Ignatius Press, 1995). For some helpful reflections on this area, see Margaret Schuster, "Preaching the Trinity," in *The Trinity: An Interdisciplinary Symposium on the Trinity*, ed. Stephen T. Davis, Daniel Kendall, and Gerald O'Collins (Oxford: Oxford University Press, 1999), 357-81.

59. Owen Cummings, "The Trinity and the Liturgy," *Priests and People* 13 (1999): 142.

60. For some helpful resources, see Ruth C. Duck and Patricia Wilson-Kastner, *Praising God: The Trinity in Christian Worship* (Louisville: Westminster John Knox Press, 1999). See also Catherine LaCugna, "Making the Most of Trinity Sunday," *Worship* 60 (1986): 210-24; Herbert McCabe, "A Sermon for Trinity Sunday," in *God Still Matters,* 233-37.

oriented toward and constituted by our relations with each other, with the cosmos, and with the triune God. It will not fear or resist the essentially paschal dimension of the Christian life, for it will recognize and acknowledge that the invitation to ever-fuller participation in the communion of the triune God involves a real self-denial, a renunciation of self, and ultimately physical death. It also inspires and motivates us to ever-fuller participation in our communion with others. As Downey explains:

> Christian life in the Spirit, the Christian spiritual life, is a journey from and toward God, the one called "Father," who is the origin and end of Love. Christian life is living for God through Christ the Word, the truth irrevocably spoken: Life endures; Love endures. It is living with and in the Spirit dwelling in the depths of the human heart, living from the desire for fuller life, light, and love recognized in the self-giving of Jesus on the cross, the perfect image of interpersonal love.[61]

This is the fullness of life to which we are called. We are created for nothing less than communion with the trinitarian God who is Love.

FOR FUTHER READING

Catechism of the Catholic Church. 2nd ed. Washington, D.C.: U.S. Catholic Conference, 2000. http://www.vatican.va/archive/ENG0015/_INDEX.HTM

Cocksworth, Christopher. *Holy, Holy, Holy: Worshipping the Trinitarian God.* London: Darton, Longman & Todd, 1997.

Downey, Michael, and Catherine LaCugna. "Trinitarian Spirituality." In *The New Dictionary of Catholic Spirituality*, edited by Michael Downey. Collegeville, Minn.: Liturgical Press, A Michael Glazier Book, 1993.

Downey, Michael. *Altogether Gift: A Trinitarian Spirituality.* Maryknoll, N.Y.: Orbis Books, 2000.

Duck, Ruth C., and Patricia Wilson-Kastner, *Praising God: The Trinity in Christian Worship*. Louisville: Westminster John Knox Press, 1999.

Fiddes, Paul S. *Participating in God: A Pastoral Theology of the Trinity*. Louisville: Westminster John Knox Press, 2000.

Hill, Jerome M. *We Have the Mind of Christ: The Holy Spirit and Liturgical Memory in the Thought of Edward J. Kilmartin.* Collegeville, Minn.: Liturgical Press, 2001.

61. Downey, *Altogether Gift,* 58.

10

Trinity and Eschatology

Always be prepared to give an account to anyone who calls you to account for the hope that is in you. (1 Pet. 3:15)

ESCHATOLOGY IS TRADITIONALLY UNDERSTOOD as the doctrine of the *eschata*, or the "last things." The "eschaton" refers both to the end and to the completion or fulfillment of creation; it means the end-time, when history has run its course. Classical approaches to eschatology treated the "last things" under headings including the End of the World, the Return of Christ, Death, Resurrection, Judgment, Purgatory, Heaven and Hell,[1] and typically addressed both the individual and the collective dimensions of the "last things" in terms of the perfection of individual life and the consummation of history and the whole cosmos. It is perhaps not really surprising that eschatology usually figured at the end, as the last piece, in outlines of Christian doctrine, following the major themes of greater import. But, situated there at the end, it appeared almost as an afterthought, and certainly not of utterly crucial importance. Karl Rahner, who was to make a highly significant contribution in re-envisioning eschatology, commented critically on the paucity of neoscholastic treatments of eschatology and on the general neglect of the area in the history of theology: "The history of the revelation of the Last Things down to and including the whole New Testament, is long and rich, but the history of eschatology is meagre in comparison with that of other sections of dogmatic theology, at least within the limits of ecclesiastical orthodoxy or in contact with this."[2]

Recent developments in Christian theology in general and in eschatology in particular have, however, radically reappraised the significance of eschatology for all Christian doctrine and the importance of its integration with other themes of theology. For example, Gustavo Gutiérrez explains: "eschatology is . . . not just one more element of Christianity, but the very key to

---

1. Limbo is not mentioned in the *Catechism of the Catholic Church*.

2. Karl Rahner, "Eschatology," in *An Encyclopedia of Theology: The Concise Sacramentum Mundi*, ed. Karl Rahner (New York: Crossroad, 1975), 434.

understanding the Christian faith."[3] Eschatology is not just another topic in Christian theology; rather, it is the essential perspective of Christian theology as a whole! So crucial and so central is eschatology to our understanding of Christian faith, that Christoph Schwöbel suggests that eschatology should figure first, not last, in our theology.[4] Our goal in this chapter is to explore the essentially trinitarian character of Christian hope and to speak of the last things, the really *ultimate* things, from an explicitly trinitarian perspective.

To articulate the "last things" is to dare to speak—not in some dispassionate way, as if the "last things" hardly concern us personally—of our deepest and most passionately held hopes for the future and of our ultimate hope, for ourselves as individuals, for our loved ones, for all humanity, and indeed for the whole cosmos.[5] In eschatology, our faith as Christians expresses itself essentially in terms of our hope. Where all Christian theology is aptly described, following Anselm, as "faith seeking understanding," one could aptly speak of Christian eschatology as "hope seeking understanding."[6] The task of eschatology is to give an account of our hope. Christian existence is, after all, essentially a way of hope. Christians are essentially people of hope. The Eucharist, as foretaste of the future and the end of all things, as "pledge of future glory" as Thomas Aquinas expressed it, is in essence a sacrament of hope. Indeed, hope itself has an essentially sacramental form; it is a visible sign of invisible grace. The church is a community of hope. Its mission is a mission of hope to a troubled and suffering world. Vatican II's Pastoral Constitution on the Church in the Modern World, *Gaudium et Spes,* begins exquisitely with reference to the hopes and joys, as well as the griefs and anxieties, of humanity today. Hope and joy are related: hope is an anticipation of joy and looks to its fulfillment. Heaven is the fulfillment of our hope (and, correlatively, hell is hope's ultimate frustration and the termination of our hope). The First Letter of Peter instructs us: "Always be prepared to give an account to anyone who calls you to account for the hope that is in you" (1 Pet. 3:15). What then is our hope? What is it that we most long for? This is the subject of our explorations in eschatology.

---

3. Gustavo Gutiérrez, *A Theology of Liberation: History, Politics and Salvation* (Maryknoll, N.Y.: Orbis Books, 1973), 162.

4. Christoph Schwöbel, "Last Things First?" in *The Future as God's Gift: Explorations in Christian Eschatology*, ed. David Fergusson and Marcel Sarot (Edinburgh: T&T Clark, 2000), 219-41.

5. Pierre Teilhard de Chardin (1881-1955) brought into focus the properly cosmic dimension of eschatology. Christ, as the *alpha* and *omega* (Rev. 1:8) of the one universal cosmic process of evolution, effects the goal of creation, the christification of the cosmos. All spheres of reality are included in the *milieu divin* (see his *The Divine Milieu: An Essay on the Interior Life* [New York: Harper & Bros., 1960]).

6. My thanks to Anthony (Tony) Kelly for this beautiful expression. See Kelly's new book on eschatology, forthcoming from Orbis in this same series.

Our day-to-day efforts and our preoccupations are so often concerned not with "the last things" but with the immediate, the here and now, the daily imperatives that demand our attention. But it takes only a serious accident or a cataclysm of some kind in our lives to cut through our many preoccupations to the core of what really matters most in our life. How quickly we recognize at those critical moments what is really important and what is not. How quickly we reorganize our thoughts, our priorities, and our focus. When life itself is at stake in some way, we realize, as if struck by lightning, that we spend so much of our energy and time on matters that aren't really of great import or significance. What is it that strikes, like lightning, as being of ultimate importance at those times? It is not material possessions—in fact, they seem so essentially immaterial and unimportant at those times. Is it not the preciousness of life itself? Do we not long for life, as Pope John Paul II observed, when addressing World Youth Day in 1993:

> Different languages have different words to express what no one would never wish to lose under any circumstances, what constitutes the expectation, longing and hope of all mankind. *But there is no better word than "life"* to sum up comprehensively the greatest aspiration of all humanity. "Life" indicates the sum total of all the goods that people desire, and at the same time what makes them possible, obtainable, and lasting.[7]

In John's Gospel, Jesus says: "I came that they may have life, and have it abundantly" (10:10). Do we not long for the fullness of life? Is our longing not something like that which Thérèse of Lisieux expressed when she said "my hopes touch on the infinite"?[8] Our hopes, our ultimate desires, and our deepest longings "touch on the infinite." It is the fulfillment of this boundless hope of which we speak when we talk in terms of heaven. There our hopes "touch on the infinite." Thérèse's own account of her childhood also tells of a time when she was invited to make her choice from a basket filled with dolls' dresses and pretty pieces of fabric. Whereas Thérèse's sister chose an item that pleased her, Thérèse exclaimed "I choose all."[9] There is a sense

---

7. Pope John Paul II, Message to the Youth of the World, On the Occasion of the VIII World Youth Day – 1993 (art 2). See http://www.vatican.va/holy_father/john_paul_ii/messages/youth.

8. Sainte Thérèse, "mes espérances qui touchent à l'infini" in Lettre A, Soeur Marie du Sacré Coeur, Manuscrit (B 2v,28), in *Sainte Thérèse de L'Enfant-Jésu et de La Sainte-Face: Oeuvres Complètes* (Paris: Cerf-Desclée de Brouwer, 1992), 224. See also *The Story of a Soul: An Autobiography of Saint Thérèse of Lisieux,* trans. John Clarke, 3rd ed. (Washington, D.C.: ICS Publications, 1996), 192, "my desires and longings which reach even into infinity." I thank Paul Chandler OCarm for his assistance with this reference.

9. Thérèse of Lisieux, *Story of a Soul*, 27.

that we too choose all. The all that we long for is the fullness of life. We long for eternal life. We long for life and for love, without limit or end and, moreover, not just for ourselves but for all creation. As Christians, we dare to hope for the perfection of creation "when God will be all in all" (1 Cor. 15:28), as Paul's First Letter to the Corinthians so expansively describes it.

In the Nicene-Constantinopolitan Creed, Christians confess that the One Lord Jesus Christ will come again to judge the living and the dead. Later, in the very last section of that perduring symbol of Christian unity, immediately following our confession of faith in the Holy Spirit—as "Lord and Giver of Life, who proceeds from the Father [and the Son].[10] With the Father and Son, he is worshiped and glorified. He has spoken through the prophets"—Christians confess that "we believe in one holy catholic and apostolic church, we acknowledge one baptism for the forgiveness of sins, we look for the resurrection of the dead, and the life of the world to come." It is no accident that our confession of faith and hope for these "last things" is so closely associated with our faith in God as Father, Son, and Spirit. The poet Dante, in his *Divine Comedy*, depicts the circles of heaven and hell and concludes with the vision in paradise of the Trinity and "the love that moves the sun and the other spheres."[11] Yet, how seldom in the tradition of Christian theology has eschatology been explicated in expressly trinitarian terms. Here indeed lies the key to an eschatology that is not isolated from the other doctrinal themes, as Schwöbel explains: "If we want to avoid the dangers of an isolated treatment of eschatology, the task consists in developing a Christian eschatology as a trinitarian eschatology."[12]

WOLFHART PANNENBERG: THE KINGDOM OF GOD AS THE GLORY OF THE TRINITY

For Wolfhart Pannenberg, who comes from the Lutheran tradition, eschatology serves as no mere addendum but as the unifying theme of his systematic theology. Indeed, Schwöbel writes: "Pannenberg's theology is perhaps the most radical attempt to understand the whole of Christian faith and theology as eschatology."[13] What is of even more interest to us is that in his the-

10. We bracket "and the Son" as a reminder that it is a later insertion into the Nicene-Constantinopolitan Creed.

11. Dante Alighieri, *The Divine Comedy: Paradise*, trans. Charles Eliot Norton (Chicago: William Benton, 1952), canto 33, line 142, p. 157.

12. Schwöbel, "Last Things First?" 238.

13. Ibid., 229. For a helpful discussion of Pannenberg's work in the wider context of the tradition of German Protestant trinitarian theology, see Simon M. Powell, *The Trinity in German Thought* (Cambridge: Cambridge University Press, 2001).

ology we find a remarkable attempt to express eschatology in expressly trinitarian terms. Readers will recall that we considered Wolfhart Pannenberg's contribution in regard to approaching a theology of creation from an expressly trinitarian perspective. It should come as no surprise that we now return to his work when considering eschatology, given that theologies of creation, usually understood in terms of a theology of the origin and preservation of the cosmos, and of eschatology, as the theology of the consummation of creation and the fulfillment of its destiny, are obviously very closely related.

It is the notion of the Reign or Kingdom of God (*basileia)*, as the central idea in the life, ministry, and message of Jesus, that grounds Pannenberg's theology. Pannenberg contrasts the prominence of the theme of the Kingdom of God in Jesus' proclamation with its lack of prominence in the expression of Christian eschatological expectation. He explains: "In view of the significance of this theme and its clear attestation in traditions about the message of Jesus, it is surprising that the theme of the kingdom of God has not played as dominant a role in Christian eschatology as one might expect."[14] Pannenberg thus insists that God and God's kingdom or rule form the central content of eschatology.

Pannenberg also notes the acute tension between the "now and already" and "the not yet" in Jesus' message of the Kingdom of God. Salvation irrupts here and now, already within reach, but it is not yet, with its consummation still to come at the end-time. This observation in itself is not exceptional. What is distinctive in Pannenberg's thought, however, is that he recognizes that this tension between the already-not yet in Jesus' life, and indeed in Christian existence, is only able to be articulated in eschatological terms. Pannenberg therefore focuses on the Kingdom of God, which is incomplete in the present order of things, as an eschatological reality. Just as Jesus proclaimed and prepared for the coming of the Kingdom, the consummation of creation will be the definite establishment of the Kingdom, when God reigns in and over all things. In other words, the eschatological consummation of the world is nothing other than the Kingdom or rule of God. Pannenberg's understanding of the Kingdom of God is consequently radically eschatological; it is "the Kingdom of God understood as the eschatological future brought about by God himself."[15] Concomitantly, Pannenberg's understanding of God is also radically eschatological. He understands God, as proclaimed in Jesus' message, as God of the coming Kingdom. We can thus begin

14. Wolfhart Pannenberg, *Systematic Theology*, 3 vols., trans. Geoffrey W. Bromiley (Grand Rapids: Wm. B. Eerdmans, 1994-98), 3:527.

15. Wolfhart Pannenberg, *Theology and the Kingdom of God*, ed. Richard J. Neuhaus (Philadelphia: Westminster Press, 1969), 53.

to appreciate just how profoundly and radically eschatology informs and forms Pannenberg's theology. Indeed, Christiaan Mostert observes that "Pannenberg's retrieval of eschatology into the centre of the theological agenda is unmatched in contemporary theology."[16] As Pannenberg himself comments: Eschatology is "not just the subject of a single chapter in dogmatics; it determines the perspective of Christian doctrine as a whole."[17]

What is even more striking about Pannenberg's systematic theology, however, is that he then connects the notions of the Kingdom of God and God as Trinity. In Pannenberg's theology, which culminates in his three-volume *Systematic Theology*, these two notions intersect. As Mostert points out: "Ultimately [for Pannenberg] the theology of the eschatological kingdom of God and the doctrine of the Trinity coincide."[18] As Mostert explains, the Kingdom of God and the Trinity are like two superimposed concentric circles.[19] For Pannenberg, the Kingdom of God *is* the glory of the Trinity. It is the power of God; it is the love that is God; it is the love that is Trinity. The Kingdom of God, as demonstrated in God's rule over the cosmos at the eschatological completion of creation, constitutes the glory of God, who is Trinity of three divine persons. That God's being (as Trinity) is God's rule (as the Kingdom of God) thus emerges as a vital principle in Pannenberg's theology. To use Pannenberg's expression: "God's being *is* God's rule."[20] Pannenberg means that God's being as Trinity simply cannot be conceived of apart from God's rule (or kingdom or reign). Consequently eschatology and Trinity are inextricably related.

The Proper Roles of the Divine Persons in the Consummation of Creation

Pannenberg proceeds to a thoroughly trinitarian approach to a theology of the consummation of creation. Having articulated, as we have seen earlier, a doctrine of creation (in terms of its origin and preservation) in explicitly trinitarian terms, Pannenberg's eschatological doctrine is concomitantly expressed in trinitarian terms. Here too he strives to expound a more explicitly differentiated treatment of the work of each of the divine persons in

16. Christiaan Mostert, *God and the Future: Wolfhart Pannenberg's Eschatological Doctrine of God* (Edinburgh/New York: T&T Clark, 2002), 20.

17. Pannenberg, *Systematic Theology,* 3:531.

18. Mostert, *God and the Future,* 5.

19. Ibid., 184.

20. Pannenberg, *Theology and the Kingdom of God,* 55. See also, e.g., Mostert, *God and the Future,* 5, 237. Pannenberg also says, "The deity of God is his rule."

God's involvement in creation and its consummation than the classical strategy of appropriation affords.

We recall the classical theological axiom that the works of the Trinity in creation are undividedly one. Through the strategy of appropriation, the work of creation is appropriated to the Father, reconciliation and redemption to the Son, and salvation and consummation to the Spirit, on the basis that each of the stages in the divine salvific plan stands in a singularly close relation to one of the divine persons. Pannenberg agrees that it is most appropriate that the third and final stage in the economy of salvation is appropriated to the Spirit.[21] But he observes that the activity of the Spirit has often been neglected in theology and that twentieth-century exegesis has brought fresh awareness of the close connection between the Spirit and eschatology. It is important to note that Pannenberg holds to the classical axiom that the three divine persons are one in essence and that their work in creation is the one work of the one God. But he would persuade us that each divine person is active in its own distinct way, in unity with the others. As Pannenberg explains, "In all its forms the activity of the Trinitarian God in creation is an activity of the Father by the Son and Spirit, an activity of the Son in obedience to the Father, and the glorifying of both in the consummation of their work by the Spirit."[22]

Pannenberg insists that the life of God is constituted by the differentiated but complementary activity of the three divine persons. "If the trinitarian relations among Father, Son and Spirit have the form of mutual self-distinction, they must be understood not merely as different modes of being of the one divine subject but as living realizations of separate centers of action."[23] The divine persons, he argues, are "direct subjects of the divine action."[24] The Spirit is the origin of life and movement, in regard both to the work of creation and to the work of the new creation. Through the Spirit, creatures come to share in the life of the triune God. This eschatological participation of creation in the life of the Trinity, Pannenberg argues, is *properly* the work of the Spirit, not just by way of appropriation.

As Mostert explains, the notion of personhood is critical to the development of his argument for differentiated and proper roles for the three divine persons.[25] Pannenberg argues that personhood, as distinct from subjecthood, consists in relationality. None of the divine persons is a divine person in iso-

21. Pannenberg, *Systematic Theology,* 3:554.
22. Ibid., 1.
23. Pannenberg, *Systematic Theology,* 1:319.
24. Ibid., 383.
25. See Mostert, *God and the Future,* 187.

lation from the others. Each divine person receives his divinity through the other two divine persons. The trinitarian relations are therefore not just relations of origin, in which the Son and Holy Spirit unilaterally, so to speak, receive their divinity from the Father. The Father also receives, so to speak, his divinity from the Son and Holy Spirit, just as they receive theirs from him. The trinitarian relations are thus relations of mutual dependence. They are characterized by mutuality and reciprocity. In this light, Father, Son, and Spirit are persons in the fullest sense. God is personal, Pannenberg argues, precisely because God is trinitarian.[26]

God as Open to and Involved in the History of the Cosmos

Pannenberg argues that, through the activity and experience of each of the divine persons in creation, God is open to and involved in the history of the cosmos. Indeed, in Pannenberg's eschatologically oriented theology, God is constituted by what each of the divine persons does in the work of creation, salvation, and consummation. In other words, the historical relations of the three divine persons are determinative of the eternal character and being of God. But we must note that Pannenberg neither intends nor brooks a process theology. Pannenberg insists that God is not "the result of history."[27] While rejecting process notions, Pannenberg argues, however, that what takes place in history affects God's very being and existence. He insists that God, through the actions of the three divine persons, is involved in the events of history, open to them, and affected by them. In other words, Pannenberg holds that the events of history "bear in some way on the God's eternal

26. See Pannenberg's discussion of the divine persons in *Systematic Theology,* 1:300-327. It can seem somewhat strange, then, that Pannenberg also proposes an understanding of the Holy Spirit as the divine force field or dynamic field of force: "The idea of the divine life as a dynamic field sees the divine spirit who unites the three persons as proceeding from the Father received by the Son, and common to both, so that precisely in this way he is the force field of their fellowship that is distinct from them both" (ibid., 383). In *Systematic Theology,* vol. 2, Pannenberg qualifies the notion: "The person of the Holy Spirit is not himself to be understood as the field but as a unique manifestation (singularity) of the field of the divine essentiality. But because the personal being of the Holy Spirit is manifest only in distinction from the Son (and therefore also from the Father), his working in creation has more of the character of dynamic field operations. . . it relates to the link and movement that connects the creatures to one another and to God. To this extent the Spirit's work in creation is by nature more than a field of divine essentiality. It relates plainly to the specificity of the person of the Holy Spirit in distinction from the Son" (pp. 83-84). Pannenberg has shown great interest over many years in the concept of the force field in physics, recognizing considerable theological potential in it. See Ted Peters's helpful comments in "Editor's Introduction: Pannenberg on Theology and Natural Science," in *Toward a Theology of Nature: Essays on Science and Faith,* ed. Ted Peters (Louisville: Westminster John Knox Press, 1993), 1-14.

27. Pannenberg, *Systematic Theology,* 1:331.

essence, existence and being."[28] While God is not "the result of history," God is affected by history, and history bears on God's essence.[29]

This is, however, to be understood eschatologically. Here we come face to face with the problem of time in our understanding of the being of God and of the relation between time and eternity and indeed with Pannenberg's somewhat idiosyncratic understanding of time, eternity, and eschatology. As Pannenberg himself comments: "The relation between time and eternity is the crucial problem in eschatology, and its solution has implications for all parts of Christian doctrine."[30] As temporal beings, we tend instinctively to situate concepts of the eschaton in a temporal context, a context shaped by notions of past, present, and future, and in a framework that is future oriented. Thus, we tend to temporalize God and the eschaton. Here it is helpful to recall Augustine's teaching that the cosmos was created with time, not in time (*City of God* 11.6). In other words, time pertains to the realm of the cosmos, not to the eternal being of God.[31] So when Pannenberg proposes that God's being remains open, and that God's essence is affected by events of history, he means this not from the perspective of the eternal divine essence but from within the realm of time.[32] So Pannenberg can speak of the Father, Son, and Spirit as separate agents of action in history, whose unity will be demonstrated at the end of history, when that unity will be shown to have been real from the beginning. Similarly, God's unity, as Pannenberg understands it, is an eschatological unity that depends on the course of history.

Mostert helpfully explains Pannenberg's thinking in terms of "retrospective permanence,"[33] meaning that, retrospectively, at the eschaton, God's being will be revealed to have been eternally what it is then. In the eschaton, and only then, what is the case in time will coincide with what is the case

---

28. Ibid., 334.

29. It is interesting to compare Pannenberg's notion of the effect of the events of history on God's eternal essence and being and von Balthasar's notion of the "enrichment" of God by the events in creation. See again Guy Mansini, "Balthasar and the Theodramatic Enrichment of the Trinity," *Thomist* 64 (2000): 499-519.

30. Pannenberg, *Systematic Theology,* 3:595.

31. Thus, Schwöbel suggests that the starting point for understanding matters eschatological is not time but God ("Last Things First?" 240). For Pannenberg, "the independence for which God has destined his creatures, and especially among them his human creatures, needs time as the form of their existence in order that creatures may bring their own lives into conformity with the future of the destiny that God has given them" (*Systematic Theology,* 3:580). As Pannenberg explains: "The duration of time is decisive for the independent existence of creatures. Only by their own, if limited, direction do they have their own existence in distinction from God and each other" (ibid., 597). "Now creaturely independence is not possible without temporality as a form of existence" (ibid., 643); see also *Systematic Theology,* 2:71-72, 95-96, 123-24.

32. See Mostert's explanation, *God and the Future,* 220.

33. Ibid., 222.

eternally. Then, and only then, it will be demonstrably clear that the cosmos is the creation of God, redeemed by God, and brought to consummation in God's Kingdom by God. The eternal being of God as Father, Son, and Holy Spirit will be revealed clearly and unambiguously to be identical with the God whose reign is proclaimed by Jesus Christ and consummated by the Holy Spirit.[34] "We shall know as we are fully known" (1 Cor. 13:12). God will "wipe away every tear" (Isa. 25:8). The revelation of God's love will be consummated.[35] The economic Trinity, active in the cosmos, will be established as identical with the immanent Trinity, the eternal God.[36] Then, and only then, will God's rule and concomitantly God's deity be confirmed. In this way, as Mostert explains, Pannenberg "argues for a view of God whose eternal being is established retrospectively from the point where eternity and time meet."[37] It is a matter of giving ontological priority to the future, of seeing God's future as the creative origin of all things in the cosmos.[38] From this perspective, God is the power of the future who, in love, brings the world into existence and who, in love, allows it to be and draws it into communion with God's triune self. At core, this love is the love of the Father for the Son, in whom and through whom the Father loves all creation.

The Kingdom of God and the Trinity

We return now to the vital nexus in Pannenberg's theology between the Kingdom of God and the Trinity. The completion and perfection of all creation at the eschaton, Pannenberg recognizes, is the Kingdom of God, demonstrated in God's rule over all creation. It coincides with the glory of the Trinity. The Kingdom of God, fully realized and revealed at the eschaton, *is* the glory of the Trinity.

In Pannenberg's theology, glorification emerges as essentially the work of the Spirit. Indeed, for Pannenberg, the work of the Spirit can be encapsulated

34. See Pannenberg, *Systematic Theology,* 3:631-32.

35. Ibid., 642-44.

36. Ibid., 646. Pannenberg concludes his three-volume masterpiece: "On the whole path from the beginning of creation by way of reconciliation to the eschatological future of salvation, the march of the divine economy of salvation is an expression of the incursion of the eternal future of God to the salvation of creatures and thus a manifestation of the divine love. Here is the eternal basis of God's coming forth from the immanence of the divine life as the economic Trinity and of the incorporation of creatures, mediated thereby, into the unity of the trinitarian life. The distinction and unity of the immanent and economic Trinity constitute the heartbeat of the divine love, and with a single such heartbeat this love encompasses the whole world of creatures."

37. Mostert, *God and the Future,* 223.

38. See Pannenberg, *Systematic Theology,* 3:527-32.

in the notion of glorification. Creation is glorified through its participation in God's glory. God is glorified in the new resurrection life of creation. The Holy Spirit is given to believers as pledge of future glorification. The work of perfection and consummation of the cosmos is realized in its transformation into the new creation and its glorification through its entry into communion with the Trinity, and Pannenberg recognizes this as preeminently and properly the work of the Holy Spirit.[39] "The whole compass of his eschatological work comes into view if we think of it as distinctly a work of glorification."[40]

Elaborating on the differentiated roles of the three divine persons in the consummation of the cosmos, Pannenberg understands that it is through the Spirit, who is the Spirit of fellowship between the Father and the Son, and who fulfills the unity of the Trinity, that creatures come to share in the life of God, for it is the Spirit who "draws them into the eternal fellowship of the Father and the Son."[41] Clearly, pneumatology and eschatology bear a special relation to each other, and Pannenberg recognizes and stresses that the work of the Spirit is inseparably linked to that of the Son throughout the history of creation, before and after the paschal mystery of Jesus. In the work of creation, the Word is the principle according to which creation is fashioned and the principle of self-distinction and differentiation within creation, while the Spirit is the source of movement and life of creatures. The work of reconciliation is accomplished by the Son, through his life, death, and resurrection, while the Spirit, who is active in the life and paschal mystery of Jesus Christ, is sent by the Son and imparted to believers, leading them to recognize the revelation of the Father in the work of the Son. The Spirit bears witness to the Son, glorifies the Son, and completes the mission of the Son. In the eschatological consummation of creation, the Spirit is the source of unity, communion, consummation, and perfection. It is the Spirit who will transform our mortal bodies into the new life of the resurrection of the dead. The Spirit is the transfiguring power that gives creatures a share in the glory of God, while the Son is agent of the last judgment, the criterion for belonging or not belonging to God and God's Kingdom. The Kingdom of God, which Jesus proclaimed and which irrupted with him, thus finds its consummation when the work of the Spirit is complete and Jesus Christ returns in glory. The lordship of the Son establishes the lordship and rule of the Father. The rule of the Father, which occurs in and through the Son and Holy Spirit, is the rule of God. It is the Kingdom of God, the glory of God, the glory of the Trinity.

39. Ibid., 622-26.
40. Ibid., 623.
41. Ibid., 626.

The Role of the Spirit in the Consummation of Creation

Eschatology and pneumatology belong together, Pannenberg argues, because the eschatological consummation of the cosmos is the work of the Spirit. Pannenberg then summarizes the role of the Spirit in the consummation of God's plan of salvation under three headings: (1) the special nature of the soteriological work of the Spirit relative to creation, (2) the Spirit as gift and the glorifying of creation, and (3) the outpouring of the Spirit and the church.[42]

In his eschatology, Pannenberg first stresses the distinctly soteriological work of the Spirit. Drawing on Augustine's understanding of the Spirit as gift, the mutual gift of Father and Son, and on the experience of the Spirit as gift in the early church, Pannenberg highlights an understanding of the Spirit as preeminently "the eschatological gift." As Pannenberg observes:

> One of the chief features common to the primitive Christian understanding of the Spirit is that the gift of the *pneuma* is an eschatological gift and that his working in the community is an eschatological event. The Spirit's work on believers is not just that of an external, invisible, and incomprehensible field of force. The Spirit is given to them as a gift. Here lies the special nature of his function relative to the salvation event. The gift of the Spirit has a soteriological function as an anticipation of the eschatological outpouring of the Spirit and is defined as a gift by the fact that Jesus Christ has given him to believers, the eschatological future of salvation having dawned already in his own person and history, so that they are aware that the Spirit they have received is the Spirit of Jesus Christ (Phil. 1:19; cf. Rom. 8:9).[43]

The work of the Spirit, Pannenberg stresses again, is closely linked to that of the Son. The Spirit teaches believers to recognize the revelation of the Father in the life and work of the incarnate Son.

Second, Pannenberg recognizes that the distinctive nature of the eschatological gift that is the Spirit is participation in the sonship of Jesus and thus entry into the trinitarian life and glory of God. He argues: "The distinctive nature of the eschatological gift of the Spirit consists, then, of the fact that by the conferring of the Spirit as a lasting possession of believers, participation

---

42. Ibid., 1-7, 7-12, 12-20.
43. Ibid., 7.

in the eternal life of God is made possible, and consequently also their resurrection to a new life in fellowship with God is guaranteed."[44] Believers are thus drawn into the Son's relationship to the Father, sharing in the glorifying of the Father by the Son and the glorifying of the Son by the Father, and therefore in the glory of God. The imparting of the Spirit, as gift, thus characterizes the soteriological phase of the Spirit's work. But the Spirit is more than simply gift. As Pannenberg argues: "the imparting of the Spirit as gift is only a transitional stage in his work in salvation history. . . . By the Spirit creatures will be made capable of independence in their relation to God and at the same time integrated into the unity of God's kingdom."[45] It is the Spirit's role as source of new life, as creative activity in bringing forth life and movement, that is the basic and essential form of the Spirit's work. The work is effectively linked to an imparting of his own ecstatic self-transcending dynamic. Creatures have movement and life in themselves, in self-distinction and independence from God. Through the work of the Spirit they enter into fellowship with God and participation in the divine life and glory. Pannenberg thus encapsulates the work of the Spirit in terms of glorification. As he explains: "The whole compass of his [the Spirit's] eschatological work comes into view if we think of it as distinctively a work of glorification."[46] The glorifying of God in creation is the work of the Spirit. It is a glorification that is mutual—the glorification of creation and the glorification of God—in the eschatological consummation:

> To the glorification of creatures as the act of God in which their being is changed to make possible their participation in God's eternal glory corresponds the glorification of God by creatures, namely, by the praise of the Creator in which creatures distinguish the Creator from themselves as the giver of their existence and their life and honor his deity by giving him thanks.[47]

Third, the Spirit's role as the source of new life also relates to the life of the church, for the outpouring of the Spirit is not just for individual believers but for the building up of the fellowship of believers, the church. The church, as fellowship of believers, is grounded on the participation of each in the one Jesus Christ, but it is the Spirit who founds the fellowship of believers, drawing them into the Son's relationship to the Father. Here too Pannenberg

44. Ibid., 12.
45. Ibid..
46. Ibid., 623.
47. Ibid., 625.

stresses that the roles of Son and Spirit are inextricably related: "The church is the creation of both the Spirit and the Son. It is the creation of the Spirit even as it is that of the risen Christ by the Word of the gospel."[48] The pneumatological and christological constitution of the church belong together, he insists, just as the Spirit and the Son mutually indwell one another as trinitarian persons: "The Spirit's work in the church always relates to Jesus and to the eschatological future of God's kingdom that has dawned already in him."[49] But it is the Spirit who enables us to perceive the eschatological consummation of the cosmos in the earthly mission of Jesus. Salvation is thus definitively actualized not in the mission of the Son but with the work of the Spirit who completes it.[50] Here too the work of the Spirit is inextricably connected to the Spirit's work in creation, as the origin of all life. Just as the first creation was created by the power of the Spirit (Gen. 1:2), our mortal life will be transformed into the new life of the resurrection of the dead (Rom. 8:11) and the world itself will be transformed into the new creation by the power of the life-giving Spirit.

CONCLUSION

We turn now briefly to summarize Pannenberg's understanding of the differentiated and proper roles of the three divine persons in creation and its consummation and to note again the consistently trinitarian character of Pannenberg's eschatology. The differentiation of the Holy Spirit from the Son is first recognized as an extension of the differentiation of the Son from the Father. Concomitantly, creaturely differentiation is grounded in the inner-trinitarian differentiation, wherein the differentiation of the Holy Spirit from the Son is an extension of the differentiation of the Son from the Father. The work of creation is described in terms of the Father, who brings creation into existence, through the Son, who is principle of self-distinction and differentiation, and the Holy Spirit, who is source of life and movement, unity and consummation. The Kingdom of God comes about through the Son's incarnation and work of redemption, and the Holy Spirit's work of consummation of the cosmos. The Father thus establishes the Kingdom of God in and through the missions of Son and Holy Spirit. The Son, through his life, death, and resurrection, reconciles creation to the Father. The Spirit

48. Ibid., 18.
49. Ibid., 21.
50. Ibid., 551.

draws believers into the sonship of the Son, and into the divine life and glory. Creation is thus drawn into the Kingdom of the Father, through the Son and Holy Spirit.

Pannenberg recognizes the inextricable connection between Jesus' life and message and Christian hope for his return and the *eschaton*, the end and consummation of creation. It is God's coming. It is reconciliation with God. It is communion with God. It is the participation of the cosmos in God's trinitarian life. It constitutes the establishment of God's Kingdom over creation, the rule of the Father through the Son and the Holy Spirit. It is the epitome of Christian hope. Pannenberg recognizes that, like the reality of God, it transcends all our concepts.[51]

Pannenberg thus relates God's being to creation in a way that is both thoroughly trinitarian and eschatological and incorporates the individual, the communal, and indeed the cosmic dimensions of eschatology. Pannenberg's eschatology is replete with trinitarian references. The result is a thoroughly relational theology—one that is deeply imbued with a sense of the three divine persons in relation to each other, and of creatures in relation to each other and to God. Once again we see that, when doctrine of the Trinity informs our thinking about God and the cosmos, the notions of relationality and of communion assume great significance.

As we come to a conclusion, it is sobering to recall that eschatology is viewed with a considerable—even healthy—measure of suspicion in some quarters, particularly by the great masters of suspicion of the twentieth century. The Marxist critique, for example, deplores and derides Christian hope in the hereafter of the *next* life as "opium of the oppressed," an opium that suppresses pain response and depresses any attempt to marshal our energies to work against injustice and oppression and to work to build a better world in the here and now of *this* life. But Christian hope in the life hereafter, properly understood, is in fact no license for complacency or oversight in regard to suffering and oppression in *this* life. Christian eschatology is called to demonstrate strongly and clearly that Christian hope for the fullness of life in the future does not imply a negation of or disregard for the present. If it is to be genuinely Christian hope, it must inspire responsible action in and for our world, here and now, as liberation theology so strongly insists. Our faith and our hope, while confident of the future that is communion in the divine life, must find expression in the love and commitments that we express in the present.

51. Ibid., 527.

FOR FURTHER READING

Alison, James. *Knowing Jesus*. London: SPCK, 1993.

———. *Raising Abel: The Recovery of the Eschatological Imagination*. New York: Crossroad, 1996.

Balthasar, Hans Urs von. *Dare We Hope "That All Men Be Saved"?* With a Short Discourse on Hell. Translated by David Kipp and Lothar Krauth. San Francisco: Ignatius Press, 1987.

Hayes, Zachary. *Visions of a Future: A Study of Christian Eschatology*. Wilmington, Del.: Michael Glazier, 1989.

Johnson, Elizabeth A. *Friends of God and Prophets: A Feminist Theological Reading of the Communion of Saints*. New York: Continuum, 1998.

Kelly, Anthony. *Touching on the Infinite: Explorations of Christian Hope*. Melbourne: Collins Dove, 1991.

Lane, Dermot A. "Eschatology." In *The New Dictionary of Theology*, edited by Joseph A. Komonchak, Mary Collins, and Dermot A. Lane. Wilmington, Del.: Michael Glazier, 1987.

———. *Keeping Hope Alive: Stirrings in Christian Theology*. Mahwah, N.J.: Paulist Press, 1996.

Mostert, Christiaan. *God and the Future: Wolfhart Pannenberg's Eschatological Doctrine of God*. Edinburgh/New York: T&T Clark, 2002.

Pannenberg, Wolfhart. *Systematic Theology*. 3 volumes. Translated by Geoffrey W. Bromiley. Grand Rapids: Wm. B. Eerdmans, 1991-98. See especially 2:136-74, 437-54; 3:1-27, 527-646.

Ratzinger, Joseph Cardinal. *Eschatology: Death and Eternal Life*. Translated by Michael Waldstein. Washington, D.C.: Catholic University of America Press, 1988.

Schwöbel, Christoph. "Last Things First?" In *The Future as God's Gift: Explorations in Christian Eschatology*, edited by David Fergusson and Marcel Sarot, 219-41. Edinburgh: T&T Clark, 2000.

Tugwell, Simon. *Human Immortality and the Redemption of Death*. London: Darton, Longman & Todd, 1990.

Conclusion

The Mysteries of Christian Faith in a Trinitarian Setting

OF THE THREE THEOLOGICAL STRATEGIES identified by the First Vatican Council in its dogmatic constitution *Dei Filius*,[1] it is the strategy of analogy that has been the most practiced in the history of theology, even though its use is not always explicitly acknowledged. In trinitarian theology, it finds its strongest expression in the psychological analogy, which first took root in the Western theological tradition with Augustine, who identified an analogy for the processions within the Godhead in the operations of the human mind or psyche, and who explored some twenty variations of what is now called the psychological analogy. Thomas Aquinas took up and refined Augustine's notion and his sophisticated explication of the processions in the Godhead by means of the psychological analogy then served as the privileged method of explanation of the mystery of the Trinity in the Western tradition until relatively recent times.

But times change and cultures shift. In modern trinitarian discourse, the psychological analogy has fallen into disrepute. Theologians of the stature of Karl Rahner, Jürgen Moltmann, and Hans Urs von Balthasar have been strident in their criticism of it. Others, such as Walter Kasper, simply dismiss it.[2] Very few positively promote it as an effective means of explicating the mystery of the Trinity. Indeed, to employ the psychological analogy these days almost calls for some kind of explanation, even an apologia, as an acceptance of its explicative value simply cannot be assumed. More often, the psychological analogy is criticized as being introspective and individualistic, and for being based more in philosophical than scriptural categories. This rejection of the psychological analogy would seem to be at least partly related to a desire in our more empirically oriented culture to render a more obviously biblically based explication of the mystery.

1. DS 3016; ND 132.

2. Walter Kasper, *The God of Jesus Christ*, trans. Matthew J. O'Connell (New York: Crossroad, 1988), 187.

In contrast to the disrepute into which the psychological analogy has fallen, the social-interpersonal model of the Trinity, albeit in a range of variations, has risen to the fore, enjoying what would seem to be almost universal favor. A survey of contemporary approaches to the mystery of the Trinity demonstrates that the social model is particularly attractive and well suited to the theological goals of liberation theologies of various kinds—for example, Latin American theology (Leonardo Boff), feminist theology (Catherine Mowry LaCugna), eco-theology (Denis Edwards)—and to ecclesiology (John Zizioulas). In comparison with the psychological analogy, the social model is esteemed as untainted by philosophical concerns and, by implication, more faithful to the biblical witness, despite the risk of tritheism which the model runs. The social model of the Trinity is also seen to be more closely identified with the Eastern tradition of trinitarian theology, where the psychological analogy, and philosophical conceptuality more generally, never took root as it did in the Western theological tradition. Hence, in much of contemporary trinitarian discourse, the contribution of the Cappadocian Fathers is applauded, while that of Augustine and Thomas Aquinas has fallen out of favor. Thus has the social model of the Trinity captured the imagination in contemporary trinitarian theology, although some theologians, most notably Jürgen Moltmann and Hans Urs von Balthasar, while sharing the negative view of the psychological analogy of many of their contemporaries, have turned instead to the paschal mystery as the privileged place of revelation of the mystery of the Trinity and of its explication.

In one way or another, all of these contemporary approaches to the mystery seek to offer a tangible point of entry into the reality of the triune God who is with us and for us, and thus to reinvest trinitarian theology with more evident meaning and value in our world and experience. Whatever the ultimate assessment of their coherence, adequacy, and value, these modern efforts to reinvest meaning in the doctrine of the Trinity serve as an indictment of the failure of the classical application of the psychological analogy to render meaning in the contemporary context. They attest to a change in the cultural milieu and the demand for new and more existentially satisfying mediations of meaning. What is particularly interesting to note among the contemporary approaches to the mystery, even if not explicitly thematized as such, is the emergence of the theological strategy of interconnection of the mysteries. While the strategy of analogy (be it the psychological analogy, the social model, or the paschal mystery) continues to be used, the strategy of interconnection, the second theological strategy identified by Vatican I, is clearly enjoying a measure of favor. Our aim in this study has been expressly to explore the insights gleaned by means of the strategy of interconnection in contemporary trinitarian theology. We turn now to review what has emerged in our study.

CHRISTOLOGY

In many ways, Christoph Schwöbel encapsulates the widespread urge in contemporary theology to move away from a substance metaphysics and toward a metaphysics of relations, when he argues for "a paradigm shift from natures to persons."[3] He calls for a Christology that is constructed from an explicitly trinitarian perspective, while also expressly rejecting the metaphysical framework of classical trinitarian theology. In Christology, "a paradigm shift from natures to persons" means, according to Schwöbel, that Jesus Christ's divinity and humanity are interpreted not in terms of the possession of a divine and human nature, but in terms of the relational dimension of the divinity and humanity of Jesus Christ, and thus the divine relations, as the divine Son to the Father and the Holy Spirit, and the relational being of humanity, as actualized in the life, death, and resurrection of Jesus.

In arguing for "a paradigm shift from natures to persons," Schwöbel effectively identifies person in terms of relations. But we must register a cautionary note at this point, for the relations between and indeed constituting the divine persons are ontologically different from the relations between human persons. The perichoretic unity of the divine persons, for example, has no analogue in interpersonal human relations. The relations are not the same, though they are analogically related. The concept of nature or substance is designed precisely to express the profound and irreducible difference between the two. As William Norris Clarke reiterates, both substance (what Clarke calls the "in-itself" dimension of being, that which is in itself and not in another) and relational metaphysics are required in order to achieve a level of adequacy and coherence in theology's task of explicating the mystery of Christ's person. So, while we can endorse Schwöbel's proposed shift in emphasis from natures to persons and his refocusing of attention on the relational dimension of personhood, we cannot agree with the complete rejection of the category of nature or substance. The concept of nature cannot simply be eliminated from the discourse.

While Schwöbel encapsulates the dissatisfaction with the classical explication and conceptuality that is so frequently expressed in modern trinitar-

3. Christoph Schwöbel, "Christology and Trinitarian Thought," in *Trinitarian Theology Today: Essays on Divine Being and Act*, ed. Christoph Schwöbel (Edinburgh: T&T Clark, 1995), 139.

ian discourse, Jacques Dupuis offers a creative and constructive contribution to contemporary Christology, while explicitly and insistently proclaiming fidelity to orthodox conciliar christological doctrine. Like Schwöbel, he too argues for a Christology that is based on an understanding of the Trinity and the interpersonal relationships between Father and Son, and between Son and Holy Spirit. Unlike Schwöbel, who effectively dismisses the category of nature, Dupuis maintains the notion of nature but insists, in accordance with Chalcedon, that we can distinguish, but not separate, the two natures and their respective operations. Dupuis argues in terms of the trinitarian rhythm of God's activity throughout salvation history and for an understanding of the presence and action of God's Word, and similarly that of the Spirit, as not restricted to the historical event of the incarnation. In other words, Dupuis maintains that the Christ-event neither limits nor exhausts the universal action of the Word and Spirit and that, from the very beginning of creation, God has revealed Godself to humankind, through God's Word and God's Spirit. As Irenaeus in the second century expressed it: God the Father saves "with two hands"—the Word and the Spirit. Dupuis' understanding of the trinitarian rhythm of the full sweep of salvation history, while not without its own hazards, is actually in close accord with the classical trinitarian teachings in regard to the invisible missions of the Word and Spirit and allows for a much more positive view of the efficacy and role of the world religions in God's salvific plan than the traditional christological understanding affords.

PASCHAL MYSTERY AND SOTERIOLOGY

While Dupuis' soteriological concern finds expression in a theology of world religions, Sebastian Moore is concerned to understand the dynamics of conversion and so to facilitate the process of conversion of the individual human person in the contemporary—essentially Western modern-cum-postmodern—context, thereby redressing the current failure to mediate religious meaning in that context. Moore therefore sets out to reconstruct what he imagines to be the first disciples' experience of Jesus' paschal mystery. His aim is to ground theology in the world of human interiority and subjectivity, and thereby to meet the concerns, sensibilities, and exigences of contemporary consciousness, by describing the process by which Jesus' story transforms each person's individual personal story. The dynamic of the paschal mystery thus emerges in Moore's exploration as the psychological pattern of the process of conversion. It reveals that our entry into the divine communion that is our destiny requires that we ourselves enter into a paschal dynamic that ultimately demands what seems to be our complete annihilation and the total renunciation of our existence.

François Durrwell also mines the interconnection of the Trinity and the paschal mystery, particularly the mystery of the resurrection, but for him its meaning is to be found not in the human psyche and the experience of conversion but in the mystery of God's being. Durrwell would persuade us that the resurrection corresponds to the inner-trinitarian mystery of the Father's generation of the Son and thus that trinitarian being and relationality are not only revealed but also realized in creation in the resurrection of Jesus Christ. In other words, Durrwell understands that, in the resurrection, the Trinity enacts itself in creation: the resurrection reveals the Father who begets the Son in the love of the Holy Spirit. Similarly, in their explorations of the nexus of the paschal mystery and the mystery of the Trinity, Hans Urs von Balthasar and Jürgen Moltmann recognize that it is no accident that the Trinity is revealed in the realm of creation precisely in the dynamic of the paschal mystery and that, concomitantly, a distinctly paschal dynamic is inherent in the nature of divine being. No wonder, then, that our entry—and, indeed, the entry of all creation into the divine communion—is an entry into a distinctly paschal dynamic that, from the perspective of daily human life in the world, seems like total annihilation. Under the impulse of trinitarian belief, an exploration of the paschal mystery thus discloses the mystery of being, both divine and human, as distinctly paschal in character. In this way, Jesus' paschal mystery presents itself as icon par excellence of both divine and human being. It is mystery of salvation precisely in revealing and in effecting our entry into the divine communion of self-giving self-yielding life and love.

CREATION

While the Christology nexus, as Schwöbel explores it, raises issues concerning traditional theological notions of nature, person, and relation, the nexus of the mysteries of the Trinity and creation raises the question of how best to understand the roles of the divine persons in the economy. Classical theology, following Augustine, understands that the incarnation is properly the visible mission of the Son, and the descent of the Holy Spirit at Pentecost is properly the visible mission of the Spirit. It also affirms that, properly speaking (that is, not merely by appropriation), both Son and Spirit have invisible missions, the goal of which is the divine indwelling in the graced human person. In terms of creation, it teaches that the work of the Trinity *ad extra* is one and undivided, and that therefore the assignment of roles to the divine persons in creation is, properly and technically speaking, by means of the strategy of appropriation: the Son and Spirit have appropriated roles, but not proper roles as such. In other words, in classical trinitarian theology, the Son and Spirit are understood to have proper missions, missions that are distinctly and uniquely and properly their own, in the work of salvation, but they do not have proper (only appropriated) roles in the work of creation. Despite Aquinas's carefully nuanced teaching in this regard (*STh* I, q. 45, a. 6), the classical trinitarian axiom, *opera trinitatis ad extra indivisa sunt* (the works of the Trinity *ad extra* are indivisible), tended to evacuate a theology of creation of real personal distinction between the divine persons, and hence of trinitarian meaning. Moreover, it attenuated a sense of the distinctly trinitarian presence *in* creation.

Modern theologians, most notably Denis Edwards and Wolfhart Pannenberg, press for a much more explicitly trinitarian understanding of the divine works *ad extra* and, in doing so, they argue for the recognition of proper (and not just appropriated) roles for the Son and Spirit in creation. Not satisfied with an understanding that the work of God *ad extra* is the work of the one undivided undifferentiated Trinity, they argue for an understanding of creation as the work of the united but *differentiated* Trinity, with each divine person having a unique role that is strictly proper—and not just appropriated—to that particular person. Neil Ormerod, in defense of the classical strategy of appropriation, argues, however, that the case for proper as distinct from appropriated roles in the work of the Trinity in the economy is ultimately not logically and theologically coherent, and that it relates to a confusion regarding the strategy of appropriation. He situates the strategy of appropriation within the framework of Bernard Lonergan's functions of meaning (cognitive, constitutive, communicative, effective).[4] He argues that, as employed in the classical understanding of the mystery of the Trinity, the strategy of appropriation operates within the cognitive function of meaning, while Edwards, for example, is working in the area of the effective function of meaning and thus, as Ormerod expresses it, "says more than can be said" in a cognitively coherent manner when he argues for proper roles in the work of creation and for God's real as distinct from logical relation to creation.[5] While Ormerod's argument might be fairly applied to Edwards's theology, it does not, I suggest, do justice to Pannenberg's work. Indeed, Pannenberg proposes a very plausible case for the notion of proper roles for the divine persons in the economy, and, moreover, he observes that it was only in the fourth century that an earlier understanding of distinction in the operation of the divine persons was overturned.

4. Bernard Lonergan, *Method in Theology* (New York: Seabury, 1972), 76-81.
5. See Neil Ormerod, *Trinity: Retrieving the Western Tradition*, forthcoming.

CHURCH

Some difficulties and limitations that are inherent in the social model of the Trinity become apparent in an exploration of the interconnection of Trinity and church. Indeed, this interconnection serves to highlight the reliance of the strategy of interconnection on the strategy of analogy, even though the analogy engaged might not explicitly figure in the argument. In other words, the strategies of analogy and interconnection are themselves inextricably interconnected. As we have seen, Leonardo Boff, Miroslav Volf, John Zizioulas, and Joseph Ratzinger all bring an explicitly trinitarian understanding to the mystery of the church, and yet they arrive at very different conclusions in regard to church structure, particularly in regard to the relationship between the local and the universal church. That trinitarian theology can be invoked in support of such diverse positions and conclusions is indicative that trinitarian theology is not the only determining feature in these arguments. More positively, the diversity of conclusions urges us to an even greater commitment to ecumenical dialogue. Theologically, the situation serves to illustrate that the social model of the Trinity cannot by itself ground an ecclesiology, and to remind us that the social model of the Trinity is just that, a model.

Admittedly, Miroslav Volf brings a much stronger notion of the limits of the analogy than does Leonardo Boff and is critical of Boff's uncritical use of the axiom that "the Trinity is our social program." But like Leonardo Boff and John Zizioulas, Miroslav Volf presses the analogy of interpersonal relations into ecclesiological service. But notice that the interpersonal analogy as explored in the tradition, preeminently in the theology of Richard of St. Victor, whereby human interpersonal relations serve as an analogy for the mystery of the Trinity, is effectively reversed here, with the interpersonal divine relations (as understood within the framework of a social model of the Trinity) invoked as analogy for human ecclesial relations. Again, we find a stress on the relational aspect of personhood and a strong rejection of an ontology of substance in favor of an ontology of relations. William Norris Clarke's argument here too holds true, in regard to seeking a better balance between the two ontologies, rather than an outright dismissal of one or the other. Nonetheless, despite its limitations, the social model offers what we might call a trinitarian value set—what Nicholas Lash has referred to as the grammar and structure of the Christian "school of discipleship"[6]—to an under-

6. Nicholas Lash, "Concerning the Trinity," *Modern Theology* 2 (1986): 183-96.

standing of church and society, wherein the values of mutuality, reciprocity, equality, and inclusion are paramount.

The psychological analogy does not figure in treatments of the interconnection of the mysteries of Trinity and church, neither in contemporary nor in classical approaches to ecclesiology. Indeed, as we have noted earlier, Thomas Aquinas, in whose *Summa* the psychological analogy finds its consummate expression, does not explicitly treat the mystery of the church, though he does treat in considerable detail the mystery of grace and the trinitarian indwelling in the human person. In other words, the psychological analogy is explicitly employed in relation to the individual but not explicitly to the collective ecclesial reality of Christian life. The work of Bernard Lonergan and Anthony Kelly effectively addresses this issue, by offering a transposition of the psychological analogy from the scholastic categories of the classical treatment into phenomenologically based categories that are more apt in the contemporary context. Their work amply demonstrates that the psychological analogy is pregnant with meaning for contemporary cosmic, ecological, psychological, political, and interfaith concerns.

We noted that Volf brings his ecclesiological-trinitarian reflections back to the paschal mystery, as does Schwöbel in his christological-trinitarian reflections. Shifting his focus from the social model of the immanent Trinity to the economic Trinity as revealed in the paschal mystery, Volf insists that to propose a social knowledge based on the doctrine of the Trinity is not so much to "project" or "represent" the triune God but, above all, to renarrate the history of the cross, the story of the triune God's descent in self-emptying love in order to take human beings into the perfect cycle of exchange in which the divine persons give themselves to each other and receive themselves back ever anew in love. It is God's passion for the salvation of the world, Volf argues, that should ground our understanding of social practice modeled on the Trinity.[7] It is in fact the paschal mystery that grounds our understanding and application of the social model of the Trinity.

THE WORLD RELIGIONS

In our exploration of the nexus of the mystery of the Trinity and world religions, neither social model, nor psychological analogy, nor paschal mystery is explicitly employed in explicating the trinitarian mystery. The mystery of the threefold being of God is simply assumed, without need for explication.

7. Miroslav Volf, "'The Trinity Is Our Social Program': The Doctrine of the Trinity and the Shape of Social Engagement," *Modern Theology* 14 (1998): 417.

Raimon Panikkar argues for an understanding of three essentially different categories of spirituality in the world religions that, he suggests, relate to three concepts of the divine, and thence to the different divine persons, an approach that resonates with the social model. The virtue of Panikkar's approach is that, in finding a point of convergence for the world's great spiritual traditions in a theology of the Trinity, it recognizes and respects the irreducible differences between the different traditions, and thus allows, as Rowan Williams has commented, for the possibility of authentic engagement between traditions *in* their particularity. In Panikkar's theology, the Trinity itself emerges as the ultimate ontological foundation for the plurality of world religions, and as all-inclusive comprehensive reality within which to make sense of human spirituality as expressed in the various patterns of religious experience. As Cousins points out, Panikkar's approach effectively fits within the vestige doctrine of Augustine, wherein the mystery of the triune Creator is reflected in and throughout all creation, including the world religions.[8]

While Panikkar takes the different spiritualities of the world religions as his point of departure, Jacques Dupuis takes the whole span of the history of salvation as the framework within which to consider the question of the plurality of religious traditions, and what he describes as the trinitarian rhythm of God's dealings with humanity throughout the history of creation, as manifested in the active presence of the Word of God throughout history and in the universal dynamic action of the Spirit of God in the world. The action of the Word is not constrained by the particularity of the incarnation event, Dupuis argues; similarly, the Holy Spirit is universally present and operative throughout salvation history; in other words, each is present and active in its own distinctive way throughout salvation history. Here Dupuis' theology bears a close correspondence with the classical understanding of the invisible missions of the Word and Spirit.

While holding fast to the Christian conviction that God's self-communication in the person of Jesus Christ is the apex and summit of God's self-revelation in salvation history, this trinitarian approach affords Dupuis the possibility of viewing other religious traditions as mediators of God's salvation, mediators of God's saving activity in the economy, through the presence of the Word of God and of the Spirit of God. In what he calls "a principled religious pluralism," Dupuis proposes a theology of religious plu-

8. Ewert Cousins, "The Trinity and World Religions," *Journal of Ecumenical Studies* 7 (1970): 476-98; see also idem, "Panikkar's Advaitic Trinitarianism," in *The Intercultural Challenge of Raimon Panikkar*, ed. Joseph Prabhu (Maryknoll, N.Y.: Orbis Books, 1996), 119-30.

ralism in which the other religions traditions converge in God's one creative plan. He argues that it is legitimate to speak of "complementarity and convergence" between Christianity and the other religious traditions. From this perspective, other religious traditions emerge as "ways" of salvation, and religious pluralism emerges as not just *de facto* but *de iure*, intended and willed by God, God who is love, and who communicates that love in boundless abundance. "A principled religious pluralism," Dupuis argues, "is based on the immensity of God, who is Love and communicates that Love."[9] The result of this interconnection with the Trinity is an expanded horizon within which to situate a Christian understanding of the mystery of redemption, without forsaking the uniqueness of Jesus as the incarnate Son of God. Such efforts as those of Dupuis and Panikkar have proved fruitful in prompting contemporary theology to articulate a more nuanced theology of world religions, one that is much more positive and inclusive, and more explicitly faithful to our understanding of God's universal salvific will.

GRACE AND THE MORAL LIFE

At the nexus of the mysteries of Trinity, grace, and the moral life, the psychological analogy demonstrates its remarkable explicative power, affording an understanding of grace in terms of God's self-communication in grace implanted or infused in the human spirit, at the level of the powers of intellect and will, by which the human person expresses him/herself in action. More than any other trinitarian analogy or model, the psychological analogy enables us to understand the dynamics of grace in terms of our participation in the very life and being of the triune God, whereby the human person actively participates in and is dynamically conformed to the understanding of the Word and the love of the Holy Spirit. A strong correlation between the Trinity and the moral life thus emerges, via the psychological analogy and the intelligibility of the dynamics of grace that it offers. In grace, through the invisible missions of Word and Spirit, the divine persons are communicated to and come to abide in the human person, thus effecting a new mode of existence, whereby the human person in his/her subjectivity participates in the trinitarian vitality of the divine life and is thus progressively conformed to the image of the Trinity of divine persons, the divine subjectivity. From this van-

---

9. Jacques Dupuis, "From Religious Confrontation to Encounter," *Theology Digest* 49 (2002): 108; idem, *Christianity and the Religions: From Confrontation to Dialogue* (Maryknoll, N.Y.: Orbis Books, 2002), 254-55.

tage point, moral action emerges as a dynamic participation in what we might call the moral consciousness of the Trinity, or "trinitarian morality," so to speak. Anthony Kelly here identifies the virtue of the psychological analogy in terms of its finely balanced emphasis on both the intelligent and the loving aspects of divine life and, correlatively, of human life and moral action. Moral action, from the perspective afforded by the psychological analogy, necessarily engages both dimensions of our self-transcending subjectivity, the intelligent and the affective. The psychological analogy thus provides not only a plausible explication of the progressive conformation of the human person in the image of the Trinity but a salutary reminder of the irreducible importance of the value judgments in moral decision making. In the contemporary world of modern moral discourse, which, as Alasdair MacIntyre has famously observed, is characterized by interminable debates on questions of value and morality and which lacks intelligibility and rationality in its deliberations, the psychological analogy, appropriately transposed into terms that are meaningful and accessible to contemporary consciousness, offers a vital corrective to the possibility of a kind of voluntarist distortion which leaves judgments of value and the concrete demands of responsible decision and loving action dangerously subject to the arbitrariness of individual assessment based on personal interest and whim.

While the psychological analogy allows for an unparalleled systematic intelligibility of the gift of grace and of the nexus between Trinity, grace, and the moral life, the social model of the Trinity nevertheless brings more explicitly interpersonal and social principles to an understanding of the moral life and its imperatives, as is demonstrated, for example, in Catherine LaCugna's trinitarian theology. LaCugna argues that trinitarian theology could be described, par excellence, as a theology of relationship, and it is here, she argues, that the practical ethical implications for a doctrine of the Trinity emerge. Based on an understanding of the Trinity as a communion of persons, LaCugna argues that Christian life is life lived according to the mystery of persons in communion. While the social model of the Trinity is unable to explicate the dynamics of grace in the human person and of the transformation that grace achieves, it clearly offers a persuasive and attractive perspective on the mystery of the Trinity in the contemporary context and highlights the values of mutuality and reciprocity in the conduct of our individual and collective lives, in a world that is very much in need of such values. Its great virtue is its explicit emphasis on the social and political-economic ramifications and ethical imperatives that necessarily follow from the trinitarian faith we proclaim, although it risks focusing on the merely functional and pragmatic aspects—and the effective function of meaning—of trinitarian theology. But inattention to the inherent limitations of the use of the social model as a basis for understanding interpersonal human relations risks eroding an understanding of the very mystery of the trinitarian communion that it seeks to reinvest with meaning. Theological discourse is always analogical, and it always demands a properly critical appreciation of its limits and its hazards. It is how that critical appreciation finds expression that is the question, particularly when one takes into account what Bernard Lonergan describes as the different realms and functions of meaning that communication of the mystery involves. Though the critical element will admittedly and necessarily be less rigorous when one's communication is geared to the constitutive, communicative, or effective function of meaning, as distinct from the cognitive function of meaning, it cannot be omitted from the communication.

SPIRITUALITY AND WORSHIP

At the nexus of the mysteries of the Trinity and spirituality, the paschal mystery brings a distinctive contribution that serves as a sobering corrective to the perspective afforded by the social model and a tendency in its application to an uncritical appropriation of the notion of trinitarian communion to human being and society. Ghislain Lafont observes that, from what he calls an "anthropological" perspective, Jesus' choice of divine communion in preference to any autonomy of existence, which is so evident in the paschal mystery, shows that the perfection of being lies in communion, as distinct from any sense of autonomy or independence. Consequently, it is communion, and not any notion that connotes autonomy, that informs and shapes our understanding of Christian spirituality. In this respect, the paschal mystery accords well with the social model of the Trinity in acknowledging the value of communion and the principle of mutuality. But the paschal mystery also shows that entry into communion with God necessarily passes through a stage of death.[10] It shows that God's self-communication and offer of communion require a renunciation of existence on the part of the human person, a surrender and transcendence of the self, a radical dying to self, and ultimately physical death. Indeed, the paschal mystery reveals that the possibility of this total *ekstasis* of self in a radical other-regarding relationality is our ultimate meaning and vocation. It is precisely through it that we enter into the life of the trinitarian communion and exchange. A distinctly paschal element thus emerges from Lafont's exploration of trinitarian relationality and divine

10. E.g., Ghislain Lafont, *Peut-on Connaitre Dieu en Jésus Christ?*, Cogitatio Fidei 44 (Paris: Les Éditions du Cerf, 1969), 241, 243.

being, as revealed in the paschal mystery and, correspondingly, for human relationality and spirituality.

The trinitarian dynamic and paschal setting of the eucharistic liturgy also serve to highlight the trinitarian and paschal rhythm of our whole lives as well as our prayer, which unfolds in continuing cycles of eucharistia, anamnesis, and epiclesis. As sign and sacrament of our unity, the Eucharist expresses and effects our entry into human community, ecclesial community, and the divine community. Indeed, in the Eucharist, the social model, the psychological analogy, and the paschal mystery find their point of interconnection and mutual correlation: Jesus' paschal mystery, wherein the mystery of the Trinity is revealed, commemorated, and celebrated; the uniqueness and specificity of the divine persons are articulated and the Trinity of persons worshipped; and the mystery of our dwelling in the trinitarian mystery and its indwelling in us, conforming us to the divine image, reconciling us and orienting us to a world of communion that is cosmic in scope and eucharistic in spirit, is progressively realized. As Christopher Cocksworth comments, worship is "The School of the Trinity": "Simply by worshipping God as Christian believers the fundamental structures of trinitarian theology are erected in our minds, hearts and spirits. We are on homeground when we look at the Trinity from the perspective of worship."[11] In the Eucharist, the all-connecting, all-embracing analogical imagination of trinitarian faith comes home, so to speak.

ESCHATOLOGY: OUR ULTIMATE END

In addressing the interconnection of the mysteries of the Trinity and eschatology, the classical strategy of appropriation and the question of the proper—and not just appropriated—roles of the Son and Spirit resurface. While Wolfhart Pannenberg holds to the classical axiom that the three divine persons are one in essence and that their work in creation is the one work of the one God, he would persuade us that each divine person is active in its own distinct way, in unity with the others, as indeed Thomas Aquinas suggested in his own carefully nuanced way (*STh* I, q. 45, a. 6). Pannenberg insists that the life of God is constituted by the differentiated but complementary activity of the three divine persons, with the divine persons as "direct subjects of the divine action."[12] The Spirit is origin of life and movement, in regard both

11. Christopher. Cocksworth, *Holy, Holy, Holy: Worshipping the Trinitarian God* (London: Darton, Longman & Todd, 1997), 124-25.

12. Wolfhart Pannenberg, *Systematic Theology*, 3 vols., trans. Geoffrey W. Bromiley (Grand Rapids: Wm. B. Eerdmans, 1991-98), 1:383.

to the work of creation and to the work of the new creation. The eschatological participation of creation in the life of the Trinity, Pannenberg argues, is properly the work of the Spirit, not just by way of appropriation. Pannenberg invokes a distinctly relational notion of personhood in his argument for differentiated and proper roles for the three divine persons and argues that personhood, as distinct from subjecthood, consists in relationality. The trinitarian relations, he stresses, are not merely relations of origin, as classically understood, but relations of mutual dependence and self-distinction, characterized by mutuality and reciprocity, whereby each of the divine persons receives his divinity through the other two divine persons. Pannenberg thus argues for proper roles for the divine persons in creation, as does Denis Edwards. He would also persuade us of the propriety of speaking in terms of properly differentiated roles of the three divine persons in the consummation of the cosmos. Glorification, he argues, is essentially and properly the work of the Spirit, while the work of reconciliation is accomplished by the Son, through his life, death, and resurrection. The end and consummation of creation are reconciliation and communion with God, and the participation of the cosmos in God's trinitarian life. For Pannenberg, this constitutes the establishment of God's Kingdom over creation, the rule of the Father through the Son and the Holy Spirit.

CONCLUSION

While the First Vatican Council articulates the classical strategies available to theology in terms of (1) analogy with the truths known naturally; (2) the interconnection of the mysteries; and (3) reference to the final end and ultimate destiny of the human person, our exploration highlights the inescapably analogical nature of the discourse at every turn, even while expressly employing the other strategies. We find that the interconnection of the mysteries is, to a greater or lesser extent, depending on the particular mystery under consideration, mediated through our understanding of the Trinity by means of the psychological analogy, the social model, or the paschal mystery. The result may seem, at first glance, to be a rather untidy and undisciplined collation. Such, I suggest, is the nature of the strategy of interconnection and the lateral exercise of the imagination that it involves. At very least, our exploration highlights that, while at any point one analogy or model may be more apt and adequate to the task, none is fully adequate to the whole task. The divine reality that theology seeks to express and affirm ever exceeds its grasp, and its grasp is ever greater than the capacities of the strategies available to it. Similarly none of the analogical avenues is apt to meet the full range of the different functions of meaning that explication and communication of the mystery involve and demand. The enormous favor that the social model of the Trinity currently enjoys needs to be matched (as indeed for any other of the analogies or models, including the psychological analogy) by a healthy appreciation of its inherent limitations and inadequacies. It is the revelation of God in the paschal mystery of Jesus that serves as the critical criterion and ultimate measure.

Our exploration has focused on the insights that emerge when a distinctly trinitarian imagination is brought to bear on the other mysteries of Christian faith. However, the strategy of interconnection, when fully engaged, should also result in an enrichment of our understanding of the mystery of the Trinity itself. Here the gains, I suggest, are generally less obvious in our study. Certainly, the notions of relationality and of communion and a more general shift to a relational ontology emerge strongly and reinforce the shift that is already strongly expressed in the favor that the social model currently enjoys. It is hardly surprising that, having embarked on a strategy of interconnection, with the mystery of the Trinity as the point of nexus, one finds that the relational dimension emerges foremost. But the potential gains for trinitarian theology emerge most clearly, I suggest, in the more creative and daring forays of the trinitarian imagination, such as are evident in the work of Hans Urs von Balthasar in relation to the paschal mystery and the understanding of the Trinity that emerges there, and in the work of Jacques Dupuis in regard to a theology of the world religions, where Dupuis stretches trinitarian thinking beyond its traditional boundaries, as classically understood, to a clearer appreciation of the roles of the Son and Spirit throughout the history of the cosmos. A full assessment of their contributions remains to be seen.

Finally, our study logically points to the development of the third strategy to which Vatican I referred in *Dei Filius*, the strategy of eschatological reference to the final end and ultimate destiny of the human person, and thus to an exploration of the mysteries of faith through an explicitly eschatological lens. Eschatology, as Pannenberg so insistently reminds us, is not just another topic or mere addendum in Christian theology; it is the essential perspective of Christian theology as a whole. In eschatology, in contemplation of the eschaton as our ultimate end, the whole theological enterprise truly comes home; the trinitarian imagination comes face to face with the reality that is the Trinity, our home.

How better to finish than with the words with which Augustine concluded his *City of God*: "I think I have now, by God's help, discharged my obligation in writing this large work. Let those who think I have said too little, or those who think I have said too much, forgive me; and those who think I have said just enough join me in giving thanks to God. Amen" (22.30).

Appendix

The *Filioque* Controversy

THE *FILIOQUE* CONTROVERSY refers to the tragically long-standing dispute concerning the question of the procession of the Holy Spirit, which resulted in the Great Schism in the eleventh century, a separation of Christianity in the East from that in the West, of the Roman from the Orthodox churches, a separation that continues today, much to the grief of Christians worldwide. The Council of Constantinople (381), which both East and West recognize as an ecumenical council of the whole church, solemnly proclaimed that the Holy Spirit proceeds from the Father. The West, however, unilaterally inserted an interpolation into the creed and proclaimed that the Holy Spirit proceeds from the Father *and the Son* (*filioque*). While the schism is usually dated at 1054, the separation was the culmination of a gradual estrangement over the preceding centuries and cannot really be dated so precisely. The tragedy is that the procession of the Holy Spirit, whom Christians worldwide revere as the divine person of unity and love, has become the point of disunity and polemic in the Christian church.

Although some modern writers persist in perpetuating Théodore de Régnon's all-too-sharp and simplistic distinction between Eastern and Western styles of trinitarian theology, in terms of Western essentialism and Eastern personalism, whereby Eastern trinitarian theology is said to proceed from the plurality of the persons, while Western trinitarian theology, following Augustine, proceeds from the divine unity,[1] the weight of scholarly opinion recognizes that differences between the Latin West and the Greek East have been grossly exaggerated in this way, and the considerable diversity within each of them just as seriously underestimated. Nevertheless some genuine distinctions gradually emerged as a result of the different circumstances in which the church in the East and that in the West evolved. The loss of political unity that occurred at the end of the third century with the division of the Roman empire into East and West, each under its own emperor, and the

1. Théodore de Régnon, *Études de Théologie Positive sur la Sainte Trinité,* 2 vols. (Paris: Victor Retaux et fils, 1892). For a critique of Théodore de Régnon's Greek/Latin paradigm, see Michel René Barnes, "Augustine in Contemporary Trinitarian Theology," *Theological Studies* 56 (1995): 237-50; idem, "De Régnon Reconsidered," *Augustinian Studies* 26 (1995): 51-79.

establishment of the second imperial capital at Constantinople in the fourth century undoubtedly contributed to the gradual separation of the church in the East and the West and to the deepening of linguistic, cultural, and ecclesiological differences between them. The church in the East, where political authority was strongly vested in the emperor, enjoyed an essentially spiritual authority, and that authority was expressed by the bishops acting collegially, a practice that was grounded in an understanding of the equality of bishops in the apostolic tradition. On the other hand, the church in the West, because of the vacuum of political authority there, assumed a political authority that was unknown in the East. Moreover, unlike the churches of Constantinople, Antioch, Alexandria, and Jerusalem in the East, the church of Rome exercised jurisdiction over a vast terrain and tended to interpret and express its authority in more universal and less collegial terms.

The insertion of *filioque* into the creed emerged in the West, where it was used to counter the reemergence of Arianism that surfaced in Spain in the fifth century, and to affirm the equality of the Son with the Father. The insertion was as much a christological issue as a trinitarian one. Theologically, the insertion was justified by Augustine's trinitarian theology, and also that of Hilary of Poitiers. It was, however, to prove a fateful interpolation. Its usage gradually spread in the West. The Third Council of Toledo (589) professed the double procession and severely anathematized any who denied it. At that point, the creed, together with the *filioque*, entered into the Latin eucharistic liturgy.

The tension between East and West increased in the seventh century. Islamic onslaughts in the East resulted in the strengthening of the power of the see of Constantinople and of the authority of its patriarch in relation to its sister churches and their patriarchs in the East. Meanwhile, in the West, the papal monarchy was emerging. The iconoclast controversy in the East exacerbated the situation. In the West, the emperor Charlemagne (768-814) took up the *filioque* cause with fervor and included the interpolated creed in the celebration of the Mass in the royal chapel and throughout the Frankish territory. The use of the interpolated Creed continued to spread through the Western church, though not in Rome. There, the papacy, while not denying the orthodoxy of the *filioque*, resisted its insertion in the creed and, indeed, the recitation of the creed in the Mass. It remains unclear precisely when the *filioque* found its way into the creed at Rome. Tradition has it that it was finally adopted in Rome in 1014, when it was used by the Pope Benedict VIII (1012-1024) in a eucharistic liturgy at the coronation of Henry II. Once adopted by Rome, however, the interpolated creed became standard throughout the church in the West, its usage now justified by claims to papal primacy. At this point, the interpolation emerged as a very serious doctrinal issue between Constantinople and Rome.

From the perspective of the East, the insertion of the *filioque* was effrontery in the extreme. First, it was an illegitimate insertion into the creed, which had been promulgated by an ecumenical council. Second, but no less important, it was theologically incorrect. The notion of the double procession violated the monarchy of the Father, as source of the Son and of the Holy Spirit. In the Orthodox tradition, going back to John Damascene, the Father is sole source within the Trinity. Many in the East would admit the statement, through the Son, *per filium*, but not *filioque*. The claim to primacy in the West together with the Christian Crusades from the West further aggravated the tension and, with the pillage of Constantinople in the Fourth Crusade, the relations between East and West were irrevocably severed.

The Latin West was uncompromising. The Fourth Lateran General Council in 1215 solemnly proclaimed the double procession of the Holy Spirit, stating that "the Holy Spirit proceeds eternally from Father and Son, not as from two principles but from one, not by two spirations but by one only."[2] The council added the anathemas: "We condemn and disapprove those who presume to deny that the Holy Spirit proceeds eternally from Father and Son, or who rashly dare to assert that the Holy Spirit proceeds from the Father and the Son as from two principles, not as from one." [3] The *filioque* was dogmatically affirmed again at the attempted reunion of East and West at the Second General Council of Lyons in 1274.[4] The primacy of the papacy was also affirmed at this council.[5] It is hardly surprising that the union was not realized, however, given that reunion effectively demanded submission to the magisterial authority of Rome. Rome regarded the council as ecumenical, but the Eastern delegates, having given their approval to the *filioque* at the council, revoked it on their return to Constantinople.

With Byzantium under renewed pressure from the Ottoman Turks, another reunion—or at least accommodation to the West for the sake of political expediency and military aid—was attempted in Ferrara-Florence in 1438-1439. Genuine dialogue was effectively subverted, however, and the *filioque* question remained unresolved. The Council of Ferrara-Florence reiterated the double procession and, moreover, affirmed the legitimacy of its insertion for the sake of clarity into the creed.[6] The Ottoman conquest followed in 1453. Dialogue ceased and, with its demise, the hope of reunion was extinguished. The opposition in the East to the *filioque* and to papal primacy continued unabated. Meanwhile, the church in the West would soon face the cataclysm of the Protestant Reformation.

2. DS 805; ND 319.
3. DS 805; ND 319.
4. DS 850; ND 321, and DS 853; ND 24.
5. See ND 803.
6. DS 1300-1302.

The history of the *filioque* controversy is a sad and sorry history of mutual misunderstanding. While the *filioque* emerged in the West as much for christological as for trinitarian reasons, it constituted an ecclesiological issue of great import in the East. The controversy is as much a matter of ecclesiology and of ecclesial authority as theology. Throughout, the truth and correctness of saying that the Holy Spirit proceeds from the Father and the Son were confused with the issue of the legitimacy of its insertion into the creed. As John Meyendorff comments: "The difficulties created by history could have been resolved if there had been a common ecclesiological criterion to settle the theological, canonical, or liturgical issues keeping the East and the West apart. But the medieval development of the Roman papacy as the ultimate reference in doctrinal matters stood in obvious contrast with the concept of the Church prevailing in the East."[7]

A range of opinions currently exists in regard to the situation. Some in the West argue for the removal of the *filioque* from the creed (as happened at the Lambeth Conference of the Anglican Communion in 1978) and a return to the original Nicene-Constantinopolitan Creed. Some perceive that the substance of the teachings in the East and in the West in regard to the procession of the Holy Spirit (*per filium*, through the Son, and *filioque,* and the Son) are in fact different perspectives on the one divine reality and essentially identical. Though the scars of the previous centuries no doubt remain, the church today would seem to be freer than ever before to consider the *filioque* question anew, free of the political tensions and the acrimony of the past, free to move to a new and gracious space of authentic dialogue and discernment.

FOR FURTHER READING

Bobrinskoy, Boris. *The Mystery of the Trinity: Trinitarian Experience and Vision in the Biblical and Patristic Tradition.* Crestwood, N.Y.: St. Vladimir's Seminary Press, 1999.

Congar, Yves. *I Believe in the Holy Spirit.* 3 volumes. Translated by David Smith. New York: Crossroad, 1997. See esp. 3:192-214.

Haddad, Robert M. "The Stations of the Filioque." *St. Vladimir's Theological Quarterly* 2 (2002): 209-68.

Kelly, J. N. D. *Early Christian Creeds.* 2nd ed. London: Longmans, 1960.

Meyendorff, John. *Byzantine Theology: Historical Trends and Doctrinal Themes.* London: Mowbrays, 1974.

7. John Meyendorff, *Byzantine Theology: Historical Trends and Doctrinal Themes* (London: Mowbrays, 1974), 91.

Selected Bibliography

Ayers, Lewis. *Nicaea and Its Legacy: An Approach to Fourth-Century Trinitarian Theology.* Oxford: Oxford University Press, 2004.

Balthasar, Hans Urs von. *Dare We Hope "That All Men Be Saved"?* With a Short Discourse on Hell. Translated by David Kipp and Lothar Krauth. San Francisco: Ignatius Press, 1987.

———. *The Glory of the Lord: A Theological Aesthetics.* Volume 2, *Studies in Theological Style: Clerical Styles.* Edited by John Riches. Translated by Brian McNeil. San Francisco: Ignatius Press, 1984; Volume 7, *Theology: The New Covenant.* Edited by John Riches. Translated by Brian McNeil. San Francisco: Ignatius Press, 1989.

———. *Life Out of Death: Meditations on the Easter Mystery.* Translated by Davis Perkins. Philadelphia: Fortress Press, 1985.

———. *Love Alone: The Way of Revelation: A Theological Perspective.* Edited by Alexander Dru. London: Burns & Oates, 1968.

———. *Mysterium Paschale: The Mystery of Easter.* Translated with an introduction by Aidan Nichols. Edinburgh: T&T Clark, 1990.

———. *Theo-Drama: Theological Dramatic Theory.* Volume 5, *The Last Act.* Translated by Graham Harrison. San Francisco: Ignatius Press, 1998.

———. *The Von Balthasar Reader.* Edited by Medard Kehl and Werner Löser. Translated by Robert J. Daly and Fred Lawrence. Edinburgh: T&T Clark, 1985.

Barnes, Michel René. "Augustine in Contemporary Trinitarian Theology." *Theological Studies* 56 (1995): 237-50.

———. "De Régnon Reconsidered." *Augustinian Studies* 26 (1995): 51-79.

———. "Rereading Augustine's Theology of the Trinity." In *The Trinity: An Interdisciplinary Symposium on the Trinity,* edited by Stephen T. Davis, Daniel Kendall, and Gerald O'Collins, 145-76. Oxford: Oxford University Press, 1999.

Bobrinskoy, Boris. *The Mystery of the Trinity: Trinitarian Experience and Vision in the Biblical and Patristic Tradition.* Crestwood, N.Y.: St. Vladimir's Seminary Press, 1999.

Boff, Leonardo. *Holy Trinity, Perfect Community.* Maryknoll, N.Y.: Orbis Books, 2000.

———. "Trinity." In *Systematic Theology: Perspectives from Liberation Theology* (Readings from *Mysterium Liberationis*), edited by Jon Sobrino and Ignacio Ellacuría, 389-404. Maryknoll, N.Y.: Orbis Books, 1993, 1996.

———. *Trinity and Society.* Translated by Paul Burns. Liberation and Theology Series 2. London: Burns & Oates, 1988.

Bonaventure. *Saint Bonaventure's Disputed Questions on the Mystery of the Trinity: An Introduction and a Translation.* Introduction and translation by Zachary Hayes. St. Bonaventure, N.Y.: Franciscan University, 1979.

Catechism of the Catholic Church. 2nd ed. Washington, D.C.: U.S. Catholic Conference, 2000. http://www.vatican.va/archive/ENG0015/_INDEX.HTM.

Cocksworth, Christopher. *Holy, Holy, Holy: Worshipping the Trinitarian God.* London: Darton, Longman & Todd, 1997.

Coffey, David. *Deus Trinitas: The Doctrine of the Triune God.* Oxford/New York: Oxford University Press, 1999.

———. *Grace: The Gift of the Holy Spirit.* Faith and Culture 2. Sydney: Catholic Institute of Sydney, 1979.

Congar, Yves. *I Believe in the Holy Spirit.* Translated by David Smith. 3 volumes. New York: Crossroad, 1997.

———. *A History of Theology.* New York: Doubleday, 1968.

———. *The Mystery of the Church: Studies by Yves Congar.* 2nd rev. ed. Baltimore: Helicon Press, 1965.

Cousins, Ewert. "Panikkar's Advaitic Trinitarianism." In *The Intercultural Challenge of Raimon Panikkar,* edited by Joseph Prabhu, 119-30. Maryknoll, N.Y.: Orbis Books, 1996.

———. "The Trinity and World Religions." *Journal of Ecumenical Studies* 7 (1970): 476-98.

Cunningham, David S. *These Three Are One: The Practice of Trinitarian Theology.* Malden, Mass./Oxford: Blackwell, 1998.

Del Colle, Ralph. *Christ and Spirit: Spirit Christology in Trinitarian Perspective.* New York: Oxford University Press, 1994.

Delio, Ilia. "Bonaventure's Metaphysics of the Good." *Theological Studies* 60 (1999): 228-46.

———. "Does God 'Act' in Creation? A Bonaventurian Response." *Heythrop Journal* 44 (2003): 328-44.

———. *Simply Bonaventure: An Introduction to His Life, Thought, and Writings.* New York: New City Press, 2001.

Downey, Michael. *Altogether Gift: A Trinitarian Spirituality.* Maryknoll, N.Y.: Orbis Books, 2000.

Doyle, Dennis M. *Communion Ecclesiology: Vision and Versions.* Maryknoll, N.Y.: Orbis Books, 2000.

Duffy, Stephen J. *The Dynamics of Grace: Perspectives in Theological Anthropology.* New Theology Series 3. Collegeville, Minn.: Liturgical Press, A Michael Glazier Book, 1993.

Dupuis, Jacques. "'Christianity and the Religions' Revisited," *Louvain Studies* 28 (2003): 363-83.

———. *Christianity and the Religions: From Confrontation to Dialogue.* Maryknoll, N.Y.: Orbis Books, 2002.

———. *Jesus Christ at the Encounter of World Religions.* Translated by Robert R. Barr. Faith Meets Faith. Maryknoll, N.Y.: Orbis Books, 1991.

———. *Toward a Christian Theology of Religious Pluralism.* Maryknoll, N.Y.: Orbis Books, 1997.

———. "Trinitarian Christology as a Model for a Theology of Religious Pluralism." In *The Myriad Christ: Plurality and the Quest for Unity in Contemporary Chris-*

tology, edited by T. Merrigan and J. Haers, 83-97. Leuven: Leuven University Press, 2000.

———. "'The Truth Will Make You Free': The Theology of Religious Pluralism Revisited." *Louvain Studies* 24 (1999): 211-63.

———. *Who Do You Say I Am? Introduction to Christology*. Maryknoll, N.Y.: Orbis Books, 1994.

Durrwell, François-Xavier. *Christ Our Passover: The Indispensable Role of Resurrection in Our Salvation.* Translated by John F. Craghan. Liguori, Mo.: Liguori, 2004.

———. *Holy Spirit of God: An Essay in Biblical Theology*. Translated by Benedict Davies. London: Geoffrey Chapman, 1986.

———. *The Resurrection: A Biblical Study*. With an Introduction by Charles Davis. Translated by Rosemary Sheed. London: Sheed & Ward, 1960.

———. *The Spirit of the Father and of the Son.* Translated by Robert Nowell. Middlegreen: St Paul, 1990.

Edwards, Denis. "The Discovery of Chaos and the Retrieval of the Trinity." In *Chaos and Complexity: Scientific Perspectives on Divine Action,* edited by R. J. Russell, N. Murphy, and A. R. Peacocke, 157-75. Vatican City State: Vatican Observatory Publications; Berkeley, Calif.: Center for Theology, 1995.

———. *The God of Evolution: A Trinitarian Theology.* Mahwah, N.J.: Paulist Press, 1999.

———. *Jesus the Wisdom of God: An Ecological Theology*. Ecology and Justice. Maryknoll, N.Y.: Orbis Books, 1995.

Emery, Gilles. *Trinity in Aquinas.* With a foreword by Jean-Pierre Torrell. Ypsilanti, Mich.: Sapientia Press, 2003.

Fiddes, Paul S. *Participating in God: A Pastoral Theology of the Trinity*. Louisville: Westminster John Knox Press, 2000.

Fortman, Edmund J. *The Triune God: A Historical Study of the Doctrine of the Trinity.* London: Hutchinson, 1972.

Fredericks, James L. *Faith among Faiths: Christian Theology and Non-Christian Religions.* New York/Mahwah, N.J.: Paulist Press, 1999.

Fullenbach, John. *Church: Community for the Kingdom.* Maryknoll, N.Y.: Orbis Books, 2002.

Hankey, W. J. *God in Himself: Aquinas' Doctrine of God as Expounded in the Summa Theologiae*. Oxford: Oxford University Press, 1987.

Hanson, R. P. C. *The Search for the Christian Doctrine of God: The Arian Controversy 318-381*. Edinburgh: T&T Clark, 1988.

Haught, John. *God after Darwin: A Theology of Evolution*. Boulder, Colo.: Westview Press, 2000.

Hayes, Zachary. "Bonaventure: Mystery of the Triune God." In *The History of Franciscan Theology,* edited by Kenan B. Osborne, 39-125. Bonaventure, N.Y.: Franciscan Institute, 1994.

———. *Bonaventure: Mystical Writings*. New York: Crossroad, 1999.

———. "Christ, Word of God and Exemplar of Humanity." *Cord* 46 (1996): 3-17.

———. *The Gift of Being: A Theology of Creation*. New Theology Series 10. Collegeville, Minn.: Liturgical Press, A Michael Glazier Book, 2001.

———. *Visions of a Future: A Study of Christian Eschatology.* Wilmington, Del.: Michael Glazier, 1989.

Hayes, Zachary, ed. *Saint Bonaventure's Disputed Questions on the Mystery of the Trinity: An Introduction and a Translation.* St. Bonaventure, N.Y.: Franciscan University, 1979.

Hide, Kerry. *Graced Origins to Graced Fulfillment: The Soteriology of Julian of Norwich.* Collegeville, Minn.: Liturgical Press, 2001.

Hill, Edmund. *The Mystery of the Trinity.* Introducing Catholic Theology Series. London: Geoffrey Chapman, 1985.

Hill, William J. *The Three-Personed God: The Trinity as a Mystery of Salvation.* Washington, D.C.: Catholic University of America Press, 1982.

Hunt, Anne. "The Psychological Analogy and the Paschal Mystery in Trinitarian Theology." *Theological Studies* 59 (1998): 197-218.

———. *The Trinity and the Paschal Mystery: A Development in Recent Catholic Theology.* New Theology Studies 5. Collegeville, Minn.: Liturgical Press, 1997.

———. *What Are They Saying about the Trinity?* Mahwah, N.J.: Paulist Press, 1998.

Hurtado, Larry W. *Lord Jesus Christ: Devotion to Jesus in Earliest Christianity.* Grand Rapids: Wm. B. Eerdmans, 2003.

Jantzen, Grace M. *Julian of Norwich: Mystic and Theologian.* London: SPCK, 1987.

Johnson, Elizabeth A. *Consider Jesus: Waves of Renewal in Christology.* London: Geoffrey Chapman, 1990.

———. "Does God Play Dice? Divine Providence and Chance." *Theological Studies* 56 (1996): 3-18.

———. *Friends of God and Prophets: A Feminist Theological Reading of the Communion of Saints.* New York: Continuum, 1998.

———. *She Who Is: The Mystery of God in Feminist Theological Discourse.* New York: Crossroad, 1992.

Jones, L. Gregory. *Transformed Judgment: Toward a Trinitarian Account of the Moral Life.* Notre Dame, Ind.: University of Notre Dame Press, 1990.

Julian of Norwich. *Julian of Norwich Showings.* Translated by Edmund Colledge and James Walsh. Classics of Western Spirituality. New York: Paulist Press, 1978.

Kärkkäinen, Veli-Matti. *Trinity and Religious Pluralism: The Doctrine of the Trinity in Christian Theology of Religions.* Aldershot, Hants, U.K.: Ashgate, 2004.

Kasper, Walter. *The God of Jesus Christ.* Translated by Matthew J. O'Connell. New York: Crossroad, 1988.

———. *Leadership in the Church: How Traditional Roles Can Serve the Christian Community Today.* Translated by Brian McNeil. New York: Crossroad, 2003.

———. *Theology and Church.* Translated by Margaret Kohl. London: SCM Press, 1989.

Kelly, Anthony. *An Expanding Theology: Faith in a World of Connections.* Newtown, NSW: E. J. Dwyer, 1993.

———. "The 'Horrible Wrappers' of Aquinas' God," *Pacifica* 9 (1996): 185-203.

———. "A Multidimensional Disclosure: Aspects of Aquinas's Theological Intentionality." *The Thomist* 67 (2003): 335-74.

———. *Touching on the Infinite: Explorations of Christian Hope.* Melbourne: Collins Dove, 1991.

———. "A Trinitarian Moral Theology." *Studia Moralia* 39 (2001): 245-89.

———. *The Trinity of Love: A Theology of the Christian God.* New Theology Series 4. Wilmington, Del.: Michael Glazier, 1989.

Kelly, J. N. D. *Early Christian Creeds.* 2nd ed. London: Longmans, 1960.

———. *Early Christian Doctrines.* Rev. ed.. New York: Harper & Row, 1978.

King-Lenzmeier, Anne H. *Hildegard of Bingen: An Integrated Vision.* Collegeville, Minn.: Liturgical Press, A Michael Glazier Book, 2001.

LaCugna, Catherine Mowry. *God for Us: The Trinity and Christian Life.* New York: HarperCollins, 1991.

———. "The Trinitarian Mystery of God." In *Systematic Theology: Roman Catholic Perspectives,* edited by Francis Schüssler Fiorenza and John P. Galvin, 1:149-92. 2 volumes. Minneapolis: Fortress Press, 1991.

Lafont, Ghislain. *Peut-on Connaître Dieu en Jésus Christ?* Cogitatio Fidei Series 44. Paris: Éditions du Cerf, 1969.

Lane, Dermot A. *Keeping Hope Alive: Stirrings in Christian Theology.* Mahwah, N.J.: Paulist Press, 1996.

Lonergan, Bernard. *Method in Theology.* New York: Seabury, 1971.

———. *Verbum: Word and Idea in Aquinas.* Edited by David B. Burrell. London: Darton, Longman & Todd, 1968.

———. *The Way to Nicea: The Dialectical Development of Trinitarian Theology.* London: Darton, Longman & Todd, 1976.

Margerie, Bertrand de. *The Christian Trinity in History.* Translated by Edmund J. Fortman. Studies in Historical Theology 1. Petersham, Mass.: St. Bede's Publications, 1982.

Marmion, Declan, and Mary E. Hines, eds. *The Cambridge Companion to Karl Rahner.* Cambridge Companions to Religion. Cambridge: Cambridge University Press, 2005.

Merriell, Donald Juvenal. *To the Image of the Trinity: A Study in the Development of Aquinas' Teaching.* Toronto: Pontifical Institute of Mediaeval Studies, 1990.

Meyendorff, John. *Byzantine Theology: Historical Trends and Doctrinal Themes.* London: Mowbrays, 1974.

———. *Christ in Eastern Christian Thought.* Crestwood, N.Y.: St. Vladimir's Seminary Press, 1975.

Moltmann, Jürgen. *The Coming of God: Christian Eschatology.* Translated by Margaret Kohl. London: SCM, 1996.

———. *The Crucified God: The Cross of Christ as the Foundation and Criticism of Christian Theology.* Translated by R. A. Wilson and John Bowden. London: SCM, 1974.

———. *History and the Triune God.* Translated by John Bowden. London: SCM, 1991.

———. *The Trinity and the Kingdom of God: The Doctrine of God.* Translated by Margaret Kohl. London: SCM, 1981.

Moore, Sebastian. "'And There Is Only One Dance': Reflections on the Trinity." *Downside Review* 119 (2001): 269-96.

———. "Are We Getting the Trinity Right?" *Downside Review* 117 (1999): 59-72.

———. *The Fire and the Rose Are One*. London: Darton, Longman & Todd, 1980.

———. *Jesus the Liberator of Desire*. New York: Crossroad, 1989.

Mostert, Christiaan. *God and the Future: Wolfhart Pannenberg's Eschatological Doctrine of God*. Edinburgh/New York: T&T Clark, 2002.

Nichols, Aidan. *Discovering Aquinas: An Introduction to His Life, Work and Influence*. London: Darton, Longman & Todd, 2002.

O'Collins, Gerald. *Christology: A Biblical, Historical, and Systematic Study of Jesus*. Oxford: Oxford University Press, 1995.

———. *The Tripersonal God: Understanding and Interpreting the Trinity*. New York/Mahwah, N.J.: Paulist Press, 1999.

O'Donnell, John J. *The Mystery of the Triune God*. Heythrop Monograph Series 6. London: Sheed & Ward, 1988.

O'Meara, Thomas F. "Grace as a Theological Structure in the *Summa Theologiae* of Thomas Aquinas." *Recherches de Théologie ancienne et médiévale* 55 (1988): 130-53.

Ormerod, Neil. "Augustine's *De Trinitate* and Lonergan's Realms of Meaning." *Theological Studies* 64 (2003): 773-94.

———. "Augustine and the Trinity: Whose Crisis?" *Pacifica* 16 (2003) 17-32.

———. "The Psychological Analogy: At Odds with Modernity." *Pacifica* 14 (2001): 281-94.

———. "The Structure of a Systematic Ecclesiology." *Theological Studies* 63 (2002): 3-30.

Panikkar, Raimon. "The Jordan, the Tiber and the Ganges: Three Kairological Moments of Christic Self-Consciousness." In *The Myth of Christian Uniqueness: Toward a Pluralistic Theology of Religions,* edited by John Hick and Paul Knitter, 89-116. Maryknoll, N.Y.: Orbis Books, 1987.

———. *The Trinity and the Religious Experience of Man*. Maryknoll, N.Y.: Orbis Books; London: Darton, Longman & Todd, 1973.

Pannenberg, Wolfhart. *Systematic Theology*. 3 volumes. Translated by Geoffrey W. Bromiley. Grand Rapids: Wm. B. Eerdmans, 1991-98.

Peacocke, Arthur. *Paths from Science towards God: The End of All Our Exploring*. Oxford: OneWorld Publications, 2001.

———. *Theology for a Scientific Age: Being and Becoming—Natural, Divine, and Human*. Minneapolis: Fortress Press, 1993.

Phan, Peter, ed. *The Gift of the Church: A Textbook on Ecclesiology*. Collegeville, Minn.: Liturgical Press, A Michael Glazier Book, 2000.

Powell, Samuel M. *Participating in God: Creation and Trinity*. Minneapolis: Fortress Press, 2003.

———. *The Trinity in German Thought*. Cambridge: Cambridge University Press, 2001.

Prabhu, Joseph, ed. *The Intercultural Challenge of Raimon Panikkar*. Maryknoll, N.Y.: Orbis Books, 1996.

Principe, Walter H. "The Dynamism of Augustine's Terms for Describing the Highest Trinitarian Image in the Human Person." *Studia Patristica* 18 (1982): 1291-99.

Rahner, Karl. "Concerning the Relationship between Nature and Grace." In *Theological Investigations,* 1:297-317. Translated by Cornelius Ernst. Baltimore: Helicon Press, 1961.

———. "Current Problems in Christology." In *Theological Investigations,* 1:149-200. New York: Seabury Press, 1974.

———. *Foundations of Christian Faith: An Introduction to the Idea of Christianity.* Translated by William V. Dych. New York: Crossroad, 1987.

———. "Nature and Grace." In *Theological Investigations,* 4:165-88. Translated by Kevin Smyth. London: Darton, Longman & Todd, 1974.

———. *A Rahner Reader.* Edited by Gerald A. McCool. New York: Crossroad, 1987.

———. "Remarks on the Dogmatic Treatise '*De Trinitate.*'" In *Theological Investigations,* 4:77-102. Translated by Kevin Smyth. Baltimore: Helicon Press, 1966.

———. "Some Implications of the Scholastic Concept of Uncreated Grace." In *Theological Investigations,* 1:319-46. Translated by Cornelius Ernst. Baltimore: Helicon Press, 1961.

———. *The Trinity.* Translated by Joseph Donceel. London: Burns & Oates, 1970.

Ratzinger, Joseph Cardinal. *Church, Ecumenism and Politics: New Essays in Ecclesiology.* Translated by Robert Nowell. New York: Crossroad, 1988.

———. *Eschatology: Death and Eternal Life.* Translated by Michael Waldstein. Washington, D.C.: Catholic University of America Press, 1988.

———. *Principles of Catholic Theology.* San Francisco: Ignatius Press, 1987.

Ruse, Michael. *Can a Darwinian Be a Christian?* New York: Cambridge University Press, 2001.

Ruusbroec, Jan van. *The Realm of Lovers.* Corpus Christianorum Continuatio Mediaeualis 104. Turnhout: Brepols, 2002.

———. *The Spiritual Espousals and Other Works.* Translated with introduction by James A. Wiseman. Classics of Western Spirituality. New York: Paulist Press, 1985.

———. *The Twelve Beguines.* Corpus Christianorum Continuatio Mediaeualis 107A. Turnhout: Brepols, 2000.

Schwöbel, Christoph. "Christology and Trinitarian Thought." In *Trinitarian Theology Today: Essays on Divine Being and Act,* edited by Christoph Schwöbel, 113-46. Edinburgh: T&T Clark, 1995.

———. "Last Things First?" In *The Future as God's Gift: Explorations in Christian Eschatology,* edited by David Fergusson and Marcel Sarot, 219-41. Edinburgh: T&T Clark, 2000.

Studer, Basil. *The Grace of Christ and the Grace of God: Christocentrism or Theocentrism.* Translated by Matthew J. O'Connell. Collegeville, Minn.: Liturgical Press, 1997.

———. *Trinity and Incarnation: The Faith of the Early Church.* Edited by Andrew Louth. Translated by Matthias Westerhoff. Edinburgh: T&T Clark, 1993.

Sullivan, Francis. *Salvation Outside the Church? Tracing the History of the Catholic Response.* Mahwah, N.J.: Paulist Press, 1992.

Tillard, Jean-Marie-Roger. *Church of Churches: The Ecclesiology of Communion.* Translated by R. C. De Peaux. Collegeville, Minn.: Liturgical Press, 1992.

———. *Flesh of the Church, Flesh of Christ: At the Sources of the Ecclesiology of Communion.* Translated by Madeleine Beaumont. Collegeville, Minn.: Liturgical Press, 2001.

Torrance, T. F. *The Trinitarian Faith.* Edinburgh: T&T Clark, 1988.

Torrell, Jean-Pierre. *Saint Thomas Aquinas.* Volume 2, *Spiritual Master.* Translated by Robert Royal. Washington, D.C.: Catholic University of America Press, 2003.

Van Nieuwenhove, Rik. *Jan van Ruusbroek: Mystical Theologian of the Trinity.* Studies in Spirituality and Theology. Notre Dame, Ind.: University of Notre Dame Press, 2003.

Volf, Miroslav. *After Our Likeness: The Church as the Image of the Trinity.* Grand Rapids/Cambridge: Wm. B. Eerdmans, 1998.

———. "'The Trinity Is Our Social Program': The Doctrine of the Trinity and the Shape of Social Engagement." *Modern Theology* 14 (1998): 403-19.

———. "Trinity, Unity, Primacy: On the Trinitarian Nature of Ecclesial Unity and Its Implications for the Question of Primacy." In *Petrine Ministry and the Unity of the Church,* edited by James F. Puglisi, 171-84. Collegeville, Minn.: Liturgical Press, 1999.

Webb, Stephen H. *The Gifting God: A Trinitarian Ethics.* Oxford: Oxford University Press, 1996.

Weinandy, Thomas G. *Does God Change? The Word's Becoming in the Incarnation.* Still River, Mass.: St. Bede's Publications, 1985.

———. *The Father's Spirit of Sonship: Reconceiving the Trinity.* Edinburgh: T&T Clark, 1995.

Williams, A. N. *The Ground of Union: Deification in Aquinas and Palamas.* New York/Oxford: Oxford University Press, 1999.

Williams, Rowan. *Arius.* 2nd ed. London: SCM Press, 2001.

———. "What Does Love Know? St Thomas on the Trinity." *New Blackfriars* 82 (2001): 260-72.

Wright, N. T. *The Resurrection of the Son of God.* Minneapolis: Fortress, 2003.

Zizioulas, John D. *Being as Communion: Studies in Personhood and the Church.* With a Foreword by John Meyendorff. Crestwood, N.Y.: St. Vladimir's Seminary Press, 1985.

———. "The Church as Communion." *St. Vladimir's Theological Quarterly* 38 (1994): 3-16.

———. "The Doctrine of the Holy Spirit: The Significance of the Cappadocian Contribution." In *Trinitarian Theology Today: Essays on Divine Being and Act,* edited by Christoph Schwöbel, 44-60. Edinburgh: T&T Clark, 1995.

———. *Eucharist, Bishop, Church: The Unity of the Church in the Divine Eucharist and the Bishop during the First Three Centuries.* Translated by Elizabeth Theokritoff. Brookline, Mass.: Holy Cross Orthodox Press, 2001.

———. "Primacy in the Church: An Orthodox Approach." In *Petrine Ministry and the Unity of the Church,* edited by James F. Puglisi, 115-25. Collegeville, Minn.: Liturgical Press, 1999.

Glossary

Actus Purus. God as pure act, the perfection of being.

ad extra. In reference to action *ad extra*, describes the work or actions of the Trinity outside of the Godhead, for example, creation, revelation, and salvation.

ad intra. In reference to action *ad intra*, describes the work or actions of the Trinity within (or inside) the Godhead, for example, the generation of the Son and the procession of the Holy Spirit.

adoptionism. The view that Jesus Christ was a man and was adopted by God at his baptism or resurrection.

appropriation. A theological strategy whereby traits or actions that are properly those of the undivided Godhead, are attributed to one of the divine persons, on the basis of their greater likeness or affinity to one person rather than to another. For example, the work of creation is traditionally appropriated to the Father, while reconciliation is appropriated to the Son and sanctification or consummation of creation to the Holy Spirit. Similarly, power is appropriated to the Father, wisdom to the Son, and love to the Holy Spirit.

circumincession, circuminsession. See perichoresis.

consubstantial. Of the same essence or being or substance.

ecclesiology. Theology of church—its nature, structure, and role.

economic Trinity. The Trinity as revealed in the realm of creation and salvation (as distinct from the immanent Trinity, as the inner-trinitarian mystery of the three divine persons).

exemplarism. The theological notion that everything in creation is based on an exemplar or model, as a replica is to a model.

filioque. Literally, "and the Son." This word was incorporated into the Nicene-Constantinopolitan Creed in the West, without the agreement of the church in the East, in reference to the procession of the Holy Spirit—that the Spirit proceeds "from the Father *and the Son.*"

generation. In trinitarian theology, refers to the origination of the Son from the Father by the process of begetting.

homoousios. "Of the same substance or being," in English, consubstantial (as distinct from *homoiousios*, "of like substance").

hypostasis. In theology, used as the Greek term for the divine person; originally used synonymously with *ousia* (substance), it was later distinguished as the term for the Three while *ousia* was appropriate to the one substance of God that was shared equally by the Three.

hypostatic union. The union of the two natures in the one person of Jesus Christ.

immutability. The inability to change; in theology it is used in reference to God as a divine perfection.

impassibility. The inability to suffer; in theology it is used in reference to God as a divine perfection.

mission, invisible. The sending of the Son and the Holy Spirit to the human person. By means of the invisible missions, the Word of Truth and the Spirit of Love are sent to the human person. The Trinity of the three divine persons thus comes to abide in the human person.

mission, visible. Those missions of the Son and Holy Spirit in which they are visibly sent; the Son is visibly present in the incarnation and the Holy Spirit at Pentecost.

modalism. That heresy that understands the three divine persons of Father, Son, and Holy Spirit to be merely different modes of God's presence in the world at different times in salvation history.

ontology. The study of being, a department of metaphysics that relates to the essence of things.

***ousia*.** The Greek term used to refer to the divine substance or being.

perichoresis. An understanding of the mystery of the divine unity whereby the three divine persons interpenetrate and coinhere in each other or mutually indwell. The Greek word was translated into Latin as *circumincessio* (from *incedere*, "to permeate and interpenetrate") and *circuminsessio* (from *sedere* and *sessio*, "to be seated"), the former conveying a more active and dynamic indwelling and usually the preferred Latin form.

***person*.** The term used in trinitarian theology to designate the Three in distinction from each other; hence Father, Son, and Holy Spirit are called divine persons.

procession. Generically refers to the origin or derivation of the Son and of the Spirit from the Father; also used specifically in regard to the origination of the Spirit (whereas begetting or generation refers specifically and only to the origination of the Son from the Father).

relation. Refers to the real and subsistent relatedness between the divine persons, in reference to their origin or procession.

Scholasticism. Refers to the methods and teaching of theology and philosophy in the schools by the so-called Schoolmen in the period 1000-1500.

spiration. The procession or breathing of the Holy Spirit from the Father.

subordinationism. An understanding of the three divine persons in the Trinity in which the Son and Spirit are understood to be lesser in divinity than the Father.

subsistent relation. Relationality constitutive of personal identity, for example, the Father is his paternity.

teleology. The study of last ends or final causes.

theodicy. Refers to the justification of the attributes of God, for example, love, justice, mercy, given the existence of evil in the world.

Theotokos. Literally, "God-bearer"; used in reference to Mary as the mother of God.

transcendental. That theological approach which addresses the necessary conditions or a priori presuppositions for the realization of the realities of Christian faith;

for example, a consideration of what necessary condition in the constitution of the human person is required for the possibility of the incarnation.

unbegottenness; unoriginate. Without origin, the characteristic of the Father.

unitarianism. As distinct from trinitarianism, the belief that God is one without intradivine differentiation.

Index